W9-CEB-814

Contents

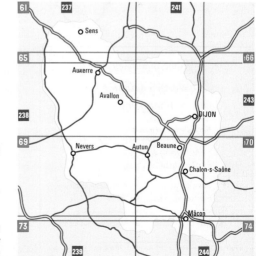

The **Michelin maps**
which accompany
this guide are:

PRINCIPAL SIGHTS

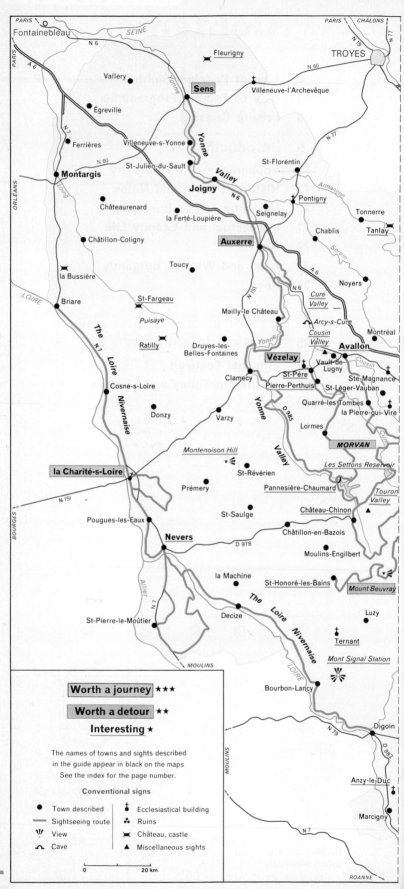

Worth a journey ★★★

Worth a detour ★★

Interesting ★

The names of towns and sights described
in the guide appear in black on the maps
See the index for the page number.

Conventional signs

●	Town described		†	Ecclesiastical building
—	Sightseeing route		∴	Ruins
╚	View		⚔	Château, castle
⌐	Cave		▲	Miscellaneous sights

0   20 km

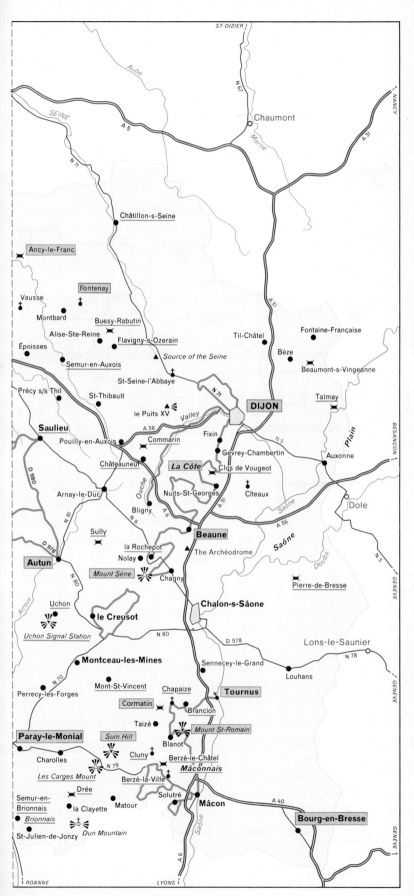

TOURING PROGRAMMES

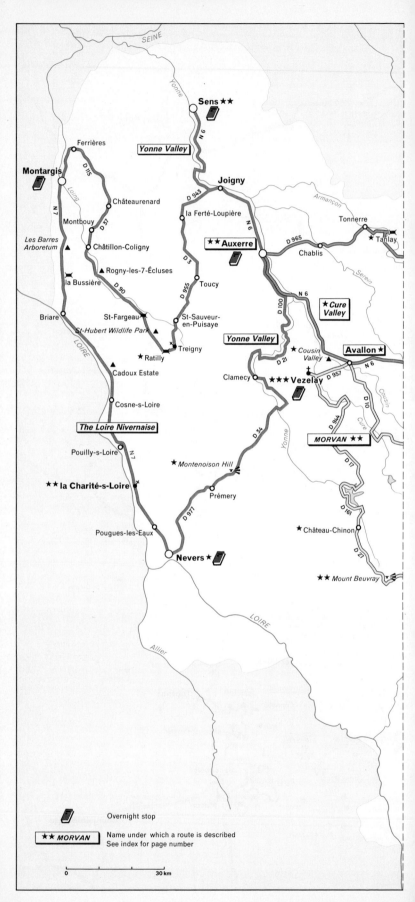

Sens ★★

Yonne Valley

Ferrières

Montargis

D 115

Joigny

D 943

Châteaurenard

Armançon

la Ferté-Loupière

Montbouy

D 37

Tonnerre

★ Tanlay

★★ Auxerre

D 965

Chablis

Serein

Les Barres
Arboretum

Châtillon-Coligny

▲ Rogny-les-7-Écluses

D 3

la Bussière

D 90

Toucy

D 955

Serein

N 6

★ Cure
Valley

D 100

Briare

St-Fargeau

St-Sauveur-
en-Puisaye

LOIRE

St-Hubert Wildlife Park

Yonne Valley

Avallon ★

N 6

★ Ratilly

Treigny

★ Cousin
Valley

▲

N 6

D 21

D 957

▲ Cadoux Estate

Clamecy

★★★ Vezelay

D 944

Cure

Cosne-s-Loire

Yonne

D 10

Cousin

The Loire Nivernaise

D 34

MORVAN ★★

Pouilly-s-Loire

N 7

★ Montenoison Hill

D 17

★★ la Charité-s-Loire

D 977

Prémery

D 161

★ Château-Chinon

Pougues-les-Eaux

Nevers ★

D 27

★★ Mount Beuvray

LOIRE

Allier

Overnight stop

★★ MORVAN   Name under which a route is described
See index for page number

0   30 km

6

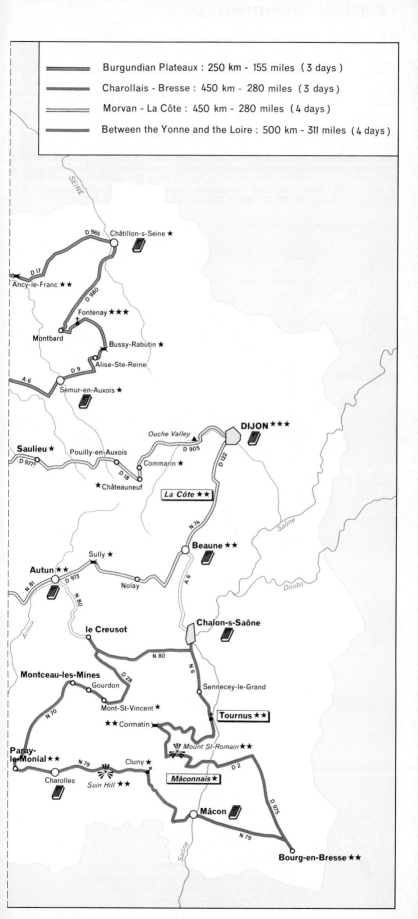

Burgundian Plateaux : 250 km - 155 miles (3 days)

Charollais - Bresse : 450 km - 280 miles (3 days)

Morvan - La Côte : 450 km - 280 miles (4 days)

Between the Yonne and the Loire : 500 km - 311 miles (4 days)

SEINE

D 965 Châtillon-s-Seine ★

D 17 Ancy-le-Franc ★★

D 980

Fontenay ★★★

Montbard

Bussy-Rabutin ★

D 9 Alise-Ste-Reine

A 6 Semur-en-Auxois ★

Ouche Valley

DIJON ★★★

Saulieu ★

Pouilly-en-Auxois

D 977 Commarin ★

D 18 Châteauneuf ★

La Côte ★★

N 74

Saône

Beaune ★★

Sully ★

Autun ★★

N 81 D 973

Nolay

N 80

A 6

Doubs

Arroux

le Creusot

Chalon-s-Saône

N 80

N 6

Montceau-les-Mines

D 28 Gourdon

Sennecey-le-Grand

Mont-St-Vincent ★

N 70

★★ Cormatin

Tournus ★★

Paray-le-Monial ★★

N 79 Cluny ★

Mount St-Romain ★★

Charolles

Suin Hill ★★

Mâconnais ★

D 2

Mâcon

D 975

N 79

Saône

Bourg-en-Bresse ★★

7

LEISURE CRUISING

Three rivers – the Yonne, the Saône and its tributary the Seille – together with several canals or stretches of canal provide about 1 200km - 1 931 miles of navigable waterway for those who would like to visit Burgundy by boat.

Some of the ports beside the waterways offer organised cruises lasting a few hours or several days (excursion craft, cabin cruisers) or cabin cruisers for hire *(see map below)*. No licence is required to hire a boat but the helmsman must be an adult; a practical and theoretical lesson is given at the beginning of the hire period. To pilot such a boat successfully one must observe the speed limits and heed the advice of the hirer, particularly when mooring or passing through locks.

For information about cruises and hiring boats *(embarkation ports are marked on the map)* apply to the Tourist Information Centre of the appropriate town or to "Bourgogne Voies Navigables", 1 and 2 Quai de la République, 89000 Auxerre, ☎ 86 52 18 99.

Information such as navigational advice, useful addresses, and tourist information along the waterways is available from Navicartes (7 quai Gabriel-Péri, 94340 Joinville-Le-Pont, ☎ 48 85 77 00), which publishes navigational maps, and from Guides Vagnon, Les éditions du plaisancier, BP 27, 69641 Caluire Cedex - France, ☎ 78 23 31 14.

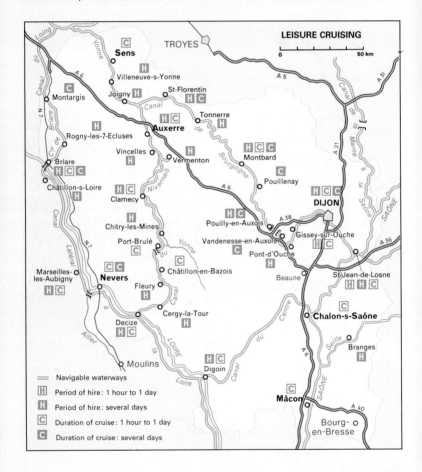

Admission times and charges for the sights described are listed at the end of the Guide.

Every sight for which there are times and charges is indicated by the symbol ⊘ in the margin in the middle section of the guide.

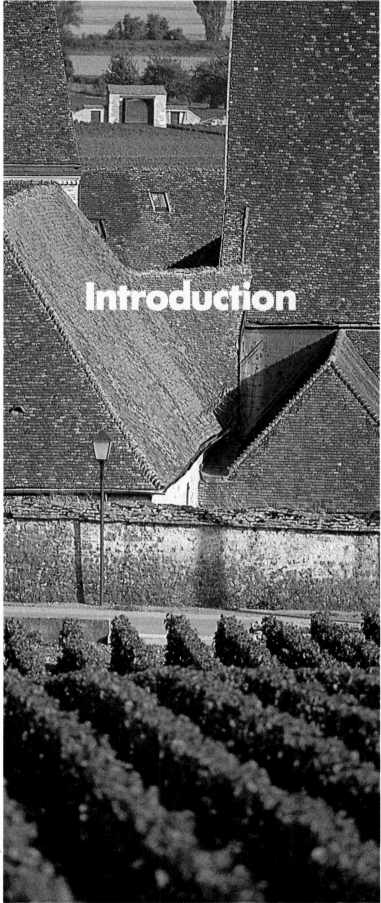

Introduction

Clos de Vougeot

APPEARANCE OF THE COUNTRY

The region described in this guide is not a natural area in the same sense as the Alps or the Paris basin. It has no physical unity and is composed of very different landscapes:

to the east, sharply dropping plains (countryside of the river Saône);

to the north and west, plains with sedimentary basins forming Basse-Bourgogne (regions of Chablis and Auxerre);

in the centre, limestone plateaux (La Côte and Arrière Côte);

and to the south, the ancient massifs and the hilly areas (massif of the Morvan, the Charollais hills, and the uplands of the Mâconnais).

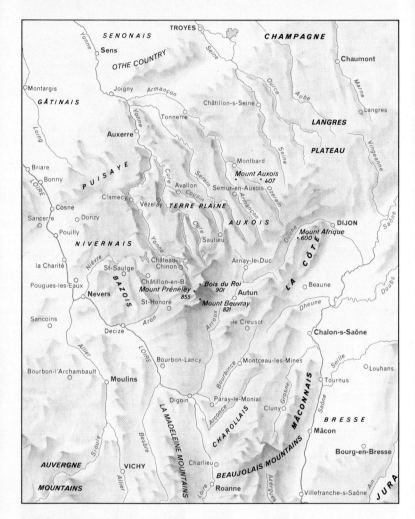

Relief characteristics. — Despite this diversity, it is nevertheless possible to pick out certain general characteristics: the northern part is linked directly with the eastern edge of the Paris basin but the Morvan, La Côte and the Mâconnais regions have very distinct characteristics.

The **Morvan,** a massif of the primary era which was first worn away by erosion and subsequently raised up once again, slopes gently towards the north. Its maximum altitude does not exceed 900m - 3000ft. To the west it dominates the Bazois depression, to the north the Terre-Plaine, to the northeast the Auxois depression and to the southeast the plains of Autun and Charollais. All these surrounding plains have made exploration of the massif itself easier and have slowly led to its development.

La Côte, at whose foot stretches the celebrated vineyard, is the edge of the last slope of the "Mountain", a high limestone plateau running from north to south, from the valley of the river Ouche to that of the river Dheune.

The region of **Mâconnais** continued to the south by the Beaujolais also has fairly marked relief. The Mâconnais uplands are still part of the limestone escarpments bordering the river Saône.

The limestone plateaux of the Châtillonnais and Basse-Bourgogne areas, which extend to the east as far as the plateau of Langres, form a poor and monotonous region, dominated here and there by rocky plateaux *(tasselots)* and cut by dry valleys. Only heavy rainfall has enabled the woodlands to survive.

The Saône to the east and the Loire to the west mark the limits of Burgundy and the Nivernais and the two rivers flow through well-cultivated alluvial plains with many meadows for grazing livestock.

Primary Era. – Beginning about 600 million years ago. Water covered the entire area of what is now France. It was in this era that an upheaval of the earth's crust took place: this upheaval or folding movement, known as the "Hercynian fold", whose V-shaped appearance is shown by dotted lines on the map below, resulted in the emergence of a number of high mountainous areas (the Armorican and Central Massifs, the Vosges and the Ardennes) including the Morvan. These mountains were formed of impermeable crystalline rocks, granite, gneiss, micaschist and mixtures of volcanic rocks, such as porphyry. The seas that covered the Parisian and Rhône basins were joined by a strait that today corresponds to the threshold of Burgundy.

Erosion, that is to say the combined action of rain, wind, frost and running water, wore away the highest parts and the Morvan was thus reduced to the state of a rocky base. The warm, humid climate brought about a thick growth of vegetation. Buried under thick layers of alluvial deposits, the remains of this vegetation were slowly turned into coal as a result of a long period of pressure. Coal-bearing deposits were formed between the Morvan and the Beaujolais massifs near the towns of Autun and Blanzy.

In this era animal life consisted of batrachians, insects, saurians and giant fish.

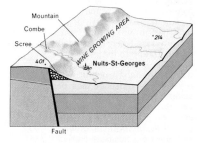

Map legend:
- Folded areas of the Tertiary Era
- Regions submerged during the Secondary Era
- Primary massifs (Hercynian folds)

Secondary Era. – Beginning about 200 million years ago. Following the slow subsidence of the Hercynian base the seas flooded the Parisian basin and, continuing their advance towards the south, covered even the highest land – Morvan, Beaujolais and Charollais – which were coated with a layer of marl and limestone. These sedimentary deposits were piled on the granite base.

After the retreat of the water, erosion again took on its work of wearing away, scouring the Morvan whose height was reduced by at least 1 000m - 3 280ft and washing away the marl and limestone deposits towards the regions of Auxois, Bazois and Châtillonnais. The layers of sediment penetrated towards the centre of the Parisian basin.

In this era reptiles became the dominant form of life and the first birds and mammals made their appearance.

Tertiary Era. – Beginning about 60 million years ago. As an after-effect of the great Alpine folding movement, the land rose once again, the seas withdrew and the Central massif was split. Its eastern edge was forced upwards and formed a series of parallel folds: the uplands of the Autunois, Charollais, Mâconnais and Beaujolais regions; the Morvan massif was also raised by this upward movement.

The huge reptiles were replaced by birds and mammals, while the vegetation was composed of plant species very similar to those of today.

Quaternary Era. – Beginning about two million years ago. The effects of erosion continued to shape the region to its present appearance: the ancient massifs (Morvan and Beaujolais) next to limestone plateaux (La Côte and Arrière Côte), sedimentary basins (Bazois, Terre-Plaine and Auxois) and low-lying plains of subsidence (valley of the Saône).

Cross section of the Morvan and Burgundy

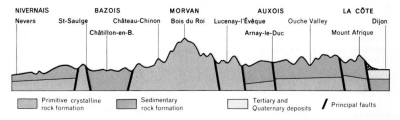

Legend:
- Primitive crystalline rock formation
- Sedimentary rock formation
- Tertiary and Quaternary deposits
- Principal faults

An original relief: La Côte d'Or. – La Côte d'Or (Golden Hill) is an escarpment created by the subsidence of the Saône plains. This escarpment is the last of a series of slopes forming the area usually known as the Arrière Côte but sometimes as the "Montagne" (Mountain).

The Côte (hill) is clearly marked by its rectilinear outline, generally speaking running north-south; the outline varies so that some of the crests reach an altitude of 200m - 656ft; elsewhere it is indented by combes or by deeper valleys.

La Côte d'Or

THE REGIONS OF BURGUNDY

From Auxois to Beaujolais and from the Saône to the Loire, the many different regions which together form Burgundy have each been able to preserve their appearance, their economy and their particular way of life.

The historical links which united them in the 15C have been strong enough to ensure that even today their common characteristics remain evident. The modern administrative divisions of the area as well as present-day economic needs have indeed turned a great part of regional activity towards Paris but this is without disturbing the links between all the different parts of a province of which Dijon is the capital in more than one sense.

Senonais. – This constitutes the northern boundary of Burgundy, abutting the regions of Ile-de-France and Champagne from which it has assimilated some characteristics, notably in physical and economic aspects. The Senonais, more fertile than the barren regions of Champagne, is reminiscent of the Brie area. Its main resource – agriculture – is rich and varied, thanks to the different types of soil and to the thick alluvium.

Gâtinais. – This region, stretching from Gien to north of Montargis, is composed of sand and clay, covered by moorland and pines and traversed by streams, most of them tributaries of the river Loing. Synonymous with for wild and uncultivated land, the Gâtinais is a shooting and fishing region that is much appreciated by Parisian sportsmen. Near Montargis, the countryside becomes greener and more humid: scattered woodlands grow where clay is to be found.

The Gâtinais, which has few riches – apart from the breeding of dairy-cows which is fairly important – looks towards Paris far more than it does towards the rest of Burgundy.

Puisaye. – This region is situated to the southeast of Gâtinais with which it has many similarities: the same soil of sand and clay, the same damp climate and the same areas of forests and pools. The Puisaye however lends itself to the cultivation of forage and to stock-breeding (one third of the region is under pasture). The mixture of woodland and grazing is its most striking feature: meadows enclosed by quickset hedges break up the monotony of the countryside.

The region is sparsely populated and homesteads are surrounded by high hedges. There are varied activities: the rearing of the white Charollais beef cattle, pigs and poultry, pottery, ochre and cement works, forestry and saw-mills.

Nivernais. – A succession of plateaux and small hills joining the Morvan massif to the east and sloping away gently as far as the valley of the Loire, the Nivernais region is above all a crossroads.

To the west of Château-Chinon stretches the **Bazois,** a rich countryside made up of well-watered land divided between the growing of cereals and forage crops on the slopes and stock-breeding in the lush meadows of the lowlands. Here the white Charollais and Nivernais cattle are fattened for the butchers' shops of Paris.

To the north of the Bazois stretches a zone of plateaux and hills sometimes reaching an altitude of 450m - 1476ft. This is the region of Clamecy and Donzy, which includes a fairly dense network of rivers – the Nièvre, Beuvron, Yonne and Nohain – and is a green land, given over both to cultivation and to stock-breeding. The presence of large forests that are being sensibly exploited has resulted in the building of two large factories at Leuglay and Prémery for the manufacture of charcoal.

From Nevers to Bonny the river Loire marks the boundary between Nivernais and Berry. The stock-breeding meadows alternate with wooded spurs.

From Pougues to La Charité the river's east bank is fairly steep and wooded whereas the west bank is flat and low. Pouilly is the centre of a well-known vineyard, which extends along the hills overlooking the Loire.

Beyond Pouilly the Loire valley becomes narrower, dominated to the west by the Sancerre hills, and then widens out again on the other side of Bonny.

Morvan. – In the aftermath of the great Alpine thrust, the edges of the granite massif of the Morvan were broken up: by wearing away at the soft layers of the lias that bordered the massif, erosion scoured out a depression that surrounds the massif on three sides; this "peripheral depression" is dominated by limestone plateaux at its outer edges. The Morvan is remarkable for the extent of its forests, the poorness of its soil and the general ruggedness of its countryside.

The size of the forests should not be allowed to eclipse the pastoral character of the region: the fields and meadows, enclosed by hedges, form a mosaic in constantly changing shades of green, brown or yellow.

The Morvan has few large towns and is characterised by its scattered hamlets, its wide open spaces and its isolated farms. The Morvan homestead, traditionally a thatched cottage, generally stands side by side with its outbuildings and stables.

Isolated by the forest as much as by the ruggedness of the country-side, the people of the Morvan have had to be self-sufficient, but progress finally succeeded in penetrating to the most isolated hamlets and farms: the thatched roofs have been slowly replaced by those of tiles or slates, crops have improved with the use of lime and fertilisers, the forests have been cleared and reafforestation with resinous trees has been carried out methodically *(p 16).*

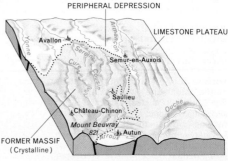

The Morvan and the surrounding area

Above all, cattle-breeding has been developed. The old breed of Morvan cattle with its red colouring has been replaced by Charollais stock.

The drainage of the Morvan region runs mainly into the basin of the river Seine and the heavy rains sometimes disturb the flow of this great river. The Yonne, the Cure and their tributaries, long used for floating of timber downstream, have had their flows regulated by reservoir-dams (Pannesière, Settons, Malassis, Chaumeçon and Crescent) where, in some cases, small hydro-electric stations have been built. However, this is still not particularly effective during the times of heavy floods in the Seine and its basin. The St-Agnan reservoir provides the water supply for surrounding towns.

Auxois. – East of the Morvan the liassic countryside of Auxois, a rich and fertile land traversed by rivers. Here lie the lush cattle-breeding meadows; the Charollais cattle are bred for meat while milk is provided by the spotted cattle from the east (Montbéliard breed) that are mostly to be found in Haut-Auxois – the region of Semur and Montbard. The Auxois draught-horses are another element in the stock-breeding industry. On the limestone spurs and bare plateaux overlooking the green valleys the use of lime and fertiliser has enabled cereal growing to be developed.

The rocky hillocks are topped by fortified townships such as Semur, Flavigny-sur-Ozerain and Mont-St-Jean or by old Roman towns such as Alésia on Mount Auxois, isolated sentinels watching over the roadways and the lines of communication.

Charollais. – Of all the regions that border the Morvan massif, the Charollais, which forms the southern part of the *département* of Saône-et-Loire, is the only one that is not a depression. It is a region of hills and plateaux with sweeping undulations. Since the marly soil makes for lush meadows, cattle-raising provides the main wealth of the area and the Charollais breed spreads as far as the regions of Auxois, Nivernais and Puisaye. The white cattle are fattened on the rich pasture-land for several months and then marketed at the large fairs to be sent on to the Paris area or exported to other European countries.

Autun Basin. – At the time of the Primary Era, this depression was a vast lake that was slowly filled in by coal-bearing deposits and bituminous schists; their presence fuelled the industrial development of the area.

The Autun region comprises: the Autun Basin proper, drained by the river Arroux, the granite ridges that dominate it from the southeast and the depression in which the rivers Dheune and Bourbince flow in opposite directions – the Dheune to the Saône and the Bourbince to the Loire. The valleys of these rivers are used by the Central Canal (Canal du Centre), which serves the mining basin of Blanzy-Montceau-les-Mines and the metallurgical centre of Le Creusot. Once extensively used as a means of water transport, the Central Canal has diminished in importance as a waterway linking Lyons and Paris. The Dheune and the Bourbince depression is a regular succession of mines and factories.

Burgundian Plateaux. – From the northern edge of the Morvan to the plateau of Langres and from Auxerre to Dijon stretches a series of limestone plateaux that form the real heartland of Burgundy. In actual fact, it is the threshold to the province of Burgundy and is the zone of contact between the basin of the Seine and that of the Saône as well as between the Vosges and the Morvan. While this heartland does not include the whole area of Burgundy, it was here, nevertheless, that the Burgundian state was born, at the very junction of the different regions that it was thus able to control.

Of fairly low altitude (400 to 500m - 1312 to 1640ft), these plateaux slope gently towards the northwest but drop abruptly in the southeast. Their dry appearance contrasts with that of the much richer and greener valleys that intersect them: those of the rivers Yonne, Serein and Armançon. From west to east, these are the plateaux of Auxerrois, Tonnerrois and Châtillonnais.

The **Auxerrois** is a rocky platform, cut by numerous valleys, where outcrops of limestone rock shine at times with dazzling whiteness. The sunny slopes have encouraged vine growing in the region of Chablis, Auxerre and Irancy as well as the cultivation of fruit trees (cherries).

The **Tonnerrois** plateau has the same appearance as the plateau of Langres, but is lower and the climate is closer to that of the Paris basin.

The **Châtillonnais** is a series of monotonous plateaux, often bare, sometimes topped by rocky outcrops and cut by dry valleys. The ranges are studded with occasional towering peaks (Mount Lassois, Signal de Bissey and the Jumeaux de Massingy). The soil is permeable; water filters through the limestone crust and reappears lower down in the form of springs *(douix)* such as the Seine at Châtillon; there is a whole network of underground streams. Although main crops suffer in years of low rainfall, they are extensively cultivated. Dairy farming is based on the brown Alpine breed of cattle. In earlier times, forest covered nearly all these plateaux. The monks of the abbeys of Molesmes, St-Seine, Fontenay and Clairvaux took an active part in clearing the trees. Later on came the exploitation of the iron ore deposits with numerous forges, foundries and nail factories existing in the 18C. Today reafforestation is the rule. Forests of resinous trees (larch, black pine, Norwegian pine, silver pine and spruce) stand beside those of deciduous trees (oak, beech, elm and ash) and the timber industry holds an important place in the economy of the area.

In the whole region, the working of quarries *(p 16)* has been a traditional source of wealth: these quarries furnish freestone, rubble and ballast.

Dijonnais. – It is in this region that one finds all the characteristics of the Burgundian countryside united in a remarkable synthesis: it is a zone of limestone plateaux, isolated, upstanding peaks, rich meadows, vast alluvial plains and hillsides covered with vines. Dijon, former capital of the Duchy and today the capital of the whole region, is the economic centre for the Châtillonnais, Haute-Bourgogne, La Côte, the plains of the Saône, the Morvan and part of southern Burgundy, but the regions of Charollais and Mâconnais are drawn more towards Lyons. The area round Dijon furnishes the city with its agricultural and stockbreeding products, while the town itself has developed a number of industries.

Set at the intersection of the main communication routes from the Mediterranean towards Paris, junction of the plains with the regions of La Montagne and La Côte, the Dijon area is a busy commercial centre served by many and varied communication links.

La Côte. — This is the edge of the last slope of the elevated land, **La Montagne** *(p 11)*, overlooking the Saône. This escarpment was caused by the cracks that accompanied the subsidence of the alluvial plain of the Saône. While the plateau of the hinterland is given over to cultivation, woods and pastures, the eastern slope is covered with vines. The villages are set in the middle of the vineyards, at the open end of the combes permitting communication with the hinterland and sufficiently low to benefit from the spring waters that are always to be found at the foot of the slopes.

"The vineyards," wrote **Gaston Roupnel**, "spread out on the low and easy slopes. Their upper edges rest on the first limestone scarps. They end lower down where the slope ceases and the plain begins with its heavy soil. This narrow and gentle rise of gravel is the real land of the vine."

One must not be surprised, therefore, if the vine-growers consider their work to be the finest and most noble of all and, since they are for the most part both owners and cultivators of the land, they generally lead a fuller life than ordinary farmers. Their houses, large and comfortable, are of the raised house (Maison en Hauteur) type: the wine vats and the storerooms are on the ground floor, while the living quarters, "as though pushed up by the cellar", are on the first floor and are reached by an outside staircase protected by a roof *(illustration on opposite page)*.

More than the type of soil (limestone that warms quickly in the spring, with sheltered sunny slopes), the attitude of the vine-growers is more progressive than in other regions: research for plants best adapted to the soil, the quest for quality rather than quantity (10 to 15 228 litre-50 gallon barrels per hectare), and arrangements that allow for the easy disposal of their products.

The vine has slowly been pushed towards the plain but without any great success. In the hinterland (Arrière-Côte), on the higher areas of the plateau, where the Hautes-Côtes are grown, the vineyards are progressively being replanted.

At the foot of La Côte, the freestone and limestone quarries of Comblanchien and Corgoloin are worked.

Mâconnais. — This region is a southerly extension of the mountainous area that forms the Côte d'Or. The difference is that the slope of the hills turns towards the interior, that is to say towards the west, while the slope of the Côte d'Or overlooks the plain of the Saône; it is a region of hills covered with vines or stock-breeding meadows.

The plains to the south of Chalon are highly productive owing to the valley of the Grosne. As in the Bresse area, cereals, sugar-beet, vegetables and poultry are the main products.

Saône Valley. — The Saône valley which is a main route for communications, stretches along the foot of the limestone plateaux. The alluvial lands of the plains round the Saône and its tributaries – the rivers Ouche and Tille – often flooded in winter, are covered with rich meadows and cultivated land. Up to the last century, forest also covered a large area. Today, the cultivation of maize, tobacco, hops, oil-producing crops and market-gardening have been added to that of wheat, sugar-beet and potatoes.

The cultivation of hops, a traditional crop in the north and northeast of France, was introduced from Alsace and flourished until the economic crisis of 1929. The acreage is now in decline.

Cattle breeding is also highly developed, notably with the spotted breed from the east which has excellent milking qualities as well as providing good meat for the butchers' shops. The latter is now closely rivalled by the black and white *pie noire* breed and the Charollais for milk and beef production respectively.

The valley of the Saône is now experiencing great economic expansion; the main centres of industrial activity are at Chalon, Mâcon and Tournus.

Bresse. — The Bresse plain stretches from the Saône to the first slopes of the Jura. The rolling countryside, composed of clay and marl, is traversed by many streams known locally as *caunes* and dotted with spinneys. Though bricks and tiles have gradually

St-Trivier-de-Courtes - Forest Farm

taken the place of cob walls and thatch the farms, standing solitary in the middle of the fields, look very much the same as they always did: long and low with a Saracen chimney *(p 165)* and a widely projecting roof providing a drying area for the maize.

The region specialises in raising beef, pork and poultry, the quality of the latter having brought fame to Bresse. The birds are marketed at Louhans or the central market at Bourg-en-Bresse. The chickens usually spend the first few months outside before being battery reared and fed on maize and buckwheat. Prior to being sold or sent to market in Louhans or Bourg-en-Bresse the capon carcases are soaked in milk.

The annual **Michelin Guide, Camping Caravaning France,**
offers a selection of camping sites with information on
situation and setting and on-site facilities and services.

While for art lovers the name of Burgundy conjures up masterpieces of the Middle Ages and the Renaissance, for all gourmets it is the synonym for good wine. The wines of Burgundy are some of the finest in the world and their fame is universal.

The joys and sorrows of Burgundian vineyards. – The cultivation of vines was introduced by the Romans and spread rapidly. The wines of Burgundy immediately gained a fame that ensuing centuries were to confirm. The names of certain vineyards (Vosne-Romanée) recall the popularity of the local wines with the Roman prefects of the province of Maxima Sequanorum.

It was mainly in the Middle Ages that lands received as gifts by religious communities were converted into vineyards by the monks, particularly the Cistercians clearing the forest; it was thus, in the 12C, that the vine-growing lands of Le Clos de Vougeot came into being. The local historian, Claude Courtépée, recalls how in 1359 the Abbot of Cîteaux, Jean de Bussières, made a gift of 30 barrels of wine from the abbey's vineyard, Clos de Vougeot, to Pope Gregory XI. The grateful Pope did not forget this handsome gift and four years later Jean de Bussières was made a cardinal. In the 15C the dukes of Burgundy were known as the "lords of the best wine in Christendom" and were regular suppliers of wine for the kings. Louis XIV favoured the Côte de Nuits while Madame de Pompadour greatly appreciated the Romanée Conti and Napoleon preferred Chambertin. In the 18C the wine business began to be organised: in Beaune, and later in Nuits-St-Georges and Dijon, the first trading houses were opened and representatives were sent out into France as well as abroad to find new markets.

Among the vine's "enemies," the phylloxera, a small insect that came from America, first appeared in the *département* of Gard in 1863. In 1878 it was found at Meursault and in a short time it had ravaged the Burgundian vineyards.

Ruin faced the entire wine-producing population of the area. Fortunately, the grafting of the French plants on to American vines checked the crisis and permitted the slow reconstitution of all the Burgundian vineyards without damaging the quality of the wines.

Distribution of vineyards. – A total of 37 500ha - 15 172 acres of vineyards, about half of which produce wines with officially registered names, are scattered in the *départements* of Yonne, Nièvre, Côte d'Or, Saône-et-Loire and Rhône.

The average annual production is about 40 000 000 gallons.

In Yonne the region of Chablis offers excellent white wines, dry and light, while the hillsides near Auxerre produce agreeable rosé and red wines (Irancy and Coulanges-la-Vineuse). Pouilly-sur-Loire, in Nièvre, produces well-known white wines (Pouilly-Fumé) with a flintlock taste which makes them similar to the nearby wines of Sancerre.

In Côte d'Or marvellous vineyards stretch from Dijon to the prestigious Santenay vineyard *(local map p 86)*. The Côte de Nuits produces the great red wines almost exclusively, of which the most celebrated are Gevrey-Chambertin, Morey-St-Denis, Chambolle-Musigny, Vougeot, Vosne-Romanée and Nuits-St-Georges. The Côte de Beaune produces at the same time a series of magnificent red wines at Aloxe-Corton, Savigny-lès-Beaune, Pommard and Volnay and some fine white wines (Corton-Charlemagne, Meursault and Puligny-Montrachet).

In Saône-et-Loire, the region of Mercurey (Côte of the Chalon area) has both high-quality red wines (Givry and Rully) and white wines (Rully-Montagny), while the Mâconnais region *(local map p 113)* prides itself on its Pouilly-Fuissé, a first-class quality white wine.

What makes Good Wine. – The quality of a wine depends essentially on the variety of grape and the soil and climate in which the vine grows but the work of the vine-grower also contributes to the final result.

Variety of Vines. – The choice Pinot Noir has for long been the "nobleman" of vines producing all the great red wines of Burgundy. At the time of the Great Dukes, it was already highly prized and an ordinance made by Philip the Bold in 1395 protected it against the Gamay (the common Burgundian vine). The Pinot Noir is native to Burgundy but has been successfully planted in Switzerland and even in South Africa, in Cape Province. The juice of the Pinot Noir grape is colourless and a special fermentation permits the production of Champagne. The Chardonnay is to white wines what Pinot Noir is to the red. This vine produces all the great white wines of the Côte d'Or (Montrachet-Meursault), the well-known wines of the Chalon district (Rully), the Mâconnais (Pouilly-Fuissé) – where it grows best – as well as the wines of Chablis. Other vine species are equally well known: the Aligoté, long cultivated in Burgundy, produces a lesser-quality white wine in the areas where Pinot Noir and Chardonnay do not grow. This white wine is mixed with blackcurrant liqueur *(cassis)* to make the now widely appreciated cocktail drink, **kir.** The drink was first concocted by a mayor of Dijon, Canon Kir.

The Soil. – This plays an important part in the "well-being" of the vine. It is the soil that allows the qualities of the vine to develop, to establish themselves and reveal their full virtues. It is in these dry and stony soils, well drained and easily warmed by the sun, that the vine grows best. The limestone soils produce bouquet wines of high alcoholic content that can be laid down for a long time (Côte de Nuits and Côte de Beaune); the soils of silica, limestone and clay yield the light wines (Chablis).

The Climate. – This also plays an important part in the growth of the vine. The general climatic conditions due to Burgundy's setting in a temperate zone, but in which the possibility of winter frosts cannot be excluded, give rise to a number of special factors. The Burgundian vineyards are generally set in terraces on the slopes of the hillsides at an altitude varying from 200 to 500m - 656 to 1 640ft. The best aspect seems to be southeast for the vineyards of Chablis, southwest for those of Pouilly-sur-Loire, east-southeast for the vineyards of the Côte d'Or (Côte de Nuits and Côte de Beaune) and east and south for the Chalon and Mâcon districts. In each village, the vineyards are divided into *climats* or sections. The names of the best situated sections, that is to say those that should normally produce the best wine, have the privilege of being added to the name of the village: thus, Beaune – Clos des Mouches. Some of these *climats* have enjoyed great fame for a long time and the name alone suffices to identify them: Chambertin, Musigny, Clos de Vougeot and Richebourg.

FORESTRY

Forests occupy a considerable area of Burgundy, about 1 000 000ha – 2 471 100 acres. The area under timber, about 30 per cent, is higher than the general average in France, which is 24 per cent. The forests, which are scattered over the whole province, are more extensive on the Burgundian plateaux (Châtillonnais, Tonnerrois and Sénonais) in the north, in the Morvan and on the Nivernais plateau in the centre and around Charolles, Cluny and Mâcon in the south.

The main timber areas are the forests of Othe, Châtillon, Bertranges, Planoise and St-Prix.

In the Morvan the forests are still impressive for the sheer area covered – a total of about 137 000ha – 338 540 acres – more than 50 % of some parishes. The most common species are beech, oak, hornbeam and birch.

From the 10C onwards the forests of the Morvan were exploited by the monks. In the 17C and 18C the timber for fuel was floated downstream to Paris *(pp 77 and 89)* or converted into charcoal where it was felled. Nowadays the Morvan is well known for the quality of its evergreens. The tall stands of spruce and pine trees are to be found particularly round Haut-Folin; over the last twenty years the Douglas fir has been used widely in replanting.

The alluvial lands bordering the Saône are covered in areas with oak forests (the Auxonne, Seurre and Chalon regions) giving a high-quality wood.

The best conifer forests are in the region of St-Prix, near Haut-Folin.

The Nivernais plateau has a magnificent oak forest producing first-class timber. Large areas of La Côte have been reafforested with broad-leaved plantations of black Austrian and Scots pines.

Several large industries are dependent on forestry: **wood distilling** and **charcoal making** (factories in Leuglay and Prémery) for the production of charcoal, acetic acid, methylene and their by-products; **sawmills;** manufacture of veneer and chipboard (in Auxerre, St-Usage, Prisse-lès-Mâcon) etc. In addition Burgundy produces the largest number of young trees of any region in France in the tree nurseries in the region of St-Florentin in the Yonne and Leuglay in Côte d'Or which supply the French and European markets.

CENTURIES OF IRON-WORKING

Since antiquity Burgundy has been an important iron-working centre owing to local outcrops of ore and vast reserves of timber for fuel. Archaeology has shown that even in the Gaulish era towns such as **Bibracte** and **Alise-Ste-Reine** *(p 36)* contained many iron-workers whose output was gladly exploited by the Romans. Evidence of extensive Gallo-Roman and medieval metal-working has also been discovered in the vicinity of Vézelay.

The **Cistercians,** who produced a great deal of iron until the middle of the 14C, played a cardinal role in the development of techniques : their invention of the camshaft enabled them to use hydraulic energy to drive small metal hammers and, by the beginning of the 13C, forge bellows. The high temperatures that could thus be attained and the better amalgamation of carbon and iron led them to discover cast iron. The forge building at Fontenay Abbey is one of the very rare relics of this industry in the Middle Ages *(p 104)*. Production grew from the 16C onwards owing to the invention of blast furnaces; the forges at **Buffon** *(p 119)* are one of the last examples of the so-called classic metallurgy, which was dependent on the combination of charcoal and hydraulic power.

Modern metallurgy was born in England in the 18C with the bringing together of coke as a fuel, the invention of the steam engine and puddling (purifying cast metal by stirring). In 1785 the blast furnaces at the **Creusot** royal foundry were the first in France to be fired by coke *(p 88)*. Unfortunately the technical success was not exploited for lack of financial support. English-style forges were not introduced in France until 1819; two years later they appeared in Burgundy in **Fourchambault** (1821) and then in **Ste-Colombe-sur-Seine** (1822). In 1836 the "Creusot collieries, forges, foundries and workshops" were bought by Schneider and in forty years became the largest metallurgical and mechanical centre in France.

In the late 18C and early 19C the development of the ironworks and related coalmines led to the founding or growth of several towns such as **Le Creusot, Montceau-les-Mines, Montchanin, Blanzy** in Saône-et-Loire and **La Machine** *(p 110)*, **Decize, Imphy, Fourchambault** and **Guérigny** in the Nièvre (where metallurgy was already well established). In the 20C foreign competition and increasing use of sources of energy other than coal led to a decline in certain centres. The metallurgical tradition survives, however, as is shown by the success since the 1950s of three big Burgundian companies: SEB (Société d'Emboutissage de Bourgogne) established in Selongey near Dijon, Vallourec, first French steel converter (Montbard) and Framatome, a branch of the Schneider group (Le Creusot and Chalon-sur-Saône).

Le Creusot - Power hammer

The key explains the abbreviations
and symbols used in the text or on the maps.

HISTORICAL TABLE AND NOTES

BC   ### Prehistoric period

Burgundy has always been a crossroads between the Paris basin and the Saône Valley, the countries of the north and those in the Mediterranean south.

A large deposit of bones discovered at Solutré *(p 157)* near Mâcon proves the existence of human habitation between 18 000 and 15 000 BC.

Antiquity

6C   Commercial exchanges with Greek traders from south Italy are already in existence, particularly around Châtillon-sur-Seine as is proved by the Vix Treasure *(p 76)*.
In the Gaulish era the country is inhabited by the **Aedui,** the most powerful tribe in Gaul with the Arverni; their capital is Bibracte *(p 55)*.

58   Under threat from the Helvetii the Aedui ask for help from Caesar who begins his conquest of the Gauls. His victory near Bibracte forces the Helvetii to return home.

52   The Arverni, led by Vercingetorix, form an alliance with the Aedui against Caesar; they are forced to capitulate at Alésia *(p 36)* in a decisive battle for the whole of Gaul.

51   *End of the Gallic War.*

AD   Roman civilisation extends into Burgundy.

1C and 3C   Autun becomes the capital of northeast Gaul and supplants Bibracte.

313   *Edict of Milan: the Roman Emperor Constantine grants freedom of worship to Christians.*

Late 4C   Christianity extends slowly into Burgundy.
The Roman Empire disintegrates under pressure from barbarians from the east.

Burgundy

5C   Burgundians, natives of the Baltic coast, settle in the Saône plain. More advanced than the other barbarians, they show evidence of an advanced civilisation and give their name to their new homeland: Burgundia which in French evolved into Bourgogne.

534   The Franks seize the kingdom of Burgundy.

800   Charlemagne becomes Emperor of the West.

814   Following the death of Charlemagne instability spreads throughout the Empire. The sons of the Emperor Louis the Pious dispute his legacy.

841   Charles the Bald defeats his brother Lothar at Fontanet (Fontenoy-en-Puisaye).

843   *Treaty of Verdun : Charlemagne's empire is divided among the three sons of Louis the Pious.*
Frankish Burgundy reverts to Charles the Bald. The Saône divides it from imperial Burgundy, Lothar's territory, the north of which becomes the County of Burgundy (or Franche-Comté).

Late 9C   Frankish Burgundy becomes a Duchy and takes in Langres, Troyes, Sens, Nevers, Mâcon.

Duchy of Burgundy

987-996   *Reign of Hugh Capet.*

996-1031   *Reign of Robert II the Pious.*

1002-1016   The King of France occupies Burgundy.

1032   Henri I, son of Robert II the Pious, to whom Burgundy returns, hands it over as a fief to his brother Robert I (a Burgundian branch of the House of Capet which survived until 1361).
Under the Capet dukes Burgundy is a bastion of Christianity: Cluny, then Cîteaux and Clairvaux *(p 30)*, reach the height of their influence.

1270   Death of Saint Louis at the siege of Tunis.

1337-1453   Hundred Years War.

1361   Duke Philippe de Rouvres dies young without issue; the line of the Capet dukes comes to an end. The Duchy passes to the King of France, John the Good, who was regent during the Duke's minority.

THE GREAT DUKES OF BURGUNDY *see also p 89*

For over a century (1364-1477) Burgundy reached the height of its power and prestige.

Philip the Bold (1364-1404). —Though scarcely more than a child, Philip fought heroically at the side of his father, King John II the Good of France, at the battle of Poitiers (1356). He earned the nickname of "the Bold" when, though wounded and a prisoner, he landed a well-aimed blow on an Englishman who had insulted the king of France. By the time he became duke of Burgundy (1364) Philip was a superb knight, tall and well-built; he loved sport and women. He devoted himself whole heartedly to his duchy and the interests of his House. His marriage in 1369 to Margaret of Flanders, the richest heiress in Europe, made him the most powerful prince in Christendom. He lived in great splendour and kept a large and magnificent household in the palace he had built where he employed painters and sculptors from Flanders. He was always luxuriously dressed; in his hat he wore twelve ostrich plumes, two pheasant feathers and two plumes from birds of India. A golden necklace with an eagle and a lion carrying his motto *En Loyauté,* set with a profusion of rubies, sapphires and pearls, was part of his daily apparel.
Philip founded the Chartreuse de Champmol in Dijon as a mausoleum for himself and his descendants. The finest marble from Liège and alabaster from Genoa were provided for the tomb which was designed in 1384 by the sculptor, **Jean de Marville.** On his death the decoration was entrusted to **Claus Sluter.** Philip the Bold spent so much money that, when he died in 1404, his sons had to pledge the ducal silver to pay for his funeral. In accordance with Burgundian custom, his widow came and placed her purse, her keys and her belt on the coffin as a sign that she renounced succession to any of her husband's goods.

John the Fearless (1404-1419). – He succeeded his father, Philip the Bold. He was a small man, weak and ugly. But he was also brave, intelligent and ambitious and had already shown his prowess during the crusade against the Turks. No sooner had he become Duke of Burgundy than he started a quarrel with the royal council against his cousin, Louis d'Orléans, brother of the mad king, Charles VI. As Louis had a knotted stick as his emblem, John took that of a plane, signifying that he would soon "plane that stick". This he achieved in 1407 by having his rival assassinated and although master of Paris he was staunchly opposed by the Orleanist party which controlled the mad king. When the leader of the Orleanist faction, the poet Charles d'Orléans, was captured at Agincourt (1415) and had left for 25 years of imprisonment in England, the leadership was taken on by Charles' father-in-law, Count Bernard VII of Armagnac.

During the struggle between the Armagnacs and the Burgundians, which set Frenchmen against each other in a civil war from which the English gained great profit, John the Fearless showed himself ready to make an agreement with the Dauphin, the future king Charles VII. He agreed to a meeting with Charles on 11 September, 1419, on the bridge at Montereau, but there he was "traitorously felled by an axe, then murdered".

Philip the Good (1419-1467) and the Golden Fleece. –

Filled with vengeance Philip the Good, son of John the Fearless, allied himself with the English and in 1430 handed over to them for the enormous sum of 10 000 *livres*, Joan of Arc whom he had captured at Compiègne. A few years later, however, Philip came to an understanding with Charles VII at the Treaty of Arras, and further enlarged his domains. Dijon thus became the capital of a powerful state which included a great part of Holland, almost all Belgium, Luxembourg, Flanders, Artois, Hainaut, Picardy and all the land between the Loire and the Jura *(see map p 19)*.

Philip, who had an even greater taste for magnificence than his predecessors, lived as a veritable sovereign. Five great officers of State, the Marshal of Burgundy, the Admiral of Flanders, the Chamberlain, the Master of the Horse and the Chancellor, surrounded the Duke, who attracted poets, painters and musicians to his court, one of the most sumptuous.

On 14 January 1429, the day of his marriage with Isabella of Portugal, Philip founded the sovereign Order of the Golden Fleece. Created in honour of God, the Virgin Mary and St Andrew, this order originally consisted of thirty-one members, all of whom swore allegiance to the Grand Master, Philip the Good and his successors. They met at least once every three years and

Dijon Fine Arts Museum
Philip the Good
by Roger Van der Weyden

wore the most sumptuous clothing: a long scarlet cloak, trimmed with grey squirrel, hung from the shoulders over a tunic of the same colour also trimmed with squirrel. The ducal motto: *Aultre n'auray* (not for others), stood out from a background of firestones, quartz, steel and fleeces. The collar that carried the fleece was made from firestones and quartz from which sparks flashed. The headquarters of the Golden Fleece was for a long time the ducal Holy Chapel at Dijon, which was destroyed during the Revolution. After being in existence for centuries, this order is today one of the most distinguished and exclusive.

When one of its members dies, his heirs must send his necklace and Fleece back to the Grand Master.

GENEALOGY OF THE HOUSES OF FRANCE AND BURGUNDY IN THE 14 AND 15 C

This chart is selective and allows one to trace
the affiliation of reigning monarchs with the
dates of their reign, their consorts and it includes
other people mentioned in the guide

PHILIP VI (1328-50)
Jeanne de Bourgogne
Blanche de Navarre

JOHN II THE GOOD (1350-64)
Bonne of Luxembourg

CHARLES V (1364-80)	LOUIS I	JOHN	PHILIP THE BOLD
Jeanne de Bourbon	Duke of Anjou	Duke of Berry	Duke of Burgundy (1364-1404)
			Margaret of Flanders

CHARLES VI (1380-1422)	LOUIS		JOHN THE FEARLESS
Isabel of Bavaria	Duke of Orleans		Duke of Burgundy (1404-19)
	Valentina Visconti		Margaret of Holland

CHARLES VII (1422-61)	CHARLES		PHILIP THE GOOD
Marie d'Anjou	Duke of Orleans		Duke of Burgundy (1419-67)
	Isabelle de France		Michèle de Valois
	Mary of Cleeves		Bonne d'Artois
LOUIS XI (1461-83)			Isabel of Portugal
Margaret of Scotland			
Charlotte de Savoie			
			CHARLES THE BOLD
CHARLES VIII (1483-98)	ANNE de Beaujeu	JEANNE de France	Duke of Burgundy (1467-77)
Anne of Brittany		Louis XII	Catherine de Valois
			Isabelle de Bourbon
	LOUIS XII (1498-1515)		Margaret of York
	Jeanne de France		
	Anne of Brittany		MARY (d 1482)
	Mary Tudor		Maximilian of Hapsburg

HOUSE OF FRANCE   HOUSE OF BURGUNDY

Charles the Bold (1467-1477). – This was the last and perhaps the most famous member of the House of Valois and Dukes of Burgundy. Tall, strongly built and vigorous, Charles loved violent exercise and hunting in particular; but he was also a cultured man who spent much of his time in study. Above all, he was passionately fond of history. He was proud and intensely ambitious, and as Commynes (historian and chronicler 1447-1511) said of him: "He was very pompous in his dress and in all other things and altogether a little too exaggerated... He wanted great glory." As his father had borne the same name as Philip of Macedonia, he dreamed of becoming a second Alexander and was constantly waging war, aimed at undermining the power of Louis XI, who on his side did everything possible to break up the Burgundian State.

Charles was killed during the siege of Nancy, which was defended by René of Lorraine. His body was found in a frozen pool, half eaten by wolves.

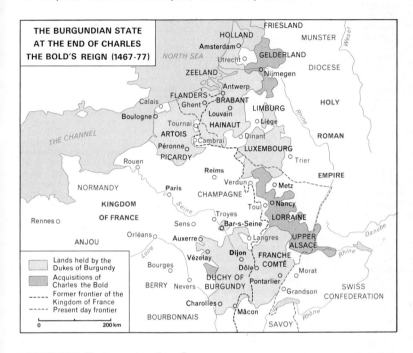

THE BURGUNDIAN STATE
AT THE END OF CHARLES
THE BOLD'S REIGN (1467-77)

Lands held by the Dukes of Burgundy
Acquisitions of Charles the Bold
Former frontier of the Kingdom of France
Present day frontier

0   200 km

Return to the Crown

1477	On the death of Charles the Bold, Louis XI annexes the royal territory of Burgundy and the Burgundian town of Picardy; deprived of a large part of her inheritance, Mary of Burgundy, daughter of the late Duke, marries Maximilian of Habsburg who thus acquires the remainder of the old Duchy *(see map above)*. Their marriage produces Philippe the Fair, whose son, Charles V, continues the struggle against France under François I.
1513	Dijon is besieged by the Imperial forces *(p 91)*.
1589-1610	*Reign of Henri IV.*
1601	Although attached to the crown, Burgundy leads a separate existence and acquires the Bresse, the Bugey and the Valmorey.
1610-1643	*Reign of Louis XIII.*
1631-1789	The Princes of Condé succeed one another as Governors of the Duchy.

19C and 20C

1814-1815	Congress of Châtillon-sur-Seine and the invasion of Burgundy by the Allies.
1822	Invention of photography by Nicéphore Niepce in St-Loup-de-Varenne.
1878	Vineyards ravaged by phylloxera.
1914	In Châtillon-sur-Seine Joffre issues the order of the day on 6 September *(p 76)*.
1940-1944	The French Resistance is active in Burgundy: Army children from Autun in combat; the Châtillonnais forests used as a refuge.
14 Sept. 1944	The Division Leclerc joins the army of De Lattre de Tassigny near Châtillon-sur-Seine.

MONASTIC LIFE IN BURGUNDY

After the turmoil of the Carolingian decline, the church used its great influence and long-established cultural tradition to resume a leading role in society; there was a great renewal of fervour for the monastic life throughout western Europe. The church owed its importance mainly to the position held by the religious orders – in particular the order of St Benedict – which became more numerous from the 10C onwards. France was in the vanguard of this religious revival and, in France, it was Burgundy that provided the driving force.

The First Religious Orders – St Benedict and his Rule. – In 529 Benedict, who was born in Norcia in Umbria, Italy, moved from Subiaco where he had at first led the life of a recluse, to Monte Cassino where he worked out his "Constitution"; it was soon to be followed by numerous monasteries. His advice, which developed into the famous "Benedictine Rule", showed great moderation; although fasting, silence and abstinence were recommended, mortification and painful penances were severely condemned. St Benedict gave an important place to manual labour in the monks' working day (six to eight hours, against four for reading and four for divine office). The abbots of the Benedictine monasteries, who were elected for life, had absolute authority. All relations with the outside world were to be avoided and the community had to make itself completely self-supporting by its own labours.
The flexibility of this rule explains its later success in Italy, Gaul and Germany, especially from the 10C onwards.

Cluny and the triumph of Benedictine Rule. – In 910, the founding of a monastery in the region of Mâcon by the Duke of Aquitaine, Guillaume le Pieux (William the Pious) marked the beginning of an important religious reform associated with the name of Cluny. The period was, indeed, propitious for such a change. The social "climate" – start of the feudal system, political turmoil and instability of royal power – brought about a mystical movement and an influx of men to the cloisters. A return to the spirit of the Benedictine Rule was marked by the observance of the great principles – chastity, obedience and fasting – but divine service occupied the greater part of the day, reducing and almost suppressing the time for manual labour and intellectual work.
The great innovation was the complete independence of the new abbey from all political power. Under its foundation charter Cluny was directly attached to the Holy See in Rome; given the remoteness of Pontifical authority, this arrangement in fact conferred complete autonomy on the order. The expansion of the Cluny order was rapid; by the beginning of the 12C there were 1 450 monasteries with 10 000 monks, scattered over France, Germany, Spain, Italy and Britain, all dependent on Cluny. Among its Burgundian filials were the abbeys or priories of St-Germain of Auxerre, Paray-le-Monial, St-Marcel of Chalon, Vézelay, Nevers (St-Sever and St-Étienne) and La Charité-sur-Loire.
This great expansion is largely explained by the personalities and the length of the "reign" of the great abbots of Cluny (Sts Odo, Mayeul, Odilo, Hugh and Peter the Venerable), who chose their own successors and surrounded themselves with men of great competence. The abbot in those days was a person of very considerable standing, sometimes more powerful than the Pope himself, whose guide and counsellor he was. Kings came to him for arbitration.
For two or three generations Cluny was the centre of a veritable empire. Its organisation however was based on an extreme centralisation and the whole weight of power was vested in the abbot of Cluny. Should this supreme power be misused, the whole structure was under threat.

Cîteaux and St Bernard. – It was precisely to fight against the luxury and the slackening of discipline among the monks of Cluny that St Bernard spoke out, "this Frenchman from Burgundy who was, by far, the strongest, most radiant and influential personality in the west". It was a strange destiny for the young nobleman born at the Château of Fontaine near Dijon, who at the age of twenty-one renounced all riches and honours and with thirty-two companions went to the monastery of Cîteaux in search of God's mercy. On his arrival in 1112, the monastery, founded fourteen years earlier by Robert de Molesmes, was passing through a grave crisis and its future seemed in jeopardy. In a short time Bernard completely transformed this difficult situation by the example and influence he exercised on all around him.
In 1115, leaving Cîteaux in full development, he went to the poor country along the borders of Burgundy and Champagne. The valley of Absinthe became "Clairvaux" (the clear valley). Bernard, now an abbot, carried out great work there. At first completely destitute, he met with enormous difficulties: a harsh climate, sickness and physical suffering due to a life of self-denial. He imposed the hardest of work on his monks as well as himself, "eating boiled vegetables and drinking spring water, sleeping on bare boards or a mean pallet, doing without heating in winter and wearing the same simple garments of wool both night and day".

The monastic foundations. – Reward was near: the fame of Bernard soon attracted to Clairvaux so many applicants for the monastic life that the abbey of Trois-Fontaines was founded in the Marne in 1121. At his death in 1153, Cîteaux had 700 monks and its influence was considerable: 350 abbeys were attached to it and among them the first four "daughters": La Ferté, Morimond, Pontigny and, above all, Clairvaux, which thanks to Saint Bernard maintained its leading role at the heart of the Cistercian order. During his abbacy Clairvaux experienced an extraordinary prosperity: from 1135 a total of 4 448 acres of forest land and 865 acres of meadows and fields belonged to the abbey, where stone buildings had replaced the wooden structures of earlier years; thus the man who seemed destined to lead a life of contemplation, a mystic convinced of the superiority of monastic life, was forced to play a political role of primary importance. Up to his death in 1153 his name was one of the greatest that the church had produced. Writer, theologian, philosopher, monk, military leader, statesman and arbiter of Europe, St Bernard was all these at the same time.

Cistercian Law. – St Bernard knew how to define Benedictine Rule, promulgated before him, in the most forceful manner and to apply it to the letter. He forbade the collection of tithes or the acquisition or purchase of land and he imposed on his monks at Clairvaux – and in a wider sense on all the monks of the Cistercian order – rigorous living conditions: their dress consisted in all seasons of a tunic of woollen serge. The food was very simple. Seven hours were set aside for repose: the monks slept fully dressed in a common dormitory on a simple straw pallet with a single woollen blanket. Every hour of the day was planned with rigorous precision: roused between 1am and 2am, the monks sang matins, then lauds, they celebrated private mass, recited the canonic hours – prime, tierce, sext, nones, vespers and compline – and took part in the community mass. Divine service thus took up six to seven hours and the rest of the time was divided between manual labour, intellectual work and pious reading.

The abbot, leader of the community, lived with his monks, ate with them, presided at worship, in chapter and at meetings. He was assisted by a prior, who took his place when he was absent.

The Cistercian Order in the 20C. – The organisation of the Cistercian order was based on the "Charter of Charity" established about 1115, a sort of link uniting the different abbeys, all equal with one another.

Today some 3 000 reformed Cistercians, governed by an Abbot General bearing the title of Abbot of Cîteaux and residing in Rome, are scattered throughout the world in about 89 abbeys, of which fifteen are in France. All the abbots of the order meet at Cîteaux on the occasion of the General Chapter.

There are a further 2 000 monks belonging to 55 abbeys or priories, of which twelve are in France, ruled by the same Abbot General but with a different General Chapter.

INTELLECTUAL AND LITERARY LIFE

Middle Ages and the Renaissance. – In the Middle Ages intellectual life centred on the churches and the monasteries: the abbey of St-Germain in Auxerre played the role of a real university in the time of Charlemagne and, a little later, the abbey of Cluny was the focal point of intellectual life.

The 12C was dominated by **St Bernard**; at Clairvaux he built up a remarkable library and was himself one of the great writers of his time. The 12C was also the era of chivalry; epic poetry was inspired by traditional legends mingled with fantastic events; ballads (chansons de geste) became a popular form of composition. The history of Burgundy provided the theme of **Girart de Roussillon,** a literary masterpiece, and the story of *La Châtelaine de Vergy*. The religious Mystery and Passion plays – a popular form of theatre – form a part of medieval literature: the *Passion of Autun* and the *Passion of Semur* were particularly popular.

In the 15C the Dukes of Burgundy patronised chroniclers, who related embellished accounts of the events marking their reigns: Commynes and Olivier de la Marche are the best known.

The humanism of the 16C is exemplified by a great philosopher and theologian, **Pontus de Thiard,** a native of the Mâconnais region, who was a member of the Pléiade. **Guy Coquille,** born at Decize, was a celebrated jurist who wrote *Coutumes du pays et duché de Nivernais*. A contemporary of theirs, **Theodore Beza** from Vézelay, was a humanist of great learning: a convert to Protestantism and successor to John Calvin in Geneva, he published many dogmatic and theological works. **Bonaventure des Périers** of Arnay-le-Duc was a witty and malicious storyteller, who was often biting and satirical.

17C and 18C. – The 17C was dominated in Burgundy by the great figure of **Bossuet,** who was born in Dijon. Two other writers associated with Burgundy are **Madame de Sévigné,** who spent her youth at the Château of Bourbilly, and her cousin, Bussy-Rabutin *(p 64)*. **Vauban** *(p 143)* was not only a great military engineer but also a writer of talent, as is shown by his *Oisivetés* and *Projet d'une Dîme Royale*.

In the 18C Jean Bouhier, President of the French Parliament, wrote *La coutume de Bourgogne*. A little later Charles de Brosses, first President of the Burgundian Parliament, revealed himself, with his *Lettres Familières sur l'Italie*, as a humanist of worth and a storyteller full of life and humour.

Buffon, Burgundian by birth and association, played an important part in the spread of French science *(p 118)*. In another field **Alexis Piron** *(p 50)* made himself known by his epigrams and his satirical comedies. **Réstif de la Bretonne,** a prolific novelist, who was also at times a philosopher, was born at Sacy near Vermenton. His work, often licentious but overflowing with an imagination that was based on reality, is a valuable source of information on society at the end of the 18C.

The Romantic and Contemporary Periods. – **Lamartine,** a native of Mâcon, was one of the great names of French romanticism and his literary influence was considerable in the 19C; in his *Méditations*, he extols the beauty of his native countryside. **Father Lacordaire,** the famous 19C preacher and writer, was born at Recey-sur-Ource. Along with the Breton, Lamennais, he founded a liberal Catholic movement and it was he who reintroduced the Dominican Order *(p 103)* to France.

Among the novelists and poets of our times, many delight in describing the most typical aspects of the province. **Colette** *(p 139),* Marie Noël and Gaston Roupnel have been faithful interpreters of Burgundian spirit and countryside. Jacques Copeau, forsaking his theatrical troupe "Le Vieux Colombier" in Paris, found in Burgundy his greatest dramatic inspiration. The poet Achille Millien has sung of the Nivernais earth and gathered together the old traditions of the people of the Morvan. Besides Claude Tillier, author of *Mon Oncle Benjamin,* Clamecy was the birthplace of **Romain Rolland** from whose pen came *Jean-Christophe* and *Colas Breugnon*. Franc-Nohain and **Maurice Genevoix** *(p 90),* from the Nivernais region, have also described the countryside they knew and loved.

The novelist **Henri Vincenot,** born in 1912 in Dijon, described the daily life of the Burgundian peasants during the early 19C and during the interwar period.

ART

ABC OF ARCHITECTURE

To assist readers unfamiliar with the terminology employed in architecture, we describe below the most commonly used terms, which we hope will make their visits to ecclesiastical, military and civil buildings more interesting.

Ecclesiastical architecture

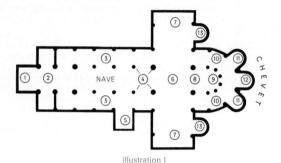

illustration I

Ground plan. – The more usual Catholic form is based on the outline of a cross with the two arms of the cross forming the transept: ① Porch – ② Narthex – ③ Side aisles (sometimes double) – ④ Bay (transverse section of the nave between 2 pillars) – ⑤ Side chapel (often predates the church) – ⑥ Transept crossing – ⑦ Arms of the transept, sometimes with a side doorway – ⑧ Chancel, nearly always facing east towards Jerusalem; the chancel often vast in size was reserved for the monks in abbatial churches – ⑨ High altar – ⑩ Ambulatory: in pilgrimage churches the aisles were extended round the chancel, forming the ambulatory, to allow the faithful to file past the relics – ⑪ Radiating or apsidal chapel – ⑫ Axial chapel. In churches which are not dedicated to the Virgin this chapel, in the main axis of the building is often consecrated to the Virgin (Lady Chapel) – ⑬ Transept chapel.

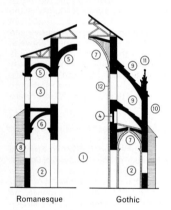

Romanesque   Gothic

◀ illustration II

Cross-section: ① Nave – ② Aisle – ③ Tribune or Gallery – ④ Triforium – ⑤ Barrel vault – ⑥ Half-barrel vault – ⑦ Pointed vault – ⑧ Buttress – ⑨ Flying buttress – ⑩ Pier of a flying buttress – ⑪ Pinnacle – ⑫ Clerestory window.

illustration III ▶

Gothic cathedral: ① Porch – ② Gallery – ③ Rose window – ④ Belfry (sometimes with a spire) – ⑤ Gargoyle acting as a waterspout for the roof gutter – ⑥ Buttress – ⑦ Pier of a flying buttress (abutment) – ⑧ Flight or span of flying buttress – ⑨ Double-course flying buttress – ⑩ Pinnacle – ⑪ Side chapel – ⑫ Radiating or apsidal chapel – ⑬ Clerestory windows – ⑭ Side doorway – ⑮ Gable – ⑯ Pinnacle – ⑰ Spire over the transept crossing.

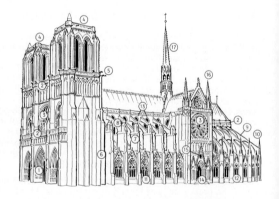

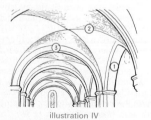

illustration IV

Groined vaulting:
① Main arch – ② Groin
③ Transverse arch

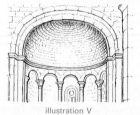

illustration V

Oven vault:
termination of a barrel
vaulted nave

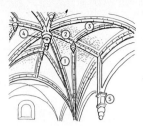

illustration VI

Lierne and tierceron vaulting:
① Diagonal – ② Lierne
③ Tierceron – ④ Pendant
⑤ Corbel

illustration VII

Quadripartite vaulting:
① Diagonal – ② Transverse
③ Stringer – ④ Flying buttress
⑤ Keystone

▼ illustration VIII

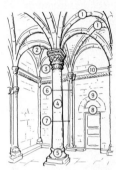

Doorway: ① Archivolt. Depending on the architectural style of the building this can be rounded, pointed, basket-handled, ogee or even adorned by a gable – ② Arching, covings (with string courses, mouldings, carvings or adorned with statues). Recessed arches or orders form the archivolt – ③ Tympanum – ④ Lintel – ⑤ Archshafts – ⑥ Embrasures. Arch shafts, splaying sometimes adorned with statues or columns – ⑦ Pier (often adorned by a statue) – ⑧ Hinges and other ironwork.

illustration IX ▶

Arches and pillars: ① Ribs or ribbed vaulting – ② Abacus – ③ Capital – ④ Shaft – ⑤ Base – ⑥ Engaged column – ⑦ Pier of arch wall – ⑧ Lintel – ⑨ Discharging or relieving arch – ⑩ Frieze.

Military architecture

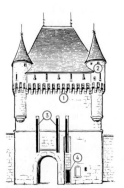

illustration X

Fortified enclosure: ① Hoarding (projecting timber gallery) – ② Machicolations (corbelled crenellations) – ③ Barbican – ④ Keep or donjon – ⑤ Covered watchpath – ⑥ Curtain wall – ⑦ Outer curtain wall – ⑧ Postern.

illustration XI

Towers and curtain walls: ① Hoarding – ② Crenellations – ③ Merlon – ④ Loophole or arrow slit – ⑤ Curtain wall – ⑥ Bridge or drawbridge.

◀ illustration XII

Fortified gatehouse: ① Machicolations – ② Watch turrets or bartizan – ③ Slots for the arms of the drawbridge – ④ Postern.

illustration XIII ▶

Star fortress: ① Entrance – ② Drawbridge – ③ Glacis – ④ Ravelin or half-moon – ⑤ Moat – ⑥ Bastion – ⑦ Watch turret – ⑧ Town – ⑨ Assembly area.

23

◀ illustration XIV

Dome on squinches:
① Octagonal dome –
② Squinch – ③ Arches of
transept crossing

illustration XV ▶

Dome on pendentives:
① Circular dome – ② Pendentive
– ③ Arches of transept crossing

◀ illustration XVI

Altar with retable or altarpiece:
① Retable or altarpiece –
② Predella – ③ Crowning
piece – ④ Altar table –
⑤ Altar front

illustration XVII ▶

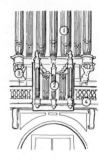

Organ:
① Great organ case –
② Little organ case –
③ Caryatid – ④ Loft

◀ illustration XVIII

Rood beam or tref: This supports the triumphal (chancel or rood) arch at the entrance to the chancel. The rood carries a Crucifix flanked by statues of the Virgin and St John and sometimes other personages from the Calvary.

illustration XX ▼

Stalls: ① High back – ② Elbow rest – ③ Cheek-piece – ④ Misericord.

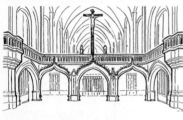

illustration XIX

Rood screen: This replaces the rood beam in larger churches, and may be used for preaching and reading of the Epistle and Gospel. Many disappeared from the 17C onwards as they tended to hide the altar.

BURGUNDY'S FINEST ROMANESQUE CHURCHES

★★★

Fontenay	Abbey Church
Vézelay	Basilica of St Mary Magdalene

★★

Autun	St Lazarus' Cathedral
La Charité-sur-Loire	Church of the Virgin
Paray-le-Monial	Basilica of the Sacred Heart
Tournus	Church of St Philibert

★

Anzy-le-Duc	Village church
Beaune	Collegiate Church of the Virgin
Chapaize	Church of St Martin
Cluny	Abbey Church of St Peter and St Paul
Nevers	Church of St Stephen
Saulieu	Basilica of St Andoche
Semur-en-Brionnais	Village church

Other Romanesque churches described in this guide

Avallon (church of St Lazarus), Bard-le-Régulier, Blanot, Bois-Ste-Marie, Brancion, la Bussière-sur-Ouche, Bussy-le-Grand, Champvoux, Châteauneuf (Saône-et-Loire), Châtillon-sur-Seine, Chissey-lès-Mâcon, Clessé, Combertault, Decize, Druyes-les-Belles-Fontaines, Échannay, Farges, Gourdon, Iguerande, Jailly, Lancharre, Malay, Mars-sur-Allier, Metz-le-Comte, Montceaux-l'Étoile, Marzy, Mont-St-Vincent, Nuits-St-Georges, Perrecy-les-Forges, Pontaubert, la Rochepot, Rouy, St-Hippolyte, St-Julien-de-Jonzy, St-Point, St-Révérien, St-Seine-sur-Vingeanne, St-Vincent-des-Prés, Taizé, Til-Châtel, Varenne-l'Arconce and le Villars.

ARCHITECTURAL TERMS USED IN THE GUIDE

Aisle: illustration I.
Altarpiece or retable: illustration XVI.
Ambulatory: illustration I.
Apsidal or radiating chapel: illustration I.
Archivolt: illustration VIII.
Arrow slit: illustration XI.
Axial or Lady Chapel: in the axis of the church; illustration I.
Barrel vaulting: illustration II.
Basket-handled arch: depressed arch common to late-medieval and Renaissance architecture.
Bay: illustration I.
Bracket: small supporting piece of stone or timber to carry a beam or cornice.
Buttress: illustration II.
Capital: illustration IX.
Chevet: illustration I.
Ciborium: canopy over the high altar or a receptacle for the Eucharist.
Coffered ceiling: vault or ceiling decorated with sunken panels.
Corbel: illustration VI.
Credence: side table, shelf or niche for eucharistic elements.
Crypt: underground chamber or chapel.
Curtain wall: illustration X.
Depressed arch: three-centred arch sometimes called a basket-handled arch.
Diagonal ribs: illustration VII.
Dome: illustrations XIV and XV.
Entombment or Holy Sepulchre: compositions covering this theme show the Placing of Christ in the Tomb and usually include seven figures around the crucified Christ.
Flamboyant: latest phase (15C) of French Gothic architecture; name taken from the undulating (flame-like) lines of the window tracery.
Fresco: mural paintings executed on wet plaster.
Gable: triangular part of an end wall carrying a sloping roof; the term is also applied to the steeply-pitched ornamental pediments of Gothic architecture; illustration III.
Gallery: illustration II.
Gargoyle: illustration III.
Glory: luminous nimbus surrounding the body; mandorla: an almond-shaped glory from the Italian *mandorla* meaning almond.
Groined vaulting: illustration IV.
High relief: haut-relief; applies to a sculpture or carved work when it projects more than one half of its true proportions from the background.
Jetty: overhanging upper storey.
Keep or donjon: illustration X.
Keystone: illustration VII.
Lintel: illustrations VIII and IX.
Lombard arcades: decorative blind arcading composed of small arches and intervening pilaster strips; typical of Romanesque art in Lombardy.
Loophole or arrow slit: illustration XI.
Low relief: bas-relief; opposite of high relief.
Machicolations: illustration X.
Mandorla: see Glory.
Misericord: illustration XX.
Moat: ditch, generally water-filled.
Modillion: small console supporting a cornice.
Mullion: a vertical post dividing a window.
Organ: illustration XVII.
Oven vaulting: illustration V.
Parclose screen: screen separating a chapel or the choir from the rest of the church.
Pepperpot roof: conical roof.
Pier: illustration VIII.
Pietà: Italian term designating the Virgin Mary with the dead Christ on her knees.
Pilaster: engaged rectangular column.
Pilaster strip: decorative feature characteristic of Romanesque architecture in Lombardy consisting of shallow projecting pilasters and blind arcading.
Pinnacle: illustrations II and III.
Piscina: basin for washing the sacred vessels.
Pointed arch: diagonal arch supporting a vault; illustrations VI and VII.
Porch: covered approach to the entrance to a building.
Postern: illustrations X and XII.
Recessed arches and orders: illustration VIII.
Rood beam or tref: illustration XVIII.
Rood screen: illustration XIX.
Rose or wheel window: illustration III.
Semicircular arch: round-headed arch.
Sexpartite vaulting: six compartments formed by three intersecting diagonals.
Spire: illustration III.
Stalls: illustration XX.
Timber framing: method of construction using a timber framework with interspaces filled with brickwork or plaster.
Tracery: interesting stone ribwork in the upper part of a window.
Transept: illustration I.
Triforium: small arcaded gallery above the aisles; illustration II.
Triptych: three panels hinged together, chiefly used as an altarpiece.
Twinned or paired: columns or pilasters grouped in twos.
Tympanum: illustration VIII.
Voussoir: illustration VIII.
Watch path or wall walk: illustration X.

ART IN BURGUNDY

It is not surprising that Burgundy has an incomparably rich artistic tradition since the necessary stimulation has always existed in the area. Since the earliest times the duchy has been a crossroads, where migrating people and many and divers influences have come together. The discovery of the Vix Treasure shows that strong currents were active in the region of Châtillon-sur-Seine *(p 75)* in about the 6C BC.

In the 15C, on the initiative of the Great Dukes, many groups of artists from Paris and Flanders settled in Dijon, which they made one of the most important artistic centres of Europe.

This penetration of foreign influences, as well as the enduring qualities of Roman civilisation and ancient traditions, combined with the expression of the Burgundian temperament led to the blossoming of a regional art that holds an honoured place in the artistic history of France.

GALLO-ROMAN ART

During their occupation, the Romans were responsible for the building of numerous monuments in Burgundy. To this day the town of Autun, built at the order of the Emperor Augustus to replace Bibracte, capital of the Aedui tribe, recalls Roman civilisation with its two monumental gateways and its vast theatre.

Excavations undertaken at Alésia, at the presumed site of the camp where Vercingetorix made his last stand before the Roman legions of Julius Caesar in 52 BC, have led to the discovery of a complete town built a little later: paved streets, the foundations of temples and a forum as well as many dwellings have been uncovered.

Other excavations carried out at the source of the Seine have revealed the ruins of a temple and a number of bronze statuettes and unusual wooden sculptures. Numerous pieces of pottery dating from Gallo-Roman times as well as examples of gold and silver work of great value were found more than fifty years ago at Vertault, not far from Châtillon-sur-Seine.

At Dijon the remains of an entrenched camp *(Castrum Divionense),* built about AD 273, have been uncovered. Excavations at Fontaines-Salées near St-Père-sous-Vézelay have revealed very extensive Gallo-Roman baths.

ROMANESQUE ART

Pre-Romanesque Art

After a period of artistic eclipse in the early Middle Ages, the Carolingian epoch, 8C-9C, saw a revival of architecture. The plans of the religious buildings were simple and the buildings of poorly cut stone were rudimentary. Part of the former crypt of St Benignus' Cathedral in Dijon and the crypts of Flavigny-sur-Ozerain and St Germanus in Auxerre are among the most ancient of these monuments.

During this period sculpture was clumsily executed: the crypt of Flavigny-sur-Ozerain, all that remains of a mid-8C basilica, contains four shafts of columns of which three appear to be Roman and the fourth Carolingian. The capitals are of great interest: they carry a decoration of flat foliage of rudimentary execution. Two of the capitals in the crypt of St Benignus' Cathedral in Dijon are decorated on each face by a man at prayer, his arms raised.

Dijon. – Capital in the crypt of St Benignus' Cathedral

Sculpted in situ the capitals show the experimental nature of the work - some sides are no more than outlines *(see illustration above)*.

During the same period, frescoes and glazed surfaces were used in the decoration of the walls of religious buildings. In 1927 fine frescoes representing amongst other scenes the stoning of St Stephen were discovered in the crypt of St Germanus in Auxerre.

Romanesque Architecture

Owing to particularly favourable conditions — numerous towns, rich abbeys and abundant building material — the Romanesque school in Burgundy showed an extraordinary vitality in the 11C and 12C not only in architecture but also in sculpture and painting; its considerable influence spread beyong the geographic limits of Burgundy.

The year 1000 saw the birth of a new impetus in the desire to build which is explained by the end of invasions, the strengthening of royal power and the discovery of new building techniques.

"As the third year after the millennium was opening," wrote Raoul Glaber, a monk of St-Bénigne at Dijon, "in all Christianity and particularly in Italy and the Gauls one saw a rebuilding of the churches... even those which did not need to be rebuilt were replaced by the Christians with even finer buildings... It seemed as if the world had shaken the dust from its old cloak in order to clothe everything in the white robes of its young churches..."

The first Romanesque churches. — Among the great builders of this period, Abbot **Guglielmo da Volpiano,** of Italian origin and related to the greatest families of his time, built a new basilica in Dijon on the site of the tomb of St Benignus. Begun in 1001, the building was consecrated in 1018.

Though this abbey completely disappeared in the 12C following a fire, the church of St Vorles in Châtillon-sur-Seine — considerably modified in the first years of the 11C by the Bishop of Langres, Brun de Roucy, a relation of Guglielmo da Volpiano — provides an example of the features of Romanesque art during this period: slipshod building methods with flat stones badly placed, massive pillars, rudimentary decoration of mural niches and cornices with Lombard arcades.

The most striking example of the architecture of this time is the church of **St Philibert** in Tournus *(p 162)*. The narthex and the upper storey of the narthex, built at the beginning of the 11C, are the oldest parts known today. In this powerful architecture, one is struck by a sobriety that is almost austere.

Cluny and its School. — Although in the beginning Romanesque art owed much to foreign influences, the following period saw the triumph of a new style from Cluny, which was to spread throughout all Burgundy and even to Switzerland.

It is at Cluny that the principal characteristics of Burgundian Romanesque architecture are to be found united for the first time.

Up to the time of the building of St Peter's in Rome in the 16C, the Abbey of Cluny was the largest church in all Christendom; its total internal length greatly exceeded that of the Gothic cathedrals that were built from the 13C onwards.

In 1247 an Italian churchman travelling through France remarked "that Cluny is the noblest Burgundian monastery of the Benedictine Black Monk Order. The buildings are so extensive that the Pope with his cardinals and entire retinue and the king and his court may be accommodated together, without upsetting the monks' routine or putting them out of their cells."

The remains of the abbey, started by St Hugh in 1088 and completed about 1130 *(see reconstruction of the abbey p 80)*, are still impressive owing to their extent and exceptional size, and allow one to recognise the general characteristics of the School of Cluny: the broken-barrel vaulting is a complete innovation for this period.

The Burgundian architects avoided the use of semicircular vaulting as much as possible and substituted broken-barrel vaulting which was far more efficient in withstanding the strains and stresses of the building. This style of vaulting consists of each bay having a transverse arch; by lessening the stress, the use of broken arches brings about a reduction in the weight on the walls and it is thus possible to raise the vaulting to a great height. The pillars are flanked by fluted pilasters in the antique style: above the narrow arches runs a false triforium of alternating bays and pilasters, which is surmounted by a clerestory. This arrangement — three storeys rising to a pointed vault — is found in many churches in the region.

The completion of so large a building, in which a great many architects and artists participated, was to make a profound impression on the construction of other churches in the Mâconnais, Charollais and Brionnais districts.

The priory church of **Paray-le-Monial** is a smaller replica of the great abbey church of Cluny. It was also conceived by St Hugh and has an identical plan of construction.

At **La Charité-sur-Loire** another priory dependent on the great abbey also shows the influence of Cluny. Other Burgun-

Autun. — Cathedral nave

dian monuments take their derivation more or less directly from the abbey of Cluny. In the church of St Lazarus in **Autun,** consecrated in 1130, a much simplified plan of Cluny is to be found; "Roman" influence is however often in evidence: on the piers fluted pilasters copied from the antique style have replaced engaged columns; on the triforium arcade the decoration is similar to that of the Arroux Gateway although this ornamentation is not without a certain heaviness *(see illustration right)*.

At **Semur-en-Brionnais,** home of the family of St Hugh, the height of the church approaches that of Cluny. On the interior of the west front, the overhanging gallery recalls a similar gallery in St Michael in Cluny.

The collegiate church of St Andoche in Saulieu is associated with the Cluny family of churches; Notre-Dame in Beaune has more points in common with St Lazarus in Autun. Among the many village churches built under the inspiration of Cluny, particularly in the Brionnais region *(local map p 63)*, those of Bois-Ste-Marie, Blanot, Montceaux-l'Étoile, Varenne-l'Arconce, Vareilles, Châteauneuf and Iguerande are noteworthy.

Vézelay and its influence. — The Cluny school was repudiated by a whole "family" of churches, the purest example of this being the basilica of St Mary Magdalene in Vézelay, though others display more varied characteristics. Built at the beginning of the 12C on a hill overlooking the valley of the Cure, Vézelay constitutes the synthesis of true Burgundian Romanesque architecture.

The essential difference between this church and earlier Romanesque buildings is that the nave has groined vaulting whereas up to that time only the side aisles had this feature, their small size mitigating the risk of the vaulting subsiding as a result of excessive lateral pressure.

This design, originally without the support of the flying buttresses which were added in the Gothic period, required the incorporation of iron bars to prevent the walls of the nave from inclining outwards.

Clerestory windows were placed directly above the main arches and opened on to the axis of each bay shedding their light into the nave. The pilasters were replaced by engaged columns, as opposed to the Cluny style. The vaulting is supported by semi-circular transverse arches.

To break the monotony of this style of architecture differently-coloured building materials have been employed: vari-coloured limestone and alternating arch-stones of white and brown.

The church in Anzy-le-Duc appears to have served as a model for the building in Vézelay; it is probable that Renaud de Semur, who came from the Brionnais region, wished to rebel against the all-powerful influence of Cluny and took as his model the church in Anzy-le-Duc, which at that time was the most perfect piece of architecture of the region. There is no lack of points of comparison: the same elevation of two storeys, the same solitary window above the main arches, the same style of semicircular vaulting and the same cruciform pillars flanked by engaged columns. This style, created in Anzy-le-Duc and perfected in Vézelay, has been copied in St Lazarus in Avallon and in St Philibert in Dijon.

Fontenay and the Cistercian School. — Cistercian architecture first appeared in Burgundy in the first half of the 12C (Cistercium was the Latin name for the town of Cîteaux). It is characterized by a spirit of simplicity in keeping with the teaching of St Bernard, who had a considerable influence on his times. He strove against the luxury displayed in some monastery churches.

With a passion and a violence that were extraordinary, he opposed the theories of the great builders of the 11C and 12C, such as St Hugh, Peter the Venerable and Suger, who considered that nothing could be too rich for the glory of God: "Why," he wrote to William, Abbot of St-Thierry, "this excessive height in the churches, this enormous length, this unnecessary width, these sumptuous ornaments and curious paintings that draw the eyes and distract attention and meditation?... We, the monks, who have forsaken ordinary life and who have renounced the riches and ostentation of the world... in whom do we hope to awaken devotion with these ornaments?"

There is however a certain grandeur in the sobriety and austerity that he advocated. The uncluttered style and severe appearance truly reflected the principles of the Cistercian rule (p 21), which regarded as noxious everything that was not absolutely indispensable to the development and spread of monastic life.

The Cistercians almost always insisted on an identical plan of construction for all the buildings of their order and themselves

Fontenay. – Nave of the abbey church

directed the work on new abbeys. The Abbey of Fontenay is a good example of the standard plan. This design and its architectural techniques is to be found throughout Europe from Sicily to Sweden. Every new monastery was another link with France and craftsmen followed the monks. It was the turn of the Burgundian Cistercian monasteries to spearhead the expansion of European monasticism. In 1135 the Cistercians adopted Fountains Abbey in Yorkshire, a recent foundation (1132); there they were to build on a largescale what was to become the wealthiest Cistercian abbey in England.

Cistercian churches. — The blind nave is covered by broken-barrel vaulting as in the architecture of Cluny (see illustration above); the side aisles are generally arched with transverse barrel vaulting and their great height enables them to take the thrust of the nave. This style is to be found in many Burgundian churches of the 12C.

The transept, also of broken-barrel vaulting, juts far out and two square chapels open into each transept arm.

The choir, of broken-barrel vaulting, is square and not very deep. It ends in a flat chevet lit by two tiers of three windows. Five windows are placed above the chancel arch and each bay of the side aisles is also lit by a window.

Often the absence of a stone belfry is evidence of St Bernard's wish to adhere to poverty, humility and simplicity. Living far from their fellow men, away from the frequented highways, the religious communities did not want to attract the attention of the faithful. Belfries, which drew attention to the existence of a church by their silhouette and the sound of the bells, were thus banished.

By avoiding all decoration of painting and sculpture, and by eliminating practically every sort of superfluous ornamentation (stained glass windows and illuminated pavements), Cistercian art achieved a remarkable purity of execution.

Romanesque Sculpture

The Cluny school of sculpture is the most significant development in the Romanesque period. The great Benedictine Abbey of Cluny attracted large numbers of sculptors and image-carvers, thus becoming almost the only creative centre from 1095 to 1115.

A delicate and plastic art was born. A new interest in nature was revealed in the varied vegetation and in the keenly observed poses of the human figures carved on the capitals in the choir (a rare survival -*i llustration opposite*). The figures, draped in flowing tunics, create an outline in harmony with the desired serenity. The influence of Cluny's sculpture was first apparent in the Church of St Mary Magdalene in Vézelay – both in the carved capitals and in the tympanum of the doorway in the narthex which shows Christ sending out his Apostles before his ascension into heaven *(illustration p 168)*. This sculpture (1120) has much in common with the doorway of St Lazarus' Church in Autun where the Last Judgement (1130-1135) contains elongated figures draped in pleated robes more closely moulded on the bodies than in Vézelay.

Cluny. – Capital in the choir

Both here and in his work in general Gislebertus *(p 40),* the sculptor of Autun, tried to express the full range of human attitudes and sentiments. The capitals in the nave and choir, which are slightly earlier (1125-1130), depict scenes from the Bible and the lives of the Saints; they provided inspiration for the vigorous talent of the artists who created St Andoche in **Saulieu.**

The two doorways of St Lazarus's Church in **Avallon,** which date from the mid-12C, reveal a desire for a new style: side by side are presented a luxuriant decoration including wreathed columns, an expression of the "Baroque tendency" of Burgundian Romanesque art, and a column statue which recalls Chartres. The round bosses on the tomb of St Lazarus in Autun (1170-1184) both by their gravity and their troubling presence indicate the trend towards the Gothic style.

The Brionnais, where there is an unusual profusion of sculpted doorways, seems to have been the oldest centre for Romanesque sculpture in Burgundy. From the mid-11C to the great projects of Cluny, this region produced a slightly rough and gauche style: the figures are bunched and their movements lack elegance. After working in Cluny, where they were summoned by Abbot Hugh of Semur, who was related to the Lords of Brionnais, the Brionnais artists introduced into their work a new grace, elongating the figures and creating less rigid compositions. These sophisticated trends appeared beside traditional elements, such as a taste for short compact figures, and evolved towards a certain mannerist decorative style (tympanum of St-Julien-de-Jonzy - *illustration p 143*).

Romanesque Painting

The crypt of the cathedral in Auxerre contains some 11C frescoes depicting Christ on horseback, holding a rod of iron in his right hand. At Anzy-le-Duc, restoration work carried out in the choir in the middle of the 19C uncovered a large collection of mural paintings which had different characteristics from those at Auxerre: very subdued, dull tints with dark outlines covering a background composed of parallel bands.

Another style (blue backgrounds) appears at Cluny and at Berzé-la-Ville, in the chapel of the "Château des Moines" (the monks' castle), where one can see a fine collection of Romanesque mural paintings *(p 54)*. These frescoes, brought to light at the end of the 19C from beneath a layer of distemper, were painted in the first years of the 12C. The use of bright paints – and not matt as at Anzy-le-Duc – is the distinctive feature of a different technique from that used up to that time. As Berzé-la-Ville, was one of the residences of the Abbots of Cluny where St Hugh came to rest on several occasions, it appears certain that these frescoes were painted by the same artists employed on the building of the great abbey. The gigantic Christ in Majesty, surrounded by six apostles and numerous other personalities, is of Byzantine inspiration and seems to have been copied from the mosaics of the Empress Theodora in the church of San Vitale in Ravenna.

This similarity between Cluniac and Byzantine art is explained by the leading rôle played by Saint Hugh, who used examples furnished by the Roman and Carolingian basilicas which were strongly influenced by Byzantine art. Thus, in architecture, sculpture and painting, the influence of Cluny was the determining factor in the art of the 12C and the destruction of the greater part of the great abbey at the end of the 18C can be considered as an irreparable loss. The remains that have come down to us give a very incomplete idea of what was without doubt the synthesis of Romanesque art.

Berzé-la-Ville. – Frescoes in the Monks' Chapel

GOTHIC ART

About the middle of the 12C and perhaps even earlier, pointed vaulting appeared in Burgundy, the prelude to a new development in architecture. The Gothic style — originating in the Île-de-France — penetrated slowly into Burgundy where it was adapted according to circumstances and trends.

Gothic Architecture

Period of transition. — In 1140 the gallery of the narthex at Vézelay was given pointed vaulting. The Cistercians were among the first to adopt this style of architecture and used it at Pontigny in about 1150. The choir of St Mary Magdalene in Vézelay, the work of the Abbot Gérard d'Arcy, was started in the last years of the 12C; the flying buttresses were not added until the 13C.

Religious buildings. — It was in the 13C that a Burgundian style emerged.

First half of the 13C. — The church of Notre-Dame in Dijon, built without interruption from 1230 to 1251, represents the most perfect and best known example of this style. Its characteristics are to be found in many religious buildings of this period in Burgundy: beyond the transept, the fairly deep choir is flanked by apsidal chapels — generally two — and ends with a high apse. The use of sexpartite vaulting permitted the replacing of the uniformly sized pillars by alternating thick and thin pillars. A triforium runs above the great arches; at the clerestory level the nave wall is set back slightly allowing for a gallery above that of the triforium.

In the outside decoration, the presence of a cornice — its form varies from one building to another — goes round the choir, the nave, the apse or the belfry and is a typically Burgundian mode of decoration.

Among the buildings constructed in this style, the most important are: Auxerre cathedral, the collegiate church of St Martin in Clamecy and the church of Notre-Dame in Semur-en-Auxois. In the latter, the absence of a triforium further enhances the effect of created by the narrow nave.

St-Thibault. – Church chancel

End of the 13C. — Architecture now became much lighter and developed a boldness that seemed to defy the laws of gravity.

The choir of the church of St Thibault in Auxois appears in such a style, with its keystone at a height of 27m - 89ft. The five-sided apse rising to a height of four storeys is of an amazing lightness. Below the highest windows is a clerestory composed of three tiers reaching to the ground; the top tier is a gallery, the middle tier is composed of pairs of radiant windows, the bottom tier consists of blind arcades.

The church of St Père has certain similarities with Notre-Dame in Dijon but it differs with regard to its height, being of two storeys with a gallery in front of the windows.

14C. — It was at this time that the Flamboyant Gothic style, characterized by the ogee arch, appeared; the number of ribs multiplied and the capitals were reduced to a simple decorative role and sometimes even disappeared completely. This period did not produce any really fine buildings in Burgundy. The church of St John in Dijon has a single nave surrounded by many chapels.

Civil architecture. — Dijon and some other towns have preserved fine mansions and houses built in the 15C by rich merchants; this is also the case at Flavigny-sur-Ozerain and Châteauneuf. Part of the palace of the Dukes of Burgundy in Dijon (the tower on the terrace and the ducal kitchens), the synodal palace in Sens and the hospital in Beaune, a triumph in wooden architecture, all date from this period. Among the fortified castles of the 13C those of Châteauneuf, built by Philippe Pot, Seneschal of Burgundy, Posanges and the ducal palace at Nevers are noteworthy.

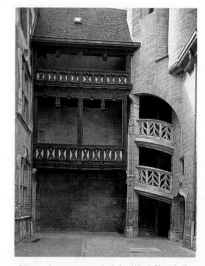

Dijon. – Inner courtyard of the Hôtel Chambellan

Book well in advance as it may be difficult to find accommodation during the season.

Gothic Sculpture

This concedes nothing in vitality and quality to Romanesque sculpture.

13C Sculpture. – The influence of the Ile-de-France and Champagne are evident in the composition and the presentation of subjects but the Burgundian temperament appears in the interpretation of some scenes, where local artists have given free rein to their fantasy and earthy realism.

A great part of the statuary of this period was destroyed or damaged during the Revolution; some examples of this 13C art remain in Vézelay, St-Père, Semur-en-Auxois, St-Thibault, Notre-Dame in Dijon, and Auxerre.

In Notre-Dame in Dijon some masks and faces are treated with an extremely elaborate realism, while others have an authenticity and an expression of such good nature that one is forced to think that they are portraits of Burgundians taken from real life. The doorway of St-Thibault-en-Auxois presents a number of scenes depicting the Virgin Mary but, more noticeably, five large statues portraying, among others, Duke Robert II and his family.

This rare example of lay personalities represented on the doorway of a church of this period is explained by the important part played by the Duke in the building of the church.

At St-Père the sculptured decoration of the west front gable is repeated in an interesting floral decoration on the capitals. It is probable that the gable of Vézelay Basilica was inspired by that of St-Père but the statues in St-Père are of much finer workmanship than those in Vézelay.

The tympanum of the Porte des Bleds in Semur-en-Auxois presents the legend of St Thomas: the figures are heavy and the draperies lack elegance – characteristics of Burgundian style. This style was modified at the end of the 13C and became more plastic: the low-reliefs on the base of the doorways on the western side of Auxerre cathedral are of a delicacy and grace never before achieved. These masterpieces were unfortunately badly damaged during the Revolution.

14C Sculpture. – The advent of the "Great Valois Dukes" in 1364 coincided with a period of political expansion and the spread of artistic influence in the Duchy of Burgundy.

In 1377 Philip the Bold began the construction at the gates of Dijon, of the Charterhouse of Champmol, which was destined to become the burial place of the new dynasty.

The duke spared no expense in the decoration of this monastery, bringing to Dijon from his northern territories a large number of artists many of whom were of Flemish origin.

Of the artists who in turn worked on the magnificent tomb now to be seen in the Guard Room in the Dijon Museum *(p 94)*, Claus Sluter (c1345-1405) is incontestably the greatest. He knew how to give the personalities he depicted an outstanding bearing, movement and vitality. His work was continued by his nephew, Claus de Werve, who abandoned the brutal realism of his uncle's style in favour of a more gentle approach. The statues of Philip the Bold and Margaret

Dijon. – Well of Moses
Head of Christ

of Flanders on the doorway of the Charterhouse of Champmol are the work of Claus Sluter; they are regarded as authentic portraits. The draperies and clothes are treated with consummate artistry and the facial expressions are of a striking realism. This tableau includes the Virgin and Child against the central pier and the donors' patron saints, St John the Baptist and St Catherine.

A new trend in sculpture emerged : statues ceased to be part of pillars and doorways; facial expressions were treated with realism and the artist, searching for likeness above all else, did not hesitate to portray ugliness or suffering.

Claus Sluter was also the artist of the great cross that was to have surmounted the well in the Charterhouse cloisters (Puits de Moïse) (illustration *above*), which luckily escaped destruction, is preserved in the Archaeological Museum in Dijon. The faces of Moses and the five prophets represented on the base of the Calvary, striking in their realism, and the costumes – flowing draperies in broken folds – studied with extraordinary detail, make this composition, which is outstanding for its vitality and great intensity of expression, one of the masterpieces of 14C sculpture.

15C Sculpture. – The tomb of Philip the Bold has given rise to many imitations: the mausoleum of John the Fearless and Margaret of Bavaria is a faithful replica; the tomb of Philippe Pot, Seneschal of Burgundy, shows more originality since it is the mourners who support the flagstone bearing the recumbent figure.

Sculpture now turned towards a style different from that of the 13C: proportions were more harmonious and the draperies simpler. The Virgin Mary in the Rolin Museum in Autun is a good example of this particular Burgundian style.

Representations of the Entombment or the Holy Sepulchre became more popular. The most remarkable of these compositions, grouping seven figures around the dead Christ, are to be found in the hospital in Tonnerre *(illustration p 161)*, in the church of Notre-Dame in Semur-en-Auxois and in the hospital in Dijon.

Some carved and gilded wooden retables were executed at this time by Jacques de Baërze: the retable of the Crucifixion and the retable of the Saints and Martyrs are on display in the Salle des Gardes of the Dijon Museum.

Two other Flemish retables of the 15C, one depicting the Passion and the other the Virgin Mary, are preserved in the little church at Ternant *(p. 160)*.

Gothic Painting

The great Valois dukes surrounded themselves with painters and illuminators whom they brought from Paris or from their possessions in Flanders. In Dijon Jean Malouel, Jean de Beaumetz and André Bellechose, natives of the north, created an artistic style remarkable for its richness of colour and detail of design, a synthesis of Flemish and Burgundian styles.

Among the best-known works, the polyptych in the Beaune Hospital by Roger van der Weyden and the paintings in the Dijon Museum are of great interest.

During the Gothic period frescoes came into favour again. Apart from the frescoes in the church of Notre-Dame in Beaune by **Pierre Spicre**, a painter of Dijon, the curious *Dance of Death* in the little church in La Ferté-Loupière *(illustration p 102)* is also noteworthy. Pierre Spicre designed the cartoons on which the tapestries in the church of Notre-Dame in Beaune were based. These works display remarkably bright colours.

The tapestries in the Beaune Hospital, ordered by Chancellor Nicolas Rolin in the 15C, are among the most beautiful of this period.

RENAISSANCE ART

Under the influence of Italy Burgundian art took a new turn in the 16C marked by a revival of the antique styles.

In architecture the transition from Gothic to Italian art met with some resistance. The church of St Michael in Dijon is evidence of this: while the nave – although started at the beginning of the 16C – is an imitation of Gothic art, the façade, built between 1537 and 1570, is a perfect example of the Renaissance style: the two towers are divided into four storeys where Ionic and Corinthian orders are superimposed alternately; but the three semicircular doorways and the porch with its abundantly-sculptured coffered vaulting are evidence of strong Italian influence.

While architecture was characterized by the triumph of horizontal lines and semicircular arches, sculpture used the antique form of medallions and busts in high relief, and sacred subjects gave way to profane.

In the second half of the 16C ornamental decoration such as that conceived by Hugues Sambin, artist of the gateway of the Law Courts in Dijon and probably a large number of mansions, was much in vogue in the city *(illustration p 175)*.

Unlike the valley of the Loire, Burgundy did not know a "blossoming" of great châteaux but prides itself on its magnificent mansions such as in Ancy-le-Franc, Tanlay and Sully. In the 16C, decorative woodwork – door panels, coffered ceilings and church stalls – assumed great importance. The twenty-six stalls in the church of Montréal, carved in 1522, are a work of local inspiration in which the Burgundian spirit appears.

CLASSICAL ART

The reunion of Burgundy with the crown of France marked the end of the duchy's political independence but its artistic role, albeit unobtrusive, remained. Classical art, first imitated from Paris and later from Versailles, is to be seen in Dijon in the arrangement of the Place Royale, in the alterations to the former Palace of the Dukes and in the building of the new Palace of the Dukes of Burgundy. Many fine mansions were built by the families of parliamentarians who were then in favour at the court and held high positions. Although keeping the characteristics of the Renaissance period, the Hôtel de Vogüé, built from 1607 to 1614, presents the new design where the living quarters are set back behind a courtyard having access to the street only by the coach gateway, the opposite façade of the house opening on to gardens.

Among the numerous châteaux built in the 17C and 18C, those of Bussy-Rabutin *(illustration p 64)*, Commarin, Grancey, Beaumont-sur-Vingeanne, Menou and Talmay should be mentioned. The sculptors – Dubois in the 17C and Bouchardon and Attiret in the 18C – had a great influence on their times. It was the same with Greuze and François Devosge in drawing and painting, and, above all, with Mignard, master-painter at the court of Louis XIV.

In music Burgundy prides itself on having given to the world **Jean-Philippe Rameau**, born in Dijon at the end of the 17C. A contemporary of Bach and Handel, he was one of the great French classical composers. Besides many pieces for the harpsichord, he composed some operas, of which one, *Les Indes Galantes*, is still popular today.

19C AND 20C ART

The transition from the 18C to the 19C is marked by **Girodet**, the celebrated son of Montargis *(p 117)*. Prud'hon and Rude, both pupils of Devosges and attached to the academic tradition, were producing paintings and sculpture at the beginning of the 19C: the work of the former is characterised by muted tones and dreamy sensual figures; the latter made a neo-classical debut but then revealed the force of his romantic temperament with the Marseillaise on the Arc de Triomphe in Paris.

They were followed by Cabet, Jouffroy and, nearer to the present, the animal sculptor, François Pompon *(p 149)* who all contributed to the artistic reputation of Burgundy. In architecture, **Gustave Eiffel** (1832-1923), an engineer from Dijon, specialised in metal construction: bridges, viaducts... The mention of his name conjures up the tower he erected in Paris for the universal exhibition in 1899; its structure is based on the principle of a web of girders.

When driving in France
use the **Michelin Motoring Atlas FRANCE**
Scale - 1:200 000.

FOOD AND WINE IN BURGUNDY

"By the glory of her vineyards," wrote one of France's most eminent gastronomic experts, "by the richness of her soil, by the excellence and quality of her natural products as well as by the talent and style of her cooks who, for centuries, have known how to keep up the finest traditions, sumptuous Burgundy is a gastronomic paradise."
This reputation has been solidly established for a very long time: Dijon has been a city of fine food since Gallo-Roman times, if one is to judge from the culinary inscriptions and signs engraved on stone tablets that are now preserved in the Archaeological Museum. In the 6C Gregory of Tours praised the quality of Burgundian wines and King Charles VI, who was still sane at the time, proclaimed the gastronomic fame of Dijon, as much for its wines as for its special dishes.
In the times of the Great Dukes of the West, cooking held an important place in the Palace in Dijon. To the present day the States-General of Burgundy and the gastronomic fair at Dijon have perpetuated this tradition of good drinking and good eating.

The raw materials. – Land of many blessings, Burgundy possesses first-class beef cattle in the regions of Auxois, Bazois and Charollais, as well as some of the tastiest game in France; it produces incomparable vegetables, many varieties of fish – white fish from the Loire and Saône and trout and crayfish from the rivers and springs of the Morvan – the most delicious mushrooms – *mousserons, cèpes, morilles* and *girolles* – snails that are famed the world over and succulent fruit (cherries from the Auxerre region).

Burgundian cooking. – This is both copious and substantial and reflects the Burgundian's temperament and his robust appetite – expecting both quality and quantity at table. Wine, the glory of the province, naturally plays an all-important part: the wine sauces, pride of the Burgundian cuisine, are called *meurettes;* basically they are made of wine flavoured and spiced and thickened with butter and flour. These sauces blend well with fish – carp, tench and eels – brains, poached eggs and beef casserole (known as *bœuf bourguignon* – Burgundian beef).
Cream is also used in the preparation of many dishes: *jambon à la crème* (cooked ham with cream sauce), *champignons à la crème* (mushrooms with cream sauce); *saupiquet*, a piquant sauce of wine and cream that accompanies ham, dates from the 15C; its name comes from the old verb *saupiquer* (to season with salt).

Burgundian specialities are numerous: snails (cooked in their shells), *jambon persillé* (ham seasoned with parsley), *andouillette* (small sausages made of chitterlings), *saupiquet, coq au vin* (cockerel cooked in wine), *pauchouse* (a stew of different fish cooked in white wine) and *poulet en sauce* (chicken cooked in a sauce of half cream and half white wine) make up the basic elements of Burgundian cooking.
In the Nivernais and Morvan regions, home-cured ham and sausage, ham and eggs, calf's head or *sansiot,* eggs cooked in wine, roast veal and *jau au sang* (a young pullet fried with bacon and small onions) figure among the traditional dishes of a well-served meal. Dijon is well known for its mustard *(moutarde),* a smooth condiment with a strong flavour.
To accompany and enhance these delicious dishes, Burgundy offers an incomparable range of great wines, both white and red (p 15).

The Cheeses. – Although they have not achieved international repute, the cheeses of Burgundy are not to be ignored. The countryside of the Yonne river produces St-Florentin, which should be eaten when the heart is still white and moist. The town of Époisses has given its name to a soft cheese which after two or three months develops a smooth reddish-orange surface, while the inside becomes the colour of butter, very smooth and creamy; the Époisses cheese has a distinctive flavour.
The goat cheeses of the Morvan region are small in size; they go well with the dry white wines of Pouilly-sur-Loire.

Spirits, Liqueurs and Tit-bits. – Among the best-known delicacies, one should mention the gingerbread and *cassissines* (blackcurrant sweets) of Dijon, the aniseed balls of Flavigny, the nougat of Nevers and the pralines (almonds browned in sugar) of Montargis. To round off a good meal, the drinking of a cassis (blackcurrant liqueur) of Dijon or a Burgundian brandy *(marc)* that has been aged in an oaken cask is particularly agreeable.

> Joyeux enfant de la Bourgogne, je n'ai jamais eu de guignon
> (Happy child of Burgundy, I have never known bad luck).

33

KEY

Sights

★★★ **Worth a journey**

★★ **Worth a detour**

★ **Interesting**

Sightseeing route with departure point indicated

Ecclesiastical building: Catholic - Protestant	Castle, Château - Ruins
Building (with main entrance)	Wayside cross or calvary - Fountain
Ramparts - Tower	Panorama - View
Gateway	Lighthouse - Windmill
Gardens, parks, woods	Dam - Factory or power station
Statue - Viewing table	Fort - Cave
Miscellaneous sights	Megalithic monument

Other symbols

Motorway (unclassified)	Hospital - Covered market
Interchange complete, limited, number	Main post office (with poste restante)
Major through road	Tourist information centre
Dual carriageway	Car park
Stepped street - Footpath	Police station (Gendarmerie)
Pedestrian street	Barracks
Unsuitable for traffic	Cemetery - Synagogue
Pass - Altitude	Stadium
Station - Coach station	Racecourse - Golf course
Metro station - Cable-car	Outdoor or indoor swimming pool
Ferry (river and lake crossings)	Skating rink - Mountain refuge hut
Swing bridge	Pleasure boat harbour
Ferry services: Passengers and cars Passengers only	Telecommunications tower or mast
	Water tower - Quarry
Airport	Reference number common to town plans and MICHELIN maps

MICHELIN maps and town plans are north orientated.

Main shopping streets are printed in a different colour in the list of streets.

Town plans: roads most used by traffic and those on which guide listed sights stand are fully drawn; the beginning only of lesser roads is indicated.

Local maps: only the primary and sightseeing routes are indicated.

Abbreviations

A Local agricultural office (Chambre d'Agriculture)	**J** Law Courts (Palais de Justice)	**POL.** Police station
C Chamber of Commerce (Chambre de Commerce)	**M** Museum	**T** Theatre
H Town Hall (Hôtel de ville)	**P** Préfecture Sous-préfecture	**U** University

Times and charges for admission are listed at the end of the guide

Additional sign

Ground plans of buildings: ▬ Extant parts. ▬ Non-extant parts.

34

Sights

Vézelay

Michelin map 🔲 north of fold 18 or 🔲 fold 2 — 16km — 10 miles northeast of Semur-en-Auxois

Alise-Ste-Reine is set on the steep slopes of Mount Auxois (407m — 1 335ft) between the Oze and Ozerain valleys overlooking the plain of Les Laumes. The first part of its name is derived from Alésia, a Gaulish, then Gallo-Roman, settlement on the plateau. The second part recalls a young Christian woman, who was martyred in the locality *(p 37)* in the 3C; her feast day in September attracts many pilgrims.

Siege of Alésia. — After his defeat at Gergovie (near Clermont-Ferrand) in the spring of 52 BC, **Caesar** retreated towards the north to join forces with the legions of his lieutenant, Labienus, near Sens. When this had been effected and Caesar was on his way towards the Roman bases, he was met and attacked by the army of Gaul, under **Vercingetorix**, near Alésia. Despite the surprise of the attack and the numerical advantage of the Gauls, they suffered a crushing defeat and Vercingetorix, fleeing from Caesar, decided to take the rest of his troops into the camp at Alésia.

Then began the memorable siege. Working with pick and shovel, Caesar's legion surrounded the camp with a double line of works, such as trenches, walls, palisades of stakes and towers: the first line of works faced Alésia to prevent any attempts to escape on the part of the besieged, the second line faced outwards to fight off any attacks by Gaulish armies trying to relieve the camp.

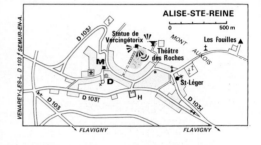

For six weeks, Vercingetorix tried in vain to break through the ring that Caesar had set up. Another rescue army of Gauls, 250 000 strong, was also powerless to reach the besieged and finally withdrew, abandoning them to their fate. With all hope of escape gone, Vercingetorix was forced to surrender and, to save his army, gave himself up to Caesar who paraded him in triumph and eventually had him strangled after imprisoning him for six years in the Tullianum in Rome.

A battle of experts. — During the last century the site of Alésia as scene of the siege was strongly questioned by some historians, who placed the combat between Caesar and Vercingetorix at Alaise, a little village in the *département* of Doubs, near the road from Ornans to Salins. To put an end to this controversy, Napoleon III had excavations carried out at Alise-Ste-Reine from 1861 to 1865. These revealed the presence of extensive military works built by Caesar's legions in the whole region of Mount Auxois, as well as the bones of men and horses and a mass of objects left behind during the siege: silver coins, millstones for cereals, weapons and weaponry. However, the erection of a huge statue to Vercingetorix on the site in 1865 did not in any way solve the problem or put an end to the polemics.

The opposing theory had a keen advocate in the erudite **Georges Colomb** (1856-1945) who, under the pseudonym of "Christophe", was the author of two well-known books for young people, *La Famille Fenouillard* and l'*Idée fixe du savant Cosinus*. More recently excavations at Chaux-des-Crotenay to the southeast of Champagnole in the Jura have revealed another site which also claims to be Alésia.

Aerial photographs and sample bores have been conducted in support of the Burgundian claim; information boards and markers placed beside the roads surrounding Mount Auxois show where these roads intersect the ditches recognised by archaeologists as Roman trenches, that is the circumvallation and contravallation created round Alésia by Caesar.

★**MOUNT AUXOIS** *time: 1 hour*

★ **Panorama.** — There is a good viewpoint from beside the bronze statue of Vercingetorix by Millet. The panorama *(viewing table)* extends over the plain of Les Laumes and the site of the Roman outworks as far as the environs of Saulieu.

⊙**Excavations (Fouilles).** — The summit of the fortified settlement *(oppidum)* was occupied by a Gallo-Roman town which derived its prosperity from its metallurgical activity. The tour *(signs and numbered sites)* indicates the different districts grouped round the forum.

The western quarter contained the theatre (which in its final form dates from the 1C AD), the religious buildings and a civilian basilica. The northern quarter was a prosperous district with shops, the bronze-workers' guild house and a large house, heated by a hypocaust (an ancient system of under-floor central heating), where a statue of the mother goddess was found in the cellar (Cave à la Mater). The artisans' quarter (southeast) is composed of small houses, some with a yard where the artisans worked at their trades. The ruins surrounded by a cemetery (southwest) belong to a Merovingian basilica, dedicated to St Reina; it was the last building to be constructed on the plateau before the population moved down to the site of the present village.

The finds uncovered during the excavations are on display in the museum in Alésia.

⊘**Alésia Museum** (Musée Alésia) (M). – Owned by the Société des Sciences of Semur-en-Auxois, this museum contains all the objects found during the excavation of the Gallo-Roman town: statues and statuettes, fragments of buildings, reconstructed façade of a Gallo-Roman chapel, coins, pottery and other objects made of bronze, iron or bone. The 4C set of sacred vessels is dedicated to St Reina. In addition various exhibits relate the siege of Alésia.

ADDITIONAL SIGHTS

Fountain of St Reina (Fontaine-Ste-Reine) (D). – It is said that a miraculous fountain gushed up from the spot where St Reina, a young Christian woman condemned to death for refusing to marry the Roman governor Olibrius, was beheaded. Up to the 18C, the curative powers of its waters were highly regarded; even today the fountain attracts many pilgrims. The nearby chapel contains a venerated statue of the saint (15C).

St-Léger. – This 7C-10C church, now restored to its original appearance, was built to the usual basilical plan with a timber roof to the nave and an oven-vaulted apse. The southern wall is of Merovingian construction; the one opposite dates from the later Carolingian period.

Theatre (Théâtre des Roches). – The theatre, which is modelled on ancient theatres, was built in 1945 for performances of the *Mystery of St Reina (p 180).*

★★ ANCY-LE-FRANC CHÂTEAU

Michelin map 🔢 fold 7 or 🔢 fold 1 – 18km – 11 miles southeast of Tonnerre

⊘The Château of Ancy-le-Franc is counted among the most beautiful Renaissance houses in Burgundy. The sumptuous interior decoration, restored in the 19C, has a marvellous unity of style.

Antoine III of Clermont-Tonnerre, Grand-Master of Waters and Forests and husband of Anne-Françoise of Poitiers (sister of the celebrated Diane) had the château built in 1546 according to plans prepared by the Italian architect, Sebastiano Serlio, who had come to the court of François I. He entrusted the interior decoration to Il Primaticcio (Italian painter, sculptor and architect who ornamented Fontainebleau; 1504-1570). In 1684 the château was sold to Louvois, Minister of War under Louis XIV. His descendants kept it until the middle of the last century when the Clermont-Tonnerre family regained possession. On the death of the last duke the château passed to his nephews, the princes of Mérode.

Exterior. – A fine avenue leads to the court of honour. The château is composed of four similar ranges linked by corner pavilions.

This style of classic Renaissance architecture was the first to be seen in France. Its simple, almost austere, character gives no hint of the considerable decoration of the inner courtyard. The vast quadrangle is large enough to belong to a real palace. The north and south ranges of buildings contain long galleries opening with three archways. The motto of the Clermont-Tonnerre family – "Si omnes, ego non: Though all renounce you, yet not I" – (between the ground-floor pillars) recalls Count Sibaud de Clermont who helped to reclaim the papal throne for Calixtus II, elected at Cluny, during the 12C Investiture Controversy. In recognition of his support Sibaud was granted the honour of bearing the pontifical tiara and keys on his coat of arms.

Apartments. – The tour of the galleries and apartments – 25 rooms – provides a chance to admire the sumptuous decoration by Il Primaticcio as well as Niccolo dell'Abbate and other pupils of Il Primaticcio. The 16C-19C furniture, for the greater part original, contributes to the harmony of the overall effect.

On the ground floor of the east and north ranges are the Caesars' Room, the Diana Room which has a fine ceiling painted in the Pompeian style in 1578, the Venus Room and the vast kitchen premises.

On the first floor, starting in the north range, are the Room of the Sacrifices decorated with 16C monochrome panels, the Room of Judith and Holofernes (depicted as Diane de Poitiers and François Ier), the Pastor Fido Cabinet, the favourite retreat of Madame de Sévigné, panelled in carved chestnut and painted with pastoral scenes by Philippe Quantin in the 17C, the library, several salons including the Blue Salon where Louis XIV slept, the dining room and the huge Guard Room (west range) with an equestrian portrait of Henri III over the chimneypiece and the **chapel** with its decorated woodwork and frescoes (1596) by André Ménassier, a Burgundian.

In the south wing the **Pharsalus Gallery,** with its vast mural paintings in shades of ochre, gives a 16C account of Caesar's victory (48 BC) over Pompey during the Roman civil war. The most delightful Flower Bedroom takes its name from the many delicately-portrayed floral species; the painting above the fireplace shows a Clermont-Tonnerre as the Huntress Diana. The painted panels of the Medea Gallery (east wing) portray the adventures of the Argonauts who sought the Golden Fleece. Finally there is another sumptuous corner room, the **Arts Salon;** under a richly-painted coffered ceiling, typical of the Henri II period, are oval medallions representing the Liberal Arts.

⊘**Motor and Carriage Museum.** – The outbuildings to the right of the court of honour house some twenty veteran cars (pre-1914: Truffault 1900, Niclaux 1903, Renault and Dion Bouton 1905) and a selection of old bicycles, a 1926 Michelin poster as well as a collection of sixty carriages.

★ ANZY-LE-DUC

Michelin map 69 fold 17 or 238 fold 48 – 20km – 12 miles south of Paray-le-Monial – Local map p 63

This village in the Brionnais region can be proud of possessing one of the most beautiful Romanesque churches in the area.

★ **Church** (Église). – Its construction probably dates from the early 11C. The beauty of ⊙ the church building is heightened by the golden tints of the stone.

The church used to have a fine doorway which is now to be seen in the Hiéron Museum in Paray-le-Monial (p 132). The whole is surmounted by a magnificent Romanesque belfry, a polygonal tower with three storeys of bays. The outbuildings of the old priory, now occupied by a farm, are dominated by a square tower. The tympanum of a very early **doorway** in the precinct wall shows the Adoration of the Magi (left) and Original Sin (right). The lintel portrays the separation of the blessed from the damned at the Last Judgment. The main doorway is still very beautiful though its decoration has been badly mutilated; the tympanum bears a Christ in Majesty.

The nave, covered with groined vaulting and lit directly by the clerestory windows, is pure and remarkable for the harmony of its lines. The capitals have been well preserved. In the nave they represent biblical and allegorical scenes. The frescoes of the apse, now in poor condition, portray the lives of St John the Baptist and Hugues d'Anzy. Those in the choir show the Ascension of Christ. One alludes to Letbaldus, provost of Semur, who in the 9C donated his property at Anzy-le-Duc for the foundation of a Benedictine house.

The ARCHÉODROME

Michelin map 69 fold 9 or 243 fold 27 – 6km – 4 miles south of Beaune

Access from the A6 motorway: via the Beaune-Tailly service area on the southbound carriageway and the Beaune-Merceuil service area on the north-bound carriageway. Access by road from Beaune by the D18 south and the D23 east (7km – 4 1/2 miles).

⊙ The archéodrome beside the Paris-Lyon (A6) Motorway (derived from two Greek words: *archaeos* = old and *dromos* = running track) presents a panorama of the history of Burgundy from the Paleolithic to the Gallo-Roman period through reconstructions of sites, places and artefacts.

The museum, which opens on to the external exhibits, traces the living conditions and activities of prehistoric and Gallo-Roman man through models and photographs and temporary exhibitions. A Gaulish dwelling stands on the central patio.

The outdoor tour includes Stone-Age huts, a settlement built on a rock spur, a tumulus grave, early iron- and bronze-working facilities and the reconstruction of more than 100m - 100yds of a fortified line (traps, trenches and defensive towers) set up by Caesar round Alésia (p 36). The Gaulish period is illustrated by a large farm (1C BC) and the Gallo-Roman period by a small sanctuary (fanum), a Roman roadside graveyard containing 15 carved tombstones (1C AD), a potter's workshop and oven and a Roman villa with its outbuildings.

ARCY-SUR-CURE

Michelin map 65 southeast of fold 5 or 238 fold 11

The River Cure divides the town into two parts linked by a large hump-backed bridge which provides a fine view of the river and Chastenay Château.

Take Rue du Pont along the west bank; turn left into Rue du Château.

On the edge of the village (left) the charming classical façade of Arcy Château (18C) comes into view approached by an avenue of trees. Further on along the narrow Chemin de Vault (turn left into the V8) the hamlet of **Val-Ste-Marie** provides a fine view of the ruins of a 14C fortified house where the lords of Arcy lived until they built the present château.

⊙ **Chastenay Château.** – *Eastern edge of Val-Ste-Marie.*

The tiny Renaissance château was erected in 1549 on the site of a 14C fortified manor house of which only part of the wall of enclosure remains. The château has mullioned windows, a charming hexagonal stair tower (north side) which was added later, and a corbelled watch-tower. The interior displays a 14C polyptych depicting the history of Joseph.

Caves. – The left bank of the Cure above Arcy village is dominated by high limestone cliffs containing a number of caves.

⊙ **Great Cave** (Grande Grotte). – The Great Cave (2.5km - 1 1/2 miles) consists of chambers and galleries decorated with stalactites, stalagmites and draperies of which only part (900m - 1/2 mile) can be visited. Where the roof is not flat it is covered in curiously shaped concretions, which a little imagination easily transforms into strange beasts and flowers or fantastic creations. Two small lakes are visible on the return; the surface of the first is covered in a fine layer of limestone.

The banks of the Cure. – *1/2 hour Rtn on foot.* A pleasant path, starting from the Great Cave, follows the west bank of the Cure at the foot of the limestone cliffs, passing a score of caves, not yet open to visitors, which include, in order, the prehistoric caves of the Horse (Cheval) or the Mammoth (Mammouth), the Hyena (Hyène) and the Fairies (Fées). The 18C naturalist Buffon visited the caves in 1740 and 1759. The Great Shelter (Grand Abri) is a huge projecting rock, which forms an impressive overhang (10m × 20m - 33ft × 66ft).

ARNAY-LE-DUC Pop 2431

Michelin map 🔢 south of fold 18 or 🔢 fold 14

This little old town with its pointed roofs overlooking the valley of the Arroux, recalls the first campaigns (1570) of the young Henri de Navarre – the future King Henri IV – at the side of Coligny, during the war between the Protestants and the Catholics. It was at Arnay – a stage-coach relay post – that the aunts of Louis XVI, Adélaïde and Victoire, were arrested at the time of the French Revolution as they were fleeing to Italy. After their visit their Christian names became very popular.

SIGHTS

St-Laurent. – The church of St Lawrence dates from the 15C and 16C. A domed vestibule (18C) opens into the 15C nave where the original stone vault was replaced in 1859 by a wooden structure like an upturned boat. The first chapel on the left contains a wooden gilt statue of St Michael (15C) beneath an interesting coffered ceiling dating from the Renaissance. The first chapel on the right contains a 16C polychrome Pietà.

Motte-Forte Tower (Tour de la Motte-Forte). – Behind the chevet of the church stands a large 15C tower, topped with machicolations, the last vestige of a large feudal castle. During the Wars of Religion the castle was almost entirely destroyed.

⊙**Regional Tableware Exhibition** (Maison régionale des Arts de la table). – *Tourist Information Centre, 15 Rue St-Jacques.* A renovated 17C building, formerly St Peter's Hospital, is the setting for an exhibition, which changes annually, on the theme of the Burgundian table: foodstuffs, cooking, specialities, tableware and local traditions. The kitchens display an imposing 18C dresser and a collection of ceramics including two plates by Bernard Palissy, the famous 16C potter.

EXCURSIONS

Bard-le-Régulier. – Pop 105. *17km - 11 miles to the west.* This hamlet has a late-12C **church** dominated by an elegant octagonal tower. It used to belong to a priory of the Augustinian Canons Regular.
Inside the church has several archaic-looking features which bely its 12C date. Round-headed arches dominate, the windows are narrow and the great piers have no capitals. The floor is also unusual as it rises in three stages to the sanctuary to compensate for the sloping terrain. As well as a 13C recumbent figure there are some 15C - 17C statues including a very elaborate one of John the Divine (late-15C stone statue). The fine 14C **stalls** (30 in all) are grouped in 4 rows, two on either side of the last bay of the choir, plus nine tall stalls. Grotesque figures from the Bestiary are carved on the armrests while the sides represent the Annunciation, the Visitation, the Nativity, the Last Supper and the martyrdom of St John the Baptist, patron saint of the church.

Bard Signal Station (Signal de Bard). – *1km - 1/2 mile east of Bard plus 1/2 hour Rtn on foot.* From the signal station (554m - 1 818ft), there is a wide view northeast over the Auxois region and southwest over Morvan.

Manlay Church. – *12km - 8 miles to the west.* This 14C fortified church is flanked on its west front by two round towers, pierced with loopholes. A square keep rises over the choir. The church was restored in 1962.

★★ AUTUN Pop 16320

Michelin map 🔢 fold 7 or 🔢 fold 25 – Local map p 124

The city of Autun is flanked by wooded hills overlooking the valley of the Arroux and the vast plain that extends westwards. The cathedral, the museums and the Roman remains bear witness to the city's past greatness.
The neighbouring forests (Les Battées and Planoise which is mainly oak trees) have enabled Autun to develop a high-quality furniture industry.

HISTORICAL NOTES

The Rome of the Gauls. – Autun, derived from Augustodunum, was founded by the Emperor Augustus as a prestige Roman town; his purpose was both to honour the Aedui, the local tribe, and to make them beholden to Rome. The splendour of the new town, which was known as the "sister and rival of Rome", soon eclipsed the contemporary Gaulish settlement of Bibracte *(p 55)*. Owing to its location on the great commercial and military road between Lyon and Boulogne the city soon grew rich and prosperous. By the 3C however this extraordinary focus of Roman civilisation suffered several disastrous invasions. All that remains today of the fortified enclosure and the numerous public monuments are two gates and traces of a Roman theatre.

The century of the Rolin Family. – In the Middle Ages Autun became prosperous once again primarily because of Nicolas Rolin and one of his sons. Born at Autun in 1376, **Nicolas Rolin,** whose name is linked with the foundation of the hospital at Beaune *(p 50),* became one of the most celebrated lawyers of his time. He attracted the attention of the Duke of Burgundy, who made him Chancellor. Despite rising to such heights, he never forgot his native town, helping to restore to it an economic activity that it had not known since Roman times. One of his sons, **Cardinal Rolin,** who became bishop of Autun, made the town a great religious centre. The completion of the cathedral of St Lazarus, the building of the ramparts to the south of the town and the construction of many private mansions date from this period.

★★ST LAZARUS' CATHEDRAL (CATHÉDRALE ST-LAZARE) (BZ)

time: 1/2 hour

In the 12C the Bishop of Autun decided to supplement the existing cathedral (destroyed in the 18C) with a new church to house the relics of St Lazarus, which had been brought back from Marseille by Gérard de Roussillon *c* 970, and to create a place of pilgrimage to rival the Basilica of St Mary Magdalene in Vézelay *(p 167)*. Construction took place from 1120 to 1146 and the cathedral was consecrated in 1130 by Pope Innocent II.

The exterior of the cathedral has lost its Romanesque characteristics; the belfry, destroyed by fire in 1469, was rebuilt in the 15C and topped by a Gothic spire. The upper part of the choir and the chapels in the right aisle date from the same period; those of the left aisle are 16C. The two towers flanking the main front, which resemble the towers of Paray-le-Monial *(p 132)*, were added in the 19C during large-scale restoration by Viollet-le-Duc. The building was seriously damaged in the 18C; the cathedral canons demolished the rood screen, the tympanum over the north door and the tomb of St Lazarus which stood behind the high altar *(p 42)*. They also plastered over the tympanum of the central door which they found grotesque; the head of Christ, being too prominent, was removed. Under its protective covering the tympanum survived the Revolution unscathed and was re-discovered in 1837; the handsome head was found among the exhibits in the Musée Rolin and was returned to its place in November 1948.

★★★ Tympanum of the central doorway. —

The tympanum (1130-35), one of the masterpieces of Romanesque sculpture, bears the signature of its creator, **Gislebertus**, beneath the feet of Christ. Nothing is known about him except that his work suggests he was trained in Vézelay and perhaps also in Cluny. Unlike his contemporaries he did not conform to the Cluniac tradition but produced his own distinctive style. His creative genius, his sense of form and his individual power of expression are everywhere evident in the cathedral sculpture. The composition of the central tympanum is a masterly solution of the problems posed by the decoration of such a large area. The theme is the Last Judgement. Despite its apparent complexity the design is deliberate. At the centre, dominating the composition, is the figure of Christ in Majesty (1) surrounded by a mandorla supported by four angels. Below are the dead summoned from the grave by four angels blowing trumpets (4,7,8,9); in the centre of the lintel an angel is separating the elect (2) from the damned (3). On the left hand of Christ the Archangel Michael confronts Satan who is trying to upset the weighing of souls by pressing on the beam of the scales (6). Behind him yawns the mouth of Hell, which is squeezed into the extreme right of the tympanum (7), while Heaven occupies the whole of the upper register with *(right)* two Apostles or Enoch, the patriarch, and Elie, the prophet, transported straight to Heaven (9) and *(left)* Mary (8) in the heavenly Jerusalem (4) and the Apostles (5) attending the weighing of souls; St Peter, distinguished by the key on his shoulder, lends a hand to one of the blessed, while a soul tries to escape by clinging to the robe of an angel.

The human being, which is the dominant subject of the tympanum, is treated with great diversity. The figures of God, his heavenly host and the biblical characters are all dressed in light finely-pleated garments. The diaphanous material, fluted at the hem, emphasises the insubstantial essence of the owners and the spiritual harmony of the heavenly kingdom.

The smaller figures of the dead, sculpted in high-relief, present a very different picture; the state of their souls is revealed through the simple but varied attitudes of their naked bodies; the more numerous elect progress in a peaceful and orderly file, their faces turned towards Christ. By contrast the fear and agony of the damned are expressed in the chaotic poses and irregular composition of the figures. Out of the parade of human beings only a few prelates

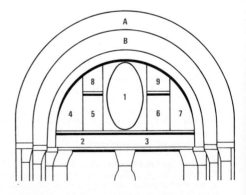

and lords among the elect *(left)* are draped with a cloak which still leaves them largely naked; it is only a distinguishing attribute not an anticipation of grace associating them with the divine figures in the upper register of the tympanum. Two pilgrims can be identified by their bags; one is decorated with a scallop shell, the other with the cross of Jerusalem. Among the damned, on the right of the person in the clutches of the devil, is an adulterous woman with serpents at her breast (symbol of lust); on the left is a miser with his money bag round his neck.

The angular lines of the procession of the damned are repeated more forcefully in Hell where the monstrous faces of the devils and the straining muscles of their misshapen limbs express their cruelty.

The whole composition is crowned by three orders of rounded arches. The outer order (A) represents the passing of time, the labours of the months alternating with the signs of the zodiac in the medallions; in the centre, between Cancer and the Twins, is a small crouching figure representing the year. The middle order (B) bears a serpentine garland of leaves and flowers. The inner order, destroyed in 1766 when the tympanum was plastered over, showed the elders of the Apocalypse.

Interior. – *(Illustration p 27 – plan below).* The pillars and vaulting date from the first half of the 12C. The Cluniac Romanesque style survives in spite of much alteration: three rows of elevation (large pointed arches, false triforium and high windows), massive cruciform pillars divided by fluted pilasters, broken-barrel vaulting with transverse ribs in the nave and rib vaulting in the aisles.

The chancel conforms to the early Christian design of an apse flanked by two apsidal chapels; the oven-vaulting disappeared in the 15C when the tall windows were inserted by Cardinal Rolin (the stained glass in the pointed windows dates from the 19C, that in the Romanesque windows from 1939). In 1766 the canons demolished the monumental tomb of St Lazarus and used its marble to cover the chancel and apse; this marble was removed in 1939.

The use of fluted pilasters surmounted by foliated capitals, which are to be found throughout the upper gallery, gives a sense of unity to the interior of the cathedral; these elements would have been familiar to the local masons from the many ancient buildings in Autun.

The majestic effect is enlivened by the carved capitals. The most admirable features are:

1) and 2) Simon the Sorcerer tries to ascend to heaven in the presence of St Peter, key in hand, and St Paul. Simon falls head first under the approving eye of St Peter. The devil (visible from the main nave) is picturesque.

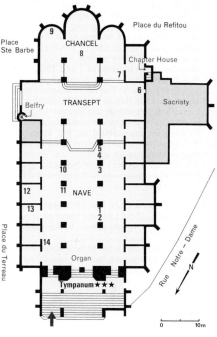

CATHEDRAL OF ST LAZARUS

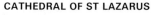

3) The stoning of St Stephen.
4) Symbolic representation of Samson pulling down the Temple.
5) The loading of the Ark, with Noah supervising from an upper window.
6) The 16C door of the sacristy.
7) Statues of Pierre Jeannin, who died in 1623, President of the Burgundian Parliament and a Minister of Henri IV, and his wife.
8) The relics of St Lazarus are placed under the high altar.
9) White marble statue of the **Virgin and Child**★ dating from the late 15C.
10) Jesus appearing to Mary Magdalene against a background of curled foliage.
11) The second temptation of Christ. Oddly enough the devil is the only figure placed high up on the roof.
12) A 16C stained glass window representing the Tree of Jesse in the burial chapel of the bishops of Autun.
13) Painting by Ingres (1834) representing the martyrdom of St Symphorian by St Andrew's Gate.
14) The Nativity. St Joseph meditating in a strange, arched chair.

Chapter House. – The chapter house was built in the early 16C using some fine **capitals**★★, made of heavily-grained stone containing mica, which originally capped the pillars in the chancel.

The most remarkable are on the right of the doorway:
– The hanging of Judas between two devils who are pulling the ropes.
– The Flight into Egypt which should be compared with the one at Saulieu.
– The Magi asleep. The Magi are seen with their crowns on, all asleep in the same bed. An angel is waking them to show them the star in the shape of a daisy. The scene is depicted with delightful simplicity.
– The Adoration of the Magi. St Joseph has been relegated to the right and seems to be waiting for the end of the ceremony.

Ⓥ **Belfry.** – The belfry (80m-262ft high) was built by Bishop John Rolin in 1462 when an earlier structure was struck by lightning. From the top *(230 steps)* there is a good **view**★ of the old roofs of the town, the Bishop's Palace, the unusual conical silhouette of the two spoil-heaps at Les Télots (relics of bituminous schist mines which once made an important contribution to the local economy) and (east) the blue hills of the Morvan.

St Lazarus' Fountain (Fontaine St-Lazare). – This charming fountain stands to the north side of the cathedral. With its dome and small lantern it was built in 1543 by the cathedral chapter. The first dome of Ionic order supports a second smaller dome of Corinthian order, and the whole is crowned by a pelican, a copy of the original which is in the Rolin Museum.

ADDITIONAL SIGHTS

★ Rolin Museum (BZ M¹). – The musem is housed in a wing of the 15C mansion built for Chancellor Nicolas Rolin and in the Lacomme mansion which in the 19C replaced the main block of the Rolin mansion.

Seven rooms on the ground floor of the Lacomme mansion house the Gaulish and Gallo-Roman collections. Relics of the oppidum at Bibracte are on display (large collection of tombstones); Gallo-Roman culture is illustrated through dress, jewellery and toilet articles (Roman helmet with a human face), through religious cults of Roman or oriental or traditional local divinities such as Epona, and through art (handsome statues and a mosaic of a naval triumph); the last room is devoted to late antiquity and the Middle Ages.

Cross the courtyard to the ground floor of the Rolin mansion.

Two rooms are devoted to masterpieces of Roman **statuary★★**; most of it is the work of the two great sculptors of the Burgundian school – Gislebertus and Martin, a monk. Gislebertus' **Temptation of Eve** expresses sensuality through the curves of the body and the plants; the carving adorned the lintel of the north door of the cathedral before 1766. Martin created part of the **tomb of St Lazarus**, which took the form of a miniature church and stood behind the altarpiece in the chancel of the cathedral until it was destroyed during the changes made by the canons in 1766. The surviving figures from the main group, which depicted the resurrection of Lazarus, are the slim and poignant figures of St Andrew and Lazarus' sisters – Martha (who is holding her nose) and Mary. The rest of the work is represented by a few fragments supplemented by a sketch.

The first floor houses 14C and 15C sculptures from the Autun workshops (15C Resurrection of Lazarus in polychrome stone) and works by French and Flemish primitive painters. The room devoted to the Rolin family contains the famous 15C painting of the **Nativity★★** by the Master of Moulins; the attention to detail and the muted colours betray the Flemish origin of the painter but the serene and solemn beauty and plasticity are characteristic of French Gothic painting. 15C Burgundian statuary is represented by the **Virgin★★** of Autun in polychrome stone and a St Catherine attributed to the Spanish sculptor Juan de la Huerta who worked in the region in the reign of Philip the Good.

The first floor of the Lacomme building displays paintings, sculptures and furniture from the Renaissance to the present day; the 17C pharmacy sign throws light on local history.

★ St Andrew's Gate (Porte St-André) (BY). – The roads from Langres and Besançon, the country of the Lingons, meet at St Andrew's Gate, one of the four gates in the Gallo-Roman fortifications, which were reinforced with fifty-four semi-circular towers.

The gateway consists of two large arches for vehicles, flanked by two smaller ones for pedestrians, surmounted by an upper arcade of ten even smaller arches. One of the guard-houses has survived by being converted into a church in the Middle Ages.

Tradition places the martyrdom of St Symphorian near this gateway.

Lycée Bonaparte (AZ B). – This former Jesuit college, built in 1709, provides a noble focal point for Place du Champ-de-Mars. The splendid wrought-iron **grille★**, dating from 1772, is adorned with gilded motifs of medallions, globes, astrolabes and lyres.

On the left, the 17C church of Notre-Dame was originally the college chapel. Notable pupils included the whimsical Bussy-Rabutin and the three Bonaparte brothers, Napoleon, Joseph and Lucien. Napoleon spent only a few months here in 1779 before going on to the military school at Brienne.

Town Hall (Hôtel de ville) (BZ H). – The building houses a large **library** including a rich collection of **manuscripts★** and incunabula.

Rolin Museum, Autun. – Temptation of Eve

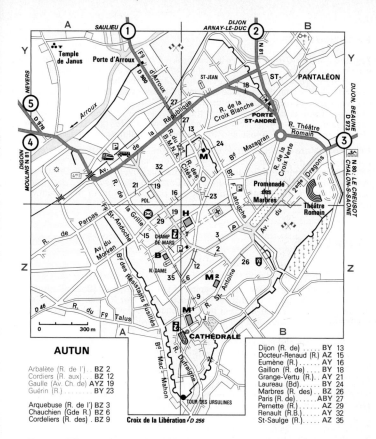

AUTUN

Arbalète (R. de l').. BZ 2
Cordiers (R. aux).. BZ 12
Gaulle (Av. Ch. de) AYZ 19
Guérin (R.)........ BY 23

Arquebuse (R. de l') BZ 3
Chauchien (Gde R.) BZ 6
Cordeliers (R. des) . BZ 9

Dijon (R. de) ..... BY 13
Docteur-Renaud (R.) AZ 15
Eumène (R.)...... AY 16
Gaillon (R. de) .... BY 18
Grange-Vertu (R.).. AY 21
Laureau (Bd)...... BY 24
Marbres (R. des) .. BZ 26
Paris (R. de).....ABY 27
Pernette (R.) ..... AY 29
Renault (R.B.)..... AY 32
St-Saulge (R.).... AZ 35

Croix de la Libération / D 256

Roman Theatre (Théâtre romain) (BYZ). — The remains reveal the size of the largest theatre in Gaul (capacity 12 000). Gallo-Roman stone fragments are incorporated into the wall of the modern bar.

Arroux Gate (Porte d'Arroux) (AY). — This was the Senonica Gate (Sens Gate) giving access to Agrippa's Way which ran from Lyons to Boulogne.
The gate is beautifully proportioned, smaller but better preserved than St Andrew's Gate. Like the latter it has two large arches for vehicles and two smaller ones for pedestrians. The arcade is surmounted by a gallery ornamented with elegant fluted pilasters capped by Corinthian capitals, which date from the reign of the Emperor Constantine. The design was an inspiration to the Cluny architects who used it extensively in Burgundy.

Lapidary Museum (BY M). — The museum is housed in St Nicholas' Chapel, a 12C Romanesque building with a Christ in Majesty painted in the apse, and in the galleries enclosing the adjoining garden. The stone fragments on display include architectural features, mosaics and tombstones from the Gallo-Roman period; sarcophagi, capitals and a "fossilised" boat from the Middle Ages as well as pieces of statuary, both ancient and modern.

Temple of Janus (Temple de Janus) (AY). — The two walls of a square tower (24m - 80ft high), which stand alone in the middle of the plain beyond the Arroux, are probably the remains of the sanctuary *(cella)* of a temple dedicated to an unknown god.

Promenade des Marbres (BY). — Near the broad, tree-lined promenade, in a French-style garden, stands a fine 17C building. It was designed by Daniel Gitard, architect to Anne of Austria, as a seminary but was later converted into a military preparatory school.

Tour of the ramparts. — This is a highly recommended walk which starts at Boulevard des Résistants Fusillés to the west of the town. Follow the ramparts in a southerly direction as far as the Tower of the Ursulines (Tour des Ursulines, BZ) a 12C keep.

Natural History Museum (BZ M²). — The museum concentrates on the geological evolution of the Autun Basin, the Morvan and Burgundy. On the ground floor amidst the mineralogical collection there are specimens of quartz (gemstones) and coal with the imprints of plants and animals (Actinodon) from the Primary Era. On the first floor there are fossils from the Secondary Era and extinct wild ox (auroch) and mammoth bones from the Quaternary. There is also a display of Burgundy's birds and insects (butterflies).

The main shopping streets are printed at the head of the street list accompanying town plans.

EXCURSIONS

★**The Liberation Cross** (Croix de la Libération). – *6km - 4 miles south of Autun*. The winding road affords a good view of the cathedral and old town, the mining tips further north *(p 41)* with the Morvan summits on the horizon.
Beyond (50m - 55yds) the entrance to **Montjeu Château** a steep path *(right - 1:5)* climbs to the Liberation Cross, a granite cross raised in 1945 to commemorate the liberation of Autun. There is a fine **view★** from the cross: in the foreground lies the Autun depression and the Arroux Valley; further off, from left to right, the mountains of Morvan, the forest of Anost and the northwestern slopes of La Côte.

Brisecou Waterfall (Cascade de Brisecou). – *2km - 1.2 miles; 45 min Rtn on foot; park in Couhard near the church*. A path beside the stream leads to an attractive wooded **site★** where the Brisecou waterfall tumbles over the rocks. On the return there is a view of the **Couhard Stone** (Pierre de Couhard) *(accessible by a path from the car park);* the unusual weathered pyramid was probably a Roman monument which dominated one of the old graveyards.

★★ AUXERRE   Pop 40 698

Michelin map ⬛⬛ fold 5 or ⬛⬛⬛ fold 10
Plan of the built-up area in the current Michelin Red Guide France

Auxerre (pronounced Aussere), the capital of Lower Burgundy (Basse Bourgogne), is built on a sloping site on a hillside beside the river Yonne. The town's fine monuments are proof of its great past; its shady boulevards, its steep and busy streets, its old houses and its pleasure boat harbour contribute to its overall interest.
From the bridges and the right bank of the river there is a very fine **view** of the town, made all the more striking as the chevets of the churches rise perpendicularly along the river bank.
The town is at the centre of a vineyard area, of which the most famous wine is Chablis. Auxerre was the birthplace of the physiologist **Paul Bert** (1833-86), who was later to enter politics and become minister during the Third Republic, and of the poet **Marie Noël** (1883-1967) whose works were full of hope and serenity.
Near a simple Gaulish village (Autricum) the Roman conquerors built the town of Autessiodurum, which, like Autun, was situated on the great road from Lyons to Boulogne. Towards the end of the 4C it was already a large town.
In the Middle Ages it was the bishops who administered the town and thus earned the title of "Defenders of the City".
Two great figures in French history have visited Auxerre. In 1429 **Joan of Arc** passed through the town twice, first with the handful of brave followers who accompanied her from Vaucouleurs to Chinon, and then a few months later at the head of an army of 12 000 men with Charles VII, whom she was taking to Rheims for his coronation.
On 17 March 1815 **Napoleon** arrived in Auxerre on his return from Elba; Marshal Ney, who had been sent to oppose him, embraced him and the Marshal's troops swelled the ranks of the Emperor's small army.

PRINCIPAL SIGHTS *tour: 1 1/2 hours*

★★**St Stephen's Cathedral** (Cathédrale St-Étienne) (BY). – The fine Gothic cathedral ⊙was built between the 13C and 16C. An earlier building, which dated from the foundation of a sanctuary by St Amâtre *c*400, burned down in 1023. Hugues de Châlon immediately began to construct a Romanesque cathedral. In 1215 Guillaume de Seignelay started all over again. In 1400 the chancel, the nave, the aisles, thec hapels and the south transept were complete. The building was practically finished by 1560.

West front. – Built in the Flamboyant style, the façade is framed by two towers with sculptured buttresses. The south tower is incomplete.
The façade is composed of four storeys of

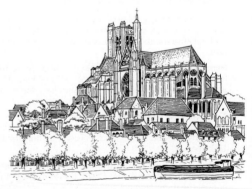

Auxerre. – The Cathedral

arcades surmounted by gables. Above the centre doorway is a rose window (7m - 23ft across) slightly recessed between the buttresses.
The sculptures on the entrance doorways (13C-14C) were mutilated in the 16C during the Wars of Religion, and the soft limestone has weathered badly.
The tympanum over the centre door shows Christ enthroned between the Virgin and St John. The lintel depicts the Last Judgment. Christ presides with the Wise Virgins on his right and the Foolish Virgins (lamps upside-down) on his left.

These twelve statuettes are placed on the engaged piers. Beneath the niches of the base (containing seated figures), there are low-reliefs in two sections: on the left the Life of Joseph (read from right to left); on the right, the Parable of the Prodigal Son (read from left to right).

The sculptures framing the north door trace the lives of the Virgin Mary, St Joachim and St Anne. The coronation of the Virgin is on the tympanum. The medallions along the base are masterly representations of scenes from Genesis.

The sculptures round the south door are 13C. The tympanum, divided into three, and the recessed arches are dedicated to the childhood of Christ and the life of John the Baptist.

Six scenes of the love of David and Bathsheba are on the upper section of the base — eight statuettes placed between the gables of the trefoiled arches symbolise Philosophy (on the right with a crown) and the seven Liberal Arts.

On the right of the doorway, a high-relief represents the Judgment of Solomon. The more interesting of the side entrances is the 14C south door, which is dedicated to St Stephen; the north door is dedicated to St Germanus.

Interior. — The nave, built in the 14C, was vaulted in the 15C. On the end wall of the south transept are four consoles supporting amazingly realistic figures. The glass of the rose window, dating from 1550, shows God the Father surrounded by the celestial powers.

The rose window of the north transept (1530) represents the Virgin Mary surrounded by angels and her own emblems.

The choir and the ambulatory date from the beginning of the 13C. In 1215 Guillaume de Seignelay, Bishop of Auxerre, who was a great admirer of the new architecture then known as the "French style" (the term Gothic was not used until the 16C), decided to pull down the cathedral's Romanesque choir; the beautiful piece of architecture, which rose above the 11C crypt, was completed in 1234.

The ambulatory is lit by a magnificent array of **stained glass windows★★** composed of 13C medallions in which blue and red are the dominant colours. They represent scenes from Genesis, the stories of David, of Joseph and of the Prodigal Son and many saintly legends. The base is emphasised by a blind arcade decorated with sculptured heads, mostly representing the prophets and sibyls.

On the left side of the ambulatory, there is a painting on wood of the 16C representing the Stoning of St Stephen.

The beautiful stained glass of the rose window dates from the 16C.

★ Romanesque crypt. — The crypt, a fine architectural unit and the only remaining element of the 11C Romanesque cathedral, is decorated with fine 11C to 13C frescoes. The scene on the vault, showing Christ on a white horse surrounded by four mounted angels, is the only example of such a representation in France. The fresco in the apse shows Christ in Majesty surrounded by the symbols of the four Evangelists and two seven-branched candlesticks.

★ Treasury. — The many interesting exhibits include a collection of 12C-13C chased enamels, manuscripts, books of hours and miniatures.

Tower. — From the top there is a fine **view** over the town.

★ Former Abbey of St Germanus (St-Germain) (BY). — Nothing remains of this celebrated Benedictine abbey built in the 6C by Queen Clotilda, the wife of Clovis, on the site of an oratory where St Germanus, the 5C Bishop of Auxerre, was buried. In the time of Charles the Bald the abbey had a famous school which attracted such teachers as Heiric and Rémi of Auxerre; the latter was tutor to St Odo of Cluny.

Abbey Church. — The upper part of the church, of Gothic style, was built from the 13C to 15C. The septuple Lady Chapel, dating from 1277, is linked to the ambulatory by a short passageway and overlies the semi-underground chapels *(see over)* which belong to the same period. In 1811 a number of bays were demolished at the western end of the church isolating the beautiful 12C Romanesque belltower (51m - 167ft high); the square base, surmounted by the belfry, makes a strong contrast with the soaring stone spire.

The interior of the church is of fine proportions.

★ Crypt. — The crypt forms a semi-underground church consisting of a nave and two aisles; the barrel vaulting dates from the Carolingian period. The confessio, raised on three steps in the centre of the crypt, provides a fine view of the Carolingian, Romanesque and Gothic vaulting; four Gallo-Roman columns, capped by composite capitals (acanthus leaves and crockets), support two millennial beams made of oak. The ambulatory is decorated by frescoes which date from 850 and are some of the oldest in France; they depict the life and death of St Stephen, two bishops and an Adoration of the Magi, in shades of red and ochre.

The vault (5m - 16ft deep), where St Germanus' body was enshrined, is covered by a ceiling spangled with painted suns (symbol of eternity), which recalls the mosaics in Ravenna where St Germanus died.

The axial chapel, dedicated to St Maxime, was rebuilt in the 13C on the site of the rotonda of the Carolingian crypt; the vaulted roof is divided by ribs into ten panels. Below is St Clement's Chapel *(access via a narrow stair in the thickness of the wall on the right on leaving St Maxime's Chapel)*. The two chapels are only partially underground owing to the steeply sloping site; some windows provide a view of the valley.

Conventual Buildings (E). — The buildings include the sacristy and the Chapter House, which date from the 12C, and the 14C **cellar** of the abbey. The **archaeological museum** houses prehistoric, neolithic and Gallo-Roman exhibits; in the former monks' dormitory the influence of Roman civilisation in Autessiodurum is recalled through Roman craftsmanship and lifestyle, religion and burials, urbanism and communications.

AUXERRE

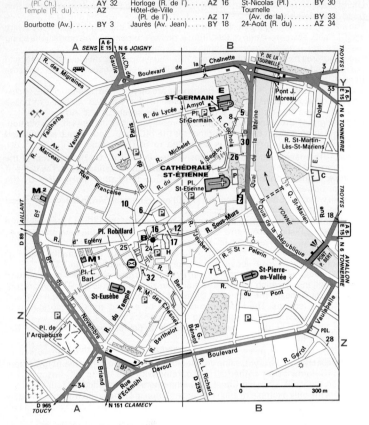

ADDITIONAL SIGHTS

Clock Tower (Tour de l'Horloge) (AZ B). – The tower was built in the 15C in the Flamboyant style on Gallo-Roman foundations; it is also known as the Gaillarde Tower (from the name of the gate which it defended) and was part of the town's fortifications. The belfry and the clock were a symbol of the communal liberties granted by the Count of Auxerre. The 17C clock has two dials apparently showing the movements of the sun and the moon. The astronomical dial was mentioned by Restif de la Bretonne, a prolific 18C novelist (Nicolas-Edme Restif 1734-1806), who served his printer's apprenticeship in a workshop at the base of the tower.

A plaque in the vaulted passage beside the Clock Tower, leading to Place du Maréchal-Leclerc, recalls **Cadet Roussel** (1743-1807), a court official, whose blighted hopes are immortalised in a famous French song.

St Eusebius (St-Eusèbe) (AZ). – The church, once part of a priory, has a fine 12C tower, decorated with multifoil arches, and a 15C stone spire.

The interior has several fine features: rib vaulting in the high hexagonal drum over the Renaissance chancel, the beautiful axial chapel and 16C stained glass. A magnificent piece of 9C Byzantine material, known as the Shroud of St Germanus, is preserved in the chapel of the fourth bay in the south aisle.

St-Pierre-en-Vallée (BZ). – The Church of St Peter is approached through a Renaissance doorway, flanked by two modern buildings in Rue Joubert. It is a classical building incorporating Renaissance elements of decoration. The highly ornamented tower is in the Flamboyant style.

⊘**Leblanc-Duvernoy Museum** (AZ M¹). – An 18C mansion houses the exhibits which include a collection of Italian pottery and black and red figured Greek ceramics, furniture and a series of magnificent 18C Beauvais tapestries including scenes from the History of the Emperor of China, pieces of national and local earthenware, portraits of the Louvois family by different painters and sculptors (including Boilly) and a collection of 17C to 20C paintings.

⊘**Natural History Museum** (AY M²). – The museum to the memory of Paul Bert *(p 44)* is set in a small botanic garden. General exhibitions on natural history.

Old Houses. – There are many interesting old half-timbered houses, mostly from the 16C, in the town centre:

Place de l'Hôtel-de-Ville (AZ 17): nos 4, 6, 16, 17, 18;
Rue Fécauderie (12): nos 23 and 28;
Rue de l'Horloge (16): no 6 and the four houses opposite;
Place des Cordeliers (AY 6): the corner house with galleries;
Rue de Paris (AY): nos 37 and 67 (handsome Renaissance house with dormer windows and a sculpted cornice);

Rue de la Draperie (AY 10): houses occupied by a bank and a jeweller's;

Place Robillard (AZ): no 5, a 14C-15C house, the oldest in Auxerre;

Rue du Temple (AZ): nos 1, 3 and 19;

Place Charles-Surugue (AZ 32) where the Cadet Roussel fountain stands: nos 3, 4, 5 and 18;

Rue Sous-Murs (BYZ) which takes its name from the walls of the Gallo-Roman city which run down one side: nos 14 and 16;

Rue de la Marine (BY 26): remains of the Gallo-Roman wall;

Place St-Nicolas (BY 30);

⊘ **Place du Coche-d'Eau** (BY 5): no 3, a 16C house where the temporary exhibitions of the **Coche d'Eau Museum** are held, and no 6.

EXCURSIONS

The Auxerre Region. – *Round tour of 40km - 25 miles - about 1 1/2 hours.* The immediate environs of Auxerre are of particular interest in April when the cherry trees are in blossom. Alternating orchards and vineyards add to the charm of the undulating country. Vast cherry orchards surround the villages on the slopes of the Yonne Valley and even extend into the valley bottom.

Take the N6 and the D596 southeast for 8km - 5 miles to St-Bris-le-Vineux.

The road rises along hillsides which take on the appearance of an immense garden interrupted from time to time by clumps of trees.

St-Bris-le-Vineux. – Pop 954. This attractive vine-growers' village has some 14C and
⊘ 15C houses and a 13C Gothic **church.** The choir and north aisle vaulting, as well as the stained glass windows, are Renaissance. Note the sculptured pulpit, and the immense fresco of the Tree of Jesse, dating from 1500, in the first bay (south side) of the choir. A small chapel, off the south aisle, contains the sarcophagus of St Cot. The hanging keystone is emblazoned with the arms of the Coligny and Dreux de Mello families.

Continue south for 5km - 3 miles.

Many picturesque glimpses of the Yonne Valley.

Irancy. – Pop 370. The village, which nestles among the fruit trees in the valley, produces the best red and rosé wine in the Auxerre vineyard. This is the birthplace of J G Soufflot (1713-80), the neo-classical architect who designed the Pantheon in Paris.

Take the GR13 south to Cravant (description p 89). Take the minor road northeast along the east bank of the Yonne; in Vincelottes cross the river; turn right into the N6.

Escolives-Ste-Camille. – Pop 424. The charming Romanesque **church,** which is set on the hillside, is entered by a narthex with round-headed arches. The octagonal spire is built of bricks set end-on. The 11C crypt used to contain the relics of St Camille, the companion of St Magnance *(p 147).*

On the northern edge of the village *(Rue Raymond-Kapps)* there are traces *(under cover)* of a Gallo-Roman town and baths (1C to 3C) and of a Merovingian cemetery *(excavations in progress).*

Return to Auxerre on the west bank of the Yonne (described in the reverse order on p 172).

Gy-l'Évêque. – Pop 355. *9.5km - 6 miles south.* The Auxerre-Clamecy road generates most of the activity in this small rural community. Beside the road stand the ruins of the **Church of St Phal** (13C-16C); the vault collapsed in 1924 *(restoration in progress).* Both the belfry and the central doorway, a fine example of Gothic art at its best, date from the 13C.

In the village *(Chemin d'Escamps)* a temporary chapel with an iron cross on the front houses a magnificent 13C wooden statue of **Christ and the Nettle** which used to be in the church.

AUXONNE   Pop 7 868

Michelin map 66 fold 13 or 243 fold 17

Auxonne (pronounced Aussone), formerly a fortified town, was for many years a frontier town where Bonaparte, then a lieutenant, did garrison duty from 1788 to 1791. The more attractive features are the castle, built by Louis XI, and the ramparts which overlook the majestic Saône and its tree-lined walks.

Lieutenant Bonaparte. – The artillery regiment La Fère had been on garrison duty at Auxonne since 19 December 1787 when Bonaparte arrived early in 1788 as a 2nd lieutenant. He was 18 years old and studying both theoretical and practical subjects at the Auxonne Royal Artillery School. As at Valence, where he had previously been on garrison duty, he was known for his serious manner and his keen desire to learn.

Worn out by long hours of study and a meagre existence imposed by lack of money he left Auxonne on 1 September 1789 for his native Corsica. At the end of February 1791 he returned accompanied by his brother Louis, to whom he acted as mentor. The Revolution was in full swing, the political scene was in ferment; young Bonaparte paid close attention to the development of events from which in a few years a new regime – his own – was to emerge.

In April 1791 he finally left Auxonne for Valence where he rejoined the Grenoble Regiment as a 1st lieutenant.

SIGHTS

Notre-Dame. – The church, which was built from the 13C to 16C, was refurbished in the 19C with a mass of gargoyles and statues. Flanking the right transept is a Romanesque 12C tower, part of an earlier church. Statues of the Prophets, restored by the sculptor Buffet in 1853, adorn the 16C porch; six of them are very free copies taken from the Well of Moses in the Champmol Charterhouse in Dijon *(p 98)*. Inside, note the beautiful late-15C statue of the Virgin with grapes, typically Burgundian, in the south apsidal chapel. It is attributed to the school of Claus Sluter. In the first chapel of the north aisle is a 16C Christ Bound and a St Anthony the hermit. The eagle-shaped lectern dates from 1652 and the choir stalls are 16C. On the fourth nave pillar on the right is a 15C painting representing St Hubert hunting. Near the church, in the centre of Places d'Armes, facing the 15C brick **Town Hall** is a **statue of Lieutenant Napoleon Bonaparte** (1857) by François Jouffroy.

⊘**Bonaparte Museum (Musée Bonaparte).** – The museum is housed in the largest tower of the castle, which was altered many times between the 15C and 19C. The first of three rooms contains Napoleonic souvenirs (a Carrara marble statue of Bonaparte by Pietreli, a Florentine sculptor); the second is devoted to prehistoric and Gallo-Roman archaeology, the third to folklore and local history.

★ **AVALLON**   Pop 9186

Michelin map 🔢 fold 16 or 🔢🔢🔢 folds 23 and 24 – Local map p 124

Avallon, perched on a granite promontory between two ravines, is in an attractive **setting**★ overlooking the valley of the Cousin. Strongly fortified, Avallon was one of the "keys" to Burgundy during the Middle Ages but, when its military role ended, Louis XIV sold the then-useless ramparts to the municipality.
The town does not lack attractions with its girdle of fortifications, its gardens and its old houses. It is also an excellent centre for excursions to the Avallon region and the Morvan.

A famous adventurer. – In 1432, when Philip the Good, Duke of Burgundy, was in Flanders, **Jacques d'Espailly**, better known under the name of Fortépice, managed to capture the majority of the castles of Lower Burgundy at the head of a band of adventurers. He even threatened Dijon. The people of Avallon, confident of the strength of their walls, slept quietly. One December night, however, Fortépice and a few men surprised the guards, scaled the ramparts, took the town and organised its defence.
Informed of these events, Philip the Good returned in haste. He directed a bombard against Avallon and the great stone boulders demolished a large section of wall. The Burgundian army rushed in but their attack was repulsed. Philip the Good sent out for more cavalry and crossbowmen. Fortépice took fright and slipped away in the night by one of the postern gates which opened on to the river, abandoning his companions to their fate.

★**THE FORTIFIED TOWN (LA VILLE FORTIFIÉE)** *time: 2 hours*

Tour of the Ramparts. – A tour of the ramparts provides a pleasant walk. The western fortifications overlook the ravine of the Potot stream. From the hospital, an 18C building facing the Auxerroise Gate (1590) bastion which is flanked by a watch tower, take Rue Fontaine-Neuve, dominated by the Vaudois Tower, to the Côte Gally bastion which overlooks a tiny promenade. Rue Fort-Mahon ( ) continues south to the Petite-Porte promenade where the Chapitre and Gaujard towers stand. The tour continues along the eastern fortifications high up above the Minimes Ravine past the Escharguet tower, which is well preserved, and the Beurdelaine Tower, the oldest tower which was built in 1404 by John the Fearless and strengthened in 1590 with a bastion crowned by a corbelled watchtower.

⊘**St Lazarus (St-Lazare).** – The church built on this site in the 4C was dedicated to St Mary; only the crypt beneath the present chancel has survived. Early in the 11C the Duke of Burgundy, Henry the Great, brother of Hugues Capet, presented the church with the head of St Lazarus, a famous relic which established a cult.
By the end of the 11C the number of pilgrims was so great that the decision was taken, in agreement with the monks who built Cluny, to enlarge the church. The chancel, the semi-domed apsidal chapels and the doorways were altered to their present appearance.
The enlarged church, which was consecrated in 1106 by Pope Pascal II, was soon too small and the façade was moved (20m - 66ft) to lengthen the nave.

Doorways. – Originally the façade had a north doorway surmounted by a belltower. The tower was damaged once by fire and several times by partial collapse; in 1633 it collapsed yet again, bringing down the doorway and part of the façade in its fall. It was replaced by the present tower built in 1670. The interesting feature of the façade lies in the two surviving doorways. The recessed arches of the left door, composed of five sculptured bands, are particularly remarkable: cherubim, the Elders of the Apocalypse bearing musical instruments, the signs of the Zodiac and the labours of the months, acanthus leaves and vine leaves appear. The decoration of the recessed arches over the little doorway is entirely of plants: garlands of roses in full bloom, wallflowers, and stylised arum lilies. A single statue of a prophet now stands against the engaged pier of the great doorway; note the elegant little columns with spiral fluting and the twisted columns alternating with straight columns. The bases of the historiated capitals of the right doorway are delicately worked.

The damaged sculptures on the tympanum and lintel of the smaller door are thought to represent the Journey of the Wise Men, their visit to Herod and to the Infant Jesus, followed by the Resurrection and the Descent into Hell. The arch stones are covered in stylised rose garlands, stocks and arum lilies.

Adjoining the west front are the remains of St Peter's Church (St-Pierre) which was the parish church until the Revolution. The nave is now used for temporary exhibitions. The terrace by the chevet provides a detailed view of the stone sculpture and a more distant view of the parkland, Parc des Chaumes, and the Cousin Valley.

Interior. — After being moved to the west the façade was found to be out of true with the axis of the nave which follows the slope of the terrain (the chancel is 3m - 10ft lower than the entrance). In the south aisle there are several 17C painted statues in wood, a 15C group of St Anne and the Virgin Mary and a 14C stone sculpture of St Michael slaying the Dragon. The rotunda-shaped chapel to the south of the choir is covered with 18C trompe-l'œil paintings.

Clock Tower (Tour de l'Horloge) (**D**). — Built in the 15C, over the gateway of La Boucherie, this fine tower is flanked by a slate-roofed turret and surmounted by a slender belfry, which served as a lookout post.

Promenade de la Petite-Porte. — The terrace laid out on the old ramparts and lined with lime trees provides a fine **view** of the Cousin Valley (100m - 300ft below) and of the Morvan mountains.

Old houses. — There are a number of 15C houses with corbelled turrets, and others from the 16C and 18C in Avallon. The tourist can discover these by taking a stroll through the old town.

ADDITIONAL SIGHTS

⊘**Avallonnais Museum** (**M**). — The museum contains one or two outstanding items in an eclectic collection.

On the ground floor, the entrance is devoted to carved stone fragments from the Gallo-Roman, Merovingian, medieval and Renaissance periods; there is a beautiful late-2C Gallo-Roman polychrome mosaic, possibly of Venus. Two rooms dealing with mineralogy and palaeontology lead to a collection of gold and silver pieces, designed between 1919 and 1971 by Jean Desprès, and a range of armour (15C to 19C).

On the second floor there is a room devoted to the memory of Étienne Flandin and his son Pierre-Étienne, politicians during the Third Republic. The next room, the prehistoric section, contains the rich collections of Abbé Parat, a 19C archaeologist who conducted many excavations in the caves beside the Cure and the Yonne. There is an exceptional collection of Roman and medieval coins and fragments of the reconstructed Gallo-Roman temple at Montmartre, dedicated to Mercury (7km - 5 miles east of Avallon).

The third floor houses 14C to 18C religious statues and an important collection of paintings and graphic art including works by Forain, Toulouse-Lautrec and Girodet, two series of 24 and 25 engravings by Jacques Callot, the famous expressionist series of the **Miserere★** (58 plates in black and white) by Georges Rouault and the first tableaux painted by him for the museum in 1895 (Stella Matutina and Stella Vespertina, while still under the influence of his master Gustave Moreau).

Les Chaumes Park (Parc des Chaumes). — 2km - 1 mile by ③ on the town plan, the N 6 or Lyon road, then right into Rue des Minimes, Chemin de la Goulotte and Avenue du Parc. Car parking at the park entrance.

From a point at the opposite end of the park from the entrance, there is a remarkable **view** of Avallon: overlooking the terraced gardens, the town stands on its granite spur and one can distinguish the ramparts, the chevet of St Lazarus and the clock tower.

EXCURSION

★ **Cousin Valley.** – *Round tour of 33km - 21 miles – about 1 hour – local map p 124. Leave Avallon by ⑤ on the town plan, the N 6 towards Auxerre. After 4km - 2 1/2 miles turn left into the D 128 to follow the Cousin Valley.*

Vault-de-Lugny. – *Description p 166.*

Take the D 427 southeast.

The road follows the river and passes a château encircled by a moat.

Pontaubert. – Pop 243. This village, set in terraces on the west bank of the Cousin, has a Burgundian Romanesque church.

Moulin des Ruats. – The road, narrow and winding, keeps close to the fast-flowing waters of the river which falls in little cascades through charming rocky scenery. Old mills have been converted into inns and stand in a pleasant setting. The road skirts the spur on which Avallon is perched and continues up the south bank of the Cousin.

Continue east on the D 427.

Méluzien. – This village stands in a charming spot at the junction of the Vaux stream and the River Cousin.

In Magny turn right into the D 75.

Moulin Cadoux. – An old hump-backed bridge crosses the river in an attractive setting.

Marrault. – On the right is an 18C château where Louis Pasteur spent several holidays, and soon after it the pool of Le Moulin on the left.

Turn right into the D 10 to return to Avallon.

The road follows a forested valley affording a pretty view of the town.

BEAUMONT-SUR-VINGEANNE CHÂTEAU

Michelin map 🔢 north of fold 13 or 🔢 fold 17

⊙ The little village of Beaumont-sur-Vingeanne has a charming 18C château of the type known as an architectural "folly" and one of the rare examples still existing in France. This château, of small but perfect proportions, was built around 1724 by Abbot Claude Jolyot, chaplain to the King, who often came here to rest, far from Versailles and the court.

A park (6ha - 15 acres) surrounds the small but delightful château, which has an elegantly-rusticated principal front with round-headed windows decorated with keystone masks.

There is fine 18C panelling in the suite of rooms on the main floor and a large vaulted chamber beneath the terrace on the garden front.

★★ BEAUNE   Pop 21 127

Michelin map 🔢 fold 9 or 🔢 fold 27 – Local map p 86

At the heart of the Burgundian vineyards lies Beaune; the name is synonymous with good wine and a visit to the city is not complete without also touring the vineyards *(p 84)* on La Côte (hillside).

Beaune also possesses incomparable art treasures displayed in the old hospital (Hôtel-Dieu), the museums and the Collegiate Church of the Virgin. The girdle of ramparts sheltering huge cellars beneath its bastions, the gardens and old houses make Beaune one of the most beautiful places in Burgundy.

HISTORICAL NOTES

The birth of a town. – First a Gallic centre and then an outpost of Rome, Beaune was the residence of the Dukes of Burgundy up to the 14C, before they moved permanently to Dijon. The original charter of communal liberties granted by Duke Eudes in 1203 is still in the town's archives.

The fortifications and towers that exist today were built from the 15C onwards. After the death of the last Duke of Burgundy, Charles the Bold, in 1477, the town stubbornly resisted all efforts to annex it by Louis XI and surrendered only after a siege lasting five weeks.

A local quarrel. – The animosity between the citizens of Dijon and Beaune was an ample source of inspiration to the Dijon poet **Alexis Piron** (1689-1773). After a shooting contest in which the marksmen of Dijon were beaten by the Beaune team, Piron composed an ode of vengeance entitled *Voyage to Beaune* in which he compared the citizens to the donkeys of their countryside – the Lasnes Brothers, merchants of Beaune, had taken the sign of the donkey as their trademark, provoking the jibes of their compatriots – and claimed that he would starve them to death by cutting the thistles from the waysides. As a result of the poem Piron was banned from Beaune but he went there nevertheless one Sunday. First he attended mass where, so he said, "those who came to ogle the women were obliged to pray to God, for, in verity, the ladies would have frightened John the Fearless."

He then went on to the theatre where he was soon recognised; the audience showed their hatred and wrath so noisily that one young spectator, anxious not to miss any of the play, cried: "Please be quiet! I can't hear anything." – "It is not for lack of ears," remarked the audacious Piron. At this new sally, the spectators flung themselves on him and it would have cost him dear if a kindly citizen of Beaune had not given him sanctuary and got him out of the town at night.

Beaune. – Courtyard of the Hospital

A great ceremony. – Each year a large crowd is attracted by the famous wine auction of the Hospices de Beaune *(p 180)*.

The Hospices de Beaune (the name covers the Hôtel-Dieu, the Charity Hospital and the hospital centre) own a very fine vineyard (58ha - 143 acres) between Aloxe-Corton and Meursault; its wines have an international reputation. It is a great honour to be a "wine-producer of the hospices".

The proceeds of the auction sales, which are known as "the greatest charity sale in the world", go to the modernisation of the surgical and medical facilities and to the maintenance of the Hôtel-Dieu.

★★ HOSPITAL **(HÔTEL-DIEU)** (AZ) *time: 1 hour*

The Hôtel-Dieu in Beaune, a marvel of Burgundian-Flemish art, was founded as a hospital by Chancellor Nicolas Rolin *(p 39)* in 1443.

The medieval building with its perfectly-preserved medieval décor has survived intact and was used as a modern general hospital until 1971 when it became a geriatric hospital.

Street façade. – The principal decorative elements of this sober façade with its tall and steeply-pitched slate roof, are the dormer windows, the weather vanes, the delicate pinnacles and lacework cresting of lead.

The roof line is broken by the bell turret surmounted by a slim spire (30m - 98ft) pointing towards the sky.

The entrance porch is surmounted by a roof of great delicacy, composed of three slate gables terminating in worked pinnacles. Each weather vane bears a different coat of arms. On the beautifully panelled door, note the ironwork grille with sharp points and the doorknocker, a magnificent piece of chased wrought-ironwork.

Courtyard (Cour d'honneur). – The buildings surrounding the courtyard give a charming overall effect at once cheerful, homely and rich, "more like a dwelling for a prince than a hospital for the poor". The wings to the left and rear have magnificent roofs of coloured glazed tiles (recently restored). The patterned roof is punctuated by turrets and a double row of dormer windows, surmounted by weather vanes adorned with heraldic bearings and small spires of worked lead.

A timbered gallery, at first-floor level, stands on light stone columns forming cloisters on the ground floor. The building on the right, erected in the 17C, on the site of outbuildings, does not mar the beauty of the overall effect. On the reverse side of the façade, the pavilions that frame the entrance doorway were built during the last century. The old well, with its wrought-iron well head and its stone curb, is graceful.

Great Hall or Poor Ward (Grand'Salle ou chambre des pauvres). – This immense chamber (52m - 171ft long by 15m - 49ft wide and 16m - 52ft high) has a magnificent timber roof in the shape of an upturned keel which is painted throughout; the ends of the tie-beams are carved in the shape of monstrous heads. The paving is a reproduction of the original flag stones. All the furniture is original or else copied from the original models.

In earlier times on feast days the twenty-eight four-poster beds were covered with fine tapestry bedspreads *(see p 53)* now displayed in the Polyptych Room. The bed-clothes, hangings and testers provide a bright note in red or white. At the end of the room stands a life-size painted wood statue (15C) of the **seated Christ bound and crowned with thorns awaiting death★**. A skull appears from underneath his tunic. The Flamboyant-style screen separating the Great Hall from the chapel was reconstructed in the 19C together with the large stained glass window. The famous altar-piece by Roger van der Weyden, ordered by the Chancellor Nicolas Rolin for this chapel and today to be seen in the Polyptych Room, used to be above the altar. The chapel exhibits a copper funerary plaque which commemorates Guigone de Salins, the wife of Nicolas Rolin and founder of the Hôtel-Dieu. The Clermont-Tonnerre collection of sacred art (priestly vestments and objects) is displayed in showcases.

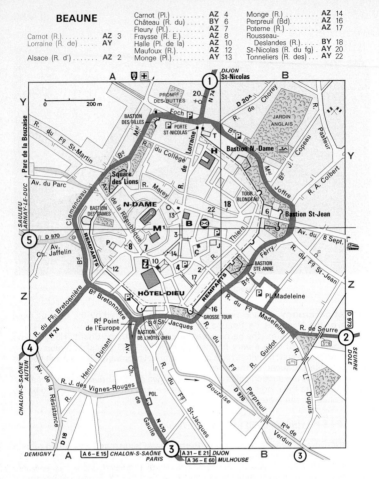

BEAUNE

St Anne's Chamber. – The linen room, visible through the windows, was originally a small bedroom reserved for "the quality". The work of the nursing nuns is illustrated by mannequins, dressed in the habits worn by the staff until 1961.

St Hugues' Room. – This ward, which was taken out of use in 1982, has been partially refurbished with its 17C décor; the beds are those in use since the end of the 19C. The frescoes, by Isaac Moillon, show St Hugues, as bishop and Carthusian, as well as the nine miracles of Christ.

St Nicholas' Room. – This ward, where those in danger of death were nursed, now houses a permanent exhibition on the history of the Hôtel-Dieu and the healing of the body and mind which it offered to the poor and sick. A glass slab in the centre reveals the Bouzaise stream which flows beneath the hospital and carried away the waste.

Kitchen (Cuisine). – *Son et lumière presentation every 15 min.* An old-fashioned scene has been set up round the huge Gothic fireplace with its double hearth and automatic spit, which dates from 1698.

The rest of the visit is conducted by a guide.

Pharmacy. – In the first room pewter vessels are displayed on a handsome 18C dresser; the second room, which is panelled, contains a collection of 18C Nevers porcelain and a huge bronze mortar.

St Louis' Room. – The walls are hung with early-16C tapestries from Tournai depicting the parable of the Prodigal Son and a series woven in Brussels early in the 12C showing the story of Jacob.

★**Polyptych Room.** – This room was designed to exhibit the famous **polyptych of the Last Judgment**★★★ by Roger van der Weyden, a masterpiece of Flemish art, commissioned by Nicolas Rolin in 1443 to grace the altar in the Poor Ward. It was extensively restored in the 19C and sawn in two to show both faces simultaneously. A huge mobile magnifying glass means it is possible to study the smallest detail and the touchingly truthful expressions of the characters.
In the central panel Christ presides at the Last Judgment; he is enthroned on a rainbow surrounded by golden clouds suggestive of Paradise; four angels, carrying the instruments of the Passion, stand at his sides in the flanking panels. St Michael is weighing the souls, flanked by angels sounding their trumpets. In attendance on the central figures are the Virgin and St John the Baptist appealing to the Saviour for mercy. Behind them are the Apostles and a few important people (including the donors) who are interceding on behalf of humankind.
At the bottom of the panels the dead rise from the earth: the just make their way to the gates of Paradise, a sparkling golden cathedral, while the damned are writhing at the entrance to the fiery pit of Hell.

The reverse side of the altar-piece is on the righthand wall. In the past only this face was ordinarily visible since the polyptych was opened only on Sundays and feast days. The fine portraits of Nicolas Rolin and his wife are accompanied by monochromes of St Sebastian and St Antony, the first patrons of the Hôtel-Dieu, and the Annunciation. On the lefthand wall hangs a beautiful early-16C *mille-fleurs* tapestry depicting the legend of St Eligius.

The tapestries hanging opposite the Last Judgment belonged to Guigone de Salins; against the deep rose-coloured background, strewn with turtle doves, are the arms of the founders of the hospital, an interlaced G and N and the motto "Seulle" (you alone) expressing Nicolas Rolin's faithful attachment to his wife. In the centre is St Antony the hermit, Guigone de Salins' patron saint.

★ COLLEGIATE CHURCH OF THE VIRGIN
(COLLÉGIALE NOTRE-DAME) (AY D) *time: 1/2 hour*

The daughter house of Cluny, begun about 1120, was considerably influenced by St Lazarus' Church in Autun *(p 40);* it is a fine example of Burgundian Romanesque art despite successive additions.

Exterior. – The façade is concealed by a wide 14C porch with three naves. The sculpted decoration was destroyed during the Revolution but the 15C carved door panels have survived.

The best view of the chevet is obtained by walking anti-clockwise round the church. Three different phases of construction – the pure Romanesque of the ambulatory and apsidal chapels, the 13C refurbishment of the chancel and the 14C flying buttresses – can be detected in the handsome proportions of the whole. The crossing tower, which is formed of Romanesque arcades surmounted by pointed bays, is capped by a dome and a 16C lantern.

Interior. – The lofty nave of broken-barrel vaulting is flanked by narrow aisles with groined-vaulting. A triforium, composed of open and blind bays, goes round the building, which has a decoration of arcades and small fluted columns inspired by those of Autun.

The transept crossing is covered by an octagonal dome on squinches. The choir, encircled by the ambulatory into which open three semi-domed apsidals, is remarkable for its proportions.

Besides the decoration of the small columns in the transept, it is worth noting the band of rosettes under the false triforium in the choir and the sculptures of certain capitals in the nave representing Noah's Ark, the Stoning of Stephen and a Tree of Jesse. The second chapel in the north aisle contains 15C frescoes depicting the Resurrection of Lazarus, which are attributed to the Burgundian artist Pierre Spicre, and a 16C *Pietà;* there are two 15C altar-pieces in the third chapel.

Off the south aisle is a Renaissance chapel with a fine coffered ceiling.

★★ **Tapestries.** – In the choir behind the high altar there are some magnificent tapestries, known as the Life of the Virgin, which mark the transition from medieval to Renaissance art. Five richly coloured panels, worked in wool and silk, trace the whole life of the Virgin in a series of charming scenes. They were commissioned in 1474, woven from cartoons by Spicre based on an outline supplied by Cardinal Rolin, and offered to the church in 1500 by Canon Hugues le Coq.

Conventual Buildings. – A Romanesque doorway in the transept leads to what remains of the 13C cloisters and the chapter house, which have both been restored.

ADDITIONAL SIGHTS

★ **Burgundy Wine Museum** (Musée du vin de Bourgogne) (AYZ M¹). – The museum is laid out in the former mansion of the Dukes of Burgundy, a building of the 15C and 16C, in which stone and woodwork complement each other harmoniously. The inner courtyard recalls the décor of a theatre and displays a reduced scale model (1:200) of the town's ramparts. The porter's lodge, on the right of the entrance doorway, is 15C. The wine cellar (14C), reached by way of a huge door, contains an impressive collection of wine presses and vats.

The entire history of the Burgundian vineyards and the cultivation of the vine is admirably presented on the ground floor. The 16C polychrome statue is known as the Virgin with a Bunch of Grapes or Our Lady of Beaune. On the first floor, a large room decorated with two immense Aubusson tapestries, one by Lurçat and the second by Michel Tourlière, is the headquarters of the Ambassade des Vins de France (Embassy of the Wines of France).

Other rooms contain collections of pitchers, bottles, wine-tasting glasses, coopers' tools as well as gold plate and souvenirs of the master-craftsmen and journeymen of the Compagnons du Tour de France, a medieval guild.

★ **Hôtel de la Rochepot** (AY B). – This 16C building possesses a pretty Gothic façade and two interior courtyards showing a marked Italian influence. Note the three tiers of galleries decorated with medallions.

In Place Monge stands a 14C belfry and a statue by Rude of **Gaspard Monge** (1746-1818), the eldest of four sons of a local shopkeeper. Monge showed an early aptitude for mathematics and physics. He invented descriptive geometry (application of geometry to construction problems) and was one of the co-founders of the École Polytechnique at the time of the Revolution. A close friend of Bonaparte, he accompanied him on his Egyptian campaign (1798-1801).

Town Hall (Hôtel de Ville) (AY H). – The town hall occupies the buildings of a former Ursuline convent (17C); the right wing houses two **museums**.

Fine Arts Museum. — The collection includes numerous works by the local artist, **Félix Ziem** (1821-1911), 16C and 17C Flemish and Dutch paintings, medieval (14C bagpipes player) and Renaissance (16C St Anne) sculpture as well as a small Gallo-Roman section.

Étienne-Jules Marey Museum. — The doctor and physiologist, Étienne-Jules Marey (1830-1904) took the first motion pictures with a single camera. On display are some of his inventions, notably the photographic rifle camera.

St-Nicolas. — *Leave by ① on the town plan, the N 74.*
This 13C church, in the vine-growers' quarter, has a Romanesque tower with a fine stone spire. A 15C timber porch covered with tiles and supported by pillars of dressed stone, shelters a 12C doorway. The monolithic tympanum depicts St Nicholas saving three young girls whom their father wished to sell.

Old houses. — Among the many old houses, the best to see are nos 18, 20, 22 and 24 Rue de Lorraine (AY), which form a fine 16C ensemble. At no 10 **Rue Rousseau-Deslandes** (BY 18) there is a house with its first floor decorated with trefoiled arcades; at no 2 **Rue Fraisse** (AZ 8) the Maison du Colombier is a pretty Renaissance house which can be seen from the square in front of the Church of the Virgin; 13 **Place Fleury** (AZ 7) is the Hôtel de Saulx (Saulx Mansion) with a pretty little tower and an interior courtyard; 4 **Place Carnot** (AZ 4) is a 16C house with attractive sculptures.

Bouzaise Park (Parc de la Bouzaise). — *Take Avenue du Parc* (AY). This is an agreeable spot for a walk with its fine shady trees and its artificial lake fed by the river.

The Ramparts. — *An external tour of the ramparts is possible on foot or by car*. The relatively well-preserved ramparts form an almost continuous wall walk (2km - 1 mile) — parts are now private property. The wall was built between the end of the 15C and the middle of the 16C of roughly rectangular blocks and is festooned with a few surviving towers and eight rusticated bastions of various shapes — the double one, originally a castle, is known as **St John's Bastion.** In places the ramparts are hidden by bushes or private houses; the encircling moat is now occupied by gardens, tennis court etc.

Tour of the ramparts. — *From Bastion St-Jean follow the outer boulevards anti-clockwise.* The north tower of **St John's Bastion** has several gargoyles and a niche occupied by a Virgin and Child and overlooks a cherry orchard in the moat.
Pass the projecting Blondeau Tower before coming to **Notre-Dame Bastion** with its mass of trees and a charming turret to cover the spur. The line of the ramparts is broken by the 18C St Nicholas Gate at the end of Rue de Lorraine. Then comes the Filles Bastion spoilt by its new roof, and the now filled-in St Martin's Bastion forming a triangular terrace **(Square des Lions)** overlooking a shaded garden. Then follows the Dames Bastion with the recent house and trees, the walk, **Rempart des Dames,** bordered by fine plane trees, and the now-abandoned Hôtel-Dieu Bastion, with a stream at its foot which served the old wash-houses. The 15C Great Tower (Grosse Tour) on the Rempart Madeleine is followed by St Anne's Bastion overgrown and still sporting a turret overlooking the moat.
The tour ends in front of the castle's south tower overlooking the hedges and bamboo in the moat. Stand back a little to obtain a better view of this outwork, crowned by a small house against a background of varnished tile roofs.

EXCURSIONS

★★**La Côte Vineyards.** — *The tours described on pp 85 to 87 may also start from Beaune.*

Montagne de Beaune. — *4km - 3 miles northwest by the D 970.*
South (about 600m - 660yds) of the statue of Our Lady of the Liberation (Notre-Dame de la Libération) stands a War Memorial; from the viewing table there is an extensive view of the attractive brown tiled roofs of the town, of the vineyard and of the Mâconnais mountains (south).

Archéodrome. — *7km - 4 1/2 miles south by the D 18 towards Chalon and the D 23 west towards Merceuil; car park before the motorway. Description p 38.*

Combertault. — Pop 185. *6km - 4 miles southeast by the D 970 and east by the D 111[1].*
The long farm buildings of the village are flanked by trees and flowers. The small ⊙ Romanesque **church,** restored in the 15C, contains several interesting statues; it consists of a short nave and a high semi-circular apse which is decorated on the outside with Lombard arcades.

Bagnot. - *24km - 15 miles northeast.* The village lies on the edge of Cîteaux Forest. The chancel of the **church,** which is Romanesque in origin, is decorated with late-15C murals called "the devils of Bagnot". The amusing and sympathetic details of the central theme, the Last Judgment, compensate for the lack of artistic skill. A calendar of the months decorates the vault.

★ BERZÉ-LA-VILLE   Pop 410

Michelin map 69 fold 19 or 243 fold 39 — 12km - 8 miles to the southeast of Cluny — Local map p 113

Towards the end of his life St Hugh of Cluny lived in the Monks' Castle (Château des Moines), a country house owned by Cluny Abbey near the priory in Berzé.

⊙ **Monks' Chapel.** — The Romanesque chapel of the priory is well known for its mural paintings, a magnificent example of the art of Cluny.

★ **Mural paintings.** – The 12C chapel, built at first-floor level on an earlier 11C building, was decorated with Romanesque frescoes *(illustration p 29)*; only those in the chancel are well preserved. The oven vault in the apse bears a mandorla containing the figure of Christ in Majesty (4m - 13ft high) surrounded by Apostles, bishops, deacons and St Peter to whom He is presenting a parchment of the Law; below the windows are groups of saints held in veneration at Cluny and martyrs emerging from simulated garments. The side walls of the apse show *(left)* the legend of St Blaise and *(right)* the martyrdom of St Vincent of Saragossa on a gridiron in the presence of Dacius, the Roman prefect.

The Byzantine influence evident in the murals, which are painted on a blue ground, is probably due to the fact that the Cluniac artists who worked at Berzé were directed by Benedictine painters from Monte Cassino in Latium where the influence of the eastern Roman empire survived until the 11C.

★ **Berzé-le-Châtel.** – *5km - 3 miles to the north. Description p 115.*

★★ BEUVRAY (MOUNT)

Michelin map 🔢 folds 6 and 7 or 🔢🔢🔢 fold 36 – 8km - 5 miles west of St-Léger-sous-Beuvray – Local maps pp 73 and 124

Access to the summit by the D 274, a one-way loop from the D 3.

The road offers one or two fleeting views through breaks in the trees.

Fortified camp of Bibracte. – The summit of Beuvray was the site of Bibracte, the capital of the **Aedui** and a Gallic *oppidum* built in 150 or 120 BC. It was a sort of fortified camp, the permanent living quarters of Gallic artisans and a refuge for the surrounding agricultural population in times of danger.

Vercingetorix made Bibracte famous by convoking a general assembly there – a veritable council of war – of all the Gallic tribes that had risen against **Julius Caesar** in 52 BC. It was there that he organised resistance to the Roman legions and was made commander-in-chief of the Gallic armies. After the capture of Alésia, Caesar twice went to Bibracte; under Augustus the *oppidum* was abandoned in favour of Augustodunum (Autun) but its name was recorded in written history by Caesar in his "Commentaries" on the Gallic War.

A monument commemorates Bulliot, whose 19C excavations were subsequently reburied; a new and ambitious programme of excavations was started in 1984. The Gallic defences (5km - 3 miles long and 3 to 4m - 2 to 2 1/2 miles wide) are known as the Beuvray Trench.

★★ **Panorama.** – From the viewpoint framed by age-old beech trees with twisted trunks, there is a magnificent panorama of Autun, the signal station of Uchon and Mount St Vincent; when visibility is good, you can see the Juras and even Mont Blanc.

BÈZE   Pop 526

Michelin map 🔢🔢 northwest of fold 13 or 🔢🔢🔢 folds 5 and 17

The little market town stands at the source of the River Bèze, a tributary of the Saône. There are several buildings of interest, notably a 13C house in Place de Verdun with pointed windows and some sculptural fragments, the 17C former priory in Place du Champ de Foire with its tower at the river's edge and the 18C church, pinpointed by its fortified 14C belfry which sports a sundial.

Source of the Bèze (Source de la Bèze). – The waters of the River Bèze, which are in effect the resurgent spring of the Venelle, gush out in a magnificent spring with a flow of $17m^3$ - 600 cubic feet per second.

⊙ **Bèze Caves (Grottes de Bèze).** – Two resurgent springs of the Tille, of which only the sinkholes (6-7m - 20-23ft) are visible, collect to form a swift-flowing underground river with a network of caves. Today these have been linked to allow boats to navigate a 300m - 328yd stretch. The visitor can enjoy the crystal-clear waters of the 18m - 60ft deep lake and the fantastically shaped concretions known as the "shell" and "Mexican hats" as well as the fine "chimney" not far from the entrance.

BLANOT   Pop 167

Michelin map 🔢🔢 fold 19 or 🔢🔢🔢 fold 39 – 10km - 6 miles northeast of Cluny – Local map p 109

A small village of old houses enclosed by fine dry-stone walls, Blanot stands in a charming setting at the foot of Mount St Romain. The church, roofed with stone slabs and the neighbouring priory, a dependent of Cluny, form a pretty ensemble.

★ **Former priory (Ancien prieuré).** – The living quarters of this 14C priory, which once belonged to Cluny, were fortified and now present a façade attractively patterned by the dry-stonework. The façade is punctuated on the left by a vaulted passageway, with a polygonal tower off centre, and a 15C round tower on the right. Several Merovingian tombs have been brought to light in front of the latter.

Church (Église). – This late-11C church has several interesting features. The apse is decorated with an open-work frieze below the eaves; the building is dominated by a curious Romanesque belfry, decorated with Lombard arcades and crowned by a widely oversailing roof. Inside, the choir is roofed with a dome on squinches.

⏱ **Caves** (Grottes). – *Leave Blanot to the north and take the D 446 to Fougnières. About 500m - 550yds beyond this hamlet, near a corner, a road leads off to the left.* The caves (over 80m - 262ft deep) were formed in the geologic period by the collapse of the roof which created a heap of huge boulders. The twenty-one chambers on show extend from the hamlet of Vivier to St Romain Mountain *(1km - 1/2 mile circuit of steep steps and low passages)*. A small showcase at the end of the tour exhibits an example of chipped-flint implements and animal bones dating from the Mousterian period (100 000 to 40 000 BC), which have been found in the caves since 1988.

BOURBON-LANCY   Pop 6507

Michelin map ▩▩ fold 16 or ▩▩▩ fold 47

On a small hill with a wide view over the valley of the Loire and the plains of the Bourbonnais, Bourbon-Lancy is both a little town with an old-world atmosphere and a well-known health resort for the treatment of rheumatic and circulatory troubles. The town is now an important engine-making centre employing over 1 200 people.

Spa town. – Five springs with temperatures ranging from 46°C to 58°C (115°F to 136°F) and yielding more than 400 000 litres - 88 000 gallons a day gush out here. The now-modernised thermal establishment overlooks a fine shaded park.

BOURBON-LANCY

Commerce (R. du)	5
Gaulle (Av. du-Gén.-de)	
	2
Autun (R. d')	3
Châtaigneraie (R. de la)	4
Dr-Gabriel-Pain (R. du)	6
Dr-Robert (R. du)	7
Gueugnon (R. de)	12
Horloge (R. de l')	13
Martyrs-de-la-Libération (R. des)	15
Musée (R. du)	16
Prébendes (R. des)	18
République (Pl. de la)	22
St-Nazaire (R.)	23

All symbols on the town plans are explained in the key p 34

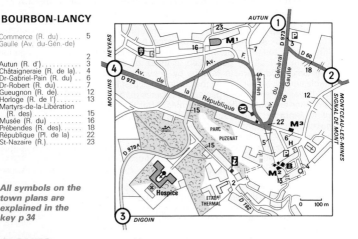

SIGHTS

★ **Half-Timbered House** and **Clock Tower** (Maison de bois and tour de l'Horloge) (B). – At no 3 Rue de l'Horloge (**13**) there is a 16C half-timbered house with a carved corner post, ogee-arched mouldings above the windows, glazed medallions and a statue. Nearby an attractive picture is created by a flower-bedecked fountain and the former belfry (now the Clock Tower with its cheeky jack o'the clock) which stands on one of the town's old gateways.

Aligre Hospice (Hospice d'Aligre). – In the chapel is a handsomely-carved pulpit given in 1687 by Louis XIV to Madame Élisabeth d'Aligre, abbess of St-Cyr. On the landing of the great staircase to the left of the chapel, there is a silver statue of the Marquise d'Aligre (1776-1843), benefactress of the hospice.

⏱ **St Nazaire Church and Museum** (M¹). – The 11C church, which was built on the basilical plan with a transept and a panelled ceiling, was part of a Cluniac priory founded by Ancel de Bourbon who gave his name to the town. Since 1901 it has housed a museum of local antiquities from the prehistoric, Gallo-Roman and Merovingian period, lapidary fragments from the local churches as well as 19C paintings and sculpture. Contemporary art exhibitions are held in the summer.

⏱ **Military Museum** (M²). – The exhibits include a large collection of uniforms and headgear belonging to different branches of the French Army during the Second Empire and the Third Republic; paintings by Merlette, a military artist.

⏱ **Bourbon-Expo** (M³). – The large hall contains a collection of obsolete agricultural machinery produced by the Puzenat factory (1902-56) which revolutionized agricultural implements at the beginning of the 20C: harrows, harvesters, threshers, tedders...

EXCURSIONS

★ **Mont Signal Station** (Signal de Mont). – *7km - 4 miles northeast plus 1/4 hour Rtn on foot.*
From the viewpoint (469m - 1539ft) there is a **panorama**★ spreading over the mountains of Morvan, the Uchon signal station, the Charollais, the Bourbon Mountain and the mountains of Auvergne in fine weather.

⏱ **St-Aubin-sur-Loire Château.** – *6km - 4 miles south.* This château, built in the second half of the 18C, is of great simplicity and perfect proportions. The façade has a slightly projecting centre. The outbuildings are handsome. Inside, magnificent tapestries decorate the main staircase. The great salon and the surrounding boudoirs have attractive panelling and furnishings of the period.

Michelin map **74** fold 3 or **243** folds 40 and 41 – Town plan in the Michelin Red Guide France

Bourg (pronounced Bourk) is and has always been the centre of the rich Bresse region, noted for its poultry which make the local markets famous. On market days or when there is a livestock fair, Bourg is picturesque and busy as crowds of farmers come into town. The annual exhibition *(p 181)* of Bresse capons and roasting chickens is held in the exhibition park. The chickens' flesh is bathed in milk making it a pearly colour. The town is also known for the manufacture of Bresse country-style furniture using fruit (walnut, wild cherry, cherry and pear) trees as well as ash. The Meillonnas pottery *(p 61)* and attractive Bresse enamels are still produced locally. The town also specialises in mechanical engineering.

These modern or traditional activities all contribute to the dynamic image of Bourg and add to its reputation as an artistic centre with one of France's brightest jewels, the outstanding works of art at Brou.

HISTORICAL NOTES

In the 10C Bourg was still a little village of thatched cottages clustered round a castle. When the family of the lords of the manor died out in the 13C the dukes of Savoy, powerful neighbours, took over the inheritance. They established the province of Bresse and made Bourg, now a busy township, its capital.

In 1536 the Duke of Savoy refused François I permission to cross his lands to invade the Milanese. The king forced his way through and, to secure his lines of communication, took possession of Bresse, Savoy and Piedmont. These territories were handed back by Henri II with the Treaty of Cateau-Cambrésis (1559).

In 1600 Henri IV invaded the region. The Treaty of Lyons (1601) forced the Duke to exchange Bresse, Bugey, Valromey and the Pays de Gex for the marquisate of Saluces, last of France's possessions in Italy. Bourg became part of France.

The Vow of Margaret of Bourbon. – In 1480 Philip, Count of Bresse, later Duke of Savoy, had a hunting accident. His wife, Margaret of Bourbon (grandmother of François I), made a vow that if her husband recovered, she would transform the humble priory of Brou into a monastery. The Count recovered but Margaret died leaving the task to her husband and her son Philibert the Handsome. Her vow however remained unfulfilled. Twenty years went by. Philibert, who had married Margaret of Austria, died suddenly. His wife saw a heavenly punishment in this. So that her husband's soul should rest in peace, she hurried to fulfil the vow of Margaret of Bourbon. She lost no time for two reasons, firstly to affirm her sovereignty and secondly to outshine her sister-in-law Louise of Savoy who was soon to become Regent of France. Nevertheless, for the past 400 years, Brou has borne witness to the married love of the two Margarets.

Ill-fated Margaret of Austria. – Margaret of Austria, the daughter of the Emperor Maximilian and the grand-daughter of Charles the Bold, was two years old when her mother, Mary of Burgundy, died. The following year, she was taken to the court of Louis XI and, in a religious ceremony, was married to the Dauphin Charles, heir to the French throne, who was also a child. The Franche-Comté was the little girl's dowry.

Five years later quarrels over the succession to the duchy of Brittany began. The heiress, the Duchess Anne, who had many suitors, was married by proxy to Maximilian, who was already known as "the penniless Emperor". On the occasion of his first marriage his fiancée had had to send him money for the journey. This time also he lacked the 2 000 *livres* necessary to go to Nantes.

Brou. – Statuette from the tomb of Philibert the Handsome

Charles VIII took advantage of their predicament: Anne of Brittany would be queen of France instead of Empress of Austria. The two unconsummated marriages were annulled; Charles repudiated Margaret of Austria, and Anne repudiated Maximilian, who was doubly embittered as father and putative husband.

At the age of seventeen the unfortunate Margaret married the heir to the Spanish throne, lost her husband after only about three months and gave birth to a still-born child. Four years later her father gave her in marriage for the third time to Philibert de Savoie, a frivolous and fickle young man. He was astute enough to acknowledge his wife's superior intelligence "intelligent enough for two" and was content to let her govern in his stead. She passed three years of complete happiness at the side of her "handsome duke". Now fate redoubled its blows: the young husband died after catching a cold while out hunting. Widowed for the second time, Margaret, now twenty-four, remained faithful to the memory of Philibert to her dying day. This high-ranking woman, well-read and artistic, who knew how to take care of herself and be obeyed, now lived only for affairs of State. In 1506 she became regent of the Low Countries and the Franche-Comté. Her wise and liberal policies brought her the fidelity, respect and affection of all living in the Comté.

Fulfilment of the Vow. – In 1506 work began on the construction of the monastery buildings. These were arranged round three cloisters, one of which was the former Benedictine priory.

The priory church was then pulled down to make room for a magnificent building to serve as the shrine for the three tombs in which were to lie Philibert, his wife **Margaret of Bourbon** and his mother.

Margaret, who was living in Flanders, entrusted the construction work to a Flemish master mason, Van Boghem, who was both architect and general contractor. He was a remarkable man, who brought life and strength to the faltering undertaking. He succeeded in erecting the fabulous building in the record time of nineteen years (1513 to 1532) but Margaret died two years before the consecration of the church.

Brou was lucky in surviving the Wars of Religion and the Revolution without suffering great damage. The monastery became, successively, a pig farm, a prison, a barracks, a home for beggars, a lunatic asylum, a seminary in 1823 and today houses Brou Museum.

★★★ BROU *Southeast of the town plan. Time: 1 hour*

Brou was once a small village clustered round a Benedictine priory, attached to Bourg. It is now part of the southeastern suburbs of that town. The church and the monastery were built in the 16C in fulfilment of the vow made by Margaret of Bourbon *(see p 57).*

A short history and the family tree of the founders are to be found in the south aisle of the church.

★★ The church

⊘The church has been deconsecrated. The building, in which the Flamboyant Gothic style is influenced by Renaissance art, is contemporary with the château of Chenonceau. On the flat ground in front of the façade there is a huge sundial which was reset in 1757 by the astronomer Lalande, a citizen of Bourg.

Exterior. – The triangular façade is richly sculptured in the central part. The tympanum over the fine Renaissance **doorway★** shows Philibert the Handsome and Margaret of Austria and their patron saints at the feet of Christ Bound. On the pier is St Nicholas of Tolentino, to whom the church is dedicated (his feast falls on the day of Philibert's death). Surmounting the ornamented doorway arch is a statue of St Andrew; St Peter and St Paul flank the doorway on the arch shafts.

The decorative sculpture includes a variety of Flamboyant Gothic floral motifs (leaves and fruit), some showing a decidedly Renaissance influence (laurel, vine and acanthus), intermingled with symbolic motifs, such as palms interlaced with marguerites. The decoration also comprises other emblems of Brou: the initials of Philibert and Margaret linked by love-knots (twisted fillet moulding festooned between the two letters) and intermingled with crossed batons, the arms of Burgundy.

The simpler north transept façade also has a pinnacled gable. The five-storey square belfry stands on the south side of the apse.

Nave. – On entering the church, one is struck by the light which bathes the nave and its double aisles. The light entering through the clerestory windows falls on the false stonework marked on the surface of the walls. The pillars, formed by numerous little columns, rise with a single thrust to the vaulting and open out into a network of ribs meeting at the carved keystones. A finely sculptured balustrade runs below the windows of the nave. The overall impression is one of elegance, richness and nobility.

In the second bay of the nave *(right)* is a 16C black marble font (1) bearing Margaret's motto.

The south transept is lit by a beautiful 16C stained glass window (2) representing Susanna being accused by the Elders *(above)* and being exonerated by Daniel *(below).*

The nave and transepts, accessible to the faithful, were separated from the chancel, reserve of the clergy and burials, by the rood screen. To its right is the Montécuto Chapel (3) which contains models explaining the construction of the church.

★★ Rood screen. – The richly decorated screen is composed of three basket-handled arches supporting seven religious statues.

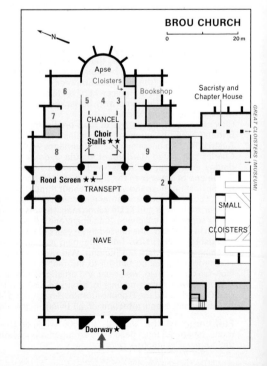

BROU CHURCH

0 ——————— 20 m

←N

Apse

Cloisters

Bookshop

Sacristy and Chapter House

6

5 4 3

7

CHANCEL

Choir Stalls ★★

8

9

Rood Screen ★★

TRANSEPT

2

SMALL CLOISTERS

NAVE

1

Doorway ★

GREAT CLOISTERS (MUSEUM)

Chancel. — This is the most important part of the church. Margaret did everything possible to obtain perfection with magnificence. Taken as a whole, the sculptured decoration of Brou borders on the excessive but the smallest detail is treated with an extraordinary mastery. One's surprise and pleasure are made all the more lively the closer one examines the decoration.

★★ **Choir stalls.** — The 74 stalls, which line the first two bays of the choir, were carved from oak in the astonishingly short time of two years (1530 - 32). The master carpenter, Pierre Berchod, known as Terrasson, had to mobilise all the wood craftsmen of the neighbourhood where wood carving was — and still is — extremely popular.

The stalls are carved in the same manner as the sculptures of the tombs and the designs appear to come from the same artist: **Jean de Bruxelles.** The seats, the backs and the canopies have an extraordinary wealth of decorative detail and statuettes; these are considered masterpieces of their kind.

The stalls on the north side have scenes from the New Testament and satirical personages. Those on the south side have personages and scenes from the Old Testament.

★★★ **The tombs.** — Many artists collaborated in the decoration of these three monuments, the high point of Flemish sculpture in Burgundy. The plans were sketched by Jean de Bruxelles, who furnished the sculptors with full-scale designs. The ornamentation and the statuary, much admired by visitors, are attributed for the most part to a Flemish workshop which was set up in Brou, in collaboration with French, German and Italian sculptors. The statues of the three princely personages are the work of Conrad Meyt, of German origin but of Flemish background.

Brou. – Chastisement (detail on a stall)

The effigies of the prince and the princesses are cut from Carrara marble. The great blocks were brought from Italy by sea and then transported up the river Rhône. The final part of their journey was by huge carts drawn by nine horses travelling at three to four miles a day.

Philibert and the two Margarets are represented, each lying on the tomb on a slab of black marble, their heads on finely embroidered cushions. Following tradition, a dog, emblem of fidelity, lies at the feet of the two princesses; a lion, symbol of strength, is at the feet of the prince. Cherubim, symbolising the entry of the three into heaven, surround the statues.

The tomb of Margaret of Bourbon (4) occupies a recessed niche hewn in the south wall of the choir.

The two other tombs differ in that they have two recumbent effigies: the first shown alive and the second dead in a shroud.

That of Philibert (5) the most sober in conception but most moving, is in the centre.

The tomb of Margaret of Austria (6), on the north, with its huge canopy of chiselled stone, prolongs the parclose. Sibyls, in the form of charming statuettes, mount guard round the effigies.

On the sole of her foot can be seen the wound which, according to legend, caused the death of the princess through blood poisoning. On the canopy the following motto is inscribed: *Fortune infortune fort une.* This can be translated as: "Fate was very hard on one woman", recalling the sad destiny of a princess whose constancy in misfortune never failed.

★★ **Stained glass windows.** — The magnificent stained glass of Brou was made in a local workshop. The windows in the centre of the apse represent Christ appearing to Mary Magdalene (upper part) and Christ visiting Mary (lower part), scenes taken from engravings by Albrecht Dürer. On the left and right, Philibert and Margaret kneel before their patron saints. The coats of arms of their families are reproduced above them in glittering colours: Savoy and Bourbon for the Duke, Imperial and Burgundian for the Duchess, as well as the armorial bearings of the towns of the State of Savoy.

★★★ **Chapels and oratories.** — The chapel of Margaret (7) opens to the north of the choir. A retable and a stained glass window, two fine works of art, deserve to be seen.

The **retable** represents the Seven Joys of the Virgin. Executed in white marble, it has come down to us in an exceptional state of preservation. It is a masterpiece of delicate workmanship, a fantastic work of art that leaves one dazed.

A scene of the Seven Joys is set in each of the niches, designed for the purpose: on the left, below, is the Annunciation; to the right, the Visitation; above, the Nativity and the Adoration of the Magi; higher still the Assumption is framed by Christ appearing to his Mother, and Pentecost.

The retable is crowned by three statues: the Virgin and Child flanked by St Mary Magdalene and St Margaret. On each side of the retable note St Philibert and St Andrew.

The **stained glass window,** in magnificent colours, is inspired by an engraving of Albrecht Dürer representing the Assumption. The glass workers have added Philibert and Margaret kneeling near their patron saints. The frieze of the window, done in monochrome, represents the Triumph of Faith. Christ, in a chariot, is drawn by the Evangelists and personages of the Old Testament: behind throng the scholars of the church and the saints of the New Testament. It is a reproduction of a design that Titian composed for his own room.

The oratories of Margaret were arranged for her personal use. Set next to the chapel (Chapelle de Madame, 8), they are placed one above the other and are linked by a staircase. The lower oratory is on the same level as the choir, the upper one is on a level with the gallery of the rood screen. These two chambers, decorated with tapestries and warmed by fireplaces, were veritable little salons. An oblique window or squint, placed below a highly original arch, allowed the princess to follow the religious services.

The nearby chapel (9), which has the name of Laurent de Gorrevod, one of Margaret's councillors, has a remarkable stained glass window representing the Incredulity of St Thomas, and a triptych ordered by Cardinal de Granvelle.

Leave by the doorway to the right of the choir to see the monastery.

★ The museum

The museum is housed in the monastic buildings which are ranged round three two-storey cloisters, unique in France. By 1506 the old Benedictine priory had become so delapidated and damp that the monks obtained Margaret of Austria's permission to rebuild beginning with the living quarters rather than the church.

Small cloisters. — First to be built of the three cloisters of Brou, the small cloisters allowed the monks to pass from the monastery to the church under cover. One of the galleries on the first floor gave access to the private apartment of Margaret of Austria; but she died before it was completed. The other gallery was to allow the princess to reach the upper chapel directly by way of the rood screen. On the ground floor the sacristy and chapter house, now made into one room, are used for temporary exhibitions. From the galleries (today a stone depository with fragments of cornice and pinnacles) enjoy the view of the south transept gable and the spire.

Great Cloisters. — This is where the monks used to walk and meditate. It gives access to the second Chapter House, now converted into the museum reception.

First floor. — A stair leads up to the dorter where the old monks' cells now house collections of painting and decorative art. On the landing and in the recess in the middle of the great corridor are some fine pieces of Bresse furniture and a showcase of 18C Meillonnas earthenware *(p 61)*.

The cells on the south side are devoted to 16C-18C art: among the Flemish and Dutch works is a fine **portrait of Margaret of Austria★** painted by B Van Orley c1518 and a triptych of the life of St Jerome (1518); the following rooms are hung with 17C and 18C examples of the Italian school (Magnasco: *Monks practising self-flagellation*) and 18C examples of the French school (Largillière, Gresly) as well as Burgundian and Lyonnais furniture (Nogaret) and objects of French religious art.

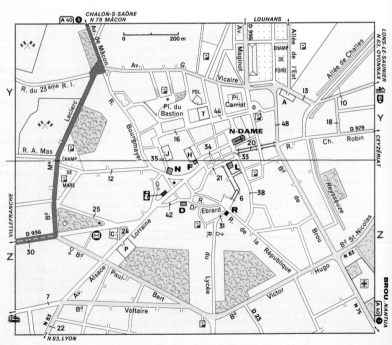

In the north gallery the rooms on the right are devoted to 19C French painting (Gustave Doré, Gustave Moreau, the Lyonnais school); those on the left exhibit the troubadour style and early-20C work. Margaret of Austria's Great State Room contains a collection of contemporary art.

In the southeast corner of the Great Cloisters is the entrance to the refectory which displays 13C-17C religious sculpture, in particular a Black Virgin (13C), a Holy Sepulchre (1443), Philibert and St Philibert from the tympanum of Brou Church (early 16C). The refectory leads into the third cloisters.

Kitchen Cloisters. – Unlike the other two these cloisters exhibit features typical of the region such as the rounded arches and the gently sloping roof of hollow tiles. The far building contains archaeological collections.

ADDITIONAL SIGHTS

Notre-Dame (Y K). – Although it was begun in 1505, the church was not completed until the 17C. The apse and nave are in the Flamboyant Gothic while a triple Renaissance doorway is the centrepiece of the façade. The central door is surmounted by a Virgin and Child, copied from a work by Coysevox (17C). The tall belfry was erected under Louis XIV but the dome and the small lantern on top are modern. A carillon plays at 7.50am, 11.50am and 6.50pm.

Interior. – The church has works or art and furnishings of interest, in particular the finely carved 16C **stalls★** in the apse. The high altar, eagle-shaped lectern, the pulpit and organ loft are all examples of 18C wood carving. The altar in the lefthand chapel is 19C. St Crepin's Chapel, third off the north aisle, has a stained glass window depicting the Crucifixion, polychrome statues and a diptych showing the Last Supper, all dating from the 16C. The mid-20C stained glass in the aisles is by Le Chevallier (north aisle) and Auclair (south aisle). Note the series of twelve 17C and 18C canvases depicting scenes from the life of the Virgin Mary.

The 13C Black Virgin, in whose honour the church was built, stands in the Annunciation Chapel to the right of the choir.

Old Houses. – There are two late-15C timber-framed houses: **Maison Hugon** (*on the corner of Rue Gambetta and Rue V-Basch* – Z L) and **Maison Gorrevod** (*Rue du Palais* – Z N). Equally attractive are the fine 17C stone façade of **Hotel de Bohan** (*on the corner by the Town Hall* – YZ F) and the 18C **Hotel de Marron de Meillonnas,** which houses the Trésorerie Générale (*Rue Teynière* – Z D). A row of medieval half-timbered corbelled houses adjoins the Jacobin Gate built in 1437 (*Rue J-Migonney* – Z R).

EXCURSIONS

St-Rémy. – Pop 551. *7km - 4 1/4 miles west.* Set in the heavily forested area of the Dombes, the town is pinpointed by its Romanesque church. The latter has a fine timberwork ceiling in the nave and harmonious Romanesque arcading in the choir.

⊘**Buellas.** – Pop 1 006. *9km - 5 1/2 miles west.* The **church** with a porch has interesting Romanesque arcading in the choir and some good statues.

Continue by the D 45 passing via Montcet.

⊘**Vandeins.** – Pop 329. *14km - 8 3/4 miles west.* The church has a 12C sculptured doorway. The fine Romanesque carving on the **tympanum★** shows Christ conferring His Blessing. Note the angels holding up the glory or mandorla which frames the figure of Christ. On the lintel the Last Supper, a less perfect work, is set between two small groups of the Damned on the arch shafts.

⊘**Montfalcon.** – *17km - 10 1/2 miles northwest.* The **church,** on its grassy mound, has above the altar a curious polychrome wood statue of the Virgin nursing the Infant. This is a good example of local 15C work.

Meillonnas. – Pop 891. *12km - 8 miles northeast.*
Meillonnas has long been famous for its earthenware which was particularly highly prized under Louis XV. Production ceased in 1866 but was restarted in 1967 on a small scale using the traditional designs. Picturesque 16C houses around the church.

★ BRANCION

Michelin map 🔢 fold 19 or 🔢 fold 39 – 15km - 9 miles southwest of Tournus – Local map p 113

The site of Brancion in the middle of the Mâconnais region is most unusual; the feudal market town is picturesquely perched on a spur overlooking two deep ravines. Brancion celebrates the feast day of St John (St Jean) by lighting bonfires in the Celtic tradition.

⊘Once through the gateway in the 14C ramparts, the visitor will be pleasantly surprised to find the imposing ruins of a fortress, the narrow streets lined with houses of medieval appearance – some of which have creepers growing all over them – the *halles* (old covered markets), and the church standing proudly at the end of the promontory. Some of the houses have been well restored.

⊘**Castle.** – This feudal castle dates back to the beginning of the 10C. The castle was enlarged in the 14C by Duke Philip the Bold, who added a wing to lodge the Dukes of Burgundy, and was destroyed by the troops of Colonel d'Ornano on 11 June 1594, during the time of the Catholic League. The keep has been restored. From the platform (87 steps), there is a good **view★** of the town and its church, the Grosne Valley and, to the west and northwest, the mountains of Charollais and Morvan.

⊘**St Peter's.** — The church is a squat building of the 12C, built in Romanesque style, surmounted by a square belfry. One is struck by the simplicity and the purity of its lines, as well as by the harmonious colours of the stone and the roofing of stone tiles. Inside there are 14C frescoes commissioned by Eudes IV, Duke of Burgundy, a recumbent effigy of Josserand IV of Brancion (13C), a cousin and companion to St Louis, who died on the Seventh Crusade, and numerous funerary stones. The 14C and 15C mural paintings on the south wall of the apse have sadly deteriorated. They represent the Resurrection of the Dead.

There is an attractive view of the valley from the church terrace, built at the end of the promontory.

BRIARE   Pop 6 327

Michelin map 🔢 south of fold 2 or 🔢🔢 fold 8

This little town on the banks of the Loire owed its prosperity at the beginning of the century to the manufacture of porcelain-like buttons made from a paste of very pure feldspar, imported from Norway. This activity produced not only a great quantity of buttons but also pearl, jet and, in particular, ceramic floor mosaics known as "Briare enamels".

The ceramics industry is still important although new industries have also come to Briare.

Briare Canal. — The canal was begun in 1604 on the initiative of Sully by the "Compagnie des Seigneurs du Canal de Loyre en Seine" but not completed until 1642. It was the first junction canal (57km - 35 1/2 miles) to be built in Europe and links the Loire Lateral Canal to the Loing Canal. The reach separating the Loire and the Seine basins extends between Ouzouer-sur-Trézée and Rogny-les-Sept-Écluses *(p 75)*.

SIGHTS

★ **Canal Bridge.** — This work of art which dates from 1890 carries the Loire Lateral Canal over the river to join the Briare Canal *(illustration p 32)*. The aqueduct (662m - 2 172ft long by 11m - 37ft wide) is made of metal plates held together by millions of rivets. The metal duct (2.20m - 7ft in depth) and the towing paths rest on 15 piles of masonry constructed by the Société Eiffel. Steps lead down to the bank of the Loire which provides a fine view of the metal structure of the aqueduct.

⊘**Car Museum.** — *South of Briare on the road to Nevers, on the right before the junction with the N 7.* The theme of the museum — the history of the automobile from 1898 to 1960 — is illustrated by about 130 vehicles (sports cars, saloon cars, convertibles) together with motorbikes, bicycles and 300 scale models. As well as many vintage cars — one of the first Panhard and Levassors (1898), a Mors (a copy of the only one, built for the Tsar in 1908), a 1907 Clément-Bayard saloon — there are racing cars (the oldest dates from 1924), touring models (including several famous names such as Bugatti, Hispano-Suiza, Cadillac), minicars built in the post-war period and a few prototypes.

The museum is housed in an old lime kiln which operated from the end of the 16C until 1914; a specialist **museum** traces the development of kilns and production techniques during that period.

EXCURSIONS

Ouzouer-sur-Trézée. — *7km - 4 1/4 miles northeast.* The village descends from the hillside to the water's edge. The late-12C Gothic **church** consists of a uniform nave leading to a square chancel in the Cistercian style. The style of Notre-Dame Cathedral in Paris is however visible in the slim clusters of columns springing from the elegant cylindrical pillars and in the broad mouldings of the pointed arches.

⊘**Pont-Chevron Château.** — *9km - 5 1/2 miles north.* Despite its classical appearance the château was built in the late 19C by Count Louis d'Harcourt. The noble white façade contrasts with the woods and lakes of the Puisaye and the Gâtinais. The great salon is decorated with hunting scenes by J B Oudry and the dining room décor consists of *trompe-l'œil* in delicate tones of pink and green.

The entrance lodge displays 2C **Gallo-Roman mosaics:** one, in black and white, depicts games, the other a polychrome god's head.

*Each year the **Michelin Red Guide France**
revises its 500 town plans which show*

    – through-routes and by-passes
    – new roads, one-way systems and car parks
    – the exact location of hotels, restaurants and public buildings.

*This up-to-date information
makes town driving less stressful.*

★ BRIONNAIS

Michelin maps 🔢 fold 17 and 🔢 folds 7 and 8 or 🔢 fold 48 and 🔢 fold 37

The small region of Brionnais, where cattle rearing is the main activity, stretches along the right bank of the Loire between Charlieu and Paray-le-Monial. In the past it was one of the nineteen bailiwicks which made up the duchy of Burgundy and Semur-en-Brionnais was its capital. It is a region of low hills from which there are pretty views of the Loire Valley, Le Forez and the mountains of Beaujolais.

A flowering of Romanesque churches. – Several attractive village churches, built under the inspiration of Cluny *(pp 22 and 29)*, are concentrated in the small area between the rivers Arconce and Sornin.

Beauty in stone. – There is an abundance of first-class building material on the spot: seams of yellowish limestone of fine grain, easy to work but also durable, provide the beautiful ochre or yellow colour of most of the Brionnais churches. When the sun is setting, the warm tones of the stone are particularly beautiful.

Decoration. – As granite and sandstone are too hard to be worked in detail, they are best employed to provide effects of line or mass, as in the churches in Varenne l'Arconce, Bois-Ste-Marie, Châteauneuf and St-Laurent-en-Brionnais; the most suitable medium for the sculptor, however, is limestone, which has been used for the beautiful façades and richly carved doorways of the locality.

Certain themes predominate; the only variations are in the attitudes and expressions of the figures. The tympanum usually shows Christ in Majesty, in a mandorla, surrounded by the four Evangelists or their symbols, or Christ ascending into heaven in a mandorla, standing on a cloud which is borne aloft by two angels.

The decoration on the lintels is particularly elaborate; multitudes thronging round the central figure of Christ in triumph, who is drawn larger than his attendants to stress the hierarchy between Christ, the Evangelists, the Virgin and the Apostles.

TOUR

★ **Anzy-le-Duc.** – *Description p 38.*

Bois-Ste-Marie. – Pop 233. Built in the 12C, the church with its open belfry and imposing apse was restored during the last century. In the south aisle the tympanum of a small doorway depicts the Flight into Egypt. Inside, the alternating red and white stones of the transverse arches of the vaulting, provide a highly decorative note. The apse, which has semi-dome vaulting, is surrounded by a low ambulatory bordered by a series of twin columns. The capitals portray foliage or ingenious and amusing scenes.

Châteauneuf. – Pop 149. The church and the château are enhanced by their woodland setting. The church, one of the latest Burgundian churches, has a massive west front. The lintel of the south doorway portrays a rather naive carving of the 12 Apostles.

Inside note the slender columns and capitals at the clerestory level and the dome on squinches over the transept crossing. The octagonal lower stage of the dome has an arcaded gallery.

Not far from the D 8 - D 113 crossroads there is the graveyard chapel.

Iguerande. – Pop 1026. The squat **church**, built at the beginning of the 12C, is perched on a rocky escarpment overlooking the Loire Valley. The church has very pure lines. The cornice corbels of the chevet are variously carved.

Inside in the nave and choir there are several strange capitals, notably the one-eyed musician (first pillar on the left). From the vicinity of the church enjoy the view across the Loire plain to Le Forez (left) and the peaks of la Madeleine (right).

Montceaux-l'Étoile. – Pop 301. Under the arch of the **church's** doorway, a single block of stone forms the tympanum and the lintel representing the Ascension, in the same manner as at Anzy-le-Duc and St-Julien-de-Jonzy. The columns supporting the recessed arches have decorative capitals.

★★ **Paray-le-Monial.** – *Description p 132.*

St Julien-de-Jonzy. – *Description p 143.*

★ **Semur-en-Brionnais.** – *Description p 153.*

Varenne-l'Arconce. – Pop 137. The **church** has a rather massive silhouette with its projecting transepts and square belfry. The sandstone was not conducive to carved decoration. The tympanum of the south doorway portrays the Holy Lamb. Inside there are several statues in wood: notably a 12C Christ and several 16C polychrome ones.

La BUSSIÈRE — Pop 656

Michelin map 📍 fold 2 or 📍 fold 8 - 13km - 8 miles north of Briare

The village lies just off the main road (N 7) in a peaceful setting of woods, lakes and cultivated fields.

Les Pêcheurs Château. – The château is an interesting example of patterned brickwork; it was built under Louis XIII in place of an earlier fortress. In 1577 during the Wars of Religion it was the scene of a bloody episode when Protestants massacred a group of priests from Gien seeking refuge in the neighbourhood. The château is surrounded by a water-filled moat and overlooks a small lake designed by Le Nôtre; there is a small exhibition on **fresh-water fishing**.

The château contains a fine collection of English and German 18C engravings, of earthenware on the theme of fresh-water fishing, and 16C leather from Cordoba. The kitchen and the laundry are on show in the basement.

★ BUSSY-RABUTIN CHÂTEAU

Michelin map 📍 south of fold 8 or 📍 fold 2

A few miles north of Alise-Ste-Reine half way up a hill stands Bussy-Rabutin Château; its highly original interior décor is an eloquent testimony of the state of mind of its owner.

The misfortunes of Roger de Bussy-Rabutin. – While his cousin, Madame de Sévigné, was very successful with her pen, Roger de Rabutin, Count of Bussy, caused nothing but trouble with his. Turenne, already irritated by his biting couplets, described him to the king as "the best officer in his armies — for writing verse". Having compromised himself, in company with other young libertines, in a now-famous orgy in which he improvised and sang couplets ridiculing the love-affair of young Louis XIV and Marie de Mancini, he was exiled to Burgundy by order of the king.

Accompanied in exile by his mistress, the Marquise de Montglat, he passed his time composing an *Histoire amoureuse des Gaules (A love history of the Gauls)*, a satiric chronicle on the love affairs of the court.

This libel took its author straight to the Bastille, where he remained for more than a year before returning to his property, alone this time as the beautiful marquise had forgotten him.

TOUR *time: 3/4 hour*

The château is protected by a moat and four round corner towers; since the 16C Bussy has consisted of only three ranges of buildings bordering a courtyard which opens on to gardens. The wings, which take the form of galleries, were decorated in the Renaissance style under Henri II. The main block was rebuilt in 1649 by Roger de Rabutin in the early Louis XIV style.

Interior. – It was Bussy-Rabutin himself who designed the interior decoration of the apartments, a gilded cage in which he spent his exile, indulging in nostalgia for army and court life and giving vent to his rancour against Louis XIV and to his amorous malice.

Bussy-Rabutin. – The château

Room of Epigrams (Cabinet des Devises). – This was the dining room. Framed in woodwork, allegorical panels and maxims composed by Roger de Rabutin form an unexpected ensemble. Views of châteaux and monuments appearing in the upper panels are interesting as historical documents. Over the fireplace is a portrait of Bussy-Rabutin by Lefèvre, a student of Lebrun. The furniture is Louis XIII.

Antechamber of the Great Warriors (Antichambre des Grands Hommes de Guerre). – Portraits of sixty-five great warriors, from Du Guesclin down to the master of the house, "master of the field, general of the light cavalry of France", are arranged in two rows round the room. Some of these portraits are very good originals. Most of them are only copies from originals of the period (17C) but they have undeniable historical interest. The woodwork and the ceilings are decorated with fleurs de lys, trophies, standards and the interlaced ciphers of de Bussy and the Marquise de Montglat.

Bussy's Room (Chambre de Bussy). – The portraits of twenty-five women are grouped here. That of Louise de Rouville, second wife of Bussy-Rabutin, is included in a triptych with those of Madame de Sévigné and her daughter, Madame de Grignan. Other personalities portrayed include Gabrielle d'Estrées, Henri IV's mistress, Madame de la Sablière, Ninon de Lenclos the famous courtesan, and Madame de Maintenon.

Gilded Tower (Tour Dorée). — Bussy-Rabutin surpassed himself in the decoration of this circular room on the first floor of the west tower where he worked. The walls are entirely covered with paintings. The subjects, taken from mythology and the gallantry of the time, are accompanied by quatrains and couplets. A series of portraits of the great personalities of the courts of Louis XIII and Louis XIV completes the ensemble.

Chapel. — The gallery of the Kings of France leads to the South Tower which houses a small oratory elegantly furnished (16C stone altarpiece depicting the Raising of Lazarus).

Gardens and park. — The park (34ha - 84 acres), which is shaped like an amphitheatre with beautiful stone steps linking the levels, makes a fine backdrop to the gardens with their statues (17C-19C), fountains and pools, apparently designed by Le Nôtre, Louis XIV's own gardener.

EXCURSIONS

Bussy-le-Grand. — Pop 298. *2km - 1 mile north.* On the hillside facing Bussy-Rabutin is the village where General Junot, made Duke of Abrantes by Napoleon, ⊘ was born. Despite its plain exterior, the 12C **church** (restored) has several interesting internal features: pillared arcades dividing the nave and aisles, a dome above the transept crossing, carved capitals, an exuberant ciborium, 17C and 18C furniture (choir woodwork, pulpit, lectern and reading desk).

Alise-Ste-Reine. — *8km - 5 miles south. Description p 36.*

Michelin Maps, Red Guides and Green Guides are complementary publications to be used together.

CHABLIS   Pop 2414

Michelin map 🔲 folds 5 and 6 or 🔲🔲🔲 fold 11

"Golden Gateway" to Burgundy, the little town of Chablis, washed by the waters of the river Serein, is the wine capital of Lower Burgundy.

Of ancient origin, these vineyards knew their greatest prosperity in the 16C. At that time, there were more than 700 vineyard owners in Chablis and the surrounding region.

Today the light, dry white wines of Chablis with their delicate taste and subtle bouquet are much prized. Their special fragrance develops about the month of March following the vintage and preserves its remarkable freshness for a long time. The vine is the Chardonnay, known in the region as Beaunois. The area in which the wine is produced extends from Maligny and Ligny-le-Châtel in the north to Poilly-sur-Serein in the south, and from Viviers in the east to Courgis in the west. "Good" wines come from both banks of the Serein on the land round Chablis but the "best" wines are grouped on the steep hillsides of the east bank: these are Vaudésir, Valmur, Blanchot, Grenouille, Les Clos, Les Preuses and Bougros. There is an annual Chablis Wine Fair *(p 180)* and a fair on the feast day of St Vincent, the patron saint of vine-growers *(p 179)*.

⊘ **St Martin.** — The church, which dates from the 12C, was the collegiate church of the canons of St-Martin-de-Tours, who set up a sanctuary for the relics of their saint after fleeing from the Normans.

On the Romanesque doorway of the south entrance, note the 13C paintings and the horseshoes nailed to the door as *ex-voto* offerings from pilgrims to the shrine of St Martin. The interior forms an attractive and uniform ensemble.

St Peter's (St-Pierre). — Only three bays remain of this Romanesque church, which is an excellent example of the Burgundian transitional style *(p 30)*. It was the parish church until 1789.

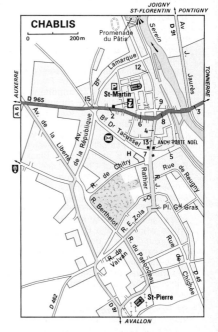

CHABLIS

Auxerroise (R.) 2	Lattre-de-T. (R. de) . . . 8
Briand (Av. A.) 3	Leclerc
Cordonniers (R. des) . . 4	(R. du Maréchal) . . . 9
Ferrières (Bd de) 5	Moulins (R. des) 12
Gaulle (Pl. Ch. de) . . . 6	Porte-Noël (R.) 13
La-Fayette (Pl.) 7	République (Pl.) 15

Chalon, an inland port situated at the confluence of the river and the Central Canal, is an active industrial and business centre; its commercial fairs are well attended. The eight-day-long carnival festivities *(p 179)* usually attract large crowds.

Chalon is also the chief town of an area of arable farming, stock rearing and of vineyards; the best wines are worthy of their great neighbours from the Côte d'Or.

Predestined as a crossroads. – Julius Caesar chose Chalon as the main warehouse for his food supplies during his campaigns in Gaul owing to its situation on the banks of the Saône, a magnificent navigable waterway, and at the intersection of a number of great roads.

During the Middle Ages the annual pelt fairs **(Foires aux Sauvagines),** which lasted two months, were among the most popular in Europe. These two fur fairs which still take place in Chalon each year are picturesque events. On these occasions, many collectors, trappers and game wardens from the Alps, the Pyrenees, the Jura, the Vosges and the Massif Central, bring every kind of pelt to Chalon: fox, badger, polecat, stoat, otter, marten, mink etc. The winter fair or *Foire Froide* (Cold Fair) *(p 180)* always draws large crowds and is the most important French fair for furs. The building of the Central Canal in the late 18C-early 19C, as well as the canals of Burgundy and the Rhône-Rhine link, developed regional commerce by waterway. In 1839 the Schneider company from Le Creusot set up a factory in Chalon at the east end of the Central Canal; it was first known as "Petit Creusot" and then "Creusot-Loire" *(p 88).* The factory specialised in heavy metallurgy and suffered the full force of the crisis in the steel industry in 1984. Since 1970 however the economic activity of Chalon has been stimulated by the arrival of other industries such as Kodak, St-Gobain, Framatome, Air Liquide and Water Queen (European leader in the production of fishing gear).

Côte de Chalon. – Between the Côte de Beaune and the Côte de Nuits to the north, and the Mâconnais and Beaujolais to the south, the Côte de Chalon appears as the poor relation. Nevertheless it produces such famous wines as Mercurey, Givry, Montagny, Rully (sparkling) and a number of fine table wines as well as superior "vin ordinaire".

The father of photography. – Joseph Nicéphore Niepce, born in Chalon in 1765, can well lay claim to the title of inventor of photography. After a short period with the Oratorians and a spell in the Revolutionary army, which he left for health reasons, he finally settled in Chalon in 1801, devoting himself to scientific research. After perfecting, with his brother Claude, an engine whose principle is the same as the jet engine, he devoted his time to lithography and in 1822 succeeded in fixing on a glass plate an image previously (1816) obtained in a darkroom, thus inventing photography. Nicéphore Niepce died in Chalon in 1833. A statue in Quai Gambetta and a monument on the edge of the N 6 at St-Loup-de-Varennes (7km - 4 miles south of Chalon), where his discovery was perfected, perpetuate the memory of this great inventor.

SIGHTS

★ **Denon Museum** (BZ M¹). – The 18C building, formerly part of an Ursuline convent, ⊘ was specially provided with a neo-classical façade when it was converted to house the museum which bears the name of one of the town's most illustrious citizens. **Denon,** a diplomat under the Old Regime, was a famous engraver and one of the first to introduce lithography to France; during Napoleon's campaign in Egypt he initiated Egyptology and then became artistic adviser to the Emperor and Grand Purveyor and Director of the Museums of France.

The museum displays an important collection of 17C to 19C paintings: the Italian school is represented by three large canvases by Giordano as well as works by Bassano *(Plan of Venice, Adoration of the Shepherds),* Solimena and Caravaggio; the golden century (17C) of Dutch painting is represented by Hans Bollongier *(Bouquet of Tulips),* Doomer, Davidsz de Heem *(Still Life);* French painting is represented by Largillière, Carle van Loo, Lagrenée, P de Champaigne and, from the 19C, Géricault's portrait of a Black Man and pre-Impressionist landscapes by Raffort, a native of Chalon. Local history is illustrated by examples of domestic traditions, the life of the Saône boatmen and a collection of local furniture. Also on display are medieval pottery, various models, 12C religious items, 16C religious sculptures and paintings, stained glass, etc. The last room is devoted to Denon and artists of his period: terra cotta figures by Clodion (female faun and children). The mezzanine gallery and its staircase are hung with contemporary works mainly by artists who won the Prix de Rome.

The ground floor is devoted to the rich archaeological collections: prehistoric flint implements from Volgu (Digoin-Gueugnon region – the largest and most beautiful stone-age relics known, which date from the Solutré period – *p 157),* many antique and medieval metal objects, a magnificent Gallo-Roman group in stone of a lion bringing down a gladiator. There are also Gallo-Roman and medieval lapidary collections.

St Peter's Church (St-Pierre) (BZ). – The church was built as the chapel of a Benedictine abbey, between 1698 and 1713 in an Italian style (19C additions) with an impressive west front. The huge nave and domed chancel are furnished with statues, some of which date from the 17C: at the entrance to the chancel St Peter and St Benet, in the transept St Anne and the Virgin bringing down the dragon. The choir stalls are attractively carved and the Regency-style organ is surmounted by a figure of Saul playing the harp.

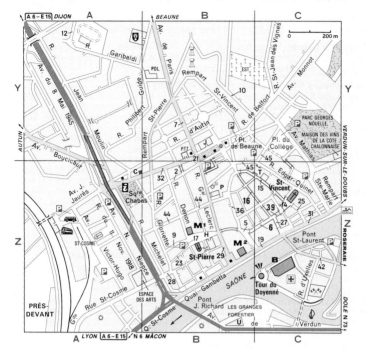

CHALON-SUR-SAÔNE

★ **Nicéphore Niepce Museum** (BZ M²). – This museum is housed in the 18C Hôtel des Messageries, standing on the banks of the Saône. The rich collection includes photographs and photographic equipment, including some of the earliest cameras made and used by Joseph Nicéphore Niepce, and his first heliographs. There are also works by well-known contemporaries of Niepce in the world of photography.

The extensive ground floor displays photographic equipment from all over the world ranging from luminous projectors and Dagron equipment for microscopic photography (1860) to the camera used on the Apollo space programme. The Niepce Room *(first floor)* contains family mementoes and the first camera (1816); the Daguerre Room displays the machinery for producing daguerreotypes; the following rooms are devoted to the first colour and relief photographs and the famous 19C cameras: the Great Chevalier camera (*c*1850), the Bertsch cameras (1860), the Damoizeau cyclographs (1890).

The last galleries *(ground floor)* are a huge room containing various old cameras (the Dubroni series, 1860; ferrotyping implements) and a small room devoted to "photosculpture".

St Vincent's Cathedral (CZ). – The cathedral of the old bishopric of Chalon (suppressed in 1790) is not uniform in appearance. The oldest parts date from the late 11C; the chancel is 13C. The neo-Gothic façade (1825) is certainly the oldest in France in this style.

The pillars in the nave are composed of fluted pilasters and engaged columns. A 15C font and a Flamboyant vault adorn the third chapel in the north transept. The north apsidal chapel contains a large contemporary tabernacle in bronze gilt (1986). A finely sculpted canopy adorns the chancel and a triptych of the Crucifixion (1608) the apse.

The 15C sacristy was divided horizontally in the 16C and the lower chamber was covered with a vault supported by a central pillar. The ante-chapel is vaulted with five pendant keystones and lit by a beautiful stained glass window depicting the woman with the twelve stars of the Apocalypse.

The south transept opens into the chapel of Our Lady of Mercy (15C *Pietà* and Renaissance tapestry) and into the 15C cloisters (restored) which contain four wooden statues; the well in the cloister garth has been restored.

The south aisle contains many burial stones; some chapels are closed off by stone screens (claustra); the last chapel contains a 16C polychrome *Pietà*.

Old houses (Maisons anciennes). – Some of the many old houses of old Chalon have a particular charm. In the streets near the cathedral there are fine half-timbered façades overlooking Place St-Vincent (note also at the corner of Rue St-Vincent the statue of a saint), Rue aux Fèvres and Rue de l'Évêché. **Rue St-Vincent** (CZ 39) forms a picturesque crossroads at the junction of Rues du Pont and du Châtelet. No 37 **Rue du Châtelet** (CZ 6) has a handsome 17C façade with low-reliefs, medallions and gargoyles. No 39 **Grande-Rue** (BCZ 16) is a fine 14C house (restored).

⊙**Hospital** (CZ B). – The Flemish-style building was started in the 16C. The first floor, the nuns' quarters, comprises several panelled rooms including the infirmary which contains four curtained beds. The buildings were extended in the 17C, and in the 18C certain rooms were decorated with magnificent **woodwork★** ; the nuns' refectory and the kitchen passage, which is furnished with dressers lined with pewter and copper vessels, are particularly interesting. The chapel (1873) has a metal structure and displays works of art from the buildings that have been demolished: woodwork decorated with coats of arms, 17C bishop's throne, rare late-15C statue of the Virgin with an inkwell. A collection of 84 18C pots is displayed in the late-18C pharmacy.

⊙**Deanery Tower** (Tour du Doyenné) (CZ). – This 15C tower originally stood near the cathedral. It was dismantled in 1907 and rebuilt at the point of the island. Near the tower is a magnificent lime tree from the Buffon nursery.

★**St Nicholas Rose Garden** (Roseraie St-Nicolas). – *4km - 2 1/2 miles northeast of Chalon-sur-Saône. Take the bridge, Pont St-Laurent* (CZ), *and continue straight on to cross the two islands, then turn left into Rue Julien-Leneuveu. A 5km - 3 mile trail (time: 1 1/2 hours) starts from St Nicholas country park and winds through the rose garden.* The garden is laid out in a loop of the Saône beyond the municipal golf course. The rose beds (25 000 bushes) are set in vast lawns shaded by conifers and young apple trees. The recommended route runs parallel with a keep-fit trail (2.5km - 1 1/2 miles). On the left of the main alley are splendid banks of roses of contrasting and harmonious hues (in flower: June-July), which are judged in an annual international competition, a small garden of rare plants (talus de la Grande rocaille) and an arboretum. On the right is an alley of old roses (mostly varieties obtained in the 19C), clumps of perennials (in flower: September), corms (irises, geraniums...), water plants, an Erica garden etc.

EXCURSION

Chalonnais. – *Round tour of 53km - 33 miles – about 2 hours.*

Givry. – Pop 2665. *9km - 5 1/2 miles west.* Givry produces wines that have been popular for a very long time. They were the *vin ordinaire* of Henri IV. The locality has the appearance of a quiet little city of the late 18C, with its fountains, its Town Hall occupying a gateway of 1771 and its **church,** an architectural masterpiece by Gauthey. The church has many domes and semi-domes; four groups of thick columns enclose the nave. The great arches of the early-19C circular hall, formerly a grain store, reveal the beautiful central spiral staircase.

Continue north for 3km - 2 miles.

⊙**Germolles Château.** – A 14C farmhouse with mullioned windows precedes the 13C fortified dwelling which was bought by the first Duke of Normandy, Philip the Bold, in the 14C and transformed into a residence for his wife, Margaret of Flanders. Still standing are the gatehouse with its round towers and superimposed chapels, the vast Romanesque-Gothic cellar and, set back from the entrance, the main block with two staircase turrets.

In Germolles turn left into a minor road to the valley of Les Vaux.

Les Vaux Valley. – This is the name given to the picturesque upper stretch of the Orbise. From Mellecey onwards the villages, which stand half-way up the slopes, are typical wine-growers' villages where the cellars are incorporated in the houses: St-Jean-de-Vaux *(the D124 branches off to the right)* and St-Mard-de-Vaux.

★ CHAPAIZE
Pop 134

Michelin map 𝟞𝟡 fold 19 or 𝟐𝟒𝟑 fold 39 – 16km - 10 miles to the west of Tournus – Local map p 113

Situated on the river Bisançon, to the west of the magnificent forest of Chapaize, the little village of Chapaize is dominated by the high belfry of its Romanesque church. The church is all that remains of a priory founded in the 11C by Benedictine monks from Chalon.

★**St Martin's Church** (Église St-Martin). – *Time: 1/2 hour.*
Between the first quarter of the 11C and the early 13C this church was built using the fine local limestone. The Romanesque edifice shows a strong Lombard influence and it is probable that Italian stonemasons worked on the building. It has a bold and harmonious belfry.

Exterior. – The original plan was basilical; the central nave was heightened and buttressed in the mid-12C. The west front is fairly plain. Both the double-arched doorway and the column-flanked window above, are round headed.

Chapaize Church

The shape of the pointed gable is repeated by the pattern of the Lombard arcades. Although set over the transept crossing, the mid-11C **belfry** is typical of those found in Lombardy. It is a surprising height (35m - 115ft) for a building of such modest size. Certain architectural contrivances emphasize this soaring effect: the imperceptibly rectangular shape, a first storey which is as tall as the two upper ones together and adorned with Lombard arcades; upper storeys marked horizontally by cornices; dissimilar openings placed on different levels with the width increasing upwards. An external staircase, added in the 18C, leads up to the base of the belfry.

The chevet was rebuilt in the 13C and modelled on the church at Lancharre *(see below)*. Its elegant simplicity harmonizes well with the rest of the building.

Stone slabs were used when the church was re-roofed in the late 14C.

A few weathered sculptures, archaic in style and limited in number, carved with floral decoration or human faces, adorn the capitals of the windows and the belfry. On the north side of the latter there is the precursor of the statue-column where a naive figure has been carved on a column.

Interior. — The stark simplicity of the interior is quite striking. The great cylindrical pillars (4.8m - 15ft in circumference) are slightly out of line and are crowned with triangular imposts. Of the total seven bays two belong to the choir. The nave arcade has very wide transverse arches which support 12C broken-barrel vaulting and also the groined vaulting of the aisles. The transept crossing is covered with an attractive **dome** on squinches and supported by semicircular transept arches. Both the apse and apsidal chapels are oven-vaulted. The former is lit by three wide windows and the latter by column-flanked openings; the one on the left is decorated with sculpted capitals. The side windows are 19C.

EXCURSION

Lancharre. — *2km - 1 mile northeast.* In this village are the remains of an 11C convent founded by the lords of Brancion. The touching ruins of the **conventual church** consist of two adjoining buildings dating from the 12C and 14C, the chevet and the transept, which is surmounted (left) by a square belfry with large ogival windows. The first bay next to the choir is all that remains of the nave, now invaded by the graveyard. The interior has several features of interest: the oven-vaulting in the vast apse and apsidal chapels; the chancel arch springing from two elegant pillars which have capitals carved with human heads; the dome on squinches surmounted by a belfry; a collection of 13C and 14C funerary tablets, some bearing engraved effigies of ladies or knights.

*With this guide use the **Michelin Maps** (scale 1:200 000) shown on p 3.*

★ La CHARITÉ-SUR-LOIRE   Pop 6 422

Michelin map 65 south of fold 13 or 238 fold 21

La Charité, which is dominated by the belfries of its handsome church, rises in terraces from the majestic sweep of the Loire. The river is spanned by a picturesque 16C stone bridge which provides a good view of the town. In the days of navigation on the Loire *(p 107)* La Charité was a busy port.

The Charity of the Good Fathers. — At first the small riverside town was called Seyr which, according to an etymology which seems to be Phoenician, means Town of the Sun. The conversion of the inhabitants to Christianity and the founding early in the 8C of a convent and a church marked the beginning of a period of prosperity which was interrupted by Arab invasions and attendant destruction.

It was in the 11C, when the present church was built, that the re-organised abbey began to attract travellers, pilgrims and poor people. The latter, knowing the hospitality and generosity of the monks, came in large numbers to ask for "the charity *(la charité)* of the good fathers" and the town acquired a new name.

La Charité river port in 1830

A check to Joan of Arc. – Fortified in the 12C, the town was to be the stake in the struggle between the Armagnacs and the Burgundians during the Hundred Years War. La Charité was initially occupied by the Armagnacs, the allies of Charles VII. In 1423 the town was taken by the adventurer **Perrinet-Gressard** who was in the service of both the duke of Burgundy, who wished to continue the struggle with Charles VII, and the English, who were anxious to delay for as long as possible a reconciliation between the Armagnacs and the Burgundians. In December 1429 Joan of Arc arrived from St-Pierre-le-Moutier *(p 145)* and besieged La Charité on behalf of Charles VII, King of France, but lack of troops and the cold weather obliged her to raise the siege. Perrinet-Gressard held the town until the Treaty of Arras in 1435 when he returned it to the king of France against payment of a large ransom and the office of town governor for life.

★★ PRIORY CHURCH OF THE VIRGIN
(ÉGLISE PRIEURALE NOTRE-DAME) *time: 1 hour*

Despite the damage incurred, this church remains one of the most remarkable examples of Romanesque architecture in Burgundy.

Eldest daughter of Cluny. – The church and its attendant Benedictine priory, a daughter house of Cluny, were built during the second half of the 11C. The church was consecrated in 1107 by Pope Paschal II; its outline and decoration were modified in the first half of the 12C.

After Cluny the priory church of La Charité was the largest church in France; it consisted of a nave and four aisles (122m - 399ft long, 37m - 120ft wide, 27m - 89ft high under the dome). It could hold a congregation of 5000 and carried the honorary title of "Eldest daughter of Cluny". At the time Cluny had at least fifty daughter houses.

Exterior. – The façade, which was separated from the rest of the church by a fire in 1559, stands in Place des Pêcheurs. Originally two towers framed the central doorway; only one (left), the 12C **St Cross Tower** (**B**), has survived. It is square in design with two storeys of windows surmounted by a slate spire in place of the original one of stone. It is decorated with blind arcades and sculptured motifs including rosettes. The two doorways are walled up; one of them has preserved its tympanum and shows the Virgin Mary interceding with Christ to obtain protection for the monastery of La Charité, represented by the monk, Gérard, its founder and prior. Scenes from the life of the Virgin are portrayed on the lintels: the Annunciation, the Visitation, the Nativity, and the bringing of the good tidings to the shepherds.

The steps of the Romanesque central doorway of which little is left, and which were replaced by a Gothic construction in the 16C, lead to Place Ste-Croix, which occupies the site of six bays of the nave destroyed in the fire of 1559.

Houses have been built into the former north aisle which was transformed into a parish church from the 12C to the 18C; the arcades of the false triforium are still visible.

LA CHARITÉ-
SUR-LOIRE

Barrère (R.) 2
Chapelains (R. des) 3
Gaulle (Pl. Général-de) . . 4
Pont (R. du) 7
Verrerie (R. de la) 8

Interior. – The church today consists of the first four bays of the original nave, the transept and the chancel. The nave, which was badly restored in 1695, has nothing of interest but the transept and the chancel constitute a magnificent Romanesque ensemble.

The transept crossing is surmounted by an octagonal dome on squinches. The arms of the transept have three bays and two apsidal chapels dating from the 11C; this is the oldest part of the church. In the south transept the second Romanesque tympanum of St Cross Tower is visible, representing the Transfiguration with the Adoration of the Magi and the Presentation in the Temple.

The choir, encircled by an ambulatory serving five radiating chapels, is of great elegance. The Lady Chapel dates from the 14C. The depressed arches of the ambulatory are sharp owing to the closeness of the high columns supporting the fine historiated capitals. A bestiary of eight motifs accentuates the false triforium; its five-lobed arcades, of Arabic inspiration, are supported by ornamented pilasters. There are good, modern stained glass windows by Max Ingrand.

Leave the church by the south transept.

★ **View of the chevet.** – The 16C pointed-vaulted passageway (Passage de la Madeleine) emerges into Grande-Rue. A covered passage, at no 45, leads into Square des Bénédictins which provides a good view of the chevet, the transept and the octagonal tower of the abbey church. Behind the chevet traces of an 11C Cluniac priory are being excavated *(closed to the public)*.

From the square take the staircase leading down to the Priory.

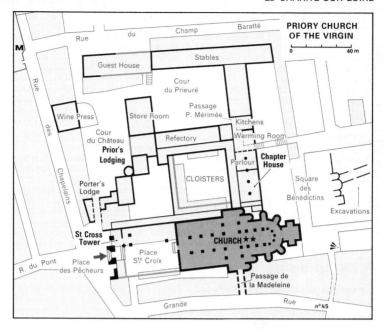

PRIORY CHURCH
OF THE VIRGIN

0   40 m

Former priory.

Former priory. – At the foot of the staircase a passageway, gained from the warming room, leads into the former courtyard of the priory, around which are grouped the main refectory, the kitchens and the stables.

The prior's lodging (early 16C) with an attractive seven-sided turret overlooks the lower courtyard (now called Cour du château).

Leave by the porter's lodge (porterie) to return to Place des Pêcheurs.

ADDITIONAL SIGHTS

Ramparts. – From the esplanade beside the college in Rue du Clos there is another attractive **view★** of the chevet with its circlet of apsidal chapels, the Loire, the old town and ramparts.

Museum (M). – Considerable space is devoted to medieval objects found during the excavations behind the church: lapidary fragments and terra cotta tiles, implements, pottery, keys, jewellery, etc. There are also sculptures by Pina (1885-1966), a pupil of Rodin, and a fine collection of Art Nouveau and Art Deco: decorative objects by Louchet, glass by Lalique, Gallé, Daum and ceramics by Deck, Delaherche.

A separate room traces the development of files and rasps; their production was an important local industry between 1830 and 1950.

Each summer there are exhibitions of contemporary art.

EXCURSION

Les Bertranges Forest (Forêt des Bertranges). – *Round tour of 45km - 28 miles.* The State forest of Les Bertranges (10000ha - 24710 acres) lies east of the Loire. It is composed of a mixture of oak trees and beeches with some firs and larch.

From La Charité take the N 151, (2). Turn right into the D 179; beyond Raveau take the D 138 towards Chaulgnes. In La Vache take the forest road leading to Rond de la Réserve (1km - 1/2 mile).

The road leads to a spring (fontaine de la Vache) beside which stands a solitary but majestic oak tree.

Turn round; turn right into the stony forest track; at the junction with La Bertherie forest track turn right again.

South of **Rond de la Réserve,** a crossroads surrounded by conifers and stands of young oak trees, lies the hamlet of Les Bois-de-Raveau. A hilly road (D 179) leads to St-Aubin-les-Forges. *Turn right into the D 117.* **Bizy** and its château overlook a fine stretch of water.

Turn right into the D 8 and right again into the D 110 to Chaulgnes.

As this scenic road climbs it affords good views of the forest and nearby villages. The final descent reveals the low-lying basin with **Chaulgnes** pinpointed from afar by its church.

Continue on the D 110; beyond Chaulgnes turn left to Champvoux.

Champvoux Church (13C) has lost all but some buttressed walls and traces of the carved doorway of its nave, but the tall triple apse with its large round-headed windows and conical roofs draws the eye; in the choir are two pillars with naive capitals and an escutcheon (dated 1668) in the axial chapel.

Take the D 110 and the N 7 to return to La Charité.

CHAROLLES Pop 3758

Michelin map 📖 folds 17 and 18 or 📖 fold 37 — Local map p 63

Chief town of the Charollais region, the land of cattle breeding and fattening, Charolles is situated in a basin with ample pastureland and forests. The town is dominated by the ruins of the former château of the Counts of Charollais; the surviving main building now serves as the Town Hall. From the public gardens, laid out as a terrace along the wall of the old fortifications, at the foot of the ivy-covered tower of Charles the Bold, there is a pleasant view of the surrounding countryside. Since 1845 Charolles has possessed a pottery industry producing finely decorated artistic work. A small museum of sculpture (32 Rue Davoine, at the far end of Promenade St-Nicolas) commemorates the local artist René Davoine (1888-1962).

Cattle rearing in the Charollais. — Charollais cattle now hold fourth place among French breeds, coming behind the black and white, Normandy and red and white breeds. Charollais now number over 3 million and are distinguished by their uniformly white colouring. They are now the French number one breed for beef production.

The herds go out to graze with the arrival of the better weather and are taken indoors again with the return of winter. Each week from April to December markets and fairs are held at which thousands of the great white cattle are sold: at St-Christophe-en-Brionnais *(p 79)* and Charolles (Wednesdays). These are always picturesque and lively occasions. It is however at Sancoins in the Cher beyond the traditional rearing area that the most important sales are held attracting buyers from all over Europe.

EXCURSIONS

★ **Les Carges Mount** (Mont des Carges). — *12km - 7 1/2 miles east.* From the esplanade where there are monuments to the underground fighters of Beaubery and the Charollais battalion an almost circular **view★** takes in the Loire country to the west, all the Charollais and Brionnais regions to the south and the mountains of Beaujolais to the east.

North of Les Carges Mount the road (D 79) descends the wooded slopes of Mount Botey *(right)* and Artus Mountain *(left)* in the heart of the Charollais.

Chaumont Château. — *16km - 10 miles to the northeast.*
The Renaissance façade is flanked by a round tower, the other façade in the Gothic style is modern. The sheer extent and size of the outbuildings are quite remarkable.

Michelin Detailed Maps 1:200 000
are regularly revised.

★ CHÂTEAU-CHINON Pop 2679

Michelin map 📖 fold 6 or 📖 fold 36 — Local maps 73 and 124

The little town of Château-Chinon, main centre of the Morvan, occupies a picturesque **site★** on the ridge that separates the Loire and Seine basins on the eastern edge of the Nivernais.

Its favourable situation on the top of a hill, a natural fortress, easy to defend and from which one can see both the highlands of the Morvan and the Nivernais plain, made this position successively a Gallic settlement, a Roman camp and a feudal castle, which gave its name to the township. During centuries of battles, sieges and great feats of arms Château-Chinon has earned its motto — "small town, great fame" *(Petite ville, grand renom).*

★★ **Panorama from the Calvary.** — *1/4 hour Rtn from Square Aligre.* The Calvary (609m - 1 998ft) is built on the site of the fortified Gallic settlement and the ruins of the former fortress.

The circular panorama is fine *(viewing table).* There is an overall view of Château-Chinon and its slate roofs, and further off the wooded crests of the Morvan. The two summits, Haut Folin (901m - 2 956ft) and Mount Préneley (855m - 2 805ft), appear to the southeast. At the foot of the hill, the valley of the Yonne opens to the east, while to the west, the view goes beyond the Bazois as far as the Loire Valley.

★ **Promenade du Château.** — A road *(starting in Faubourg de Paris and returning by Rue du Château)* encircles the hill halfway up the slope. Through the trees there are glimpses of the Yonne Gorge as well as the countryside which is visible from the Calvary.

⊘ **Septennate Museum.** — The buildings (18C) of a former convent of Poor Clares at the top of the old town now house the official presents received by François Mitterrand (former mayor of Château-Chinon) in his capacity as President of the Republic since 1981. There are photos of the heads of state he has met, of honorary insignia and decorations together with many examples of arts and crafts from all over the world.

⊘ **Costume Museum.** — The museum, which is housed in the Hôtel de Buteau-Ravisy, exhibits a large collection of French civilian dress, fashion accessories and folk traditions (reconstructions).

Fountain. — The monumental fountain opposite the town hall, composed of independent articulated sculptures, is the work of Jean Tinguely and Niki de Saint-Phalle.

EXCURSIONS

★★ 1 Mount Beuvray
(Mont Beuvray). — *Round tour of 73km - 45 miles — about 2 hours — see adjoining local map. Leave Château-Chinon by the D 978 going east.*
The winding and picturesque road passes through open hilly country; numerous villages and hamlets are terraced on the hillsides set amid a multitude of fields enclosed by quickset hedges.

Arleuf. — Pop 864. Almost all the western gable ends of the houses are slated to protect them against the rain.

Continue east.

Beyong the wood there is a good view *(left)* of the highlands of Anost Forest.

East of Pommoy turn right into the D 179 to the Gorges de la Canche (p 126).

South of the bridge over the Canche the pleasant setting *(right)* of the dam and reservoir comes into view.

At La Croisette turn righ into the forest road.

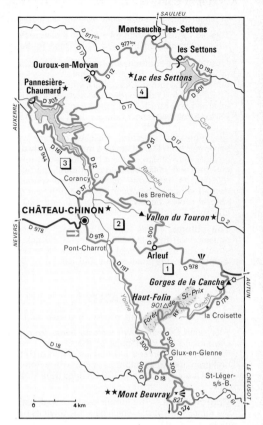

The magnificent pines and spruces of the **St-Prix Forest** flank the road. At the roundabout is the turning (right) which loops north to the ski-lift at **Haut-Folin** *(p 125).*

Make a detour south (14km - 9 miles Rtn) via the D 500 through Glux and Anvers; turn left into the D 18 and right into the D 300.

★★ Mount Beuvray. — *Description p 55.*

Take the D 300 and D 197 north through the Upper Yonne Valley to return to Château-Chinon.

★ 2 Touron Valley (Vallon du Touron). — *Round tour of 29km - 18 miles — about 1 hour — Local map above. Take the D 978 east to Arleuf; turn left into the D 500 going north.*

After a short climb (1.5km - 1 mile) the road traverses the steep Touron Valley; beyond Les Brenets the forested slopes of the Haut-Folin are visible to the south. The road continues northwest through the lush hillside pastures where the herds of Charollais cattle graze.

Turn left into the D 37 to return to Château-Chinon.

★ 3 Pannesière-Chaumard Dam. — *Round tour of 38km — 24 miles - about 1 1/2 hours — Local map above. Michelin maps 69 fold 6 and 65 fold 16 or 238 folds 23 and 24. Follow the roads which go all round the reservoir. Description p 132.*

★ 4 Les Settons Reservoir (Lac des Settons). — *Round tour of 64km - 40 miles — about 2 1/2 hours — Local map above. Michelin maps 69 fold 6 and 65 folds 16 and 17.*

The route from Château-Chinon to Montsauche-les-Settons is described on p 123. From Montsauche-les-Settons take the D 977bis and the D 12 west.

Ouroux-en-Morvan. — Pop 1 010. From the church and Place Centrale two streets lead ro a fine **viewpoint★** from which is visible part of the Pannesière-Chaumard Reservoir in its hilly setting *(1/4 hour Rtn).*

Take the D 17 and D 12 south; beyond Courgemain turn left into a minor road to les 4 Vents.

This winding road affords numerous views of the Morvan highlands and the Pannesière-Chaumard Reservoir *(description p 132).*

Turn left into the D 12; south of Corancy turn right into the D 37 to return to Château-Chinon.

★ CHÂTEAUNEUF   Pop 62

Michelin map 🗺 southwest of fold 19 or 🗺 folds 14 and 15

This old fortified market town, set in a picturesque **spot★**, is famous for its fortress, which commanded the road from Dijon to Autun and all the surrounding plain.

★ **Castle.** – The southern approach (D18^A) provides a spectacular view immediately ⏱after crossing the Burgundy Canal.

In the 12C the lord of Chaudenay, whose ruined castle stands on an attractive site in Chaudenay-le-Château *(6km - 3 1/2 miles south)*, built this fortress for his son; it was enlarged and refurbished at the end of the 15C in the Flamboyant Gothic style by Philippe Pot, Sénéchal of Burgundy. It was presented to the State in 1936 by its then owner, Count G de Vogüé.

The impressive structure, enclosed by thick walls flanked by massive towers, is separated from the village by a moat. Formerly there were two fortified gates; today a single drawbridge, flanked by huge round towers, gives access to the courtyard and the two main buildings. Although partially ruined, the guest pavilion has retained its handsome ogee-mullioned windows. The other wing with its high dormer windows has been restored; the vast guard room, the chapel (1481) and several rooms decorated in the 17C and 18C can be visited. From the circular chamber there is a panoramic view of the Morvan plain.

★ **The village.** – This forms a picturesque ensemble with its well-preserved old houses, built from the 14C to the 17C by rich Burgundian merchants, its narrow streets and the remains of its ramparts. Note in particular an interesting old pewter workshop in the main street and carved or ogee door lintels.

CHÂTEAURENARD   Pop 2 241

Michelin map 🗺 north of fold 3 or 🗺 fold 8

This small Gâtinais town took its name from the 10C castle built on the hilltop overlooking the right bank of the Ouanne.

There are still several old houses, the most attractive of which is the 15C half-timbered one with sculptures in Place de la République. Also visible on the left bank of the Ouanne is the early-17C Château de la Motte (private) standing in its attractive park.

Church (Église). – The former castle chapel, dating from the 11C-12C, stands amid the ruins of the castle which gave the town its name. Some of the castle towers are more or less intact. A fortified gateway between two towers gives access to the church.

A well precedes the west front with its gable belfry crowned by a lantern turret. From the open space nearby (12C oil press) there is a good view of the town below.

Except where otherwise stated, all itineraries in town are designed as walks.

CHÂTILLON-COLIGNY   Pop 1 786

Michelin map 🗺 fold 2 or 🗺 fold 8

The town is situated on the banks of the river Loing and the Briare Canal which are bordered by old wash-houses. It was the birthplace, in 1519, of **Admiral Gaspard de Coligny,** a victim of the St Bartholomew's Day massacre (1572). In 1937 a monument was erected (over the site of the room where he was born) in the park of the château, by Dutch subscription, in order to recall the marriage of Louise de Coligny, daughter of the admiral, to William the Silent, Prince of Orange. As the male line of the Coligny family died out in 1657, the Châtillon demesne reverted to the Montmorencys and then to the Montmorency-Luxembourg line.

In 1893 the French writer Colette married Willy (Henri Gauthier-Villars) at Châtillon-Coligny, where she lived with her brother, Dr Robineau.

Château. – When the Maréchal de Châtillon replaced his medieval castle with a magnificent Renaissance residence in the 16C he retained the polygonal Roman-esque keep (26m - 85ft high) built between 1180 and 1190 by the Count of Sancerre. The 12C keep and its underground access passages survived the Revolution but all that remained of the 16C building were three huge terraces.

⏱**Museum.** – The chief exhibits of the museum, which is housed in the former 15C workhouse, are portraits and documents belonging to the Coligny and Montmorency families who owned the Châtillon estates. The very fine pedestal table from the Louis-Philippe period is decorated with Sèvres plaques depicting the Maréchal de Luxembourg and the Constables of Montmorency. A small room is devoted to local archaeology from the Iron Age to the Merovingian period.

The construction of the seven locks at Rogny was begun on the orders of Henri IV in 1605 and completed in 1642. The project which carried the Briare Canal from the Trézée Valley to the Loing Valley was a considerable achievement for the period. The locks were in use until 1887 but have now been by-passed by a new series of six locks, more widely-spaced, which causes less delay to the traffic on the canal. The nearby church dating from the 16C and 17C is flanked by a belfry which itself abuts one of the gateways of the town wall.

EXCURSIONS

Montbouy. – Pop 619. *6km - 3 1/2 miles north*. To the north of the village the ruins of a 2C Gallo-Roman amphitheatre are visible.

Cortrat. – Pop 61. *12km - 8 miles northwest via Montbouy*. This small country **church** has a **tympanum★** engraved in a strange primitive style, representing the Creation.

⊙ **Les Barres Arboretum.** – *8km - 5 miles northwest*. The arboretum belongs to the National School of Engineers for the Forestry and Water Boards. The arboretum has some collections and experimental plantings which are over 150 years old and contains 3000 different species of trees and shrubs.

Rogny-les-Sept-Écluses. – Pop 735. *10km - 6 miles south*.
Young fir trees have been planted to replace those that once stood beside the seven locks which form a staircase. Though there is seldom water passing through the locks the place is still attractive.

CHÂTILLON-EN-BAZOIS   Pop 1179

Michelin map 𝟞𝟡 north of fold 5 or 𝟚𝟛𝟠 fold 35 — Local map p 124

Châtillon-en-Bazois stands on both the river Aron and the Nivernais Canal. It is an important centre for inland cruising in Burgundy. The boatbuilding yards are overlooked by a 16C-17C château with a 13C round tower, which stands between the river and the canal.

Church (Église). – The chapel on the left of the entrance contains a painting by Nicolas Mignard *(Baptism of Christ)*; on the right of the entrance is the 14C tombstone of Jehan de Châtillon. The altar frontal in the chancel is a stone altarpiece (1423) which portrays a *Pietà* surrounded by the Apostles.

EXCURSION

Rouy. – Pop 532. *10km - 6 miles west*. The 12C Romanesque **church** has a fine Gothic belfry which is ornamented with pillared arcades on the first storey and twin bays on each face of the second. The painting on the vault of the apse portrays Christ conferring his blessing flanked by an angel and a devil.

★ # CHÂTILLON-SUR-SEINE   Pop 7963

Michelin map 𝟞𝟝 fold 8 or 𝟚𝟜𝟛 fold 2

The trim little town of Châtillon is set on the banks of the young Seine, which is joined here by the abundant waters of the river Douix, flowing from a resurgent spring. Sheep-breeding has for several centuries been the main source of wealth on the dry plateaux of the Châtillon region (Châtillonnais) and up to the 18C Châtillon was the centre of a very flourishing wool industry.

A hundred years later. – A hundred years separate the two major events in the history of Châtillon. In February 1814, while **Napoleon I** was defending the approaches to Paris foot by foot, a congress was held in Châtillon between France and the countries allied against her – Austria, Russia, England and Prussia. Napoleon rejected the harsh conditions laid down, the fighting resumed and ended soon afterwards with the downfall of the Empire.

CHÂTILLON-SUR-SEINE

Abbaye (R. de l')	2
Bourg-à-Mont (R. du)	3
Courcelles-Prévoires (R.)	4
Herriot (Av.)	6
Joffre (Pl. Maréchal)	7
Lattre de Tassigny (R. de)	8
Philandrier (R.)	10
Résistance (Pl. de la)	12
8-Mai (Pl. du)	13

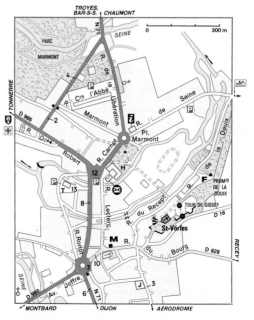

All maps and town plans are north orientated

In September 1914 French troops retreated in the face of a violent attack by the Germans. **General Joffre,** Commander-in-Chief of the French armies, set up his headquarters at Châtillon-sur-Seine, where he issued his famous order of 6 September.

"We are about to engage in a battle on which the fate of our country depends and it is important to remind all ranks that the moment has passed for looking back..." The German advance was halted and the French counter-attack on the Marne became a great victory.

★**Museum** (M). – The exhibits are displayed in the Philandrier house, an attractive Renaissance building. There are several interesting Gallo-Roman pieces – pottery, vases and statuettes – discovered in the 19C and early 20C during local excavations, particularly at Vertault *(20km - 12 miles west of Chatillon)*. The pride of the museum is however the extraordinary archaeological find made in January 1953 at Mount Lassois near Vix.

★★**The Treasure of Vix.** – The treasures were found in a 6C BC grave containing the remains of a woman: jewellery of inestimable value, the debris of a state chariot, countless gold and bronze items and a huge bronze vase (1.64m - 5ft high, 1.45m - 4 1/2ft wide and 208kg - 459lbs in weight). The rich decoration of the vase – sculptured frieze made of applied panels in high relief portraying a row of helmeted warriors and chariots, Gorgons' heads on the handles – reveals a highly-developed art form influenced by the archaic Greek style. The showcases contain the other items found in the tomb of the Gaulish princess: a massive golden diadem, bronze and silver goblets, wine jugs, bracelets and other jewellery.

Vix Vase – Gorgon Head handle

★ **Source of the Douix** (F). – The source of this river is to be found in a spot of astonishing beauty, at the foot of a rocky escarpment (over 30m - 98ft high) set in lovely green scenery. This resurgent spring collects the waters of other small springs and infiltrations of the limestone plateau. The normal flow is 132 gallons a second but this can reach 660 gallons in flood periods. The promenade, laid out on the rocky platform, affords a view over the town, the valley and the swimming-pool.

St-Vorles. – Built on a shaded terrace from which the view extends over the lower town and the valley, the church dominates the Bourg quarter, city of the bishops, which remained independent until the 16C.

The 11C building, with Lombard arcades, has been greatly altered; the belfry dates from the 13C. The underground chapel of St Bernard is part of the original church where St Bernard used to come and pray as a child. The chapel now contains a very fine Renaissance Holy Sepulchre.

EXCURSIONS

Mont Lassois (Mont Lassois). – *7km - 4 miles.*
Mount Lassois, also called St Marcel's Mount, (100m - 329ft) dominates the surrounding plain.

The summit is crowned by St Marcel's Church, a 12C Romanesque building roofed with stone shingles. It was at the foot of the hill near the river Seine that the "Treasure of Vix", now in the museum in Châtillon-sur-Seine, was found.

Montigny-sur-Aube Château. – *22km - 14 miles northeast.* The 12C tower (restored) is all that remains of a feudal fortress which was replaced in the 16C by four ranges of buildings round a courtyard. The façade facing the village of the surviving south wing is composed of the three classical orders – Doric, Ionic and Corinthian – superimposed. The **chapel,** now separate from the château, is a fine example of the classical Renaissance style: architectural austerity contrasting with rich ornamentation.

*The **Michelin Detailed Map** Series (1:200 000)*
covers the whole of France; use these maps

When choosing a lunchtime or overnight stop
*as all towns listed in the **Red Guide***
are underlined in red on the maps.

When driving into or through a town
as the reference numbers used on the maps
*also appear on the town plans in the **Red Guide.***

CÎTEAUX ABBEY

Michelin map 65 south of fold 20 or 243 fold 16 — 14km - 9 miles east of Nuits-St-Georges.

⊙ Cîteaux, like Cluny *(p 80)*, is an important religious centre in western Christendom. It was here, among the "cistels" or reeds that Robert, Abbot of Molesme, founded the Order of Cistercians in 1098 *(p 20)*, an off-shoot of Cluny, which under the great driving force of St Bernard, who joined the community in Cîteaux in 1112 and eventually became abbot, spread its influence throughout the world.

The abbey of La Trappe *(see the Michelin Green Guide Normandy Seine Valley)*, which was attached to Cîteaux in 1147 and reformed in 1664, has given its name to several monasteries which joined the Strict Observance. They did not amalgamate however until 1898 but followed parallel courses. Today the Order is divided into two branches: Cistercian monks who may devote themselves to a pastoral or intellectual life, such as teaching, and the more numerous Trappist monks who follow a strictly contemplative vocation.

During the Revolution Cîteaux nearly perished in its entirety; the monks were expelled and did not return until 1898 (when the abbey was again proclaimed the mother house of the Order); the church containing the tombs of the first dukes of Burgundy and of Philippe Pot (now in the Louvre) was entirely destroyed. All that remains are relics of the library, faced with 15C enamelled bricks,which incorporates six arches of a Gothic cloister and a vaulted room on the first floor. There is also a handsome 18C building near the chapel and another late-17C building beside the river.

CLAMECY   Pop 5 826

Michelin map 65 fold 15 or 238 fold 22

Clamecy is situated in the heart of the pretty country of the Vaux d'Yonne, junction point of the Morvan, the Nivernais and Lower Burgundy. The old town, with its narrow winding streets, is perched on a spur overlooking the confluence of the rivers Yonne and Beuvron. There are many pleasant walks along the hillsides.

Clamecy remains "the town of beautiful reflections and graceful hills" described by **Romain Rolland** (1866-1944), the French writer and philosopher, who is buried in the Nivernais not far from his native town. The writer's bust stands in front of the museum.

Bethlehem in Burgundy. – It is hard to understand why a bishopric existed at Clamecy, especially when there were already bishops at Auxerre, Nevers and Autun. One has to go back to the Crusades to find the answer.

William IV of Nevers, who left for Palestine in 1167, contracted the plague there and died at Acre in 1168. In his will he asked to be buried in Bethlehem and bequeathed to its bishops one of his properties in Clamecy, the hospital of Pantenor, on condition that it should be a refuge for the bishops of Bethlehem in the case of Palestine falling into the hands of the infidels.

When the Latin kingdom of Jerusalem fell, the bishop of Bethlehem took refuge at Clamecy in the domain bequeathed to the bishopric by William IV. From 1225 up to the French Revolution, fifty bishops succeeded each other at Clamecy. This episode is recalled in the dedication of the modern church (1927) of Our Lady of Bethlehem (Notre-Dame de Bethléem).

Corporations and brotherhoods. – Corporations were once held in honour in Clamecy. Those of the butchers, tanners, cobblers, and apothecaries were prosperous. The Revolution put an end to these organisations but they later re-formed under the name of "Brotherhoods". There were seven of them, each of which carried the banner of its patron saint: St Crispin (cobblers), St Anne (carpenters), St Honoratus (bakers), St Fiacre (gardeners), St Nicholas (watermen and raftsmen), the Ascension (all trades using ladders), and St Eligius (blacksmiths). Only the brotherhoods of St Nicholas and St Eligius have survived; they celebrate their corporative feast day each year.

The floating of free logs. – This method of moving timber, which goes back to the 16C, brought wealth to the river port of Clamecy for over three hundred years. It was first tried by Gilles Deffroissez and then organised on the river Cure by a rich timber merchant from Paris, **Jean Rouvet**.

The logs, cut in the forests of the Upper Morvan, were piled along the banks of the rivers and marked with their owners' signs. On an agreed day, the dams holding back the rivers were opened and the logs were thrown into the "flood" which carried them in a mass down to Clamecy. This was the floating of *bûches perdues* (free logs). All along the banks an army of workmen regulated the flow of logs as best they could.

At Clamecy, a dam stopped the wood, the timbermen with their long hooks "harpooned" the logs, dragging them from the water and putting them in piles according to their marks. This was known as the *tricage*. In mid-March, at the time of the flood-water, immense rafts of wood, called "trains" and sometimes consisting of 7 063 cubic feet of wood, were sent by the Yonne and the Seine towards Montereau and Paris.

The building of the Nivernais Canal brought to an end this method of transportation by "trains" with the introduction of barges. In 1923, the last "train" of wood left Clamecy.

Today all this logging activity has ended on both the Yonne and the Cure but Clamecy continued to operate the largest industrial charcoal factory in France until 1983 using supplies from the local forests.

SIGHTS

★**St Martin's Church.** – The church was built between the end of the 12C and the beginning of the 16C. The rich Flamboyant decoration on the façade and the high platform tower contrasts with the austerity of the rest of the building. Episodes in the life of St Martin are illustrated on the arch stones over the door (damaged at the Revolution).

The interior reveals the rectangular plan and the square ambulatory. The rood screen was constructed by Viollet-le-Duc to counteract the bowing of certain pillars in the chancel. In the nave there are two small galleries: one in the triforium and one below the clerestory. The first chapel in the south aisle contains an early 16C triptych of the Crucifixion and two low-reliefs from the 16C rood screen (destroyed in 1773) which depict the Last Supper and the Entombment. The organ is by Cavaillé-Coll (1862).

Old houses (Maisons anciennes). – It is a pleasure to stroll through the picturesque streets looking for old houses. *From Place du 19-Août take Rue de la Tour and Rue Bourgeoise; turn right into Rue Romain-Rolland and Rue de la Monnaie. Take Rue du Grand-Marché and Place du Général-Sanglé-Ferrière to return to Place du 19-Août.*

⊘**Romain Rolland Museum of Art and History** (M¹). – The museum is installed in the Duc de Bellegarde's mansion. Paintings include French and foreign works by Hell Bruegel, Pieter II, Vernet and Carracci. There is Nevers and Rouen pottery, ceremonial objects belonging to the corporations and an archaeological collection. One room is devoted to the floating of logs down the rivers while a second with a fine timberwork ceiling contains contemporary works. An underground passage leads to the Romain Rolland rooms which exhibit souvenirs of the author and various editions of his works.

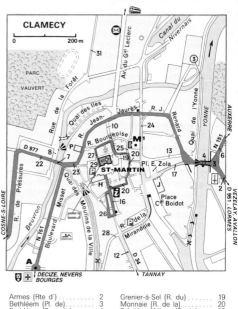

Armes (Rte d')	2	Grenier-à-Sel (R. du)	19
Bethléem (Pl. de)	3	Monnaie (R. de la)	20
Bethléem (Pont de)	4	Président-Wilson (R. du)	22
Bethléem (R. du Fg de)	6	Randan (R. Porte)	23
Beuvron (Pont du)	7	République (Av. de la)	24
Beuvron (Quai du)	8	Rolland (R. Romain)	25
Collège (R. du)	10	Sanglé-Ferrière (Pl. du Gén.)	26
Crot-Pinçon (R. du)	12	Tour (R. de la)	27
Davy (R. Marié)	13	Victoires (Pl. des)	28
Grand-Marché (R. du)	16	19-Août (Pl. du)	29
Gravière (R. de la)	17	43-Tirailleurs (R. des)	31

Views of the town. – The approach to Clamecy from Varzy (D 977) provides a glimpse of the old town with its red-brown roofs and the tower of the church of St Martin.

From Quai des Moulins-de-la-Ville there is also an attractive view of the houses overlooking the mill-race.

From Quai du Beuvron the picturesque Quai des Îles is visible.

The Bethlehem bridge, on which stands a tall statue in memory of the loggers, provides a good overall view of the town and its quays.

Upstream on the point overlooking the Nivernais Canal and the river stands a bronze bust of Jean Rouvet *(p 77)*.

Man of the Future (A). – Bronze statue of Caesar erected in 1987.

EXCURSIONS

Tannay. – Pop 699. *12km - 8 miles southeast.* The road passes through **Amazy**, where the 16C Gothic church is worth a visit.

Tannay is terraced on a hillside overlooking the left bank of the river Yonne, in the middle of vineyards laid out on the well-exposed slopes of the limestone hills. The white wine produced is very good, dry and with a pleasant bouquet.

The **church of St-Léger**, a former collegiate church, was built from the 13C to 16C and still has great charm. The vaulting of the nave is supported by "palm tree" pillars without capitals.

⊘**Metz-le-Comte Church.** – *14km - 9 miles southeast.*

Standing apart from the village on a hillock, the church of Metz-le-Comte and the fine trees growing in the surrounding graveyard make a picturesque **beauty spot★** which is reached by a steep climb.

This Romanesque church was altered in the 15C; the aisles are covered with broken barrel vaulting and the attractive roof of flat stones reaches almost to the ground. From the terrace behind the church, the **view★** extends east to the Avallonnais and the Morvan and north to the valley of the Yonne.

La CLAYETTE

Michelin map ⬚⬚ southeast of fold 17 or ⬚⬚⬚ fold 37 — Local map p 63

The little town of La Clayette (pronounced in the region as "Claite") — well known for its annual horse races and jumping competitions — lies in terraces above the valley of the Genette, a fast-running river, which forms a lake shaded by plane trees.

Château. — The château, built in the 14C, was altered and modernised during the last century. It is surrounded by a moat in which great carp swim. The vast turreted outbuildings and 17C orangery have considerable character.

EXCURSION

Drée Château. — *4km - 2 1/2 miles north by the D 193 then a road to the left.* The 17C château of Drée is a well-balanced construction consisting of a main building with two wings at right angles. From the wrought-iron entrance, framed by two magnificent cedars, there is an excellent view of the façade. Ionic columns, forming a portico, support a balcony and, on the first floor, a sculptured coat of arms. The beautiful yellow colour of the stone and the high slate roof give the building a particular beauty.

St Christophe-en-Brionnais. — *Pop 648. 12km - 7 1/2 miles west.* For five centuries the small town has attracted a lively crowd to its weekly cattle markets (Thursday mornings) for the Charollais breed. The animals arrive about four in the morning and three sales take place between 6.15 and 8 o'clock: bulls and lean beasts, grass-fed calves and bull calves, and beef cattle for slaughter. Next to the market are some 120 waiting pens and 50 marshalling platforms. In autumn over 3 000 cattle are brought to market each Thursday.

★ CLOS DE VOUGEOT CHÂTEAU

Michelin map ⬚⬚ fold 20 or ⬚⬚⬚ folds 15 and 16 — 5km - 3 miles north of Nuits-St-Georges — Local map p 86

The walled vineyard of Clos-de-Vougeot (50ha - 124 acres), owned by the abbey of Cîteaux from the 12C up to the French Revolution, is one of the most famous of La Côte.

Stendhal tells how Colonel Bisson, on his return from Italy, paraded his regiment in front of the château and made them present arms in honour of the celebrated vineyard. Since 1944 the château has been owned by the **Brotherhood of the Knights of the Tastevin** (la Confrérie des Chevaliers du Tastevin). Ten years earlier in 1934 a small group of Burgundians met in a cellar in Nuits-St-Georges and decided to fight against the slump in wines and to form a society whose aim was to promote "the wines of France in general and, in particular, those of Burgundy". The Brotherhood was founded and its renown grew fast and spread throughout Europe and America. Each year several chapter meetings of the order, well-known throughout the world, are held in the 12C Great Cellar of the château. Five hundred guests take part in these banquets, at the end of which the Grand Master and the Grand Chancellor, surrounded by high dignitaries of the Brotherhood, initiate new knights according to strictly observed rites that are based on the Divertissement in Molière's *Malade Imaginaire.*

During these plenary chapter meetings, the knights of the Tastevin celebrate the first of the **"Three Glorious Days"** *(Trois Glorieuses — p 181)* in the château on the eve of the sale of the wines of the Hospices of Beaune, which is held in the town on the following day *(p 51).* The Monday is devoted to the *Paulée de Meursault (p 87).*

⊘ **Tour.** — *Time: 1/2 hour.* The château was built during the Renaissance period and restored in the 19C. The rooms visited include the Great Cellar (12C) where the "disnées" (banquets) and the ceremonies of the Order are held, the 16C kitchen with its huge chimney and ribbed vault supported by a single central pillar, and the monks' dorter which has a spectacular 14C pitched roof. *Presentation of slides (1/4 hour) about the Brotherhood of the Knights of the Tastevin.*

The name of Cluny evokes the high point of medieval spirituality. The order of Cluny (p 20) exercised an immense influence on the religious, intellectual, political and artistic life of the West. Up to the time of the Revolution, each century left the mark of its style on Cluny. From 1798 to 1823 this centre of civilisation was ransacked but from the magnificence of what remains one can get an idea of the majesty of the basilica. For a good overall view of the town, climb the Cheese Tower (Tour des Fromages).

Promising beginnings. – Founded in the 10C by William the Pious, Duke of Aquitaine, the abbey of Cluny developed rapidly owing to the fact that, by Pontifical decree, it was exempt from the jurisdiction of the bishop and was responsible for other abbeys and priories under its obedience, whose collective unity was a strong force against the depredations of the times. Under the leadership of abbots of great worth, such as St Odo, St Mayeul, St Odilon, St Hugh and Peter the Venerable, Cluny became the chief abbey of the order, being responsible only to the Holy See and independent of all temporal power. The abbot in those days was a person of very considerable standing, sometimes more powerful than the Pope himself, whose guide and counsellor he was. Kings came to him for arbitration.

The abbey had enormous prestige: its dependencies were scattered throughout all the provinces of France and were established as far away as Italy, Germany, England, Poland, Spain and Switzerland.

Cluny, light of the world. – "Wherever the wind blows, the abbey of Cluny holds riches" was once a local saying. More than 10 000 monks were under its authority, it possessed about 1 450 dependencies, of which some 200 were fairly large, and in the year 1155 the mother-abbey alone had 460 monks. Prayer, study and teaching were the main objectives of the community.

The youth of Europe came from all countries to this capital of learning. "You are the light of the world", Pope Urban II, himself from Cluny as were many other Popes, said to **St Hugh** in 1098. When St Hugh died in 1109, having started to build the magnificent abbey church that Peter the Venerable, abbot from 1122 to 1156, was to finish, he left the abbey in a state of great prosperity.

Decline. – Rich and powerful, the monks of Cluny slowly slipped into a way of life that **St Bernard** condemned. He denounced the bishops who "cannot go four leagues from their house without a retinue of sixty horses and sometimes even more... Will the light shine only if it is in a candelabrum of gold or silver?".

The 14C saw the decline of Cluny's influence and power. Its abbots divided their time between the abbey and Paris where, at the end of the 15C, Jacques d'Amboise rebuilt the mansion erected after 1330 by one of his predecessors, Pierre de Châlus. This private lodging was often used by the kings of France, and gives an idea of the princely luxury with which the abbots of Cluny surrounded themselves.

Falling *in commendam* in the 16C, the rich abbey became nothing but a quarry for spoils. It was devastated during the Wars of Religion and the library was sacked.

Destruction of the abbey. – In 1790 the abbey was closed; its desecration began when the revolution was at its height. In September 1793 the local authority gave the order for the tombs to be demolished and the material sold. In 1798 the buildings were put up for sale and bought by a property speculator from Mâcon who demolished the nave. Little by little the magnificient abbey church was destroyed. By 1823 only what is visible today was left standing.

★**OLD ABBEY** *time: 1 hour*

⊙Most of the abbey church of St Peter and St Paul, called Cluny III, was built between 1088 and 1130 by the abbots St Hugh and Peter the Venerable. The foundations of two previous 10C and 11C buildings have been uncovered, together with those of a Gallo-Roman villa, south of the 12C basilica on the site of the former cloisters in the southeast corner of the present cloisters.

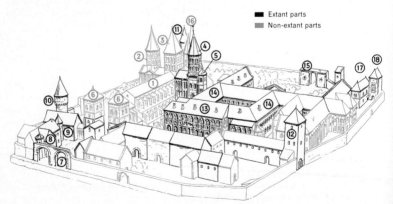

Cluny Abbey at the end of the 18C

1) Abbey Church of St Peter and St Paul - 2) Les Bisans Belfry - 3) Choir Belfry - 4) Holy Water Belfry - 5) Clock Tower - 6) The Barabans - 7) Main Gate - 8) Palace of Jean de Bourbon - 9) Palace of Jacques d'Amboise - 10) Fabry Tower - 11) Ronde Tower - 12) Cheese Tower - 13) Pope Gelasius' Façade - 14) Cloistral Ranges - 15) Garden Gate - 16) Lights Belfry - 17) Flour Store - 18) Mill Tower

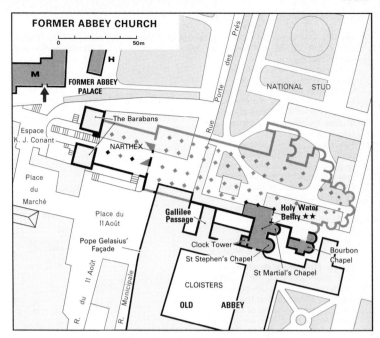

FORMER ABBEY CHURCH

0 — 50m

FORMER ABBEY PALACE

Espace K. J. Conant

The Barabans

NARTHEX

Place du Marché

Place du 11 Août

Pope Gelasius' Façade

R. du 11 Août

R. Municipale

NATIONAL STUD

Prés

des

Porte

Rue

Galilee Passage

Holy Water Belfry ★★

Clock Tower

St Stephen's Chapel

St Martial's Chapel

Bourbon Chapel

CLOISTERS

OLD ABBEY

Cluny III, symbol of the primacy of the Cluniac Order, then at its most powerful, was the largest Christian church (177m - 581ft long) until the reconstruction of St Peter's in Rome (186m - 610ft long). It consisted of a narthex, a nave and four aisles, two transepts, five belfries, two towers, 301 windows and 225 decorated stalls. The painted apsidal vault rested on a marble colonnade. It is difficult to imagine the full extent of the old building as only the south transepts remain standing.

Narthex. – The site of the narthex is now bisected by Rue Kenneth J Conant. During excavations in 1949 the base of the south end of the façade was uncovered, together with the footings of the doorway which was flanked by the square Barabans towers of which only the foundations survive. Subsequently the south aisle of the narthex was uncovered revealing a wall of uniform construction with pilasters attached to semi-columns.

The long Gothic façade (restored) in Place du 11-Août is named after Pope Gelasius who died at Cluny in 1119. By standing well back one can see the belfry and the high clock tower. To the rear are the Hugh stables.

Cloisters. – The 18C monastic buildings form a harmonious group enclosing the vast cloisters; two great flights of stone steps with wrought-iron railings occupy two corners. There is a handsome sundial in the garth.

Galilee Passage. – The 11C passage, which was used by the great Benedictine processions, linked the Galilee (a covered porch) of Cluny II with the south aisle of the great church of Cluny III.

Traces of the Church of St Peter and St Paul. – From the dimensions of the **south transepts** it is possible to calculate the audacious size of the whole basilica. Its height (30m - 98ft under the barrel vaulting, 32m - 105ft under the dome) is exceptional in Romanesque architecture. The church consisted of three bays; the central bay, surmounted by an octagonal cupola on squinches, supports the handsome **Holy Water Belfry★★**. St Stephen's Chapel (St-Etienne) is Romanesque; St Martial's Chapel dates from the 14C. The right arm of the smaller transept contains the Bourbon Chapel with its late-15C Gothic architecture and a Romanesque apse. The contrast between them emphasises the transition from Romanesque to late-Gothic art.

Monastic buildings. – The buildings, which house the School of Arts and Crafts, were nicknamed Little Versailles owing to the elegant classical east façade.

Flour Store (F). – The storehouse (54m - 177ft long) was built in the late 13C against the early-13C Mill Tower (tour du Moulin); in the 18C it was truncated (by about 20m – 65ft) to reveal the south end of the façade of the cloister building overlooking the gardens.

The low storeroom with its two ranges of ogive vaulting houses sculptures including a doorway with recessed arches from Pope Gelasius' palace (see above).

The **high chamber,** with its beautiful oak roof, makes an effective setting for various pieces of sculpture from the abbey. The very fine **capitals** (illustration p 29) and column shafts saved from the ruins of the chancel of the abbey church are exhibited by means of a scale model of the chancel: the eight capitals on their columns are set in a semi-circle round the old Pyrenean marble altar consecrated by Urban II in 1095. They are the first examples of the Burgundian Romanesque sculpture which was to blossom in Vézelay, Autun and Saulieu. The two models, of the great doorway and of the apse of the basilica, were designed by Professor Conant, the archaeologist who directed the excavations from 1928 to 1950.

ADDITIONAL SIGHTS

★**Ochier Museum** (M). – This museum is in the former abbey palace, a gracious building of the 15C, built by Abbot Jean de Bourbon, and is contemporary with the Cluny Mansion in Paris.

Pieces of the great doorway of the abbey church and capitals from the narthex, found during excavations carried out by the American archaeologist K J Conant are on display together with some outstanding works of lay sculpture. The rooms of the palace, complete with their chimneypieces, house a certain number of items that belonged to the abbey (lectern, Paschal candlestick, chests) as well as 4 000 books, including the works of Prud'hon, who was born at Cluny. The cellars are devoted to the Gallo-Roman collections of the museum. There is also a centre for Cluniac studies.

Town Hall (Hôtel de ville) (H). – This now occupies the building erected for Abbots Jacques and Geoffroy d'Amboise at the end of the 15C and beginning of the 16C. The garden front has an original decoration in the Italian Renaissance style.

Cheese Tower (Tour des Fromages) (D). – From the top (120 steps) of this 11C tower there is a good view of Cluny: the abbey, the Holy Water Belfry, the flour store and adjoining mill tower, the belfry of St-Marcel and Notre-Dame.

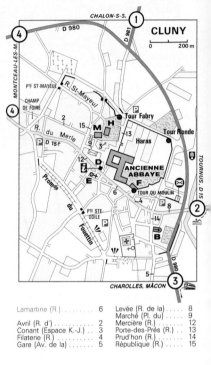

Lamartine (R.)	6	Levée (R. de la)	8
		Marché (Pl. du)	9
Avril (R. d')	2	Mercière (R.)	12
Conant (Espace K.-J.)	3	Porte-des-Prés (R.)	13
Filaterie (R.)	4	Prud'hon (R.)	14
Gare (Av. de la)	5	République (R.)	15

Fabry and Ronde Towers (Tour Fabry et tour Ronde). – The Fabry Tower (1347) with its pepperpot roof is visible from the garden near the town hall and the older Ronde Tower can be seen from the Fabry Tower.

National Stud (Haras National). – In 1806 Napoleon I decided to establish 23 studs. The one at Cluny was constructed with the stones of the neighbouring abbey. The various stable buildings house about sixty stallions most of which are away during the breeding season (March to mid-July) at Burgundy's nine subsidiary stables.

Romanesque houses. – Cluny has preserved fine Romanesque dwellings: at no 25 Rue de la République, a 12C house, and no 6 Rue d'Avril, the 13C mint (restored).

St Marcel (B). – This church has a fine octagonal Romanesque **belfry**★ of three storeys, topped by a graceful 15C polygonal brick spire (42m - 138 ft high). There is an excellent view of the belfry and the apse from the road (D 980).

Notre-Dame (E). – The square in front of the church has an 18C fountain and old houses. The church, built shortly after 1100, was altered and enlarged in the Gothic period. It was originally preceded by a narthex of which only the flagging remains. The 13C doorway is badly weathered.

The interior is a good example of Cluniac architecture. The lantern tower has carved brackets. The stalls and panelling date from 1644. The stained glass in the choir is modern.

Promenade du Fouettin. – Formerly part of the town's fortifications this promenade is bordered by centuries-old lime trees. There is a good view over the town and the Grosne Valley from the terrace at the southern end of the promenade.

EXCURSION

St-Vincent-des-Prés. – Pop 98. *14km - 9 miles northwest.* Above the apse of the small 11C Romanesque **church** rises a belfry decorated with blind arcades; the apse also is decorated with arcades and engaged columns.

The broken barrel vaulting above the nave and aisles is supported by four enormous round piers and two slimmer pillars with capitals; one is carved with scrolls, the other with fleur-de-lys. The chancel rises to a dome on squinches; the apse to oven-vaulting.

Further north *(1.5km - 1 mile)* **Bezornay** perches astride the ridge overlooking the plain. The ruins of the wall of enclosure, and a defensive tower and the old chapel (now a private house) with its curious apse shaped like a reversed cone, date from the Middle Ages when the hamlet was a dependency of Cluny.

Michelin map ⚉⚉ folds 18 and 19 or ⚉⚉⚉ fold 14

This little village of the Côte d'Or is the proud possessor of a handsome château.

★ **Château.** — Two late-14C towers survive from the feudal castle. Beyond them the
⊙main building (1702) rises to a fine French-style roof. The left wing was rebuilt in the
reign of Louis XIII over a Gothic chapel. The rooms open to the public (left wing)
present a décor and furniture which date from 1750 and some very beautiful 16C
tapestries. The chapel houses a 15C Burgundian Virgin and a 16C Entombment. The
Great Salon is hung with a full-length portrait of Charles X by Baron François Gérard.

Échannay. — Pop 86. *3km - 2 miles northeast.* In the choir of this small Romanesque
church is a beautiful marble retable dating from the 16C.

★★ CORMATIN CHÂTEAU

Michelin map ⚉⚉ fold 19 or ⚉⚉⚉ fold 39 — 13km - 8 miles to the north of Cluny

Cormatin was built in the aftermath of the Wars of Religion between 1605 and 1616
by the Governor of Chalon, Antoine du Blé d'Huxelles. The architecture is under-
stated in the style of Henri IV and was probably designed by Jacques II Androuet du
Cerceau, architect to the king. Originally the château consisted of three wings round
three sides of a courtyard; the south wing collapsed in 1815 during conversion to a
cloth weaving factory. The façades are in the "French rustic" style recommended by
du Cerceau: absence of the classical orders (except for the two monumental doors
in the courtyard), high stone base, matching quoins and window surrounds. The
broad moat and the impressive corner pavilions with watch-towers and cannon
suggest a defensive concept confirmed by traces of a rampart (demolished in the
late 17C) which closed the fourth side of the courtyard.

⊙**Interior.** — The north wing contains a magnificent grand **staircase** in an open
well (1610); the straight flights of steps, flanked by vigorous balusters, open
directly on to the central well. It is the oldest and largest stair of this kind (25m -
82ft high), successor to the Renaissance stairs in two flights separated by
a wall.

The sumptuous Louis XIII décor in this wing is the work of Marquess Jacques du Blé
(son of Antoine) and his wife Claude Phélypeaux, who were close friends of Marie
de' Medici and the literary salon of the Précieuses. They intended that their summer
house should reflect the sophistication of Parisian fashion by using the artists and
craftsmen who had worked for the Queen at the Luxembourg Palace. The gilt, the
paintings and sculptures which cover the walls and ceilings are proof of an informed
mannerism; each painting has an allegorical meaning reaffirmed in the symbolism
of the decorative motifs and the colours used for the panelling.

The ante-chamber of the Marchioness (daughter and sister of Government minis-
ters), which was created in the middle of the Protestant revolt (1627-8), is in homage
to Louis XIII who is represented above the chimneypiece: the red panelling (colour
of authority) celebrates the activites and virtues of the King. The Marchioness' room
has a magnificent French ceiling in gold and blue, symbol of fidelity; the great
painting of Venus and Vulcan, a work of the second Fontainebleau school, symbolises love and the baskets of fruit and flowers on the woodwork represent plenty. One
of the oldest "heavenly" ceilings, made fashionable by Marie de' Medici, adorns the
landscape room. The
sumptuous baroque
décor in the **St Cecilia
Room★★★**, Jacques du
Blé's tiny study, is dom-
inated by very blue
lapis-lazuli and rich
gilding which reflected
the glow of the candle-
light so necessary in a
study; the figure of St
Cecilia accompanied by
the cardinal virtues rep-
resents moral harmony.
Also on view are the
kitchens and the Nea-
politan bed of Cécile
Sorel in a room in the
west wing which was
refurbished at the turn
of the 19C.

Park. — There are fine
views of the château
from the grounds
which have been laid
out with various fea-
tures: a box maze with
a belvedere-aviary, a
pond, an English gar-
den, a grass theatre, a
vegetable garden and a
canal (200m - 219yds
long).

Cormatin Château. – St Cecilia's Room

Cosne is a small industrial town set on the east bank of the Loire where the Nohain Valley meets the latter. It is a very pleasant town to visit and more so now that it is by-passed by the N7.

A much-coveted arsenal. – In the 18C Cosne was famous for its forges which produced cannons, muskets and sea anchors. It could import coal from the Nivernais *(p 107)* and export its products cheaply down the Loire to the Atlantic ports. In 1738 the forges in Cosne were bought by Jacques Masson, who already owned other forges including the one at **Guérigny;** in 1745 they were all purchased by Babaud de la Chaussade who gave them his name. They became so prosperous that in 1781 Louis XVI acquired them for 2 500 000 *livres* but he never paid the owner who died in poverty. The forges began to decline in importance and manufacture was concentrated in 1782 at Guérigny which continued to supply the navy until 1971.

⊘**St Agnan.** – The church, once part of a Cluniac priory, has preserved its Romanesque doorway and apse: the latter is supported by magnificent buttresses rising to the cornices and flanked by two smaller apsidals set well back.
Behind the church on a promenade bordering the Loire are two items produced by the Royal Foundry: a pair of late-17C gates and an anchor dating from 1861 (2 580kg - 2 1/2 tons).

⊘**Museum.** – The museum is housed beside the River Nohain in a building called the Guard House (Corps de Garde) which contains a magnificent Renaissance **chimneypiece★** . Its theme is the middle Loire: fishing, shipping, trade. The exhibits include landscape paintings, model boats, articles used by the boatmen and old photographs. Upstairs is a rich collection of modern art: Vlaminck, Chagall, Utrillo, Dufy, Derain.

EXCURSION

⊘**Cadoux Estate (Domaine de Cadoux).** - *10km - 6 miles north by the N 7.*
An old barn now houses a small craft and agricultural museum with displays of 19C agricultural and craft items.

*The **Michelin Motoring Atlas France** is complementary to the yellow sheet maps, which slip conveniently into pocket or handbag with the local Green Guide. The atlas, the guides and the sheet maps are valuable aids to the motorist in France.*

★★ La CÔTE

The celebrated vineyards of the Côte d'Or (Golden Hillside) stretch from Dijon to Santenay (60km - 37 miles) forming a triumphal way for those who love good things to eat and drink. Each place bears a famous name; each village and each hillside has a claim to glory. This is the region of the great wines.

THE GREAT WINES OF BURGUNDY

Natural conditions. – The Côte is formed by the eastern edge of "The Mountain", whose rectangular shape is cut by transverse combes in the same way as the blind valleys of the Jura vineyards. Between Dijon and Nuits-St-Georges, the cliffs and rocks of these combes are a favourite spot for the rock-climbers of Dijon. The vineyards cover about 8 000ha - 19 768 acres in the Côte d'Or and 10 000ha - 24 711 acres in the Saône-et-Loire and are planted with first-quality vines (Pinot Noir and Chardonnay). They are set in terraces overlooking the plain of the Saône at an altitude varying from 200m to 300m – 686ft to 984ft.
While the summits of the hills are covered with box-trees or sometimes crowned with small woods, giving a Mediterranean appearance, the vineyards occupy the limestone slopes, well exposed to the morning sun – the best – and sheltered from cold winds. This position makes the grapes extremely sweet which in turn gives the wine a high alcohol content. Only the southern and eastern-facing sides of the combes are planted with vines; the northern slopes are often covered with woods. In addition, the slopes facilitate drainage; vines like dry soil and the slope is therefore an important factor in the quality of the grape-harvest.

The great wines. – For the greater part of its run through the vineyards the N 74 separates the "noble" wines from the others. The great wines are generally on terraces halfway up the slopes. The high-quality Pinot Noir, king of Burgundian vines, is the only plant for the great red wines. The great white wines are produced from the Chardonnay and Pinot Blanc vines. After the crisis brought about by the phylloxera beetle at the end of the 19C, the vineyards were entirely replanted with American rootstocks, on to which have been grafted the historic Burgundy vines. South of the Dijon vineyards the Côte d'Or is divided into two parts, the Côte de Nuits and the Côte de Beaune. The wines of both are well known; those of Nuits for robustness; those of Beaune for their delicacy.

Each district has its own hinterland with vineyards higher up in the hills, where the wines are known as Hautes-Côtes, and although they do not pretend to be "noble", in a good year they may give pleasure to the most knowledgeable connoisseur. The **Côte de Nuits** extends from the village of Fixin to the southern limit of the Corgoloin region. Its production is almost entirely of great red wines. Its most famous wines, from north to south, are: Chambertin, Musigny, Clos-Vougeot, and Romanée-Conti. Particularly rich and full-bodied, the wines take eight to ten years to acquire their unequalled qualities of body and bouquet.

The **Côte de Beaune** extends from the north of Aloxe-Corton to Santenay and produces great white wines as well as excellent red wines. These wines mature more rapidly than those of the Côte de Nuits but grow old earlier. Its principal wines are: Corton, Volnay, Pommard and Beaune for the red wines, less full-bodied than those of the Nuits but very smooth, and Meursault and Montrachet for the rich and fruity whites. The great wines, enhanced by delicious cooking, make the Côte a celebrated roadway in the world of gourmets and connoisseurs.

★★THE VINEYARDS

① From Dijon to Nuits-St-Georges

32km - 20 miles – about 1 1/12 hours – Local map p 86

The road goes along the foot of hillsides covered with vines and passes through villages with world-famous names.

★★★**Dijon.** – *Time: 4 hours. Description p 91.*

Leave Dijon by the D 122, known as the "Route des Grands Crus" (Road of the Great Wines).

Chenôve. – Pop 19 528. The Clos du Roi and Clos du Chapitre recall the former owners of these vineyards, the Dukes of Burgundy and the canons of Autun. The great wine cellar of the Dukes of Burgundy **(Cuverie des ducs de Bourgogne)** contains two magnificent 13C presses (some say they are early-15C replicas) which were capable of pressing in one go the contents of 100 wine casks.

Nearby *(on leaving the cellar turn left and first right)* there are picturesque vine-growers' houses, some dating from the 13C, in Rue Jules-Blaizet.

Marsannay-la-Côte. – Pop 5942. Part of the Côte de Nuits, Marsannay produces popular *rosé* wines, obtained from the black Pinot grapes.

Fixin. – *Description p 102.*

Brochon. – Pop 811. Brochon, which is on the edge of the Côte de Nuits, produces excellent wines. The **château** was built in 1900 by the poet Stephen Liégeard who coined the phrase Côte d'Azur (the Azure Coast) for the Provençal coast and Mediterranean sunshine. The name has stuck long after the poet has faded into obscurity, together with his poem which was honoured by the French Academy.

Gevrey-Chambertin. – *Description p 106.*

At Morey-St-Denis rejoin the N 74.

Vougeot. – Pop 197. Its red wines are highly valued.

★ **Clos de Vougeot Château.** – *Description p 79.*

Chambolle-Musigny. – Pop 364. The road from Chambolle-Musigny to Curley (north-west) passes through a gorge, Combe Ambin, to a charming beauty spot: a small chapel stands at the foot of a rocky promontory overlooking the junction of two wooded ravines.

Reulle-Vergy. – Pop 84 *(8km - 5 miles west of Chambolle-Musigny).* This village has a 12C church and a curious town hall, built on top of a washing house. Opposite the town hall a barn now houses a **museum** describing the arts and traditions associated with the Hautes Côtes wines. Themes covered include the day-to-day work in the vineyards, archaeology (items from the Bronze Age, the Gallo-Roman and medieval periods), the flora and fauna, daily life in the 19C (costumes and everyday objects) and the history of the region (evocation of the medieval poem of the Mistress of Vergy).

From l'Etang-Vergy take the D 35 and D 25 south and east to Nuits-St-Georges.

Nuits-St-Georges. – *Description p 131.*

Vosne-Romanée. – Pop 530. *2km - 1 1/4 miles north of Nuits-St-Georges.* These vineyards produce only red wines of the highest quality; they are choice and delicate. Among the various sections *(climats)* of this vineyard, Romanée-Conti and de Richebourg have a worldwide reputation.

② From Nuits-St-Georges to Chagny

115km - 72 miles – about 4 hours – Local map p 86

The itinerary follows in part the N 74 and also some of the picturesque roads of the Burgundian part of "The Mountain".

Nuits-St-Georges. – *Description p 131.*

Comblanchien. - Pop 572. *4.5km – 2 1/2 miles south of Nuits-St-Georges.* This township is known for the limestone that is quarried from its surrounding cliffs. The stone is very beautiful and is often used for facings, replacing the more costly marble.

South of Comblanchien turn right to Arcenant, 9km - 5 1/2 miles northwest.

Beyond Arcenant raspberry and blackcurrant bushes border the road. During a fairly stiff climb, there is a good view over Arcenant, the arable land and the deep gorge of the **Combe Pertuis.**

From Bruant take the D 25, D 18 and D 2 south to Bouilland.

During the long run downhill, there is a view of **Bouilland** and its circle of wooded hills.

From Bouilland take the D 2 south.

Beyond the hamlet of La Forge the road is dominated on the left by the rocky escarpments crowning the hill and on the right by the rock known as the pierced rock *(roche percée)*. Soon after there is the cirque of the Combe à la Vieille on the left. The road then follows the fresh, green and narrow valley of the Rhoin, between wooded slopes. Shortly before **Savigny-lès-Beaune** the valley opens out.

From Savigny take the minor road west to Aloxe-Corton (3km - 2 miles).

Aloxe-Corton. — Pop 198. This village (pronounced Alosse), the northernmost village of Côte de Beaune, is of ancient origin. The Emperor Charlemagne owned vineyards here and Corton-Charlemagne, "a white wine of great character", recalls this fact. Red wines are produced almost exclusively at Aloxe-Corton, "the firmest and most forward wines of the Côte de Beaune". The bouquet improves with age and the wine remains full-bodied and cordial.

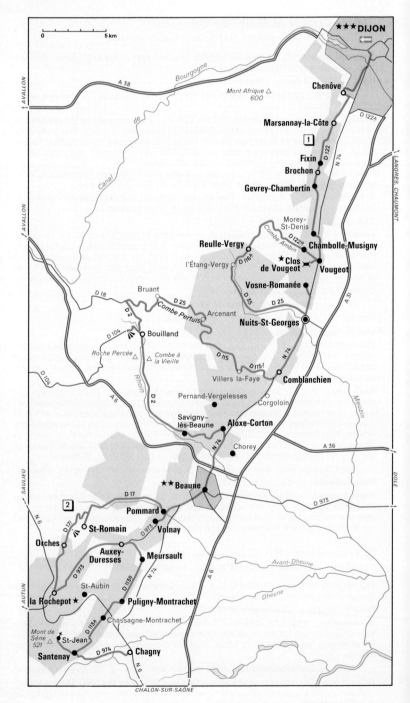

The vineyards are shown in green — Black dots indicate the great wines

★★ Beaune. – *Time: 1 hour. Description p 50.*

Pommard. – Pop 606. *3km - 2 miles southwest of Beaune by the N 74 and D 973.* The fairly large village of Pommard takes its name from an ancient temple dedicated to Pomona, the goddess of fruits and gardens. These vineyards of the Côte de Beaune produce red wines that are "firm, dark red, full of candour and worth keeping". These wines were greatly appreciated by Ronsard, Henri IV, Louis XV and Victor Hugo.

Volnay. – Pop 411. *1km - 1/2 mile southwest of Pommard by the D 973.* Its red wines have a delicate bouquet and a silky taste. It is said that King Louis XI was fond of them. From the esplanade, below the small 14C church with its squat belfry, there is a good view of the vineyards.

Return to Pommard; take the D 17 west to St-Romain (9km - 5 1/2 miles).
The road follows the green valley floor between wooded slopes.

St-Romain. – Pop 250. This township is made up of two quite distinct parts: St-Romain-le-Haut perched high on a limestone spur, surrounded by a semicircle of cliffs, with the ruins of its 12C-13C castle (short visitor trail marked out) on the southern edge. Lower down in St-Romain-le-Bas stands the **town hall**. The attic rooms of the latter house displays on local archaeology and ethnology.

North of St-Romain turn left into the D 17¹ to Orches and La Rochepot.
As the road approaches **Orches**, in its attractive rocky site, there is a fine **view★** of St-Romain, Auxey, Meursault and the Saône Valley.

★ La Rochepot. – *Description p 140.*
From La Rochepot take the D 973 northeast skirting the château.
The road follows a narrow valley and prior to Melin crosses a series of limestone escarpments worn by erosion.

Auxey-Duresses. – Pop 345. This village is set in a deep combe leading to La Rochepot and its château. The vineyards of Auxey-Duresses produce fine red and white wines which, before the law of nomenclature, were sold as Volnay and Pommard. The church, with its fine 16C triptych, is worth a visit.

Meursault. – Pop 1 646. *2km - 1 1/4 miles southeast of Auxey.* This little town, dominated by the beautiful Gothic stone spire of its church, is proud of producing both red and white wines of high quality. It owes its name to a valley that clearly divides the Côte de Meursault from the Côte de Beaune. This valley, known as the Rat's Leap (*Saut du Rat* – in Latin *Muris Saltus*) is said to have given the present name of Meursault. Its white wines, with those of Puligny and Chassagne-Montrachet, are considered "the best white wines in the world". They have a slight taste of hazelnuts and an aroma of ripe grapes which gives a freshness to the subtle qualities of taste and bouquet.

Meursault wines have the rarity of being both dry and mellow at the same time. The *Paulée de Meursault*, last of the "Three Glorious Days of Burgundy" *(p 79)*, is a well-known local fête. At the end of the banquet, to which each guest brings bottles of his wine, a literary prize is awarded. The happy laureate receives a hundred bottles of Meursault.

Puligny-Montrachet. – Pop 528. *4km - 2 1/2 miles south of Meursault.* The white wines of Puligny-Montrachet, like those of Meursault, are excellent. Alexandre Dumas, connoisseur of note, declared that this wine "should be drunk while kneeling with the head uncovered".

The red wines of this old walled vineyard are full-bodied and have subtle qualities of taste and bouquet.

Santenay. – Pop 1 014. *6km - 3 1/2 miles southeast of Puligny.* The three localities that go to make up Santenay – Santenay-le-Bas, Santenay-le-Haut and St-Jean – are spread along the banks of the river Dheune as far as the first slopes of Mount Sène or the Montagne des Trois-Croix. Santenay derives its reputation not only from its vast vineyards but also from the local mineral water, which contains lithia and is very salty. **St John's Church** stands at the foot of a semicircle of cliffs; a wooden porch protects the round-headed doorway which opens into the 13C nave; the 15C vaulting in the chancel contains an unusually high number of ribs. Two 15C painted wooden statues of St Martin and St Roch contrast with a 17C Virgin and dragon by the local sculptor J Bésullier.

Chagny. – Pop 5 604. *4.5km - 3 miles east of Santenay.* This commercial and industrial town makes a good place to stop for a gastronomic meal. There are several interesting buildings.

Le CREUSOT

Michelin map 🔠🔠 fold 8 or 🔢🔢🔢 fold 26
Town plan in the current Michelin Red Guide France

The rural setting of Le Creusot, on the northeast border of the Massif Central, contrasts with its industrial character. The blast-furnaces and rows of brick-built workers' houses have been replaced by modern industrial plants.

LE CREUSOT BASIN

The basin is a natural depression containing the towns of Montceau-les-Mines, Blanzy, Montchanin and Le Creusot, from which it takes its name. It is an important passage, used by the Dheune and Bourbince rivers and now by the road, canal and railway, linking the Saône and the Loire river valleys.

Development of industry. – Although iron ore was mined in the Middle Ages in the region of Couches, the discovery of vast coal deposits at Épinac, Le Creusot and Blanzy in the 17C marked the real origin of the industrial development of the whole area. Mining was pushed to its maximum during the last century to supply fuel for the growing steel industry of Le Creusot. Today, mining operations continue at the Blanzy pit to supply the thermal power station, Lucy III.

While certain localities, such as Couches and Perrecy-les-Forges, have seen their activity slowly decline, Le Creusot has become in the 20C the focal point of the whole basin.

The Central Canal (Canal du Centre). – In this hilly region, the canal is a vital artery, serving different industrial centres. The building of a canal was first envisaged at the start of the 17C but it was only in 1794, when Le Creusot began to develop as a steel town, that it was opened for navigation. From Chalon, where it leaves the Saône, to Digoin where it joins the Loire, the canal goes up the valley of the Dheune *(p 89)* and then down that of the Bourbince.

Various industries are established along the banks of the canal. Although the canal's industrial importance has declined, the waterway now provides good possibilities for cruising.

Promising beginnings. – At the start of the 16C the inhabitants of Le Creusot began to exploit the outcrops of coal and to trade with the surrounding localities. The scarcity of coal-bearing deposits in Le Creusot itself forced the industries of this town into processing the primary materials, extracted from the iron mines and the quarries of the region, into finished products.

Industrial exploitation really began in 1769 and by 1782, "The Royal Foundry of Montcenis" consisted of a foundry and blast-furnaces.

City of steel. – In 1836 **Joseph-Eugène Schneider**, forge-master at Bazeilles, and his brother, **Adolphe Schneider**, set themselves up at Le Creusot, at that time a little township of 3000 inhabitants. The rapid expansion of the Schneider works was to contribute to the wealth of the town, which from that date increased its population tenfold. The construction of steam and marine engines began the following year. In 1843 the invention of the power hammer by one of the factory's engineers, M. Bourdon, resulted in the forging of heavy castings. From that time, besides products for the railways, the factories produced equipment for the great electrical power stations, for ports, factories and mines, etc.

About 1867 steel made its appearance and was used at that time mainly for sheets of armour plating and guns. The iron ore originally came from the Couches region. In 1924 the old power hammer was superseded by the great furnace (forge) equipped with 7500 - 11300 tonnes hydraulic presses. In 1949 the Schneider works were reconstituted as the Société des Forges et Ateliers du Creusot with factories in the communes of Le Creusot, Le Breuil, Torcy and Montchanin. In 1970 the company amalgamated with the Compagnie des Ateliers et Forges de la Loire to form Creusot-Loire. Following the European steel crisis, Creusot-Loire filed for bankruptcy in 1984. The works were acquired by CLI, a subsidiary of Usinor-Sacilor, by Alsthom Creusot Rail and by Framatome. The Creusot factory has also diversified with the establishment of SNECMA, the development of the textile sector and the creation of a nucleus of technological skills directed to high energy and electronics.

The industrial heritage and tourism. – In a region rich in reminders of its industrial past (mines, foundries, factories, workshops and workers' settlements) there is now an effort to exploit this industrial heritage for tourism. An association, founded in 1983, now promotes and organises guided tours from its headquarters in La Verrerie Château *(see below)*.

SIGHTS

Power hammer. – The 100 tonne power hammer, standing on the southern outskirts, symbolises the paramount importance of industry to the town. This particular machine was in use from 1876 until 1924 and enjoys a worldwide reputation.

Place Schneider. – A statue of Eugène Schneider, one of the founders of the industrial empire, stands at the centre of the square. On the east side at the edge of a vast wooded park stands La Verrerie Château.

⊘ **La Verrerie Château.** – The former home of the Schneider family was acquired by the municipality in 1971 and now houses a specialist **museum** and the headquarters of the Communauté Urbaine le Creusot-Montceau which covers 16 communes. The château is named after a glass factory, making crystal ware for Queen Marie-Antoinette, which was transferred in 1787 from Sèvres to Le Creusot where it prospered for many years; in 1833, when it was bought by the St-Louis et Baccarat group, the works in Le Creusot were closed down.

In front of the château and in contrast with its dazzling white façade stand two huge conical glass-firing ovens. They were converted in 1905, one into a delightful **miniature theatre** and the other into a chapel which is now used for temporary exhibitions. A collection of 18C and 19C bronze cannons is arrayed in the courtyard. Nearby is the **Technical Centre** which displays examples of the metallurgical and mechanical activities of Le Creusot (articles, models, paintings).

⊘ The specialist **museum** is devoted to two themes: the history of Le Creusot, its locality and inhabitants (model of the metal works at the end of the 19C); the history of the Schneider dynasty and its achievements.

Peak Road (Promenade des Crêtes). — *Follow Rue Jean-Jaurès, Rue de Longwy, the D 28 (towards Marmagne) and a sharp righthand turn to join the Peak Road.* The switch-back road overlooks the Le Creusot basin. A clearing in the woods *(viewing table)* provides an overall view of the town and its surroundings. Further on another viewpoint reveals the extent of the old Schneider works and the central position, in this context, of La Verrerie Château.

EXCURSIONS

St-Sernin-du-Bois. — *Pop 1 652. 7km - 4 1/2 miles north.* St-Sernin is built on the edge of a lake serving as a reservoir. The castle is a great square keep dating from the 12C.

⊘ **Brandon Château.** — *10km - 6 miles northeast.* The medieval fortress was built on the site of a Roman camp for purely military purposes. Alterations made under Louis XIII included the refurbishment of the living quarters in the upper courtyard. The lower courtyard contains the 12C stables and a 14C postern gate. From the castle there is a good view of the surrounding countryside, St Vincent Mount and the Charollais mountains.

East of Le Creusot. — *37km - 23 miles — about 2 hours.*

Couches. — Pop 1 532. *16km - 10 miles northeast.* The House of the Templars (maison des Templiers) is a handsome 17C building with a loggia and colonnade. On the
⊘ outskirts of the town stands the 15C **château** of Margaret of Burgundy. According to local tradition the wife of Louis X spent the end of her life at Couches in relative freedom after leaving Château-Gaillard where she had been confined for adultery. Although much restored, the château has retained some of its early defences: a drawbridge, part of the curtain wall, traces of towers and the upper and lower courtyards linked by a huge gateway. Visitors may see the 15C chapel (contemporary statues and altarpiece), the prison tower and the 11C square keep which was slightly altered in the 14C and 15C (weapons, Aubusson tapestries).

From Couches take the D 978 southeast; in St-Léger turn right into the D 974.

Dheune Valley. — The road first passes between the Dheune and the Central Canal, with its series of locks (9 in all although only 6 are in working order). After Les 7 Écluses the road runs along an embankment between the canal cutting and the pool of Longpendu which flows into the Saône by way of the Dheune and into the Loire by way of the Bourbince. In La 9ᵉ Écluse the Canal House is organised by the
⊘ district of **Écuisses** as part of the Industrial Heritage Museum.

Montchanin. — Pop 6 303. An industrial centre with many foundries. There is good fishing in the many pools in the neighbourhood which supply water to the canal.

Take the D 28 northwest past Torcy Pool to return to Le Creusot.

★ CURE VALLEY

Michelin map ▓▓ folds 5, 6, 15 and 16 or ▓▓▓ folds 10, 11 and 23

The river Cure, which has a larger basin than the Yonne, is a typical Morvan river. Owing to its strong flow of water the Cure is popular with canoeists and a good venue for canoe and kayak competitions.

A vanished activity. — It was on the Cure in the middle of the 16C that the first attempt was made at logging *(p 77)*. The building of the reservoir at Les Settons *(p 156)* in the 19C was intended to assist in this activity.
Since the disappearance of logging the reservoir is used only to regulate the flow of the Cure and to feed the Nivernais Canal during the summer.
Since 1930 several hydro-electric power stations have been established in the basin of the Cure: the Crescent dam (1930-33) upstream from Chastellux; the Malassis dam (1929-30) near Domecy-sur-Cure; the Chaumeçon dam (1933-35) on the Chalaux.

FROM AUXERRE TO VÉZELAY

60km - 37 miles — 4 1/2 hours excluding visits to Auxerre and Vézelay

★★ **Auxerre.** — *Time: 1 1/2 hours. Description p 44.*

From Auxerre to Cravant follow the itinerary described on p 172.

Cravant. — Pop 756. This one-time fortified village stands at the confluence of the Cure
⊘ and the Yonne. The 13C **church** has a Renaissance choir and tower. Walks have been laid out along the former moats.
Although regulated along its course by successive reservoirs, the Cure preserves the character of a fast river. The road follows the Cure fairly closely at this stage, running through wooded or vineyard countryside.

Vermenton. — Pop 1 166. This town stands on the banks of the Cure. The church has a handsome 12C tower. The doorway has remains of mutilated column-statues.

Arcy-sur-Cure. — *Description p 38.*

Voutenay-sur-Cure. — Pop 193. A village in a charming situation at the foot of wooded hills. South of Voutenay, from a righthand bend in the road, Vézelay is visible in the distance.

Notre-Dame-d'Orient. — *East of Sermizelles.* A rough track (sign) leads to the summit which is crowned by a 19C octagonal chapel surmounted by a stone statue of the Virgin Mary. From the foot of the statue (39 steps) there is a good view of the Cure Valley.

Behind is the modern pilgrimage chapel of Notre-Dame-d'Orient.

★★ **Vézelay.** — *Time: 1 hour. Description p 167.*

DECIZE
Pop 7 522

Michelin map 屈屈 folds 4 and 5 or 屈屈屈 fold 34

The best view of the town is from the summit of the Vauzelles Côte (viewing table).

Waterway crossroads. — The town is built on an island of the Loire, on a rocky eminence, which was once crowned by the château of the Counts of Nevers. It is at a junction of several waterways, standing at the mouth of the **Nivernais Canal,** where it flows into the Loire Lateral Canal on the left bank. The communicating stretch of water was impounded by a dam downstream. The Nivernais Canal was built, in stages, between 1784 and 1842 and covers the 170km - 106 miles from Auxerre to Decize. It is one of France's most winding waterways and now has very little barge traffic. The southern stretches are well adapted for water sports and cruising.

Celebrities of Decize. — These include the legal expert, **Guy Coquille** (1523-1603), author of a *Commentaire de la Coutume du Nivernais.* Henri IV tried many times to obtain the services of this man but Guy Coquille preferred to remain in his home province of Nivernais of which he was so great a son.

Decize was also the birthplace of **Saint-Just** (1767-94), a member of the National Convention, who was a close friend of Robespierre. A member of the Revolutionary Comité de Salut Public, named Commissioner of the Army of the Rhine, and later of the Army of the North, he took part in the capture of Charleroi and the victory of Fleurus. Arrested by the Convention on Thermidor 9 (11th month of French Revolutionary calendar, corresponding to July-August), he went to the scaffold the next day with Robespierre, Lebas and Couthon.

Another local figure was the author and Academician, **Maurice Genevoix** (1890-1980) who won the prix Goncourt in 1925 for his novel *Raboliot;* all his work celebrates the bounty of nature which leads man to reflect on morality.

⊙**St-Aré.** — The choir of this 11C church is built on a **double crypt** dating from the 7C, which before the Revolution contained the tomb of St Aré, bishop of Nevers. At his death, the legend says, it was his wish that his body be placed in a boat which was then pushed out into the waters of the Loire; it floated upstream and finally rested on the bank at Decize. The crypt is one of the few Merovingian constructions still in existence. There is a 16C statue of the Underground Virgin Mary and low-reliefs of the same century.

In the church are 15C bronze stoups and the reliquary of St Aré.

Promenade des Halles. — A fine promenade shaded by tall plane trees.

DIGOIN
Pop 11 341

Michelin map 屈屈 fold 16 or 屈屈屈 fold 48 — Town plan in the Michelin Red Guide France

The town is well situated at the junction of several valleys, namely the Loire, Arconce, Arroux and Bourbince and also a network of canals. The link between the Loire and the Saône is achieved by joining two of the canals by means of a canal-carrying bridge.

Notre-Dame-de-la-Providence. — This 19C church is a mixture of both Romanesque and Byzantine styles. The carved tympana of the west front date from the period 1976-8. The spacious interior is bathed in light from the attractive stained glass.

⊙**Pottery Documentation Centre (Centre de Documentation sur la Céramique).** — The displays cover the geographical distribution of the most important sources of raw material (clay), the different manufacturing processes (moulding, coiling, wheel throwing, decoration, glazing, firing...) and the tools and equipment used locally, today and in the Gallo-Roman period.

Finally there is a selection of both antique and present-day pieces: Digoin and Sarreguemines ceramics, local stoneware and pottery, tiles...

The chapter on Practical Information
at the end of the Guide lists
– local or national organisations providing additional information
– admission times and charges.

Michelin map 🔢 fold 20 or 🔢🔢 fold 16 — Local map p 86

Surrounded by magnificent vineyards, the former capital of the Dukes of Burgundy is famous for the many fine monuments which mark its long and glorious history. Dijon, an important regional centre and university town, is also a major junction on which converge the roads and railways of Europe. Spreading out from the city, a network of highways, railways and waterways lead off in all directions to Paris, the Mediterranean, Germany, Switzerland and Italy. As a result of this privileged situation, Dijon has developed as an important commercial and industrial centre. The two main industrial zones are to the south and northeast.

HISTORICAL NOTES

Creation of the Dukes of Burgundy. — The Roman fortress that bore the name of Divio, set on the great military highway from Lyons to Mainz, remained a place of secondary importance for many centuries. Sacked, pillaged, burnt and rebuilt many times, Dijon played no great part in history until 1015, the year in which Robert I, Duke of Burgundy, chose it as the capital of his duchy.
In 1137 a terrible fire completely devastated the town. Duke Hugues II rebuilt it on a larger scale and enclosed it together with the Abbey of St Benignus within a new city wall, composed of fortified ramparts, pierced by eleven gates. William's Gate (Porte Guillaume), the last gate to be demolished, was replaced in 1788 by the present triumphal arch.

The "Great Dukes of the West". — In 1364 Philip the Bold, fourth son of King John II the Good, of France, received the duchy of Burgundy as a legacy on the death of his father. He was the first member of the House of Valois which for the next 100 years was to transform Dijon, attracting many artists and giving it magnificent monuments. The reign of the Valois marked the most brilliant period in the history of Dijon. These four dukes of the House of Valois, Philip the Bold, John the Fearless, Philip the Good and Charles the Bold (Le Téméraire), were among the richest and most powerful princes in all Christendom. Their enormous wealth and the display of magnificence with which they surrounded themselves earned them the title of "the Great Dukes of the West" *(see p 18 for the genealogy of the Houses of France and Burgundy in the 14C and 15C).*

An argument without reply. — On 7 December 1513 the town of Dijon was facing one of the greatest disasters in its history. An army of 30 000 Swiss, Germans and men of the Franche-Comté was at its gates. The Governor of Burgundy, La Trémoille, had only 6 000 or 7 000 men to defend the city. What could he do but negotiate? The Swiss however were inflexible.

DIJON

Aiguillottes (Bd des)	**A** 2	Clomiers (Bd des)	**A** 15	Mansart (Bd)	**B** 38
Allobroges (Bd des)	**A** 3	Fauconnet (R. Gén.)	**AB** 23	Ouest (Bd de l')	**A** 41
Briand (Av. A.)	**B** 4	Fontaines-lès-Dijon (R.)	**A** 25	Parc (Cours du)	**B** 42
Castel (Bd du)	**A** 6	Gabriel (Bd)	**B** 26	Pompon (Bd F.)	**A** 43
Champollion (R.)	**B** 8	Galliéni (Bd Mar.)	**AB** 27	Saint-Exupéry (Pl.)	**B** 52
Chanoine-Kir (Bd)	**A** 9	Gaulle (Cours Gén.-de)	**B** 28	Schuman
Châteaubriand (R. de)	**B** 12	Jeanne-d'Arc (Bd)	**B** 33	(Bd Robert)	**B** 54
		Kennedy (Bd J.)	**A** 34	Strasbourg (Bd de)	**B** 55
		Magenta (R.)	**B** 36	Trimolet (Bd)	**B** 56
		Maillard (Bd)	**A** 37	26ᵉ-Dragons (R. du)	**B** 65

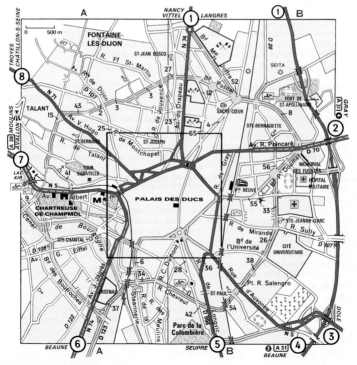

They had opened fire and had already made breaches in the walls when La Trémoille had an inspiration of pure genius. Heading a procession of wagons all loaded with wine, a new group of negotiators was sent out to parley with the besiegers. What a Godsend! The soldiers drank, they soon became fuddled and the Swiss agreed to lift the siege. France had to pay 400 000 écus and evacuate the Milan region. The king never really understood anything about this "marvellously strange" treaty and consequently refused to ratify it but Dijon and Burgundy had been saved.

The progress of the town. – Although deprived of its position as capital of a State after the union of Burgundy and France, Dijon nevertheless retained an important administrative role. The Governors of the province still kept their head-quarters there. The "States" of Burgundy (a regional assembly of deputies, clergy, the nobility and the Third Estate) held their meeting regularly every three years in the old ducal palace which was especially arranged for these solemnities; the town opened its richly decorated mansions in a series of brilliant civic receptions. At the end of the 18C, Arthur Young (English writer, 1741-1820) declared that "Dijon is a fine town; although the houses are built in old-fashioned style, the streets are well paved and have pavements, something that is very rare in France". At that time however Dijon had less than 20 000 inhabitants.

A centre of regional activity in Burgundy, Dijon is also proud of the great wines (p 15) produced by the local vineyards and of several famous gastronomic specialities: mustard, gingerbread, blackcurrant liqueur and snails.

It is however to the development of communications, which began in 1850, that the town owes its present great progress. Dijon has become one of France's great rail junctions. The town is also served by an extensive motorway network and an airport.

★PALACE OF THE DUKES AND STATES-GENERAL OF BURGUNDY (PALAIS DES DUCS ET DES ÉTATS DE BOURGOGNE)
time: 3 hours – plan p 95

The remains of the ducal palace are now surrounded by buildings in the classical style.

Place de la Libération. – This is the former Place Royale. In the 17C, when the town was at the height of its parliamentary power, it felt itself to be a capital and decided to transform the ducal palace, which had stood empty since the death of Charles the Bold, and to re-arrange its approaches. Plans for the fine semicircular design were drawn up by Jules Hardouin-Mansart, the architect of Versailles, and were carried out by one of his pupils from 1686 to 1701: the arcades of the Place de la Libération, surmounted by a stone balustrade, enhance the main courtyard. The old King's House (logis du Roi), a handsome ensemble marked by strong horizontal lines and terminating in two wings at right angles, is dominated by the high tower of Philip the Good.

Main Courtyard (Cour d'honneur). – There was a pretty vaulted room in the entrance, which is today a public passageway.

Take the passageway to the right communicating with the courtyard, Cour de Bar.

Bar Courtyard (Cour de Bar). – The **tower** (Tour de Bar, **B**), built by Philip the Bold in the 14C, preserves the name of an illustrious prisoner who was kept there by Philip the Good: René d'Anjou, Duke of Bar and Lorraine, Count of Provence, who was known as "King René".

The charming 17C **staircase** (**D**) by **Bellegarde**, which goes round the tower, leads to the north gallery of the same period. Note the statue of the sculptor **Claus Sluter** by Bouchard and the old **well** backing on to the ducal kitchens.

Leave by the passage leading to the Rue Rameau and then turn left.

★★ Fine Arts Museum (Musée des Beaux-Arts).
– The Fine Arts Museum is installed in the former ducal palace and in the eastern wing of the Palace of the States-General. An engraved plaque, on the wall to the right of the entrance, shows the layout of the Gallo-Roman fortress which covered the central area of Dijon.

Ground Floor. – On the left, at the far end of the rooms devoted to temporary exhibitions (**2**), are the **ducal kitchens** (**3**), built in 1435. The six huge chimneys were scarcely sufficient for the preparation of feasts worthy of the Burgundian court the vaulting converges on the central vent.

To the right of the reception the first room traces the history of the ducal palace (model) and of the museum. Downstairs (**1ᴬ**) on the left is a 13C sculpted altar front (the Calling of St Peter).

The **Chapter House** (**1**) of the former 14C ducal Chapel (missing together with its treasure) illustrates the evolution of religious sculpture – an art form held in high regard in Burgundy – from the 14C to the 17C; the two tombs of Jean Dubois are of particular interest. Also on display are precious works of art: 15C stained glass windows, reliquaries, 16C silver gilt altar pieces together with St Robert's cross (11C) and a cup belonging to St Bernard.

On the half-landing of the grand staircase stands a statue of Joan of Arc (**1**) by **François Rude** (1784-1855).

First Floor. – On the landing is the old door of the Dijon law courts, carved by Hugues Sambin (16C), and some fine medieval and Renaissance pieces of religious gold and silver ware and carved ivory. The first two rooms in the suite overlooking the courtyard (**1**) are also devoted to Renaissance art: furniture, medals, enamels and paintings (*Woman at her Toilet* by the Fontainebleau school – late 16C); the third room is hung with 17C Burgundian paintings (Tassel, Quentin).

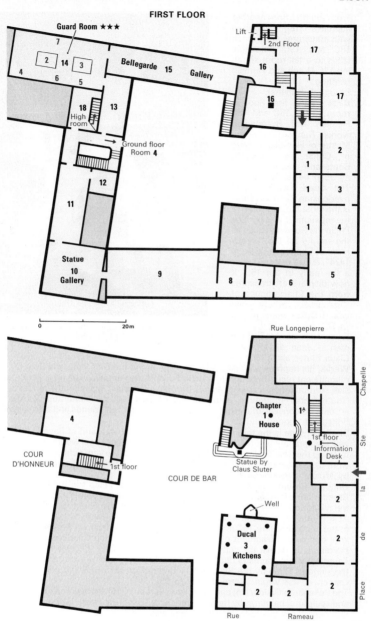

FIRST FLOOR

GROUND FLOOR

The next room (**2**) is devoted to 14C to 16C Italian painting, particularly works by the Tuscan primitives (P Lorenzetti) and Florentines (*St Peter Walking on the Water* by Vasari – 1574). The next two rooms (**3** and **4**) are hung with 15C and 16C German and Swiss paintings; the best are by Schongauer *(Annunciation)*, Conrad Witz and the Master of *The Carnation of Baden* (altar piece of the Passion). The following rooms present French paintings in chronological order: rooms **5** and **6** are devoted to the 17C and the reign of Louis XIV: Philippe de Champaigne (*Presentation in the Temple*, Le Sueur, Le Brun, François Perrier; rooms **7** and **8** are devoted to the late 17C and the 18C: works by Rigaud, Coypel, Mignard, Largillière, etc and the sculptor Jean Dubois. The large room (**9**) is hung with paintings by La Fosse, Nattier (portrait of Marie Leszczynska), Van Loo (portrait of Louis XV).

The **Statuary Gallery** (**10**) in the corner of the West Wing, which contains copies of ancient works and 19C pieces including *Hebe and the Eagle of Jupiter* by Rude, has a fine view of Place de la Libération; the ceiling depicting the fame of Burgundy and Prince Condé is by Pierre Paul Prud'hon. The Condé Salon (**11**) is decorated with woodwork and stucco of the Louis XVI period; it displays 18C French art: furniture, terracottas and paintings, sculptures by Coysevox (bust of Louis XIV), Caffieri (busts of Rameau and Piron). The Empire Salon (**12**) presents furniture and paintings of the period (Prud'hon).

The Prince's Staircase, which is built against the Gothic façade of the old Dukes' Palace, leads down to the Arms Room (**4**) on the ground floor: weapons and armour from the 13C to the 18C.

From the first floor another staircase (18), decorated with miniatures and French 18C and 19C paintings, leads to a tall room showing 17C Dutch and Flemish painting (Jan "Velvet" Brueghel, Rubens).

Back on the first floor in room 13 are 15C and 16C Flemish and Burgundian works: *The Nativity* by the Master of Flémalle, a Head of Christ by Aelbrecht Bouts and a saint reading by Jean de la Huerta.

The **Guard Room★★★** (14) overlooking Place des Ducs is the most famous room in the museum. It was built by Philip the Good and used as the setting for the "joyous entry of Charles the Bold in 1474"; it was restored after a fire early in the 16C. It now displays art treasures from the Charterhouse of Champmol, where the Grand Dukes were buried *(p 98)*.

From 1385 to 1410 three men — Jean de Marville, Claus Sluter and Claus de

Dijon Fine Arts Museum. — Detail from the tomb of Philip the Strong

Werve, his nephew — worked successively on the tomb of Philip the Bold (2). The magnificent recumbent figure, watched over by two angels, rests on a black marble slab surrounded by alabaster arches forming a "cloister" to shelter the procession of "mutes" and "mourners" composed of 41 very realistic statuettes. The funeral procession consists of clergymen, Carthusians, relatives, friends and officials of the Prince, all hooded and dressed in mourning.

Similar in style is the tomb of John the Fearless and Margaret of Bavaria (3) which was erected between 1443 and 1470. The two altarpieces in gilt wood commissioned by Philip the Bold for the Charterhouse of Champmol are very richly decorated; they were carved between 1390 and 1399 by Jacques de Baerze and painted and gilded by Melchior Broederlam.

Only the Crucifixion altarpiece (4) near the tomb of Philip the Bold has retained Broederlam's famous paintings on the reverse side of the wings: the Annunciation, the Visitation, the Presentation in the Temple and the Flight into Egypt.

At the other end is the altarpiece of the Saints and Martyrs (5).

In the centre is a late-15C altarpiece of the Passion (6) from an Antwerp workshop and, opposite, a fragment of a 15C tapestry (7) depicting Charlemagne visiting a building site. Above the central altarpiece, between two 16C wall hangings from Tournai, hangs a tapestry dedicated to Our Lady of Good Hope after the raising of the siege of Dijon by the Swiss on 11 September 1513 *(p 91)*; it comes from the Church of the Virgin (Notre-Dame) *(p 95)*.

The Bellegarde Gallery (15) and the following rooms (16) are devoted to 19C painting and sculpture: paintings by Henner, Géricault, Tissot (*Japanese Woman in her Bath*) and sculptures by Rude, Canova, Carpeaux and Dampt.

The second-floor galleries, which are accessible from here, provide a chronological review of the museum's French collections.

The last two rooms on the first floor (17) are hung with 16C and 17C Italian paintings: Veronese, Titian, Guido Reni, Guardi...

Second Floor. — This floor and the attic are devoted to the collections belonging to the Granville donation and the Robin legacy. Works by **François Pompon** (1855-1933 — *p 149*), a great animal sculptor, are displayed in a room apart. The rest of the floor presents a variety of paintings, drawings, engravings and sculptures from the 16C to the present; among the artists are Georges de la Tour *(Blowing out the Lamp)*, Géricault, Delacroix, Daumier, Courbet, Gustave Moreau and several painters of the Barbizon school, Rodin, Maillol, Bourdelle.

The section on modern and contemporary art contains canvases by the Impressionists and post-Impressionists — Manet, Monet, Boudin, Cézanne, Cross, Vuillard as well as Picasso, Juan Gris, Marcoussis, Gleizes; the collection of contemporary paintings includes works by Domec, Adolphe Peterelle, Rebeyrolle, Charles Lapicque, Nicolas de Staël, Jean Bertholle, Alfred Mannessier, Jean Messagier, Georges Mathieu. There is also an interesting collection of African sculptures and masques.

Place des Ducs-de-Bourgogne. — From this little square, one can imagine what the palace must have looked like at the time of the Dukes. The handsome Gothic façade is that of the Guard Room, dominated by Philip the Good's Tower.

Return to the main courtyard by the vaulted passageway which gives access to Philip the Good's Tower.

⊙Philip the Good's Tower (Tour Philippe-le-Bon) (E). – The tower (46m - 151ft high) was built by Philip the Good in the 15C. From the terrace at the top (316 steps), there is a fine **view★** over the town, the valleys of the Ouche and the Saône and the first foothills of the Jura mountains.

Take the covered passageway to reach the Flore Courtyard.

Flore Courtyard (Cour de Flore). – The buildings surrounding the courtyard were finished just before the Revolution in 1789. In the northeast corner is the **Chapel of the Elect (F)**; its interior decor and the doors date from the period of Louis XV. Mass was celebrated in the chapel during the sittings of the States of Burgundy. Under the porch which gives access to Rue de la Liberté (former Rue Condé) is a magnificent staircase leading to the **Chamber of the States of Burgundy (L)** which was designed in 1735 by Jacques Gabriel, father of the architect who designed the Petit Trianon at Versailles.

Take the passageway north into Rue des Forges.

★Rue des Forges. – This is one of the most characteristic old streets of the town.

Hôtel Chambellan. – *No 34 inner courtyard.* The 15C house, which was built by a rich family of drapers, has a very fine spiral staircase; the central column rises to a flamboyant palm-tree vault supported by the statue of a vine-grower carrying a basket.

Milsand House. – *No 38.* The Renaissance façade is lavishly decorated in the style of Hugues Sambin.

Former Hôtel Aubriot. – *No 40.* A classical doorway contrasts with the elegant 13C arcaded façade of the former Aubriot mansion, built by the first bankers of Dijon. This was the birthplace of Hugues Aubriot, provost of Paris under Charles V. He was responsible for building the Bastille, several of the bridges over the Seine, notably the St-Michel Bridge, and the first vaulted sewers.

Hôtel Morel-Sauvegrain. – *Nos 52, 54 and 56.* 15C façade.

★Church of the Virgin (Notre-Dame). – This is a good example of 13C Gothic architecture in Burgundy. With only a restricted space in which to work, the master mason showed astonishing technical prowess.

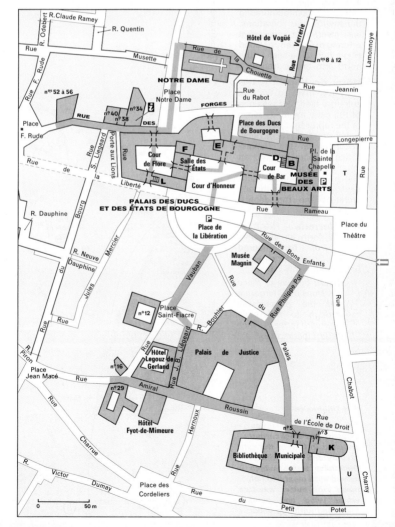

Exterior. – The façade is original. Above the great porch with its three bays, closed in laterally as is the porch at Autun, two delicately arcaded galleries are underscored by three tiers of gargoyles. Two graceful bell-turrets top the towers hidden by the façade: that on the right carries the Jacquemart clock brought from Courtrai by Philip the Bold in 1382 after his victory over the rebellious Flemish.

The clock has quite a history. It broke during the journey on an ox-wagon and on its arrival at Dijon had to be recast. The name of Jacquemart describing the figure of "the man who strikes the bell of the clock with a hammer" first appeared in 1500. The people of Dijon were very fond of him and in 1610 considered that his continued celibacy must be weighing very heavily on the poor man. So he was given a female companion.

In 1714 the poet Aimé Piron took pity on this brave couple, who seemed to have undertaken a vow of chastity. They were given a son, Jacquelinet, "whose hammer strikes the little bell for the half-hours"; in 1881, a daughter was added, Jacquelinette, who strikes the quarter-hours.

Interior. – The overall effect is harmonious; the triforium of small tapering columns is of great delicacy. Note the height of the transept crossing beneath the lantern tower. The boldly conceived choir, ending with a polygonal chevet, is sober and graceful.

The stained glass windows of the south transept date from the 13C. The 15C fresco has been restored. The chapel situated to the right of the choir houses the statue of Our Lady of Good Hope. This Black Virgin, of the 11C, has been the object of particular veneration since the Swiss raised the siege of the town on 11 September 1513; the tapestry given at that time as a votive offering is now to be found in the museum (p 94). After Dijon had been liberated without damage from the German occupation on 11 September 1944, a second tapestry, made by Gobelins, commemorating the town's two liberations, was given as a new votive offering to Our Lady of Good Hope. It is to be seen in the north arm of the transept.

⊘**Hôtel de Vogüé.** – This early-17C mansion with its colourful tiled roof was one of the early meeting places of the representatives of the province. A portico richly decorated in the Renaissance style opens into an inner courtyard.

The mansion is now occupied by the offices of the city architect and the department of cultural affairs.

Rue Verrerie. – Nos 8, 10 and 12 form an attractive group of half-timbered houses. Some of the beams have been richly carved.

Return by way of Place des Ducs de Bourgogne and the passageway through to the main courtyard to reach Place de la Libération.

A la Dijonnaise

Two Dijon specialities – mustard and blackcurrants – are used to flavour the local savoury and sweet dishes. Dijonnaise sauce, which is served with meat and fish, is made with butter, mustard, white wine and vinegar, thickened with egg yolks.

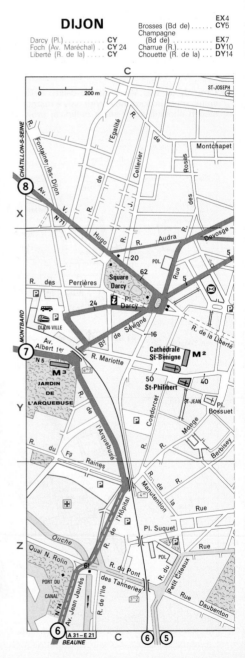

★**THE LAW COURTS QUARTER** *time: 1 hour*

Leave from Place de la Libération (plan p 95) by way of Rue Vauban to the south.
No 12 Rue Vauban has a classical façade adorned with pilasters and pediments, overlooking the inner courtyard.

Hôtel Legouz de Gerland. – Take the Rue Jean-Baptiste Liégeard to the left to skirt this mansion with its Renaissance façade pinpointed by four watch-turrets. The classical inner façade may be seen from 21 Rue Vauban.

At the corner of Rues Vauban and Amiral-Roussin stands a half-timbered house (no 16) which once belonged to a carpenter. This craftsman embellished his shutters with linenfold panelling and some of the beams with scenes of his craft. The house almost opposite, at no 29, has an elegant courtyard which is screened off by a curved balustrade.

Hôtel Fyot-de-Mimeure. – *No 23 Rue Amiral-Roussin.* The façade in the pretty interior courtyard is in the style of Hughes Sambin, a pupil of Leonardo da Vinci; he described himself as a woodcarver but, although he may have designed the decoration, he probably did not do the work.

⊘**Municipal Library (Bibliothèque Municipale).** – *Enter by no 3 Rue de l'École-de-Droit.* The 17C chapel of the former college of Les Godrans (**K**), founded in the 16C by the rich Dijon family of this name and directed by Jesuits, has been transformed into a reading room.

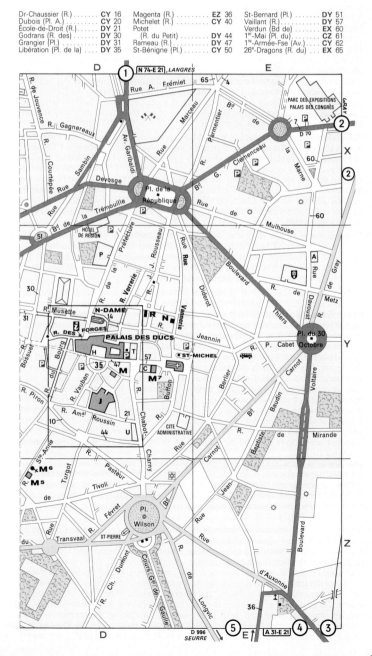

The large rooms on the first floor have been luxuriously arranged with 18C furnishings. This library contains amongst its 300 000 or more items precious illuminated manuscripts, including some executed at Cîteaux during the first thirty years of the 12C. The Well of Love (Puits d'Amour), from a house which was demolished when the library was extended, has been rebuilt in the courtyard *(enter by no 5 Rue de l'École-de-Droit)*.

Follow Rue du Palais to reach the Law Courts.

Law Courts (Palais de Justice). — This building was formerly the Burgundian parliament. The gabled façade, in the Renaissance style, has a covered porch supported by columns. The door is a copy of a work by Sambin (pupil of Leonardo da Vinci) (the original is in the Fine Arts Museum). The huge Lobby (Salle des Pas-Perdus) is covered by a **vaulted ceiling★** like an upturned boat. Opposite the entrance the tiny Chapel of the Holy Ghost contains a screen of carved wood.

⊙**Magnin Museum (Musée Magnin).** — This national museum is laid out in an elegant 17C mansion, which still has its period furnishings and obviously belonged to an art lover. Besides canvases by the great masters, the museum displays a well-chosen collection of paintings by French and foreign artists, either ignored or forgotten, who lived between the 16C and 19C.

ADDITIONAL SIGHTS

★ **Charterhouse of Champmol (Chartreuse de Champmol)** (A). — *Town plan p 91.* ⊙*Entrance: 1 Boulevard Chanoine-Kir.*
A psychiatric hospital now occupies the site of this monastery, destroyed during the French Revolution in 1793. At the entrance is a 15C doorway which escaped destruction.
The first Dukes of Burgundy were buried at Cîteaux but Philip the Bold wanted an almost-royal burial place for himself and his heirs and in 1383 he founded the charterhouse which was consecrated five years later by the Bishop of Troyes. The best artists of the period contributed to the magnificent undertaking but nothing remains except the tombs of the dukes, the retables preserved in the Dijon Museum, and two works by Claus Sluter (end 14C), the sculptor from Haarlem who became the leader of the Burgundian-Flemish school of art: the chapel doorway and Well of Moses which stands in a courtyard.

★★ **Well of Moses** (Puits de Moïse) (A V). — *Walk round the buildings to reach the courtyard.*
In fact the well is the socket of a polychrome Calvary made between 1395 and 1405 to decorate the font in the great cloisters *(the painting is barely visible)*. It is named after the figure of Moses, probably the most impressive of the six huge and strikingly life-like statues which surround the hexagonal socket; the other five figures are the prophets — David, Jeremiah, Zachariah, Daniel and Isaiah. The angels beneath the cornice are the work of Claus de Werve, Sluter's nephew; with touching veracity each one through a different pose expresses his suffering before the Calvary (which has disappeared).

★ **Chapel doorway.** — The doorway, which is now inside the chapel, consists of five statues sculpted by Claus Sluter between 1389 and 1394. Duke Philip the Bold and Margaret of Flanders, his wife, are presented kneeling, watched by their patron saints (St John the Baptist and St Catherine), on each side of the Virgin Mary and Child who are portrayed on the central pier.

St Benignus' Cathedral (Cathédrale St-Bénigne) (CY). — *Plan p 96.* The ancient abbey church, pure Burgundian-Gothic in style, is the last to occupy this site. In 1001 Abbot **Guillaume de Volpiano** built a Romanesque basilica with a large crypt to replace an earlier ruined church; he added a three-storey rotunda to the east which was consecrated in 1018. In 1271 the church collapsed on to the crypt. The present Gothic church was built against the rotunda but during the Revolution the upper parts of the rotunda were destroyed and the crypt filled in. The base of the rotunda and part of the crypt, the only relics of the Romanesque building, were excavated in 1843. The west front of the Gothic church is supported by massive buttresses and projections flanked by two great towers crowned by two octagonal storeys with conical roofs of multi-coloured tiles. Within the porch, which is surmounted by a delicately pierced gallery, is the old 12C Romanesque doorway in the centre of the Gothic façade; it is topped by a tympanum, the work of the Bouchardon brothers, which came from St Stephen's Church (now the Chamber of Commerce — DY). The transept crossing is marked by a tall spire (93m - 305ft) in the Flamboyant style, restored in 1896.
The **interior** is quite austere; its lines are unadorned: plain capitals, simply moulded arcades in the triforium, little columns extending unbroken from the vault to the floor in the crossing and to the tops of massive round pillars in the nave. Since St Benignus lost its own works of art during the Revolution, it has provided a home for tombstones and pieces of sculpture from other churches in Dijon. The organ (1743) is by Riepp.

★ **Crypt.** — The only remaining traces of the Romanesque crypt consist of part of the ⊙transept with four apsidal chapels on the east side and a trench in the middle containing the remains of a sarcophagus which was probably used for the burial of St Benignus, the first Burgundian martyr who died in the 3C; there is a pilgrimage to his tomb on 20 November. The sarcophagus faces a broad opening in the lower storey of the **rotunda★★** which echoes the highly symbolic architecture of the tomb of Christ in Jerusalem built in the 4C; only eight rotundas of this type are known in the world. Three circles of columns radiate from the centre; some have retained their original capitals decorated with palm leaves, interlacing, monstrous animals or praying figures, rare examples of pre-Romanesque sculpture *(p 26)*. The eastern end of the rotunda opens into a 6C chapel which may be a "cella" (sanctuary).

★ **Archaeological Museum** (CY M²). – *Plan p 96*. The museum is housed in the west wing of the now non-existent cloisters of the old abbey of St Benignus. The 11C Romanesque cellars display a collection of Gallo-Roman sculptures; several tomb-stones, including those of a butcher and a wine merchant, represent the daily life of the period; a pillar depicting several divinities from Mavilly provides an interesting insight into Gaulish religion in Burgundy. The collection of ex-voto offerings, made of wood (in the Gaulish tradition), as well as of bronze and stone, includes human figures and parts of the human body; they come from a healing sanctuary near the source of the Seine which is personified by the bronze statuette of the goddess Sequana.

The monks' dorter (13C) on the ground floor is devoted to medieval sculpture from Dijon: a bust of Christ *(illustration p 31)* by Claus Sluter for the Calvary of the Charterhouse of Champmol is accompanied by architectural fragments; at the end of the bay is a Christ on the cross, attributed to Claus de Werve; flanking it are two Romanesque tympana from St Benignus.

The second floor presents household goods from different periods, from the Palaeolithic to the Merovingian period: pottery typical of the Chasséenne culture (Burgundian neolithic), a golden bracelet (1.3kg - 46oz) found at la Rochepot (9C BC), a hoard of Bronze Age objects found at Blanot (belt, greaves, leather and golden necklaces, bracelet), weapons consecrated at the Gaulish sanctuary at Mirebeau, several stone carvings of Gallo-Roman gods typical of the region (mother-goddesses from Alésia, a god with birds, a god with a mallet).

St-Philibert (CY). – *Plan p 96*. Built in the 12C and altered in the 15C, the church has been deconsecrated.

Square Darcy (CY). – *Plan p 96*. The square takes its name from the engineer who brought drinking water to Dijon in 1839. The basins and fountains are complemented by a background of greenery.

At the entrance is Pompon's (1855-1933) imposing statue of a **polar bear.**

★ **Arquebuse Gardens** (Jardin de l'Arquebuse) (CY). – *Plan p 96*. This park owes its name to the Company of Harquebusiers, who occupied the site in the 16C. All the western part is taken up by the botanical gardens (3500 different species), which were founded in the 18C and joined to the Promenade de l'Arquebuse. In addition there is an arboretum, tropical glasshouses and a vivarium. Magnificent trees surround the colourful banks of flowers.

Natural History Museum (CY M³). – *Plan p 96*. The museum, which was founded in 1836, is housed in the old barrack of the crossbow men (1608). It displays regional geological and mineralogical collections (fossil of an ichthyosaurus and the giant carapace of a glyptodon) and describes the fauna of the various Burgundian habitats; there is an important section on animals and also on insects from all over the world.

Grévin Museum (A M⁴). – *Plan p 91*. Historic tableaux composed of waxwork figures illustrating 17 episodes in the history of Burgundy between the 6C BC and the present.

Rude Museum (DY M⁷). – *Plan p 97*. The transept and chancel of St Stephen's Cathedral, which was deconsecrated at the Revolution, now house original works, plaster casts, copies and a few drawings by the sculptor of the Marseillaise on the Arc de Triomphe in Paris *(p 32)*.

Excavations in the chancel have revealed the foundations of the crypt of the 11C church and of the Gallo-Roman wall of enclosure (3C).

★ **St Michael** (DY). – *Plan p 97*. The church, which was begun early in the 15C in Flamboyant Gothic style, was consecrated in December 1529, although its façade was eventually completed in the full Renaissance style; the two towers framing it were finished in the 17C.

The façade, on which the three classical orders are superimposed, is the most curious part of the building. The porch, which juts far out, is pierced by three doorways: a long frieze of ornamental foliage and grotesque decorations runs along the upper part of the porch for its whole length. Under it, in medallions, are busts of the prophets Daniel, Baruch, Isaiah and Ezekiel, as well as of David with his harp and Moses with the Tablets of the Law. The right doorway dates from 1537 and is the oldest of the three.

The Last Judgment, presented on the tympanum of the central doorway, is the work of a Flemish artist: Nicolas de la Cour. The statue of St Michael on the pier dates from the 16C and replaces the original one which was destroyed during the Revolution. It rests on a finely sculptured console. The sculptures on the console were inspired by both pagan traditions and sacred texts; close together one can identify David, Lucretia, Leda and the Swan, Hercules, Apollo, Venus, Judith, the Judgment of Solomon, St John the Baptist and Christ appearing to Mary Mag-dalene.

The interior is Gothic in style. Note the height of the choir, which like St Benignus lacks an ambulatory, and the 18C woodwork. There are four paintings by Franz Kraus, an 18C German painter: *Adoration of the Shepherds* and *The Flight into Egypt* (deteriorated) in the north transept; *Adoration of the Magi* and *Presentation in the Temple* in the Holy Sacrament Chapel, which also has a fine Flamboyant altar. The last chapel on the left on entering contains a fragment of a 15C Entombment.

House of the Caryatids (Maison des Cariatides) (DY R). – *Plan p 97. 28 Rue Chaudronnerie*. This house built in 1603 has 12 caryatids on the street front.

Rue Vannerie (DY). – *Plan p 97*. Nos 39 and 41 (**N**) are 18C mansions. At no 66 is a Renaissance mansion with ornamental windows flanking a watch-tower by Hugues Sambin.

Colombière Park (Parc de la Colombière) (B). – *South of plan p 91*. This is reached by way of an avenue of magnificent trees. Clumps of flowering shrubs are intersected by paths and green lawns, all once part of the Condé Princes park. A section of the Roman road *Via Agrippa* which linked Lyons to Trier can be seen in this park.

⊘**Burgundian Folklore Museum** (DZ M⁵). – *Plan p 97*. An old Bernardine convent houses the regional and urban ethnographical collections of Perrin de Puycousin (1856-1949), a native Burgundian. Daily life, ceremonies and Burgundian traditions in the 19C are evoked through a very lively display of costumes, furniture, domestic implements and other mementoes.

⊘**Museum of Sacred Art (Musée d'art sacré)** (DZ M⁶). – *Plan p 97*. The late-17C church of St Anne, with its circular plan and dome, now houses a collection of 14C-19C sacred art: vestments, old wooden statues including a late-12C Virgin in Majesty as well as an elegant baroque altar dating from 1769. Note in particular the canopy of the monumental marble altar with stucco decoration and statues (Visitation and cherubim) by Jean Dubois *c*1672.

EXCURSIONS

Talant. – Pop 11 665. *Plan p 91* (A). Climb up to the church on the highest point (355m - 1 165ft) of the old village. The 13C **church** (restored) has an interesting collection of statues: Virgin and Child (14C), two *Pietà* (15C), Saints with Christ bound (16C), two Entombments (16C, the finest is in the south aisle), a medieval Christ suspended from the choir roof and a painted low-relief showing scenes from the life of St Hubert on the inside of the west front.

From the viewing table beside the church there is a wide **view★** over Dijon, the Ouche Valley and the Chanoine Kir Reservoir which is now an important watersports centre.

Mount Afrique (Mont Afrique) – *12km - 8 miles west – about 1 hour*. The path following the edge of the plateau offers good views of the Dijon area.

Val-Suzon. – *Round tour of 40km – 25 miles - about 1 1/2 hours. Take the N 74 north and after 5km - 3 miles turn left into the D 996.*

Messigny-et-Vantoux. – 18C **château**.

On leaving Messigny turn left into the D 7.

The river Suzon flows between wooded slopes. The valley widens out into a basin at **Ste-Foy.** Before Val-Suzon areas of scree appear on the hillsides.

At Val-Suzon-Haut turn left into the N 71 which climbs steeply.

The road affords an attractive view of Val-Suzon-Bas and the valley.

DONZY
Pop 1 890

Michelin map 🆖 fold 13 or 🔢 fold 21

Seat of a powerful barony in the Middle Ages, whose lords became the Counts of Nevers, Donzy still has a Gothic church and some old houses.

Donzy-le-Pré. – *1km - 1/2 mile west of Donzy by the D 33 and the D 163*. These ruins were once part of an early-12C priory dependent on the Order of Cluny. The 12C **tympanum** is a masterpiece of Burgundian sculpture and portrays the Virgin and Child between the Prophet Isaiah and the Angel of the Visitation. The recessed arches are adorned with dogtooth motifs and foliage.

EXCURSION

⊘**Les Granges Château (in Suilly-la-Tour).** – *6km - 4 miles southwest of Donzy-le-Pré*. This elegant classical château dates from 1605. The top storey is adorned with dormer windows. The curtain wall flanked by round towers also encloses numerous outbuildings and a chapel.

⊘**Menou Château.** – *13km - 8 miles east*. The château was built between 1672 and 1684 by Armond-François de Menou; it passed through the female line to the Damas-Crux and then early in the 19C to the Blacas who sold it in 1987. Two pavilions project from the corners of the main building; the central projection is surmounted by a lantern. The interior, which was refurbished in the 19C, contains some rooms in the Restoration style. On the first floor, however, the Sun Room and its adjoining study have retained their 18C decor of painted woodwork and a ceiling decorated with allegorical scenes.

Help us in our constant task of keeping up to date.

Send your comments and suggestions to

Michelin Tyre PLC
Tourism Department

Davy House
Lyon Road
HARROW Middlesex HA1 2DQ

DRUYES-LES-BELLES-FONTAINES   Pop 309

Michelin map 65 northeast corner of fold 14 or 238 fold 22

⊘The hilltop location of the ruins of the 12C feudal **castle** of Druyes make an impressive sight. They are seen to best advantage in the late afternoon from the south, either from the D 148, a picturesque and hilly road, or from the D 104, which provides an excellent view of the village and castle with the old railway viaduct in the foreground.

The 14C fortified gateway on the road to Courson-les-Carrières (D 104 north) gives access to the rock on which the old town and castle stand; only the external walls and the porch-tower, incorrectly called the keep, remain.

The 12C Romanesque church in the lower village has a fine doorway.

Near the church is the picturesque source of the River Druyes.

DUN MOUNTAIN

Michelin map 73 fold 8 or 243 fold 38

The summit of Dun Mountain **(Montagne de Dun)** (721m - 2365ft) is reached from the road between Chauffailles and St-Racho.

From the promenade beside the chapel, traces (reconstructed in 1900) of an old stronghold destroyed by Philippe-Auguste, there is a semi-circular **view★**: to the east, of the Grosne Depression and the Champ-Juin Pass; to the northeast, of the St-Cyr peak and Grande-Roche; to the north, over the Charollais and Arconce Valley; to the northwest, of the Clayette region and to the west, of the Brionnais and Loire Valley.

ÉGREVILLE   Pop 1345

Michelin map 61 folds 12 and 13 or 237 fold 43 - 19km - 12 miles southeast of Nemours

This small agricultural town in the Gâtinais region has a **château** dating from the 12C. In the 16C the château was rebuilt by François I's favourite, Anne de Pisseleu – better known as Duchesse d'Étampes. It was remodelled in the following century by Marshal de la Châtre, one of the leaders of the Catholic League, who surrendered Orléans to Henri IV in return for a considerable financial reward and the confirmation of all his titles, in particular his marshal's baton.

The composer Jules Massenet (1842-1912) spent the last years of his life in the château which he bought in 1899.

Covered market (Halles). – This 16C covered market has an impressive chestnut timber roof and an arcade on the gabled south side (1638). Together with the 13C-15C church with its massive belfry-porch, it makes a charming picture.

ÉPOISSES   Pop 820

Michelin map 65 fold 17 or 243 fold 1 - 12km - 8 miles west of Semur-en-Auxois

Époisses is a pleasant village, on the plateau of Auxois, a livestock-rearing district which is known for its cheese.

It is said that Époisses was the seat of royal power in the 6C Kingdom of Burgundy, notably of Brunehaut and her grandson King Thierry II. It was the latter that the Irish St Columbanus (540-615) rebuked for his degeneracy. St Columbanus had founded a monastery at Luxeuil-les-Bains in the Vosges and having incurred the displeasure of Brunehaut he left for Gubbio in Italy via Switzerland.

★ Château. – The château is set slightly apart from the village and is enclosed by two ⊘fortified precincts ringed by dry moats. The buildings in the outer courtyard form a small village clustered round the church, once part of a 12C abbey, and a robust 16C dovecot.

To see the four towers which link the living quarters walk round the outside of the inner precinct before crossing the second moat. The entrance is in the keep; the Condé Tower (named after the prince who lived there) is a 13C building of rubble and stone, a rare combination in Burgundy; the rustic octagonal tower was built in the 14C; the Bourdillon Tower, at the end of the west wing, is the oldest tower (10C), restored in 1560.

A balustraded terrace precedes the court of honour, which is marked by the presence of a well with an attractive wrought-iron wellhead. The château was remodelled in the 16C and 17C and the southern range was demolished during the Revolution. The Guitaut family, owners of the château since the 17C, have preserved many mementoes of famous people who have stayed here.

Interior. – In the entrance hall Renaissance portraits are set into the panelled walls. The small room beyond has a richly painted ceiling. The salon's Louis XIV furniture includes chairs covered with Gobelins tapestries.

On the first floor the portrait gallery is hung with paintings of 17C and 18C personalities (Charles de Sévigné, son of the famous marquise). Opening off this on one side is the less elaborately decorated King's Bedroom where Henri IV is said to have slept, and on the other side, Madame de Sévigné's Room with its attractive 16C painted ceiling. When in Burgundy she often stayed at Époisses, with the Guitaut family, as her own Bourbilly Château *(p 152)* was by then in a state of dilapidation.

FERRIÈRES

Pop 2417

Michelin map 61 fold 12 or 237 fold 43

Ferrières was the great monastic centre of the Gâtinais. The town with its network of winding narrow streets clusters at the foot of the old Benedictine abbey, one of the founts of Carolingian learning.

St Peter's and St Paul's Abbey (Ancienne abbaye St-Pierre et St-Paul). — Leave the car on the shady esplanade, which is marked by the beautiful slim cross of St Apollina.

Abbey church. — The church in the Gothic style has an unusual **transept crossing★** built in the 12C as a rotunda supported by eight tall columns. This may well be the remains of a 9C Carolingian structure.

The five stained glass windows in the choir are Renaissance. In the north transept there is a collection of 14C-17C statues and a curious baroque liturgical object , a sort of hanging pyx: a gilt palm tree interlaced with vine tendrils, used to display the Holy Sacrament.

Abbatial buildings. — The open space below the former cloisters provides a view of the south side of the church and the Chapel of Our Lady of Bethlehem, which has been rebuilt many times since the 15C and has a long and venerable tradition as a place of pilgrimage.

Lower town. — An arm of the Cléry has been diverted giving this quarter a certain charm. One of the wash-houses is still in use. The bridge affords a **view** of the tanning mill's sluice, the old rooftops and the spire of the abbey church.

La FERTÉ-LOUPIÈRE

Pop 630

Michelin map 65 fold 4 or 238 fold 9 - 18km - 11 miles southwest of Joigny

Detail from the Dance of Death

⊘This is an old fortified market town (*ferté* means strongpoint). The 12C-15C **church** contains some very unusual **mural paintings★** which were executed on dry plaster at the end of the 15C and the beginning of the 16C. In 1910 the distemper which had covered them was removed and they were protected. The paintings stretch along the left wall of the main nave above the three first arches. Subjects include the portrayal of the three dead men and the three live men and a Dance of Death *(Danse Macabre)*, consisting of forty-two figures representing all walks of life. This is both an historical document and a moral lesson (death comes to all: none escapes him). The larger pillars are decorated with *(right)* the Annunciation and *(left)* St Michael the Archangel slaying the dragon.

FIXIN

Pop 883

Michelin map 65 fold 20 or 243 folds 15 and 16 — 10km - 6 miles southwest of Dijon — Local map p 86

It is said that some of the wine produced by this village is among the best wine of the Côte de Nuits. Fixin is known for a touching example of loyalty. Noisot, a former major in the grenadiers during the Napoleonic Wars, had his friend the sculptor **François Rude** *(p 32)* erect a monument in 1847 in his own park to the glory of the Emperor. This is known as *Napoleon Awakening to Immortality*. Faithful unto death, the old soldier wished to be buried "standing before his emperor".

The 10C church of the neighbouring hamlet of Fixey is said to be the oldest in the Côte d'Or.

⊘**Noisot Park (Parc Noisot).** — *In the centre of the village take Rue Noisot up to the car park. Follow the avenue of fir trees leading to the entrance (signposts).*

A small museum containing souvenirs of the imperial campaigns is housed on the first floor of the park attendant's house. A stairway leads to François Rude's monument showing **Napoleon Awakening to Immortality** and continues to Noisot's tomb. From the belvedere there is a good view of the Saône Valley, the Jura and the Alps. From behind the museum another path leads to fountains and a flight of 100 steps that Noisot had built to commemorate the Hundred Days (Cent Jours) between Napoleon's return from Elba and arrival in Paris and the second abdication after Waterloo.

★ FLAVIGNY-SUR-OZERAIN — Pop 438

Michelin map 65 north of fold 18 or 243 fold 2

Flavigny is built in a picturesque **spot★**, perched on a rock isolated by three streams. Seat of an abbey since the 8C and a fortified township in the Middle Ages, Flavigny has today lost its former importance. Its narrow streets, flanked by old mansions, its fortified gateways and the remains of its ramparts recall its past grandeur. Today, Flavigny is chiefly known for the production of aniseed-flavoured sweets, which were first made in the 9C.

SIGHTS

Park the car on the Esplanade des Fossés. No cars allowed beyond this point.

St-Genest. — This 13C church, built on the site of an even earlier religious building, was altered in the 15C and 16C.
It has a stone central gallery dating from the beginning of the 16C. Other galleries run along the top of the aisles and the first two bays of the nave, something that is very rare in Gothic architecture. They are enclosed by 15C wooden screens. The stalls are early 16C.
Among the many interesting statues, note the **Angel of the Annunciation**, a masterpiece of the Burgundian school, in the last chapel on the right in the nave, and a 12C Virgin nursing the Infant Jesus, in the south transept.

Former Abbey (Ancienne abbaye). — A Benedictine abbey, founded in the 8C, consisted of a great church, St Peter's Basilica, and the usual conventual buildings. The latter were rebuilt in the 18C and now house the aniseed sweet factory. There are interesting remains from the Carolingian period of St Peter's.

St Reina Crypt. — The upper level of the double-decker Carolingian apse, reached by steps from the nave, contains the high altar. The lower chamber, built *c*758, contains the tomb of St Reina. Following her martyrdom at Alise *(p 37)* her remains were buried here in 864. The finely carved pillar is a good example of Carolingian decorative work.

Chapel of Our Lady of the Pillars. — In 1960 excavations revealed the existence of a hexagonal chapel with ambulatory beyond the crypt. The style recalls the pre-Romanesque rotundas of St Benignus in Dijon and Saulieu.

Tour of the town. — Starting from the 15C Town Gate (Porte du Bourg) with its impressive machicolations, take Chemin des Fossés and Chemin des Perrières to reach Valley Gate (Porte du Val) flanked by two round towers. Nearby is the Maison Lacordaire, a former Dominican monastery founded by **Father Lacordaire** (1806-61) *(p 21)*.

Old houses. — Many houses have been restored; they date from the late Middle Ages and the Renaissance and are decorated with turrets, spiral stairs or delicate sculptures.

EXCURSION

Frolois Château. — *17km - 10 1/2 miles northwest*. The de Frolois family was already in residence on the site in the 10C; all that remains of the much restored medieval stronghold is the residential block dating from the 14C and 15C.
The room on the first floor belonging to Antoine de Vergy (the de Frolois heir) is decorated with a French ceiling bearing his arms and cipher. The ground floor was altered and refurbished in the 17C and 18C: fine Bergamo tapestries (late 17C).

★ FLEURIGNY CHÂTEAU

Michelin map 61 fold 14 or 237 fold 33 — 15km - 9 miles northeast of Sens

The entrance front of this fine 13C château encircled by a moat presents both massive round corner towers and finely worked pediments. The entrance passageway, flanked by towers, leads to the inner courtyard, now open towards the park since the destruction of the far wing. The inner façades have a strong Renaissance imprint, with their decorative brick patterns and stone trims and the ground-floor arcade.
The guard room has a large sculptured chimneypiece. One of the rooms has a delightful series of 17C painted wooden panels. The chapel has a handsome coffered ceiling with hanging keystones, which, like the stained glass, is the work of Jean Cousin (1500-90).

FONTAINE-FRANÇAISE — Pop 859

Michelin map 66 north of fold 13 or 243 fold 5

This pleasant spot, set between two pools, was once the seat of a powerful family; it formed an enclave in Burgundy that was directly dependent on the crown of France. It was near here that on 5 June 1595 **Henri IV** at the head of 510 knights defeated the combined Spanish and League forces, 15 000 strong, commanded by the Constable of Castille and the Duc de Mayenne. A monument recalls this victory which led to the general pacification of the kingdom.

EXCURSIONS

St-Seine-sur-Vingeanne. – Pop 294. *5km - 3 miles east.* There is a 16-18C château in the village.

The **church** is in the Burgundian-Romanesque style and is surmounted by a belfry of three storeys.

There is a handsome 19C stained glass window in the choir, and at the top of the nave, to the right looking at the altar, a 16C Christ of Compassion in coloured stone.

⊘**Rosières Castle.** – *10km - 6 miles southeast.* The castle is now a farm. The earlier buildings – the massive keep, a 15C tower, the moat, the gate and a small tower which was part of the fortifications – are well preserved; so too is the pavilion with a typical Louis XIII-style stair which was added in the 17C.

★★★ FONTENAY ABBEY

Michelin map 🔢 southwest of fold 8 or 🔢 fold 2

The abbey of Fontenay, nestling in a lonely but verdant valley, is a particularly good example of what a 12C Cistercian monastery was like, self-sufficient within its boundaries.

A Second Daughter of St Bernard. – After he had become Abbot of Clairvaux, Bernard founded three religious settlements one after the other: Trois-Fontaines near St-Dizier in 1115, Fontenay in 1118, and Foigny in Thiérache in 1121. Accompanied by twelve monks, he arrived near Châtillon-sur-Seine at the end of the year 1118 and founded a hermitage there. After he had returned to Clairvaux, Bernard found that the monks he had left under the direction of Godefroy de la Roche had attracted so many others that the hermitage had become much too small. The monks moved into the valley and established themselves where the abbey stands today.

Up to the 16C the abbey was prosperous with more than 300 monks and converts but the regime of Commendam – abbots nominated by royal favour and interested only in the revenues – and the disorders caused by the religious wars brought about a rapid decline. The abbey was sold during the French Revolution and became a paper mill.

In 1906 new owners undertook to restore Fontenay to its original appearance. They tore down the parts which had been added for the paper mill and rebuilt the abbey just as it was in the 12C *(plan p 105).* The many fountains from which the abbey takes its name are today the most beautiful ornaments of the gardens surrounding the buildings.

Fontenay Abbey. – Cloister garth

⊘**TOUR** *time: about 3/4 hour.*

The main doorway of the porter's lodge is surmounted by the coat of arms of the abbey; the upper floor dates from the 15C. On going under the archway, note the niche below the staircase: the opening made at the bottom used to permit the watch-dog, on guard inside, to keep an eye also on the hostel, the long building on the right of the inner courtyard, where pilgrims and travellers were lodged.

After the porch, walk along beside a large 13C building, which used to house the visitors' chapel and the monks' bakehouse, remarkable for its round chimney. Today this houses the reception area and a small museum. Further on to the right is a magnificent circular dovecot.

Abbey Church. – Built during the lifetime of St Bernard, the church was erected from 1139 to 1147, owing to the generosity of Ebrard, Bishop of Norwich, who took refuge at Fontenay. The church was consecrated by Pope Eugenius III in 1147. It is one of the most ancient Cistercian churches preserved in France.

The expression "monastic simplicity" is particularly suited to the architectural art of the Cistercians *(details and illustration p 28).*

The façade, stripped of all ornament, is marked by two buttresses and seven round-headed windows, symbolising the seven Sacraments of the church. The porch has disappeared but the original corbels that supported it are still in place. The leaves and hinges of the doorway are exact reproductions of the original folding doors.

Interior. – The Cistercian rules and plans of design have been scrupulously observed *(see p 20)* and despite the relatively small dimensions of the building (length: 66m - 217ft, width of transept: 30m - 98ft), the general effect is one of striking grandeur.

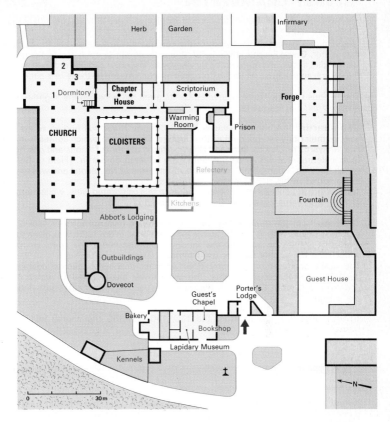

The nave, of broken-barrel vaulting, has eight bays; it is supported by aisles of transverse barrel vaulting, forming a series of communicating chapels, lit by small semicircular bays. The blind nave receives its light from openings in the façade and from those set above the chancel arch.

In the huge transept, the arrangement of the barrel vaulting and the chapels in the transept arms is similar to that in the aisles. In the north transept arm, note the statue (1) of Our Lady of Fontenay (end of the 13C); her smile and ease of pose recall the Champagne school.

The square chancel (2) with its flat chevet, is lit by a double row of windows in triplets (symbol of the Trinity). Tombstones and the remains of the 13C paving of small squares of glazed stone, which once covered the floor of the choir and a great part of the church, have been assembled here. On the right, there is the tomb (3) of the nobleman Mello d'Époisses and his wife (14C). The stone retable of the former Gothic high altar (late-13C) has been damaged.

The night stair to the monks' dormitory is in the south transept.

Dormitory. – The monks slept on straw mattresses on the floor and each sleeping compartment was screened off by a low partition. The magnificent oak timberwork roof is late 15C.

Cloisters. – The cloisters, on the south side of the church, are a magnificent example of Cistercian architecture, both elegant and robust. Each gallery has eight bays marked by fine buttresses; the semicircular archways, except for those of the doorways giving on to the garth, are divided by double arches resting on coupled columns.

The **chapter house,** with quadripartite vaulting and water-leaf capitals, communicates with the eastern cloister by way of a magnificent doorway. The monks' workroom or scriptorium is situated at the end of the east range. From the latter a doorway leads to the warming room. The two fireplaces were the only ones allowed in the abbey apart from those in the kitchen.

The prison is open to view; so too is the forge which was built beside the river to provide water power to activate the hammers and bellows (p 16).

The monks raised medicinal plants in the gardens next to the infirmary, which is set apart from the other buildings.

The path back to the entrance passes in front of the water tower, its fountain cascading down into the fish pond (trout).

A road which goes behind the abbey buildings leads to a very fine beech grove in the forest of Fontenay.

GEVREY-CHAMBERTIN
Pop 2 582

Michelin map 🔢 fold 20 or 🔢 folds 15 and 16 — 12km - 8 miles south of Dijon — Local map p 86

This village is typical of the wine-growing community immortalised by the Burgundian writer, **Gaston Roupnel** (1872-1946). It is situated at the open end of the gorge, Combe de Lavaux, and surrounded by vineyards. The older part lies grouped around the church and château while the Baraques quarter crossed by the N 74 is altogether busier.

The famous Côte de Nuits, renowned for its great red wines, starts slightly to the north *(p 84)*.

Chambertin. — Among the wines of the Côte de Nuits, full-bodied wines that acquire their body and bouquet as they mature, Chambertin, which comes from the two vineyards of Clos de Bèze and Chambertin, is the most famous and one of the most celebrated wines of all Burgundy. The "Champ de Bertin" (Field of Bertin), which became "Chambertin", was the favourite wine of Napoleon I and was always to be found in his baggage-train, even on campaigns.

Today there are only 28ha - 69 acres producing this celebrated wine, while there are 400ha - 988 acres producing Gevrey-Chambertin.

Château. — In the upper village stands the square-towered fortress, lacking its portcullis; it was built in the 10C by the lords of Vergy. In the 13C it was given to the monks of Cluny who enlarged the windows and installed a fine spiral staircase, wider than the simple ladders used hitherto.

The great chamber on the first floor with its uncovered beams contains a beautiful late-14C credence table. The great tower has retained its watch room and bowmen's room. Beneath the basket-handle vaulting in the cellars past vintages are stored.

Church (Église). — Dating from the 13C, 14C and 15C the church still has a Romanesque doorway.

JOIGNY
Pop 10 488

Michelin map 🔢 north of fold 4 or 🔢 fold 10

Joigny, whose townsfolk have the name of "Joviniens", is a busy, picturesque little town set at the gateway to Burgundy on the borders of the forest of Othe. It is built in terraces on the side of St James' Hill (Côte St-Jacques), overlooking the river Yonne. From the Yonne bridge, which has six 18C arches, there is a pretty view of the river, the quays, the shady promenades and the town built in the shape of an amphitheatre.

The Revolt of the Maillotins (Maul-bearers). — In 1438 the people of Joigny rebelled against their lord of the manor, Count Guy de la Trémoille, attacked and captured his castle, and put the Count to death with blows from their mauls or mallets, tools used by the wine-growers of those days. Since that event the "Joviniens" have been known as Maillotins (Maul-bearers) and the maul figures in the town's coat of arms.

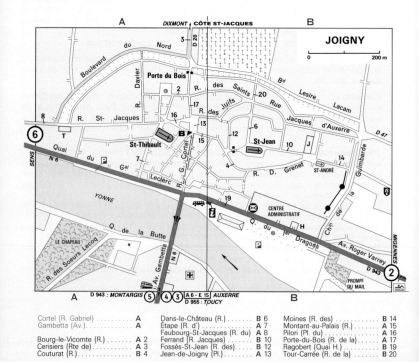

Cortel (R. Gabriel) . . . . A	Dans-le-Château (R.) . . . . . . B 6	Moines (R. des) . . . . B 14
Gambetta (Av.) . . . . A	Étape (R. d') . . . . A 7	Montant-au-Palais (R.) . . . . . . A 15
	Faubourg-St-Jacques (R. du) A 8	Pilori (Pl. du) . . . . A 16
Bourg-le-Vicomte (R.) . . . . . A 2	Ferrand (R. Jacques) . . . . . . B 10	Porte-du-Bois (R. de la) . . . . . A 17
Cerisiers (Rte de) . . . . A 3	Fossés-St-Jean (R. des) . . . . B 12	Ragobert (Quai H.) . . . . B 19
Couturat (R.) . . . . B 4	Jean-de-Joigny (Pl.) . . . . A 13	Tour-Carrée (R. de la) . . . . . . B 20

SIGHTS

St Theobald's Church (St-Thibault) (A). – The church, built in both the Gothic and the Renaissance style between 1490 and 1529, is dominated by a 17C square tower crowned by a delicate belfry. Above the door is an equestrian statue of St Thibault (1530) by the Spanish sculptor Joan de Juni (Jean de Joigny). Inside the church, the chancel slants to the left; this rare asymmetry is emphasised by the chancel vaulting, which has an unusual hanging keystone. There are many works of art *(plan in the north aisle level with the pulpit)*: paintings and sculptures including a charming **Smiling Virgin**★, a 14C stone statue *(against the 4th pillar on the right facing the pulpit)*, and a series of low-relief Renaissance sculptures from the old rood screen including Christ in hell *(in the east chapel)*.

St John's Church (St-Jean) (B). – A belfry-porch precedes the west front of this church which lacks transepts but has a pentagonal chevet. The Renaissance-style coffered ceiling has carved medallions framed by decorated ribs.
The south aisle contains a 15C Holy Sepulchre in white marble, ornamented with low-reliefs and the 13C recumbent figure of the Comtesse de Joigny. The tomb is lavishly sculptured and includes the figures of the countess' children. The Louis XV woodwork and the furnishings of the sacristy came from Vézelay.

Porte du Bois (A). – This 12C gateway, flanked by two round towers, was once part of the medieval wall, part of which can be seen in Chemin de la Guimbarde (B).

Old houses (Maisons anciennes). – A stroll through the narrow streets in the vicinity of the churches of St Theobald and St John will reveal several half-timbered houses dating from the 15C and 16C. Most of these were badly damaged, either during the bombardments of 1940 or a gas explosion in 1981, but have been restored. The best-known house is the corner one (A **B**), called the Tree of Jesse.

★ **View from the Côte St-Jacques.** – Michelin map 🔲 south of fold 14 or 🔲 fold 10. *1.5km - 1 mile north by the D 20.*
The road climbs in hairpin bends round St James' Hill (Côte St-Jacques). From a right-hand bend there is a fine semicircular **panorama**★ over the town and the valley of the Yonne.

EXCURSIONS

⊘ **Laduz Folk Museum.** – *15km - 10 miles south.* The museum at the southeast entrance to the village recalls rural working life before 1914; the tools and products of about fifty craftsmen are on display together with a large collection of old toys and many of the carved figures which were popular in the past.

⊘ **Fabulous Museum (La Fabuloserie).** – *25km - 15 1/2 miles west by the D 943.* At **Dicy** there is a museum of unsophisticated or "over the top" art which displays unusual and spontaneous works created from a variety of material by untrained people without reference to accepted artistic norms. The world of the irrational extends into the garden where more works are exhibited in the open air.

These are the **Michelin Maps** *to use with this guide*

The LOIRE NIVERNAISE

Michelin maps 🔲 folds 2, 12 and 13 and 🔲 folds 3, 4, 5 and 16 or 🔲 folds 8, 20, 21, 33 to 35, 47 and 48

The stretch of the Loire from Digoin to Briare, which borders the Nivernais region, is neither as large nor as impressive as the river below Orléans. It is nonetheless attractive owing to the scenery through which it passes and its character – sometimes listless and sometimes spirited; the flow of water varies from 1 000 or 1 400 cubic ft a second in summer to 250 000 and even 280 000 cubic ft when it is in spate.
In summer the Loire is little more than a trickle making its way with difficulty among the great golden sand banks; here and there the willow bushes provide a splash of green. From October to June the river completely fills its bed, sweeping along like a great grey snake, in complete contrast with the summer months.

Navigation on the Loire. – Although the most irregular of French rivers, the Loire once knew intensive navigation.
In the days when highways were rare, and often poor, the waterways were much used. By the 4C there was an established organisation for navigators of the Loire. Later, in the 14C, a powerful organisation was established known as "The Company of Merchants using the river Loire and other rivers by going up and down them". This company levied duties on all goods being transported on the Loire and its tributaries, and imposed tolls.
From Roanne to Orléans, a whole population of boatmen earned their living by transporting all kinds of merchandise on lighters, barges and other vessels – some of which had mast and sail: agricultural products from the Charollais and the Morvan, earthenware from Nevers and wood and coal from the Forez.
Traffic was particularly heavy on the downstream journey when one could cover up to twenty miles a day. On the other hand, the return trip upstream was difficult owing to the fast current and the rivermen generally preferred to demolish their boats, sell the planks, and return on foot to their starting point.

Travellers readily adopted this form of locomotion. The rivermen, who were rough and sometimes violent, evolved a manner of speech from their voyages and their adventures that could hardly be described as polished and, perhaps, at best as truculent, so that the "tourists" of those days were well advised not to listen to their conversation for fear of soiling their own vocabulary; unless, like the parrot "Vert-Vert" *(p 127)*, they were too weak and fell into temptation.

Just before the French Revolution in 1789, a regular passenger service was organised on the three sections of the river, Roanne-Nevers, Nevers-Orléans and Orléans-Nantes.

In the 19C steam navigation gave a new impetus to the river traffic. Regular services by a number of companies were instituted between Nevers and Orléans. The arrival of the railways sounded the knell of the river traffic. In 1862 the last company suspended its services. *For further details see the English edition of the Green Guide Châteaux of the Loire.*

Remains of the past. — The river banks, once so lively with the constant movement of the boats, are deserted today. The quays alone where the vessels once moored bear witness to the past; the inns and hostelries with their signs, reminiscent of the old-time river life, are disappearing.

Some chapels dedicated to St Nicholas, the patron saint of rivermen, still exist as at Nevers or have been partly demolished as at La Charité-sur-Loire. It is common in churches along the Loire to find wooden models of 17C sailing ships hanging from the roof beams; these used to be carried in procession in honour of St Nicholas.

FROM DIGOIN TO NEVERS *106km - 66 miles — about 4 hours*

Digoin. — *Time to visit the museum: 1 1/2 hours. Description p 90.*

Leave Digoin by the D 979 which crosses the Arroux then follows more or less closely the east bank of the Loire.

On leaving St-Aubin note its château on the right.

St-Aubin-sur-Loire Château. — *Description p 56.*

Bear right into the D 979A to Bourbon-Lancy.

Bourbon-Lancy. — *Description p 56.*

Leave Bourbon-Lancy by the D 973; turn right into the D 979.

The road now runs at some distance from the river but offers occasional views of the river and its islands, especially north of Charrin.

Decize. — *Description p 90.*

Leave Decize by the N 81 going northwest.

Béard. — The tiny 12C Romanesque church has a charming **belfry;** the two storeys are pierced on each face by pairs of round-headed arches.

Continue north. On the north side of Imphy turn left into the D 200.

Chevenon. — *Description of the castle p 130.*

Take the D 13 northwest to Nevers.

From the bridge over the Loire there is a good view of Nevers *(p 127)*.

★ **Nevers.** — *Time: 1 hour. Description p 127.*

FROM NEVERS TO BRIARE *94km - 58 miles — about 3 hours*

★ **Nevers.** — *Time: 1 hour. Description p 127.*

Leave Nevers by the D 504 going southwest along the north bank of the Loire.

There is an attractive view of the confluence of the Loire and Allier opposite **Bec d'Allier.**

Continue to Marzy.

Marzy. — *Description p 129.*

Take the D 131 north; in Fourchambault take the D 8 to Pougues-les-Eaux.

Pougues-les-Eaux. — *Description p 137.*

Take the N 7 which once again follows the river bank.

At La Charité a picturesque hump-back bridge dating from the 16C spans the majestically wide river linking the town to the island, Ile du Faubourge de Loire.

★ **La Charité-sur-Loire.** — *Time: 1 hour. Description p 69.*

Continue north on the N 7.

Pouilly-sur-Loire. — Pop 1 738. The town is famous for its vineyards which produce white wines with a characteristic earthy taste and aroma.

North of the town *(N 7)* there is a viewpoint overlooking the river and a string of midstream islands.

Cosne-sur-Loire. — *Description p 84.*

Take the N 7 north for 10km - 6 miles to Cadoux.

Cadoux Estate. — *Description p 84.*

The tour ends at Briare where the amazing bridge by Gustave Eiffel carries the canal over the river.

Briare. — *Description p 62.*

LORMES

Michelin map 📖 fold 16 or 🔲🔲🔲 fold 23 — Local map p 124

Built on the side of a hill, Lormes stands on the dividing line between the Morvan and Nivernais regions. It is a popular summer resort and makes an excellent centre for excursions.
Charming and picturesque roads lead to the dams of Pannesière-Chaumard, Chaumeçon and Le Crescent, as well as to the reservoir of Les Settons.

★ **Panorama.** – From near the Income Tax Office (Perception), Rue du Panorama climbs steeply to a modern church built in Romanesque style at the top of a hill (470m - 1 542 ft).
From the cemetery terrace there is a vast panorama stretching from wooded summits of the central Morvan (southeast) to the farmlands of the Bazois and the Nivernais (southwest), dotted with villages and interspersed with little woods. On the horizon (centre) stands the hill of Montenoison.

★ **Mont de la Justice.** – 470m - 1 542 ft. *1.5km - 1 mile northwest. Leave Lormes by the D 6 going west; at the bottom of the hill turn right into La Justice Pass. From the pass there is a path (left) to the summit (viewing table):* fine **panorama**★ of Vézelay (north), the Yonne depression and the hill of Montenoison (west), the Bazois (southwest) and beyond the belfry of Lormes to Morvan and the peak of Haut-Folin.

EXCURSION

Chaumeçon Dam (Barrage de Chaumeçon). – *17km - 11 miles east by the D 6.* The road winds through wooded valleys with outcrops of rocks. Once out of the trees the road passes through a countryside of wooded crests and green valleys.

> *After crossing the dam turn left into the D 235.*

The road climbs upwards, overlooking the reservoir which is a favourite fishing place, encircled by wooded heights.
After Vaussegrois, the road goes down steeply, crossing a small valley and coming to the bank of the reservoir whose curving shore it follows before crossing the dam to reach Plainefas.

The key explains the abbreviations and symbols used in the text or on the maps.

LOUHANS

Pop 4 198

Michelin map 🔟 northwest of fold 13 or 🔲🔲🔲 fold 29

Louhans is a picturesque little town and is an important centre for butter, eggs and Bresse poultry, which is known as Louhannaise poultry. The town is also known for its pig and cattle markets.

SIGHTS

⊘ **Hospital** (Hôtel-Dieu). – The 18C building contains two large public rooms divided by a wrought-iron screen. Each curtained bed bears a plaque indicating for whom the bed was intended – usually the benefactors offered a bed to the inhabitants of a particular town.
The **pharmacy,** decorated with Louis XIV woodwork, displays a beautiful collection of hand-blown glass vessels and Hispano-Moorish lustreware. There is also a most unusual Burgundian wood-carving of the Virgin of Mercy kneeling before the dead Christ (early-16C).

Grande-Rue. – The arches of the old houses, which date from the late Middle Ages, provide a picturesque scene.

Church. – This building has been greatly restored with stone and brick and is roofed with glazed tiles. On the left is a belfry-porch and large chapel with turreted pavilions.

⊘ **Print-Room of the old Independent.** – This annexe of the specialist museum of the Burgundian region of Bresse *(p 135)* is housed in the old premises *(29 rue des Dôdanes)* of the Independent (l'Indépendant), a Bresse newspaper abandoned in 1984 after a hundred years of publication. The old machines are still in place; the offices have been reconstructed.

EXCURSION

⊘ **Rancy Museum of Makers and Menders of Chairs.** – *12km - 7 1/2 miles southwest by the D 971 on the outskirts of Rancy.* Chair-making, which at the beginning of the 19C was a long-established part-time occupation in Rancy and Bantanges, had become a full-time job by the end of the century. Today the centre is the second most important French producer of straw-bottomed chairs. This annexe of the specialist museum of Burgundian Bresse *(p 135)* illustrates the development of the different stages in this manufacture from the making of the wooden frame to the addition of the straw seat.

LUZY

Michelin map 69 fold 6 or 238 fold 36 — Local map p 124

This medieval town is a pleasant spot on the banks of the Alène on the southern edge of the Morvan region. The 14C tower of the Barons of Luzy still stands on the highest point (272m - 892ft).

⊙**Tapestries in the Town Hall.** — One of the rooms in the Town Hall (Hôtel de Ville) is hung with 17C Aubusson tapestries representing scenes from the life of Esther. The series comprises two main compositions and six panels. The colours have retained an attractive freshness. The imposts of this room's two doorways are painted with gallant scenes by the school of Lancret.

EXCURSION

⊙**Tibetan Monastery of Kagyu-Ling** (Monastère tibétain Kagyu-Ling). — *18km - 11 miles west by the D 228, D 47 and D 114 to the Château de Plaige north of La Boulaye.*
It is unexpected to find a Buddhist centre in Burgundy. The monastery was founded in 1974 in the Château of Plaige which is surrounded by a park (8ha - 20 acres). The purpose of the community of four Tibetan lamas and about thirty western bonzes is to explain their doctrine and Himalayan culture.
Oriflammes and banners greet the visitor, as well as a "stoupa", a monument (symbol of the enlightenment of the Buddha) containing two statues of the Sage which is crowned by a dome and conical spire. The **temple,** a sort of rectangular three-storey pagoda (19.5m - 64ft high), is built of concrete faced with painted and gilded plaster. The monastery also houses a study and translation centre for the Tibetan language and sacred texts.

La MACHINE

Michelin map 69 fold 4, 5 or map 238 fold 34; 7.5km - 4 1/2 miles north of Decize

Although their existence was known in antiquity, the coal deposits in La Machine were not fully exploited until the 16C. At first limited and rudimentary, the mines began to be exploited on an industrial scale under Colbert who recommended the excellent quality of the Nivernais coal to the King for fuelling the military arsenals. The town takes its name from an extraction machine installed on the site in 1670. In 1864 the mine was bought by the Compagnie Schneider du Creusot *(p 88)* and nationalised in 1946. Foreign competition and the ever-increasing use of other sources of energy caused the mine to close in 1974.

⊙**Museum.** — Housed in the old administration building, the museum traces the history of the site *(audiovisual presentation: 8 min)*, the daily routine at the pit bottom and the social life of the people of La Machine since the 19C.

⊙**Simulated Mine.** — *Follow the sign opposite the museum to Puits des Glénons.* In the past the miners were trained in a simulated mine. The site now presents a reconstruction showing the wooden supports and the different extraction techniques: dynamiting, mining, evacuation of the coal...

MÂCON

Michelin map 69 fold 19 or 243 fold 39 — Local map p 113

Mâcon spreads along the west bank of the Sâone between the river and the Mâconnais Heights where the terraced slopes are covered in vineyards. The round roof tiles mark it as a southern town. Its lively atmosphere is due partly to the marina and its great reach of water and partly to the National French Wine Fair *(p 180)*. The Mâconnais wines *(p 112)* complement the delicious culinary specialities of the region *(quenelles de brochets, pauchouse, poulardes à la crème, coq au vin* – pike fish balls, fish stewed in white wine, chicken in cream sauce and chicken in red wine sauce). Mâcon is the meeting point of the main roads from the Paris Basin to the Mediterranean coast and from Lake Geneva to the banks of the Loire. It has always been a busy crossroads; since ancient times waves of invasion have left their mark, such as the prehistoric civilisation excavated at Solutré *(p 157)*. At the end of the Roman period Mâcon, then known as Matisco, was invaded by the Barbarians.

A Prince of Romanticism. — Alphonse Prat de Lamartine, who was born in Mâcon in 1790, was drawn to literature very early in life and steeped himself in Racine, Rousseau, Chateaubriand, Ossian and the Bible. His great love for a young woman, Mme Charles, whom he extolled as Elvira, directed him to the vocation of poetry. His *Meditations*, published in 1820, were the first step in a brilliant literary career which was accompanied by a no less brilliant career in politics. His prolific output included his poems *Jocelyn* and *The Fall of an Angel*, his novel *Graziella* and his history *The History of the Girondins.*
Lamartine was an embassy Secretary from 1821-30; he was elected Deputy for the North in 1833 and as Minister of Foreign Affairs played an important part in the events of June 1848. In 1849 he was forced out of political life and went to live in his native Mâconnais. The end of his life was beset by financial problems and family grief; he died in Paris in 1869.
Memories of Lamartine are still alive in Mâcon. His admirers will not fail to do the "Lamartine Circuit" in the neighbourhood of Mâcon *(p 114);* they will want to see his father's house, Hôtel d'Ozenay (15 rue Lamartine), where he lived until his marriage and where, so it is said, he composed his first verses.

MÂCON

Barre (Pl. de la)	AYZ 2
Barre (R. de la)	BZ 3
Laguiche (R. Ph.)	BZ 8
Lamartine (R.)	BYZ 9
Poissonnière (Pl.)	BZ 13
Pont (R. du)	BZ 14
Sigorgne (R.)	BZ 19

Dombey (R.)	BZ 5
Gaulle (Av. du Gén.-de-)	BY 6
Paix (Square de la)	BY 10
Perrier (R.)	AY 12
Préfecture (R.)	BY 15
St-Étienne (Pl.)	BY 17
St-Nizier (R.)	BZ 18
Strasbourg (R. de)	BY 20
Ursulines (R. des)	BY 21
11-Novembre 1918 (R. du)	ABZ 22
28-Juin-1944 (R.)	BY 24

SIGHTS

★ **Ursuline Municipal Museum** (BY M¹). — The museum, which is housed in an old ⊙17C Ursuline convent, contains sections on prehistory, Gallo-Roman and medieval archaeology, regional ethnography, paintings and ceramics.

Ground Floor. — The history of Mâcon is traced from antiquity to the present day. The prehistoric section presents articles from the excavations at Solutré *(p 157)* and other regional sites: flint-cutting techniques, tools, weapons and ceramics from the palaeolithic to the iron age. The rooms following after are devoted to the Gallo-Roman period (statuettes, tools, pottery kiln, collection of funerary urns from the Mâcon necropolis), to medieval archaeology (Merovingian weapons and burials, lapidary fragments) and to sculpture from the 12C to the 17C. The convent chapel is used for temporary exhibitions.

First Floor. — This gallery is devoted to regional ethnology and to local traditions: general characteristics of the Mâconnais, the River Saône and its activities, stone carving, vine husbandry and the traditional pottery of the Saône Valley.

Second Floor. — This gallery contains 17C and 18C furniture, French and foreign earthenware and paintings: 16C Flemish works, paintings by the Fontainebleau school; 17C and 18C French and Nordic works (Le Brun, Ph de Champaigne, Greuze); 19C romanticism (Corot), academics and symbolists (Bussière); 20C post-Cubist canvases (Gleizes, M Cahn) and contemporary works (M Bill, G Honneger, T-L Boussard).

Old St Vincent (Vieux St-Vincent) (BY). — In the fervour of Revolutionary madness the people of Mâcon destroyed the twelve churches of their town, not even sparing the ancient cathedral of St Vincent. The narthex, two octagonal towers and the intervening bay are all that escaped destruction; the beginning of the nave is still visible. In the **narthex** one can see the 12C tympanum; the carvings were damaged during the Wars of Religion. Five rows of superimposed sculpture depict scenes from the Last Judgment; the Resurrection of the Dead, Paradise and Hell are still distinguishable.

⊙**Lamartine Museum** (Musée Lamartine) (BZ M²). — The Hôtel Senecé is a mansion in the pure Regency style and was the seat of the Academy of Mâcon when it was founded in 1805. The rooms possess paintings, tapestries and furnishings of the period. A collection of documents recalls the life and work, both literary and political, of Lamartine.

Half-timbered House (BZ D). — A charming Renaissance house with finely sculptured small columns stands at 22 Rue Dombey, on the corner of Place aux Herbes. Grotesque carvings and fantastic animals decorate the coping.

View from the St-Laurent Bridge (BZ). — This 14C bridge, restored in the 19C, links Mâcon with the suburb of St-Laurent and the Bresse region. From the bridge there is a good view of the quays and the town, dominated by the towers of the old cathedral.

Upstream the Saône opens out into a magnificent broad reach (300m - 330 yards) where the French rowing championships *(see Practical Information)* are held.

⊙**Hospital** (Hôtel-Dieu) (BY B). – This 18C building was designed by Melchior Munet, one of Soufflot's pupils. The Louis XV **dispensary★** has a fine collection of pottery of that period. The Louis XV-style panelling is as remarkable as the woodwork of the windows which is in perfect harmony with the general decor.

EXCURSIONS

⊙**St Andrew (St-André)** . – *9km - 6 miles east*. The **church,** which stands alone in the middle of a cemetery, was built at the end of the 11C by the monks of Tournus.
A magnificent and elegant octagonal **belfry★**, capped by a stone spire (restored in the 19C), rises above the apse which is flanked by apsidal chapels. Carved capitals and slim columns adorn the chancel.

Lamartine Heritage Trail. – *70km - 44 miles – about 3 hours. Description p 114.*

*The diagram on page 3 shows the **Michelin Maps** covering the Guide;*
the chapter headings specify the appropriate map for the locality.

★ MÂCONNAIS

Michelin map 69 folds 19 and 20 and 73 folds 9 and 10 or 243 folds 39 and 40

The delightful and varied landscape of the Mâconnais extends from Tournus to Mâcon, between the Valley of the Saône and the Valley of the Grosne (west).

GEOGRAPHICAL NOTES *see also p 14*

The terraced Mâconnais Heights on the west bank of the Saône terminate at the northern end in the Chalon Plain north of Tournus. On the west they are separated from the Charollais by the Grosne Valley; in the south they merge imperceptibly into the Beaujolais country.
The Mâconnais does rise to dramatic heights (Signal de la Mère Boitier 758m - 2487ft) but the countryside is attractive and varied. The forested peaks and the barren sunless slopes contrast with the well-watered meadows in the valleys; the terraces bordering the Saône and the hillsides which catch the sun are planted with vineyards.
The Mâconnais contains features more typical of the Mediterranean region to the south: instead of high pointed roofs of slates or flat tiles one sees low-pitched roofs covered with rounded tiles known as Roman or Provençal. The region is a borderland between the North and the South. The climate is less harsh than in northern Burgundy.

THE WINES OF THE MÂCONNAIS

The monks of Cluny planted the first vines in the Mâconnais, of which the Chardonnay, the Pinot and the Gamay are the best known.

The king and the wine producer. – Although he was only a simple vine-grower from Chasselas, **Claude Brosse** decided to try his local wines on the Paris market. He filled two hogsheads with his best wine, loaded them on to a cart drawn by two oxen and after a journey of 33 days arrived in the capital. In Versailles he attended mass in the presence of the King who noticed his great stature. After the service Louis XIV desired to see the unknown man.
Without the least embarrassment Claude Brosse explained the purpose of his journey and how he hoped to sell his wine to some noble lord. The King asked to taste the wine on the spot and found it much better than the products of Suresnes and Beaugency then being drunk at court.
The wines of Mâcon became very popular with the courtiers and acquired their titles of nobility; the bold wine-producer continued to convey the produce of his vineyards for sale in Paris and Versailles.

The extent of the vineyards. – The Mâconnais vineyards meet the Beaujolais vineyards on their southern border; they extend from Tournus in the north to St-Vérand in the south and include the region of Pouilly-Fuissé, which produces fine white wines. Annual wine production in the Mâconnais is about 200 000hl - 4 400 000 gallons, two-thirds of which are white wines.

The main wines. – Up to the 19C the vineyards of the Mâconnais produced only a medium-quality wine known as "grand ordinaire"; now they produce good red wines and particularly good white ones.

The white wines: these come from the Chardonnay stock, the great white grape vine of Burgundy and Champagne. The most celebrated is Pouilly-Fuissé. This wine has a beautiful green-gold colour, it is dry and crisp; when young it is fruity but with age acquires a bouquet. Pouilly-Loché, Saint-Vérand, Pouilly-Vinzelles, Mâcon-Lugny and Mâcon-Viré, members of the same family as Pouilly-Fuissé, are also well known. The other white wines are sold under the names of White Burgundy, White Mâcon and Mâcon-Villages. They are produced from the Pinot-Chardonnay stock.

The red wines: without pretending to equal the great wines, these can be considered as excellent value. Fairly full-bodied and fruity, they are generally produced from the Gamay stock, which is a black grape with a white juice.

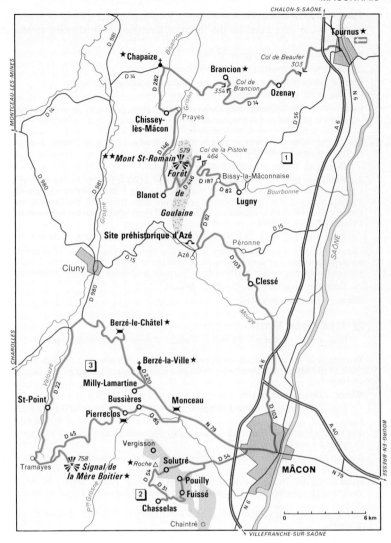

The Pouilly vineyard is shown in green

1 **LA MONTAGNE**

From Tournus to Mâcon

71km - 44 miles — about 3 1/2 hours — Local map above

This drive passes through a picturesque region of fine views and wide panoramas, as well as Romanesque churches *(signposted itinerary)* and many other interesting buildings.

★**Tournus.** — *Time: 1 hour. Description p 162.*

Leave Tournus by ③ on the town plan, the D 14.

The road climbs rapidly, providing views over Tournus, the Saône Valley and the Bresse region. Southwest of the Beaufer Pass the countryside has many valleys and the crests are covered with boxwood and sometimes by pines.

Ozenay. — Pop 266. Set in a little valley, Ozenay has a small 13C castle and a rustic 12C church.

Beyond Ozenay outcrops of rocks appear here and there on the slopes.

Most houses have a porch and covered balcony forming a loggia.

From the Brancion Pass, take the road to the old market town of Brancion, picturesquely perched on a promontory.

★**Brancion.** — *Description p 61.*

Returning to the Pass, go as far as Chapaize, which is pinpointed by its fine belfry.

★**Chapaize.** — *Time: 1/2 hour. Description p 68.*

Opposite the church in Chapaize take the road to Lys; turn left.

Chissey-lès-Mâcon. — Pop 250. The 12C church with an elegant belfry, typical of Cluny, has curious historiated capitals.

Continue east to Prayes; turn right into the D 146.

Take the D 446 northeast.

Blanot. – *Description p 55.*

A picturesque road traverses the forest of Goulaine before climbing to Mount St-Romain.

★★ **Mount St-Romain.** – *Description p 146.*

Continue northeast to La Pistole Pass; turn right.

East of Bissy-la-Mâconnaise lies the Mâconnais vineyard country.

The D 82 leads to Lugny.

Lugny. – Pop 879. Nestling amid green scenery, Lugny produces an excellent white wine and is situated on the Mâconnais Wine Trail *(route des vins du Mâconnais).* The town has a modern wine co-operative.

⊘Beside the ruins of a fortress stands the **church** which has a 16C stone altarpiece portraying Jesus with the twelve Apostles.

Return to Bissy; take the D 82 south to Azé.

⊘**Azé Prehistoric Site.** – The **museum** displays over 2000 artefacts found locally. An arboretum precedes the entrance to the **caves;** the first (208m - 682ft long) served as a refuge for cave bears (many bones), prehistoric man, the Aedui, the Gallo-Romans etc; the second cave contains an underground river which can be followed for a stretch (800m - 2625ft).

Take the D 15 east; in Péronne take the D 103 southeast to Clessé.

⊘**Clessé.** – Pop 627. This vine-growers' village (co-operative) has a late-11C **church** with a polygonal tower and varnished spire, similar to the one on the fine octagonal belfry with its twinned openings and arcading. The nave is covered with a timberwork roof.

Continue south on the D 103 to Mâcon.

Mâcon. – *Description p 110.*

② THE VINEYARD

Round tour of 20km - 12 miles – about 2 hours – Local map p 113

The circuit in the immediate environment of Mâcon is a pleasant drive in the very heart of the Mâconnais vineyards, through a countryside of varied and picturesque scenery.

Mâcon. – *Description p 110.*

Leave Mâcon by ④ on the town plan, the N 79; turn left into the D 54 to Pouilly.

Pouilly. – This hamlet gives its name to various wines: Pouilly-Fuissé, Pouilly-Loché and Pouilly-Vinzelles. These wines are highly appreciated and go well with certain Burgundian specialities *(p 33).*

Beyond this village the orderly patterns of the vineyards spread over the gentle curves of the hillsides.

Fuissé. – Pop 355. This is one of the communes (Chaintré, Fuissé, Solutré, Pouilly and Vergisson) producing Pouilly-Fuissé, classed as one of the world's great white wines *(p 112).*

Fuissé is a pleasing village, typical of a community of rich and prosperous vine-growers.

Between Fuissé and Solutré, the road affords splendid views over the neat patterns of the vineyards.

Chasselas. – Pop 140. This village is dominated by an outcrop of grey rock which appears amidst the heath. The village has developed a vine that produces a well-known dessert grape.

The rock of Solutré, looking like the prow of a ship, stands out against the sky.

Solutré. – *Description p 157.*

In the background appear the valley of the Saône, the Bresse countryside and the Jura mountains. After Solutré the road enters the heart of the vineyard and affords a pretty view of the village of **Vergisson** and its rocky outcrop, a fine limestone escarpment.

Return to Mâcon.

③ LAMARTINE HERITAGE TRAIL

70km - 44 miles – about 3 hours – Local map p 113

All those who are interested in souvenirs of Alphonse de Lamartine or who appreciate the elegiac style of his poetry will be attracted by this tour which passes through the countryside he knew, the scenes and views from which he drew his inspiration.

Mâcon. – *Description p 110.*

Take the N 79 west.

⊘**Monceau Château.** – This was one of Lamartine's favourite residences, where he lived as a great vineyard owner but where his creditors pursued him at the end of his life. It was in a little building, known as "La Solitude", in the middle of the vineyards, that he wrote his *Histoire des Girondins.*

Milly-Lamartine. – Pop 206. An ironwork grille stands before the house where the poet lived from the age of seven. The 12C church has been restored. At the top of the village, in front of the Town Hall, there is a bronze bust of the poet and a good view over the vineyards. It was at Milly that Lamartine composed his first meditation, *L'Isolement.*

★**Berzé-la-Ville.** – *Description p 54.*

From the road (D 17) one sees the imposing mass of Berzé-le-Châtel Castle with its impressive fortifications.

★**Berzé-le-Châtel Castle.** – This feudal ⊙castle was once the principal seat of the most important barony in the Mâconnais. Henri IV made it a county. The castle protected the southern approaches to Cluny from its highly attractive site on the vineyard covered slopes.

Take the D 17 and the N 79 west and the D 22 south up the Valouze Valley to St-Point.

St-Point. – Pop 273. The **church,** in the style of Cluny, has a fresco of Christ in Majesty in the apse. It also pos- ⊙sesses two pictures painted by Madame de Lamartine, who rests close to her husband and other relatives in the little chapel nearby. To the left of the church, a small door opens on to the park of the **château.**

Alphonse de Lamartine

This château was Lamartine's favourite residence and was considerably altered between 1833 and 1855. Inside one can see his study, his bedroom and his salon, which contain many souvenirs. These include portraits by his wife, letters from personalities of the period and a 17C Gobelins tapestry (Battle of Zama).

South of St-Point beside the road (D 22) lies an artificial stretch of water which is used as a leisure and water-sports centre. East of Tramayes the picturesque road offers wide views.

★**La Mère Boitier Signal Station** (Signal de la Mère Boitier). – *A steep road leads up to a car park. 1/4 hour Rtn on foot.* From the signal station (758m - 2 487ft), the highest point of the Mâconnais region, there is a fine **panorama★** *(viewing table)* of the Suin Hill to the northwest, the St-Cyr Mountain to the west and the Bresse and Jura to the east.

Take the D 45 northeast to Pierreclos.

⊙**Pierreclos.** – Pop 781. Mademoiselle de Milly who appears as Laurence in *Jocelyn* lived in the 17C château.

Bussières. – Pop 393. **Abbot Dumont,** Lamartine's first master and his great friend, whom he immortalised in *Jocelyn*, rests by the chevet of the little church.

Return to Mâcon by the D 45 and the N 79.

MAILLY-LE-CHÂTEAU

Pop 501

Michelin map 🔲 south of fold 5 or 🔲 fold 11

The old fortified town stands on an escarpment overlooking the River Yonne. A shady terrace provides an attractive **view** of the loop in the river and a stretch of the Nivernais canal; in the distance are the hills on the edge of the Morvan. From the end *(right)* of the terrace one can see the lower town at the water's edge and the 15C bridge with its little chapel.

SIGHTS

St Adrian. – This 13C fortified church, supported by heavy buttresses, has a powerful-looking belfry ornamented with gargoyles. The west front in an early Gothic style has a sharp-pointed gable and an arcade with semicircular arches resting on statue-columns (three atlantes and an angel).

Cemetery chapel. – This 12C chapel (restored) has a flat east end and a charming bell-turret with trefoil openings. The interior, lit by six small round-headed windows, is adorned by wall paintings depicting the life of Christ.

*Don't get lost - use **Michelin Maps***

*The **Michelin Detailed Map** Series (1:200 000) covers the whole of France, showing*

- *the road network*
- *the width, alignment, profile and surface of all roads from motorways to footpaths*
- *emergency telephones.*

These maps are a must for all drivers.

MARCIGNY

Michelin map 🔢 north of fold 7 or 🔢 fold 48 - Local map p 63

The charming little town with its old houses occupies an attractive site on the western slopes of the Brionnais not far from the Loire.

SIGHTS

⊘**Mill Tower Museum (Tour du Moulin).** – The fine 15C mill, once the property of a Benedictine priory, has unusual decoration of cannon balls on the wall and a magnificent **timberwork roof★** *(top floor)*. The **museum,** devoted to local history, displays ancient pottery, Italian majolica and interesting 12C-17C sculptures; an apothecary's shop with 113 Nevers drug-jars aligned on the shelves; two 16C Nevers pottery sweetmeat dishes by Bernard Palissy.

Old houses (Maisons anciennes). – There are half-timbered houses near the church and an imposing 18C mansion between Place du Cours and Place Reverchon.

EXCURSION

⊘**St-Martin-du-Lac Carriage Museum.** – *2km - 1 1/4 miles south.* The museum, near Château de la Garde, displays late-18C and 19C carriages and harnesses.

MATOUR

Pop 1 231

Michelin map 🔢 south of fold 18 or 🔢 fold 38

Matour lies on the borders of Mâconnais, the Charollais and the Beaujolais near the source of the Grosne surrounded by wooded mountains. Fields of crops occupy the lower slopes. The peaks are covered with forest, partly composed of pine trees, but they nevertheless provide extensive views.

EXCURSIONS

St-Cyr Mountain (Montagne de St-Cyr). – *7km - 4 miles northwest by the D 211; after 4km - 2 1/2 miles turn left.* A path to the right leads up to the viewing table on the summit (771m - 2530ft): fine **panorama** of the Charollais Mountains.

Pezanin Arboretum. – *9km - 6 miles north by the D 987 going east and after 4km - 2 miles by the D 95 going northwest.* The arboretum (20ha - 49 acres) which was planted between 1903 and 1923 in an attractive setting around a fine stretch of water, contains trees and bushes from all over the world - about 400 species of deciduous and evergreen trees.

MONTARGIS

Pop 17 629

Michelin map 🔢 south of fold 12 or 🔢 fold 8
Conurbation plan in the Michelin Red Guide France

Montargis, the chief town of the Gâtinais, a region known for shooting and fishing, is dominated by its château which is now occupied by a school. The pleasant town stands on the edge of a forest (4 000ha - 9 884 acres) at the junction of three canals – the Briare, the Loing and the Orléans – and at the confluence of three rivers. The main river, the Loing, widens out into **Les Closiers Lake** (water-sports centre).

Confectionery and Canine Skill. – Montargis has two claims to fame: the invention of **pralines,** grilled almonds with a sugar coating, which were first produced in the 17C by the Duke of Plessis-Praslin's cook and the medieval legend of a dog which by identifying its master's murderer was instrumental in the criminal's execution.

MONTARGIS

Dorée (R.)
République (Pl. de la)... 36

Ancien-Palais (R.)....... 3
Baudin (Bd.)............. 4
Belles-Manières (Bd).... 5
Bon-Guillaume (R.)...... 6
Chaussée (R. de la).... 10
Cormenin (R.)........... 12
Fg d'Orléans (R. du).... 18
Ferry (Pl. Jules)........ 20
Laforge (R. R.)......... 23
Mirabeau (Pl.)........... 27
Moulin-à-Tan (R. du).... 28
Pêcherie (R. de la).... 30
Poterne (R. de la).... 32
Pougin-de-
    Maisonneuve (R.)..... 33
Tellier (R. R.) 39
Vaublanc (R. de)....... 41
18-Juin-1940 (Pl. du).... 45

*Use Michelin
Maps with
your Michelin Guide*

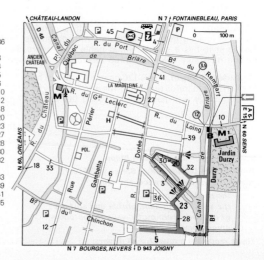

SIGHTS

The canals. – *Round tour of about 1 hour.* The old part of Montargis is criss-crossed by waterways – the Briare Canal, smaller canals and branches of the rivers – which are spanned by 127 road and foot bridges.

Take the Boulevard Durzy from the bridge which is level with the Girodet Museum.

Briare Canal. – The sight of barges and locks filling and emptying attracts anyone out for a stroll. The canal, which was built in 1642 to link the Loing to the Loire (*commemorative plaque – B*) skirts the town to the north and east; the water courses which embellish the old part of the town were used in the past to regulate the Loire which was always liable to burst its banks.

Montargis. – Canal

Boulevard Durzy. – Shaded by plane trees the boulevard is bordered on one side by the Briare Canal and on the other by the Durzy Garden. At the southern end is an elegant metal hump-back footbridge over the canal. From this footbridge there is an attractive view of two locks.

Cross the canal by the bridge and carry straight on.

Boulevard Belles-Manières (5). – The boulevard runs parallel to a narrow canal with footbridges giving access to the houses, built on the foundations of the rampart towers.

From the east end of Boulevard Belles-Manières turn left into Rue du Moulin-à-Tan; leave Place de la République on the left and take Rue Raymond-Laforge.

Rue Raymond-Laforge (23). – The bridges over the two canals provide views of the old houses and the wash houses lining their banks and of the decorative barges, acting as large window boxes, which are tied up to the quays.

Return several yards to take Rue de l'Ancien-Palais up the finger of land.

At the end of Rue de l'Ancien-Palais turn right into a vennel which is prolonged by a bridge offering a perspective along the second canal.

Turn right again into Rue de la Pêcherie.

The half-timbered houses in this district have been restored. From Place Jules-Ferry Rue Raymond-Tellier leads to a bridge providing another **canal landscape** which stretches as far as the Briare Canal.

Turn around. Turn left into Rue de la Poterne and take the bridge over the Briare Canal to reach the Boulevard Durzy.

⊙**Girodet Museum (M¹).** – The building, Hôtel Durzy, was designed in the 19C as a museum. It is surrounded by a charming garden, planted at the same time, which contains an arcade from a 13C building belonging to the Templars.
The museum is devoted to the painter, **Anne-Louis Girodet** (1767-1824), a native of Montargis, who was a pupil of David and a leading light of both neo-classicism and romanticism. There is also an important collection of work by the romantic sculptor, Henry de Triqueti (1804-74) who designed the doors of the Madeleine Church in Paris. On the first floor the first gallery is hung with 15C to 18C French and Italian paintings, a St Jerome by Zurbaran and 16C and 17C Dutch and Flemish paintings.

★ **Girodet Collection.** – The square salon and the second gallery are devoted to Girodet; among his 20 works are the extraordinary *Flood* on which the painter spent four years of study, portraits of Doctor Trioson, his adopted father, of Mustapha, together with the sketch and the replica, painted by Girodet himself, of two famous canvases in the Louvre: *The Sleep of Endymion* and *The Entombment of Atala*.
The second gallery, in which one of Girodet's pupils has painted the local monuments on the ceiling, is hung with works by 19C French artists such as Bonvin, Lancrenon, Chaplin, Ribot *(The Poacher)*, Carpentier *(portrait of Girodet)*; the display case contains precious earthenware and porcelain including a 19C Sèvres service and a rare breakfast service by Dagoty (early-19C).

⊙**Gâtinais Museum (M²).** – The archaeological museum is housed in a 15C tannery. The ground floor is devoted to the Gallo-Roman sites at Sceaux-en-Gâtinais and Les Closiers where excavations uncovered a necropolis and a cult complex near a theatre. The other section contains articles from Merovingian burial sites at Grand Bezout. The first floor is devoted to prehistoric regional archaeology; it also contains a small Egyptian section (two sarcophagi, a mummy) from the Campana collection.

Michelin map 🔢 southeast of fold 7 or 🔢 fold 1

Montbard rises up the slope of a hill that impedes the course of the River Brenne; it has become an important metallurgical centre specialising in steel tubes and pipes. The memory of Buffon has obliterated that of the Counts of Montbard, who built the fortress that was to become a residence of the Dukes of Burgundy.

A GREAT SCHOLAR

Georges-Louis Leclerc de Buffon. — Born at Montbard in 1707, Buffon was the son of a counsellor of the Burgundian parliament. At a very young age he showed his passionate interest in science and went on several journeys to France, Italy, Switzerland and England in order to satisfy his desire to study nature. In 1733, when he was only 26, he entered the Academy of Science, where he succeeded the botanist, Jussieu.

His nomination to the post of Administrator of the King's Garden (Jardin du Roi) and museum, now the Jardin des Plantes, in 1739 was to be decisive in his career. Hardly had he taken over his new position than he conceived the vast plan of writing the history of nature. From then on he devoted all his energies to this gigantic task. The first three volumes of his *Histoire Naturelle (Natural History)* were published in 1749 and the other 33 volumes followed during the next forty years.

In 1752 Buffon was elected to the French Academy. The honours that were showered on him, just reward for his work and his ability, never had any effect on him. The crowned heads of all Europe and all the leading figures of his times sought his friendship and were honoured to obtain it.

Helped by the naturalist, Daubenton (1716-99), Buffon reorganised the Jardin du Roi, considerably augmenting the collections of the natural history museum.

Buffon at Montbard. — Buffon did not really care for Paris and the distractions offered him in the capital did not allow him to work as he wished. So he came back to Montbard, his real home. He set up **forges** *(see opposite)* on his estate to the northeast of Montbard which he directed himself. As lord of Montbard, he razed the central keep and the annexes of the château, keeping only the outer walls and two of the ten towers. Inside he laid out terraced gardens and planted trees of different species as well as flowers and vegetables. It was at Montbard, where he led the life he liked most, that Buffon wrote the greater part of his huge work. He died in Paris, in the Jardin du Roi, in 1788.

SIGHTS

★ **Buffon Park (Parc Buffon).** — In 1735 Buffon bought Montbard Château, which dates from before the 10C and was by then in ruins; he demolished all but two towers and the fortified wall of enclosure. The gardens which he laid out, slightly altered over the years, now form the Buffon Park. The paths and alleys provide a number of pleasant walks.

Aubespin Tower (Tour de l'Aubespin). — Buffon used its height (40m - 131ft) to conduct experiments on the wind. The gargoyles and merlons date from a 19C restoration. From the top there is a fine **view** of the town and its surroundings. The first of the three rooms contains souvenirs of local history.

St Louis Tower (Tour St-Louis). — The mother of St Bernard was born here in 1070. Buffon lowered the tower by one storey and used it as his library.

Buffon's Study (D). — It was in this small pavilion with the walls covered with 18C coloured engravings of various bird species that Buffon wrote most of his *Natural History*.

Buffon's Chapel. — Buffon was buried on 20 April 1788 in the vault of a small chapel adjoining the Church of St Ursa (St-Urse) which stands outside the old castle precinct.

MONTBARD

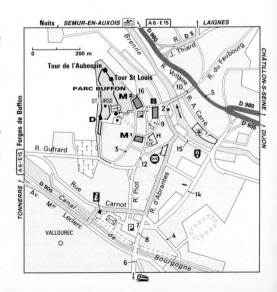

Except where otherwise stated, all recommended itineraries in towns, are designed as walks

Hôtel de Buffon (B). – Buffon built the large and comfortable mansion from which he had direct access to his gardens and his study.

⏱**Fine Arts Museum** (Musée des Beaux-Arts) (M ¹). – The museum is housed in the former chapel (1870) of the Buffon Institute. It contains a magnificent wooden triptych (Adoration of the Shepherds) by André Ménassier (1599), 19C and 20C paintings and sculptures. Three of the artists represented here are natives of Montbard: the sculptor Eugène Guillaume and the painters Chantal Queneville and Ernest Boguet. There are also works by Yves Brayer, Maurice Buffet and three sculptures by Pompon.

⏱**Old Stable Museum** (M²). – Buffon's stables now house a museum devoted to the great naturalist and to his place in the history of Montbard.

EXCURSIONS

⏱**Buffon Forge.** – *7km - 4 1/2 miles northwest.* In 1768 when Buffon, the great French naturalist, was 60 years old he built a forge for the commercial exploitation of his discoveries about iron and steel and to continue his experiments with minerals on a large scale.

His industrial complex was built on two levels: on the lower level were the production shops beside a channel containing water diverted from the River Armançon; on the upper level above the flood line were the houses and other facilities.

The **workshops** consist of three buildings separated by two water channels which supplied hydraulic energy to the bellows and trip hammers: the blast furnace was reached from the upper level by a huge internal stair which divided into two flights serving platforms where the pig iron was drawn off; next came the refinery, the forge itself, where the pig iron was recast and beaten with the trip hammer into iron bars, and the slitting mill where the bars could be reworked into semi-finished products. Further on is the basin where the raw mineral was washed before being smelted.

⏱**Château de Nuits.** – *18km - 11 miles northwest.* The castle was built in 1570 during the Wars of Religion. The attractive Renaissance façade of pediments and pilasters was formerly screened by a fortified wall. The east façade, facing Armançon (the old border between Burgundy and Champagne), has retained its austere defensive appearance. The vaulted cellars leading to the east terrace contain a kitchen with an indoor well which enabled the castle to hold out against a siege. Among the state rooms are a salon with a Renaissance chimneypiece, an 18C Venetian bedroom and a 19C dining room (neo-Baroque chimneypiece).

In this guide the length of time indicated
– for sightseeing is the average time required for a visit
for touring allows one to enjoy the views and the scenery.

MONTCEAU-LES-MINES   Pop 26 949

Michelin map 𝟞𝟿 folds 17 and 18 or 𝟤𝟦𝟥 folds 25 and 26
Town plan in the current Michelin Red Guide France

The town developed rapidly from 1856 with the working of the Blanzy coal basin. The industrial sector also includes metallurgy and heavy engineering (lifting machinery and boiler making) electrical engineering and the hosiery trade.

⏱**Fossil Museum.** – Local mining has uncovered many fossils contemporary with the formation of the coal seam 300 million years ago. Three rooms illustrate the countryside at the end of the Primary Era through the presentation of fossils of animals (amphibians, fish and crustaceans) and vegetable matter (ferns, "stick" of calamite). There is a plan of the different coal deposits in the Blanzy-Montceau basin.

Blanzy. – Pop 6 968. *3km - 2 miles northeast.* Set beside the Central Canal the town prospered with the development of coal mining and from 1860 knew a rapid expansion. In 1970 Michelin built a tyre factory in the industrial zone. As well as the smelting works, activities include plastics, plumbing and construction materials.

⏱**Men and Mining.** – The winding gear (22m - 72ft high) marks the pit-head of the St Claude shaft which was active from 1857 to 1881. It has been re-equipped to show the evolution of mining methods: lamp room; machine room (to operate the cage and the pumps); galleries (130m - 142yds) demonstrating coal cutting and coal hauling and pit props. The exhibition room explains the old mine *(20 min audiovisual presentation on the formation and exploitation of coal)*.

EXCURSION

Gourdon. – Pop 819. *9km - 6 miles southeast.*
A narrow road climbs steeply to Gourdon from where there is a good **panorama★** over Montceau-les-Mines, the Blanzy basin, Montcenis, Le Creusot and in the distance ⏱the Morvan Mountains. This small village has an 11C Romanesque **church,** with a blind triforium and clerestory and a series of interesting capitals.

★ MONTENOISON HILL

Michelin map 65 fold 14 or 238 fold 22 – 10km - 6 miles northeast of Prémery

On the top of one of the highest hills of the Nivernais region, **Butte de Montenoison** (417m - 1 368ft), there are remains of a large castle built in the 13C by Mahaut de Courtenay, Countess of Nevers. Go to the left of the chapel and climb to the Calvary erected on an old feudal mound. From this point *(viewing table)* there is a wide **panorama★** of the Morvan highlands. In clear weather one can make out the church in Lormes.

MONTRÉAL   Pop 191

Michelin map 65 fold 16 or 238 fold 24 – 12km - 7 1/2 miles northeast of Avallon

Montréal, the "Royal Mount" of Queen Brunhilda (d 613), dominates the west bank of the River Serein. The medieval township is among the most characteristic of Burgundy: the sheltering ramparts, the old houses, the church which is famous for its carved choir stalls and the vast horizon which is visible from the graveyard.

Old town. – The town is entered by the Lower Gateway (Porte d'En Bas) which has fine 13C arcades. The main street is lined by picturesque old houses (15C and 16C).

Church. – This 12C primitive-Gothic building was restored by the architect and writer, Viollet-le-Duc (1814-78). The Upper Gateway (Porte d'En Haut) which stands in front of the church serves as its belfry. The main doorway with semi-circular archivolts and cusped arch shafts and piers is surmounted by a rose window. Inside, a 12C stone gallery at the end of the nave is supported by a delicate little column.

The twenty-six **stalls★** of carved oak dating from the 16C and attributed to the Rigolley brothers of Nuits-sous-Ravières are extremely fine work. All the subjects dealt with, for the most part from the New Testament, are of equal worth. The two artisans have shown themselves having a drink during a pause in their work.

Montréal. – Altar piece in the church

A magnificient alabaster **altarpiece★** of the 15C *(damaged when it was stolen)*, which originally came from England, stands on the left of the choir. The scenes portray the life of the Virgin Mary.

Also note the 15C pulpit and lectern, a triptych and a statue of Our Lady carved in wood, and the handsome tombstones.

Panorama. – From the terrace, at the end of the cemetery behind the church, the view spreads over the whole valley of the Serein, the Auxois, Terre-Plaine and, in the distance, the mountains of the Morvan. In the plain (northeast towards Thizy) stands a large fortified farm, so typical of Burgundy.

EXCURSION

Talcy. – Pop 57. *5km - 3 miles north.* The village which occupies a sunny slope on the edge of the Talcy Plateau is dominated by a Romanesque **church;** the bricked-up doorway of the manorial chapel *(right of the entrance)* has fine Renaissance decoration.

Gourmets should look in the current **Michelin Red Guide France**
for the restaurants with stars.

Michelin map 🔟 fold 18 or 🔢 fold 26

The Charollais village stands on a bluff, on the watershed between the Loire and the Saône. It is one of the highest peaks (603m - 1 987ft) in the Saône-et-Loire *département,* where an old Celtic mid-summer custom is perpetuated when a bonfire is lit on about St John's Day (24 June) to celebrate the return of summer *(see p 180).*

SIGHTS

★★ **Panorama.** – At the entrance to the village a sharp righthand turn leads up to a TV and meteorological station. From the top of an old mill, converted into a belvedere *(telescope and viewing table),* there is an almost complete panorama: the Morvan mountains (northwest), the Le Creusot and Autun basins (north), the mountains of the Mâconnais (southeast) and Charollais (southwest).

Church. – The church, built at the end of the 12C, was formerly a priory of Cluny Abbey. A gallery surmounts the square porch. Above the doorway is a carved tympanum, now badly damaged, showing Christ in Majesty between two figures which are believed to be St Peter and St Paul. There is transverse barrel vaulting, similar to that in St Philibert in Tournus, in the nave and groined vaulting in the aisles. The transept crossing is surmounted by a dome on squinches.
From the open space beside the graveyard there is an attractive view of the many small valleys to the north.

⊙ **J Régnier Museum** (Musée J.-Régnier). – The old 15C salt warehouse (restored) now houses a collection of articles (from the neolithic to the medieval period) found in regional archaeological excavations. One room is devoted to Romanesque art.

★★ MORVAN

Michelin maps 🔟 folds 15, 16 and 17 and 🔟 folds 6, 7 and 8 or 🔢 folds 23, 24, 35 and 36 and 🔢 folds 13 and 25

The Morvan Massif is not served by any main roads but it receives a growing number of visitors who are attracted by its vast forests, its rocky escarpments, its valleys and picturesque sites; canoeists appreciate the mountain streams, fishermen line the banks of the rivers, lakes and reservoirs.
Although the Morvan is a distinct natural region between the Nivernais and Burgundy, it has never been a separate political or administrative entity; it has no historically-established borders. Only its physical characteristics distinguish it from its neighbours. From a distance it is recognisable by its vast and sombre forests; in Celtic etymology "morvan" means "black mountain" *(montagne noire).*

GEOGRAPHICAL NOTES *see also pp 10 and 12*

Lower and Upper Morvan. – The Morvan covers a quadrilateral area (70km - 43 1/2 miles long by 50km - 31 miles wide) stretching from Avallon to St-Léger-sous-Beuvray and from Corbigny to Saulieu.
Seen from the north the Morvan appears as a vast, slightly undulating plateau, which rises slowly towards the south. The northern section (maximum altitude 600m - 2 000ft) descends in terraces sloping gently into the Paris basin; this is the Lower Morvan (Bas Morvan).
It is the southern section, the Upper Morvan (Haut Morvan), south of Montsauche, which contains the higher peaks: Mount Beuvray (821m - 2 694ft), Mount Preneley (855m - 2 805ft), the Massif du Bois du Roi or Haut-Folin (901m - 2 956ft). Although the peaks do not attain very great altitudes, it is because they end suddenly above the Autun basin that the region is said to be mountainous.

Countryside of water and forest. – The heavy rainfall and the melting snow turns the smallest stream into a torrent. As the ground is composed of non-porous rock covered with a layer of granitic gravel (a sort of coarse sand), the Morvan is like a sponge full of water: the rivers – Yonne, Cure, Cousin and their tributaries – become turbulent watercourses. Dams and reservoirs (Pannesière-Chaumard, les Settons, Crescent, Chaumeçon) have been built to regulate the flow when the rivers are in spate or the water level is low, so as to supplement the output of hydro-electric power when necessary; St Agnan provides a reservoir of drinking water.
The characteristic feature of the Morvan Massif is the forest which covers a third and often half of the surface area. Gradually the beeches or oaks are being replaced by fir trees. Timber is no longer floated to Paris by water as tree trunks *(p 77)* but is now transported by lorry to nearby factories for cabinet-making and particularly charcoal production.

LIFE IN THE MORVAN

A rough and unfertile country, the Morvan has for a long time been the butt of gibes from its neighbours. In Burgundy they say: "Nothing good comes from the Morvan, neither good people nor a good wind", an unjust statement which expresses the superior attitude of the rich Burgundians towards the Morvan people, whose countryside has neither vineyards nor fertile fields. Since they could extract only small profit from the soil of their native land, the Morvan men often "came down" to the surrounding plains of Bazois or Auxois, rich lands of cattle-breeding and cultivation, while the women found work as wet-nurses.

The Morvan wet-nurses. – In the 19C in particular wet-nursing was a most profitable occupation for the Morvan women.

In the towns at this period it was not considered proper for young mothers to nurse their children and the Morvan women were excellent wet-nurses. Some went to Paris "to provide food", some stayed at home to nurse the babies entrusted to their care. Countless Parisian children spent the first months of their lives in the Morvan during this period.

Present resources. – Today the Morvan is still far from being a rich and prosperous region and its population continues to decline. Cattle-rearing on a small scale is no longer a profitable proposition. Forestry, however, is a new resource instituted since the Second World War by the planting of evergreens to provide raw material for the developing timber industries.

Another sector of commercial progress is tourism in the Avallonnais and the Morvan.

In the highest parts of the Massif, southeast of Château-Chinon, a skiing centre has been established with downhill runs (Haut-Folin – *p 125*) and cross-country routes.

The **Morvan Regional Nature Park,** created in 1970, covers the greater part of the region and contributes to its attraction to visitors.

LOWER MORVAN (LE BAS MORVAN)

A description of this northern area is given on p 121.

① From Vézelay to Château-Chinon

97km - 60 miles – about 3 1/2 hours – itinerary ① *on the local map p 124.*

This road enters the Morvan from the north and the scenery becomes hillier and more varied after Lormes. The altitude increases southwards.

★★**Vézelay.** – *Time: 1 hour. Description p 167.*

Leave Vézelay by the D 957 east towards Avallon.

Vézelay and its basilica, set high on their rocky outcrop, are still visible from St-Père.

★**St-Père.** – *Time: 1/4 hour. Description p 144.*

Take the D 958 south.

The road follows the upper Cure Valley, which becomes a wooded gorge.

Excavations at Fontaines Salées. – *Description p 145.*

★**Pierre-Perthuis.** – *Description p 136.*

Continue south on the D 958. Turn left into the D 453 and left to the dam.

Malassis Dam (Barrage de Malassis). – This small dam and hydro-electric power station on the Cure are intended to regulate the flow of water and in particular any irregularities caused by the Bois-de-Cure Power Station upstream.

Continue southeast.

After Domecy-sur-Cure, the road becomes very winding; it overlooks the enclosed river valley.

After crossing the river in St-André-en-Morvan, take the road east to Chastellux.

Chastellux Château comes into view, perched on a hillock dominating the Cure.

Chastellux-sur-Cure Château. – This château was altered in the 13C and restored in 1825 and has been the seat of the Chastellux family for over a thousand years.

The best view of the château is from the viaduct which carries the D 944 across the Cure. The building clings to a rocky slope amidst much greenery, overlooking the wooded gorge.

A track (left) descends steeply, affording views of the Crescent Dam and Reservoir, in a setting of lush meadows and wooded hillsides.

Crescent Dam (Barrage du Crescent). – Built between 1930 and 1933 this dam impounds the Cure downstream from its junction with the Chalaux. By its sheer mass the dam retains the accumulated waters flowing from the Cure and the Chalaux. It has a maximum height of 37m - 122ft and a total length of 330m - 1 083ft.

The reservoir of water (14 million m^3 - 494 million cu ft) is used by the Bois-de-Cure power station to generate electricity and helps to regulate the flow of the Seine.

Drive south for 13.5km - 8 miles to Lormes.

Lormes. – *Description p 109.*

South of Lormes turn left into the D 17.

Ouroux-en-Morvan. – *Description p 73.*

After 1.5km - 1 mile turn right into the D 12 in the direction of Chaumard.

The last mile or so of this downhill run towards the Pannesière Reservoir provides superb bird's-eye views of this stretch of water.

Before Chaumard, turn sharp right into the D 303, which runs along the bank of the reservoir and across the dam. Turn left into the D 944 and left again into the D 161 which leads to the reservoir.

★**Pannesière-Chaumard Dam** (Barrage de Pannesière-Chaumard). – *Description p 132.*

Take the road south along the west shore of the lake to Château-Chinon.

★**Château-Chinon.** – *Description p 72.*

② From Château-Chinon to Saulieu

59km - 37 miles – about 3 hours – itinerary ② on the local map p 124.

The road affords charming views over Les Settons Reservoir and the upper valley of the Cure.

★ **Château-Chinon.** – *Description p 72.*

> *Leave Château-Chinon by the D 944; turn right into the D 37.*

After a bridge over the Yonne, you will see **Corancy** on the left, clinging to its hillside. The winding road follows the small valleys at mid-slope level.

> *North of Planchez turn right to Les Settons Reservoir.*

★ **Les Settons Reservoir** (Lac des Settons). – *Description p 156.*

After crossing the River Cure the road (D 501) follows the east shore of the reservoir. After turning north the road (D 193) climbs, offering pretty views over the reservoir and its wooded islands, to the charming resort of Les Settons which overlooks the reservoir and the dam.

Montsauche-les-Settons. – Pop 746. This village is the highest resort (650m - 2 133ft) in the massif. The village stands at the centre of the Morvan Regional Nature Park. Like Planchez, this township was rebuilt following almost total destruction in 1944.

> *Take the D 977bis northeast.*

The road descends rapidly into the Cure valley and crosses the river just before Gouloux.

Gouloux Leap (Saut de Gouloux). – *Access by a path (right) from the first bend in the road after the bridge over the Cure. 1/4 hour on foot Rtn.* Just upstream from its confluence with the Cure, the Caillot flows over an attractive waterfall.

The road continues east through the forest and across a plateau, dotted with woods and pools, before reaching Saulieu, on the eastern edge of the Morvan.

★ **Saulieu.** – *Time: 1/2 hour. Description p 148.*

③ From Saulieu to Avallon

55km - 34 miles – about 2 1/2 hours – itinerary ③ on the local map p 124

The proposed route between Saulieu and Avallon, both small towns situated on the borders of the Morvan, enters the massif through vast forests in picturesque scenery.

★ **Saulieu.** – *Time: 1/2 hour. Description p 148.*

> *From Saulieu take the D 977bis west; turn right into the D 26ᴬ to Dun-les-Places.*

The road crosses a plateau dotted with woods and pools and then wooded countryside.

Breuil-Chenue Forest. – West of Les Fourches *(2km - 1 mile)* a track (right) leads to the information centre in a former forestry lodge. Nearby there is a pen containing fallow deer with observation posts from which to view the animals. A nature trail *(1 hour)* and a forest trail lead to a fine beech wood.

Dun-les-Places. – Pop 528. North of the village *(access by the minor road and a path to the camp site)* stands a calvary (alt 590m - 1 936ft); the road provides good views of the Morvan peaks.

> *Take the picturesque road north through Le Vieux-Dun. After crossing the River Cure turn right into a forest track.*

La Pérouse Rock (Rocher de la Pérouse). – *From the parking place a steep footpath climbs to the rocky summit (200m - 656ft); 1/2 hour on foot Rtn.*

From the top there is an interesting **view** over the isolated Cure Valley and the rounded summits of the massif.

> *Continue along the forest track; turn right then left into the D 10 to Quarré-les-Tombes.*

Quarré-les-Tombes. – *Description p 139.*

Beyond Marrault, Avallon comes into view.

After passing through wooded country the road (D 944) runs parallel with the Cousin into Avallon, a picturesque town built on a rock spur.

★ **Avallon.** – *Time: 1/2 hour. Description p 48.*

TERNIN VALLEY (VALLÉE DU TERNIN)

④ From Saulieu to Autun

45km - 28 miles – about 1 hour – itinerary ④ on the local map p 125

Picturesque drive up the valley.

★ **Saulieu.** – *Time: 1/2 hour. Description p 148.*

> *Leave Saulieu by the D 26 going southwest.*

The road climbs steeply and crosses a plateau before following the **Ternin Valley.** There is an attractive view (left) of the water held back by the **Chamboux Dam** (completed in 1985). The river winds between small green hills with wooded summits.

South of Alligny-en-Morvan (D 20) the valley narrows but widens out again as the road (D 980) approaches Chissey-en-Morvan, the only place of any size, apart from Lucenay-l'Évêque.

★★ **Autun.** – *Time: 1/2 hour. Description p 39.*

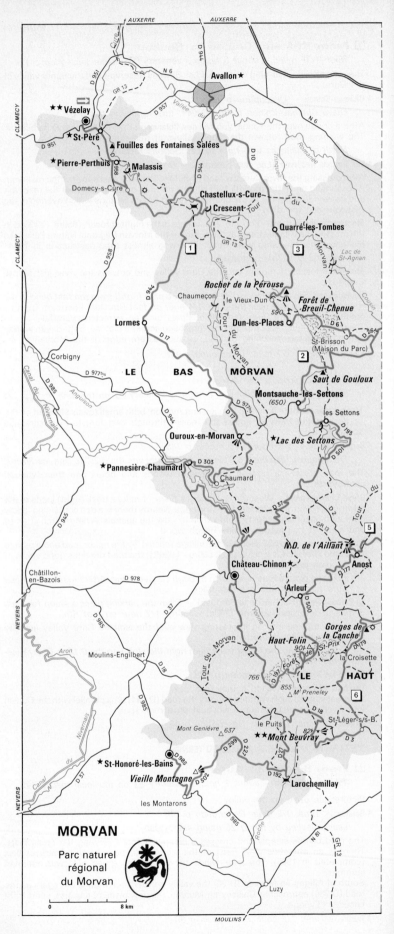

MORVAN

Parc naturel
régional
du Morvan

0   8 km

UPPER MORVAN
(LE HAUT MORVAN)

A description of this southern region is given on p 121.

5 From Château-Chinon to Autun

84km - 52 miles — about 2 1/4 hours — itinerary 5 on the local map, left

This drive crosses several forested massifs and offers far-reaching views.

★ **Château-Chinon.** – *Description p 72.*

Leave Château-Chinon by the D 27 going south.

A view opens out towards the west of a landscape of meadows, arable fields and woods. The road then rises steeply before entering **La Gravelle Forest.**

This is the threshold between the drainage basins of the Seine (Yonne to the east) and the Loire (Aron and its tributaries to the west).

At one point quite near to the summit (766m - 2513ft) there is a view to the right of bleak broom-covered moorland. The road then leaves the forest. Another good panorama opens out southwards over a small dam nestling at the bottom of a green hollow dominated by the wooded crests which mark the limit of the Morvan.

Turn left into the D 197; turn right into the forest track (steep gradient 16% - 1:6) which passes through the state forest of St-Prix.

Haut-Folin. – The slopes of this peak have been developed for skiing by the French Alpine Club.

Turn left into the Bois-du-Roi forest track and left again into the Haut-Folin forest track.

The Haut-Folin (901m - 2956ft), the highest peak in the Morvan, is crowned by a telecommunications mast.

The Bois-du-Roi forest track continues west through the **St-Prix Forest,** a magnificent stand of spruce and fir trees with immense trunks.

Turn left into the D 500 to Arleuf.

Arleuf. – *Description p 73.*

East of Arleuf turn left into the D 177; in Bussy take the D 88 to Anost.

Anost. – Pop 848. Set in a pleasant and picturesque spot, Anost offers the tourist the choice of numerous walks, especially in the forests (signposted forest trails).

Notre-Dame de l'Aillant. – *Access by the D 2 north and 1/4 hour on foot Rtn.* From beside the statue there is a semicircular **panorama★** over the Anost Basin and beyond the hills of the Autun depression.

Further north (D 2) are wild boar in an enclosure. Northeast of Anost the winding road (D 88) affords views of the hills and their wooded crests.

Cussy-en-Morvan. – Pop 505. This small village is curiously built on a hillside in an attractive beauty spot. The **church** has an interesting statue of the Virgin and Child dating from the 15C.

Continue on the D 88 which descends steeply; in Mortaise turn right into the D 980.

Between Lucenay-l'Évêque and Reclesne the downhill drive affords views of Autun surrounded by an arc of wooded hills.

★★ **Autun.** – *Time: 1/2 hour. Description p 39.*

⑥ From St-Honoré-les-Bains to Autun

79km - 49 miles – about 2 hours – itinerary ⑥ *on the local map p 124*

This drive through the highest part of the Morvan is both varied and picturesque. After Les Montarons the route follows a succession of picturesque local roads and passes the Vieille Montagne and the foot of Mount Genièvre.

★ **St-Honoré-les-Bains.** – *Description p 142.*

Take the D 985 south; in Les Montarons turn left into the D 502.

Vieille Montagne. – *Car park. 1/2 hour on foot Rtn.* From the clearing a path leads to the belvedere in its pleasant setting; there is an extensive view, partly blocked by trees, of Mount Beuvray and La Gravelle Forest.
Between Le Niret and Sanglier the road (D 299) skirts the foot of Mount Genièvre.

Turn right into the D 227, then left into the D 192 and right into the D 27.

Larochemillay Château comes into view perched high on its rocky site.

Larochemillay. – Pop 417. This 18C **château** replaced an earlier feudal fortress. From its remarkable site the château dominates the Roche Valley.

Take the D 27 north; in Le Puits turn right into the D 18; after 5km - 3miles turn right into a one-way road with very steep gradients (20% - 1:5) to Mount Beuvray.

★★ **Mount Beuvray.** – *Description p 55.*

Continue east to St-Léger; take the D 179 north.

La Canche Gorge (Gorges de la Canche). – The road follows the gorge along the side of a hill in a wild landscape of rocks and trees. There is a fine viewpoint in a bend to the left *(partly screened by trees).*
At the bottom of the gorge can be seen the white building of La Canche hydro-electric power station.

Turn right into the D 978 to Autun.

★★ **Autun.** – *Time: 1/2 hour. Description p 39.*

MOULINS-ENGILBERT   Pop 1732

Michelin map 🔢 fold 6 or 🔢🔢🔢 fold 35 – Local map p 124

Moulins-Engilbert on the borders of the Bazois and the Morvan is one of the main centres of the Nivernais; it lies at the foot of its old castle. There is a happy harmony between the roofs and turrets grouped about the slate spire of the Gothic church tower.
The town is well-known for its Charollais cattle fairs which traditionally took place on the first Tuesday of the month. Nowadays every Tuesday brings the bustle of the electronic auction, the latest way of selling cattle: the cattle are herded into the ring; each seat is equipped with a button which the buyer presses to register a bid; a panel shows the weight of each animal, its lot number and the progress of the bidding which is anonymous.

Commagny. – *2.5km - 1 1/2 miles southwest by the road towards Decize; at the top of the hill turn left into the steep climb to the priory.*

⊙ The former Benedictine **Priory** is attractively situated above the Bazois meadows. The apse of the small Romanesque church is decorated with five arcades, alternately open and blind; the decor resembles Lombard arcading in which tall pilasters rise to a frieze of small arches.
Above the small graveyard rises the well-preserved façade of the 15C prior's lodging, flanked by a belfry and a high round tower. There is a fine view of the chevet of the church from the entrance to the property *(walk round by the foot of the tower).*

GREEN TOURIST GUIDES

Architecture
Fine Art
History
Geography
Picturesque scenery
Touring programmes
Town and site plans

Guides for the holidays

Michelin map 🔢🔢 folds 3 and 4 or 🔢🔢🔢 fold 33
Plan of the built-up area in the current Michelin Red Guide France

Situated a few miles from the confluence of the Loire and the Allier, Nevers is the capital of the Nivernais region and the town of fine pottery.
From the great bridge of reddish-brown sandstone that spans the river Loire, there is an overall view of the old town, set in terraces on the side of a hill and dominated by the high square tower of the cathedral and the graceful silhouette of the ducal palace.

Julius Caesar checked. – In 52 BC, before undertaking the siege of Gergovie, Caesar made the fortified town into an important food and forage depot for his army. Noviodunum Aeduorum, generally considered to have been the Roman name for Nevers, was situated on the borders of the territory of the Aedui tribe. On hearing the news of his check before Gergovie, the Aedui immediately attacked Noviodunum and destroyed it by fire, thus imperilling Caesar's whole position in Gaul.

Pottery and spun glass. – Luigi di Gonzaga, the Duke of Mantua's third son who became Duke of Nevers in 1565, brought artists and artisans from Italy.
He developed the glass industry as well as the art of enamelling, which became very fashionable. The town's products – spun glass was generally used in the composition of religious scenes – were sent by boat on the Loire to Orléans and Angers. Luigi di Gonzaga introduced artistic earthenware in Nevers between 1575 and 1585. The three Italian brothers Conrade, "master potters in white and other colours", taught their art to a group of local artisans. Little by little, the shape, the colours and the decorative motifs, which at first reproduced only the Italian models and methods, evolved into a very distinctive local style. About 1650 the pottery industry was at its height – with twelve workshops and 1 800 workers.
⏱The Revolution of 1789 dealt the industry a grave blow. Today, three **workshops,** two of them employing artisan craftsmen, maintain the reputation of this traditional craft.

The parrot "Vert-Vert". – The history of the parrot is told in a piece of light verse written by J-B Gresset in 1733.
The famous parrot once lived with the Visitandines in Nevers, coddled and spoiled but impeccably educated. When the Visitandine nuns at Nantes heard of the prodigious reputation of this marvellous parrot, they begged their sisters at Nevers to let them have him for a few days. The nuns at Nevers were reluctant but finally they agreed. Vert-Vert went off for his visit to Nantes but during his voyage in the river boat the Loire rivermen and some Dragoons taught him a vocabulary considerably less virtuous than that he had learned with the nuns:

> "For these Dragoons were a godless lot,
> Who spoke the tongue of the lowest sot,
> ... Soon for curses and oaths he did not want
> And could out-swear a devil in a holy font."

The nuns in Nantes were horrified at his lurid maledictions; Satan's myrmidon was quickly sent back to Nevers. Brought before the convent's Council of Order, Vert-Vert was condemned to a period of fasting, solitude and, worst of all, to silence. After honourably serving his sentence, Vert-Vert returned to favour once again among the nuns of Nevers but, as in the past, he was spoiled and he died of over-indulgence:

> "Stuffed with sugar and mulled with wine,
> Vert-Vert, gorging a pile of sweets,
> Changed his rosy life for a coffin of pine."

OLD TOWN *time: 1 1/2 hours*

Start from the Porte du Croux and follow the itinerary shown on the plan.

★**Le Croux Gate (Porte du Croux)** (Z). – This handsome square tower with machicolations and corbelled turrets, topped by a high roof, is one of the last remnants of the town's fortifications. It was built in 1393, at the time when the fortifications, set up two centuries earlier by Pierre de Courtenay, were being enlarged.

⏱The tower houses the **Nivernais Archaeological Museum** which contains ancient sculptures (Greek and Roman marbles) and a large collection of Romanesque sculptures.

> *Take Rue de la Porte-du-Croux then turn right into Rue St-Genest.*

Nevers Museum. – Nevers earthenware plate
(late 17C - early 18C)

⊙ **Municipal Museum** (Z M¹). – The museum, which is housed in the buildings of an old abbey, has a fine collection of **Nevers pottery★** including pieces in the Italian, Persian, Chinese and Nivernais traditions. Among the polychrome and monochrome earthenware there is a statue (1636) of the Virgin with an Apple and a Nevers blue dish depicting Venus and Mercury.

Other pieces include delicate enamels and spun glass and sculptures by Jean Baffier.

Return to the crossroads and turn right into Rue des Jacobins.

★ **St-Cyr-et-Ste-Julitte Cathedral** (Z B). – This vast basilica, displaying all the
⊙ architectural styles from the 10C to the 16C side by side, was consecrated in 1331 before being completed and then altered several times. The plan is characterised by two apses at opposite ends of the nave: Romanesque to the west and Gothic to the east. This arrangement, which was common in the Carolingian period and is to be found in some cathedrals on the banks of the Rhine, notably at Speyer, Worms and Mainz, is rare in France.

Exterior. – Walk round the building which bristles with buttresses, pillars, flying buttresses and pinnacles to see the sequence of the different styles and to admire the square tower (52m - 171ft high) standing against the south arm of the transept. The tower is flanked by polygonal buttresses; the lower storey is 14C, and the other two, richly decorated with niches, statues and arcades, are 16C.

Interior. – The most striking feature is the sheer size of the nave with its triforium and clerestory and the choir encircled by the ambulatory.

The Romanesque apse, named after St Julitta, raised by thirteen steps and with semi-domed vaulting, is decorated with a very indistinct 12C fresco representing Christ surrounded by the symbols of the Evangelists. The 13C nave is off-centre. The 16C clock has a jack o' the clock. Statuettes decorate the base of the triforium columns.

★ **Ducal Palace** (Palais Ducal) (Z). – The former home of the Dukes of Nevers was begun in the second half of the 15C by Jean de Clamecy, Count of Nevers, who was eager to move out of his old fortress which stood on the site of the present Town Hall. The palace was completed at the end of the 16C by the Clèves and Gonzagas. It is a most beautiful example of civil Renaissance architecture. The great round towers at the rear give on to a courtyard that overlooks Rue des Ouches. The ochre façade is surmounted by a slate roof and flanked by twin turrets; the beautiful canted tower in the centre rising to a small belfry contains the grand staircase; a most graceful effect is created by the placing of the windows which follow the spiralling of the stairs. The modern low-reliefs recall the legend of the Knight of the Swan *(Chevalier au Cygne)*, an ancestor of the house of Clèves, who inspired the tale of Lohengrin. The dormer windows are flanked by caryatids and the chimneys resemble organ pipes. On the left turret a plaque recalls that several princesses of the Nivernais became Queens of Poland.

Cross Place de la République in front of the Ducal Palace.

Montée des Princes (Z N). – From the terraced garden beyond the Palace Yard there is a good view of the Loire.

Turn left into Quai de Mantoue then Rue du Commerce.

Belfry (Y F). – The vast 15C building, which is dominated by a pointed belltower, once housed the covered markets and the council chamber.

Follow Rue du Commerce; turn right into Place Guy-Coquille; turn left into Rue St-Étienne.

★ **St Stephen** (St-Étienne) (Y D). – This beautiful Romanesque church, which once belonged to a priory of Cluny, has remarkable purity of style and homogeneity. It was built from 1063 to 1097, at the instance of Guillaume I, Count of Nevers.

The chevet, best seen from Rue du Charnier, has a magnificent tiered arrangement of apse and apsidals. The transept tower, of which only the base remains, was destroyed together with the two towers surmounting the façade, at the time of the French Revolution.

The façade is sober. A line of brackets indicate the former existence of a porch. Apart from the capitals in the ambulatory, the interior is devoid of sculpture but its attraction lies in its fine proportions and the golden colour of the stone. The six bays of the nave are covered by barrel vaulting with transverse arches; there is groined vaulting in the aisles. A Romanesque altar stands in the chancel (restored). The transept crossing is covered by a dome on squinches. The row of windows beneath the vault is of impressive boldness and the two galleries of the triforium open to the nave are also remarkable.

Return south; turn right into Rue Francs-Bourgeois and then Rue des Ardilliers.

Paris Gate (Y E). – This triumphal arch was built in the 18C to commemorate the victory of Fontenoy; mediocre verses by Voltaire in praise of Louis XV are engraved on it.

North of the gate turn left into Rue du Rempart, left again into Rue Hoche and finally right into Rue St-Martin.

St Mary's Chapel (St-Marie) (Y). – This is the former chapel, now deconsecrated, of the 7th convent of the Visitandines founded in France. At the request of the bishop of Nevers, Mademoiselle de Bréchard, a lady of the Nivernais, who had become a nun of the Visitation and Mother Superior of the convent of Moulins, was sent by St Francis of Sales to found this convent.

The façade, of Louis XIII style, is covered with Italian-type ornamentation: niches, entablatures, columns and pilasters.

Ramparts Promenade (Z). – A well-conserved section of the town walls, built by Pierre de Courtenay in the 12C, stretches from Le Croux Gate southwards to the Loire. Several of the original towers (Tours du Hâvre, St-Révérien and Gogin) are still standing. The ramparts are bordered to the west by gardens.

NEVERS

ADDITIONAL SIGHTS

⊘ **Convent of St-Gildard** (Y). – *Pilgrimage from April to October.* It was this convent that **Bernadette Soubirous**, acclaimed at Lourdes for her many visitations, entered in 1866. She died there in 1879 and was canonised in 1933. Her embalmed body rests in a glass shrine in the chapel of the convent which is the mother house of the Sisters of Charity and Christian Instruction of Nevers.

⊘ A small **museum** retraces the saint's life and work and displays some of her personal effects. The fine low-relief portraying scenes from the life of the Virgin originally belonged to the church of St-Gildard.

⊘ **Ste-Bernadette-du-Banlay.** – *Take Avenue Colbert* (Y) *and then Boulevard de-Lattre-de-Tassigny.* From the outside this church (1966) has all the massive appearance of a blockhouse. Inside however the well-lit nave has a great feeling of spaciousness.

EXCURSIONS

Marzy. – Pop 2 792. *5.5km - 3 miles west by the D 131.* This village has an interesting 12C Romanesque church, surmounted by a graceful, two-storey belfry; it contains 17C and 18C statues. Return to Nevers by the road that runs alongside the river. There is a good view of the **Bec d'Allier**, where the Loire and Allier meet.

The countryside between the Loire and the Allier. – *Round tour of 82km - 51 miles – about 4 hours.* In the upper part of its course the fast-flowing Allier makes straight for the Loire. The calm of this green, hedgerow countryside is disturbed only by the sound of traffic on the busy N 7. The area is bordered by the Loire, the Allier and the Forest of Perray in the south. Towns are rare and fine mansions are hidden on their estates, where the main activity is the large-scale fattening of white Charollais cattle. During the Hundred Years War the area was the theatre for the exploits of the adventurer, Perrinet-Gressard *(p 70)*.

Leave Nevers by the N 7 going south. After 14km - 9 miles turn left in the direction of the Magny-Cours Racing Circuit.

⊘ **Magny-Cours Racing Circuit.** – *Follow the signs.* Between Magny-Cours and St-Parize-le-Châtel this circuit has a school for racing drivers and is the venue for international racing events and, more recently, of Formula 1 and motorcycle Grand Prix competitions.

St-Parize-le-Châtel. – Pop 982. This community, with its gaseous waters, was already a flourishing village in Gallo-Roman times. The waters are still sought after (source to the east of the town). The church, built on a terrace, dominates the countryside and has a remarkable 12C crypt. The historiated capitals can be interpreted variously – some say they are instrument-playing animals, acrobats and fantastic figures illustrating the Deadly Sins. The other capitals have pagan motifs (chimaera or emblems), foliage and rosettes. There is an interesting Carolingian sarcophagus.

Take the D 203 and the D 978^A southwest for 11km - 7 miles.

St-Pierre-le-Moûtier. – *Description p 145.*

Take N 7 south; after 8km - 5 miles turn left; in Chantenay-St-Imbert take D 522 east.

Le Perray Forest. – The dense woodland (2 200ha - 5 436 acres) is relieved by several pools. The Rond du Perray is a vast clearing among the trees from which several woodland rides radiate deep into the forest. Cut timber is stacked round the outskirts of the forest. Le Perray Massif continues west through Chabet Forest.

North of the forest turn right into the D 978ᴬ; in Les Raguet turn left into the D 13 through Luthenay-Uxeloup.

North of Luthenay on the east side of the valley stands **Rozemont Castle** (13C), one of the lairs of Perrinet-Gressard.

Continue on the D 13 downhill and north beside the river.

⊙**Chevenon.** – Pop 646. The **castle** occupies a strategic site controlling the valley. The pink colour of the stonework softens the massive and forbidding aspect of this tall building. The main wing flanked by two great round towers formerly had a moat. The castle was built in the 14C in the reign of Charles V by Guillaume de Chevenon, Governor of Vincennes.

Return to Nevers by the D 13.

The road follows the Loire Lateral Canal whose calm waters reflect the peaceful scenery. The river is hidden by an alluvial bank.

NOLAY   Pop 1 582

Michelin map 🗺 fold 9 or 🗺 folds 26 and 27 – 15km - 9 miles northwest of Chagny

Nolay, on the river Cosanne, is the home town of **Lazare Carnot** (1753-1823), "organiser of the victory" at the time of the Convention. His statue stands before the house where he was born, which has remained in the Carnot family.

Overall view. – There is a good general view of Nolay and the valley of the Dheune from the northern approach to the town *(2.5km - 1 1/2 miles by the D 33).*

Old covered market (Vieilles halles). – This was built in the 14C and the timber roof is covered by limestone slabs.

Church. – This 15C building, altered in the 17C and restored following a fire, is surmounted by a curious stone belfry. The 16C jack o' the clock has been restored. Inside there are several statues including a 14C one of St James *(first chapel on the right)* and a 15C one of St Benedict *(ambulatory).*

EXCURSIONS

★ **La Rochepot.** – *5km - 3 miles east of Nolay by the D 973.* The road goes through a smiling undulating countryside. *Description of La Rochepot p 140.*

La Tournée Valley. – *5km - 3 miles north on the Vauchignon road which is narrow and winding; 1/2 hour Rtn on foot.*

On the right rise the **cliffs of Cormot** (les falaises de Cormot), excellent terrain for rock climbing; the "Dame de Paris" is the most precipitous point.

On leaving Vauchignon turn left into a road which ends after 1.5km - 1 mile.

The road ends by a bridge at the foot of high rock walls.

A footpath (left) climbs through trees to a cave, a beauty spot, where the River Cosanne descends in a waterfall on to pink granite rocks.

Another footpath leads across the fields to a rock circus known as the World's End **(Cirque du Bout du Monde);** in this remarkable **setting★** of limestone peaks a waterfall (28m - 92ft) descends in a thin stream.

NOYERS   Pop 837

Michelin map 🗺 fold 6 or 🗺 fold 12

⊙Noyers (pronounced Noyaire) is a picturesque little town held in the bend of the river Serein and surrounded by its ramparts and sixteen round towers. The streets with names recalling the past are lined with old half-timbered or gable-ended houses, which lend the town a certain charm.

Cellars with access directly from the street remind us that this is vineyard country.

TOUR time: *3/4 hour*

Place de l'Hôtel-de-Ville. – Around the square there is a mixture of 14C-15C half-timbered houses and others with arcades. The town hall has a 17C façade with a curvilinear pediment, pilasters and balconies of wrought ironwork.

Take Rue du Marché-au-Blé which leads to the square of the same name.

Cornmarket (Place du Marché-au-Blé). – This triangular-shaped square is overlooked by more old houses. Note in particular the one on the right with arcades and a gable end.

The Rue de l'Église leads to the church and the museum.

Notre-Dame Church. – This vast late-15C church has a Renaissance west front flanked by a square tower with gargoyles. Buttresses shoulder the impressive chevet. Note on the north side the curious sculpture of a recumbent effigy.

⊘**Museum** (Musée). – Collection of naive paintings.

>*Return to Place du Marché-au-Blé then turn left under the arcade into Rue du Poids-du-Roy.*

Rue du Poids-du-Roy. – In this picturesque alley note on the left just after the arcade a charming 15C half-timbered house with carved corner posts. The Rue du Poids-du-Roy ends in a covered passageway which opens on to the tiny **Place de la Petite-Étape-aux-Vins** bordered by half-timbered houses. The house on the left is adorned with three naive statues of saints.

The main street (left), **Rue de la Petite-Étape-aux-Vins,** also lined with old houses, leads to Place du Grenier-à-Sel. At the far end of this square in **Rue de la Madeleine** there is a Renaissance house (left) with a Greek inscription.

>*Return to Place du Grenier-à-Sel.*

Passage Hardy (left) leads to the riverside promenade shaded by plane trees. The promenade along the bank of the Serein passes the seven round towers which were once part of the town's defensive system.

Enter by the square fortified gateway, Porte Peinte, and follow Rue Porte Peinte, passing on the left a large half-timbered house, to reach Place de l'Hôtel-de-Ville.

NUITS-ST-GEORGES   Pop 5461

Michelin map 🖼 southwest of fold 20 or 🖼 fold 16 – Local map p 86

This friendly and attractive little town is the centre of the vineyards to which it has given its name *(p 84)*. It is proud of the famous wines which have a world-wide reputation.

The fame of the wines of Nuits goes back to Louis XIV. When the royal doctor, Fagon, advised the king to take some glasses of Nuits and Romanée with each meal as a tonic, the whole court wanted to taste it.

Among the most famous of the wines Nuits St-Georges, produced from the vineyards since the year 1000, is the best known.

St Symphorien. – This vast church was built at the end of the 13C although it is pure Romanesque in style. The flat chevet is pierced by a large rose window and three windows flanked by small columns and sculptures. A massive belfry surmounts the transept crossing.

The lofty nave, which is covered with groined vaulting, contains an 18C organ loft and a rare late-16C wooden cylinder decorated with open-work carving to enclose a spiral staircase. Traces of frescoes (including the martyrdom of St Christine) and 16C inscriptions are visible in the aisles.

Other buildings. – There are two fine 17C edifices: the belfry of the former Town Hall and the St-Laurent Hospital. The present Town Hall is 18C. The modern church of Notre-Dame has stained glass (1957) by J J Borghetto.

⊘**Archaeological Museum** (Musée archéologique). – The museum contains Gallo-Roman and Merovingian finds from the archaeological excavations at les Bolards, near Nuits-St-Georges.

⊘**Military Museum.** – It displays 19C and 20C French uniforms and headgear and recalls the battle of Nuits-St-Georges on 18 December 1870 when the Prussians were defeated.

EXCURSION

⊘**Cussigny Château.** – *10km - 6 miles southeast.* The Château, which was built about 1742, presents two identical façades. Following alterations in the 19C only the south wing remains.

The entrance hall contains a large Charles X billiard table and the winter garden is furnished with Louis XV, Louis XVI and Empire furniture. The gardens are designed in the formal manner and the 18C outbuildings include an attractive dovecot. The château is lit by gas lanterns.

OUCHE VALLEY

Michelin maps 🖼 folds 19 and 20 and 🖼 fold 9 or 🖼 folds 14, 15 and 16

Situated at the western limits of the countryside behind Dijon, the valley of the Ouche links up with the area of the Auxois. The valley, set between limestone plateaux, is rich green open land fit for cultivation and pastures. The Burgundy Canal follows its course from the Pont d'Ouche.

Burgundy Canal. – Completed in 1832, this 242km - 150 mile canal acts as a link between the rivers Yonne and Saône, from Laroche (altitude 84m - 276ft) to St-Jean-de-Losne (altitude 182m - 597ft).

It follows the valleys of the Armançon and the Ouche which are at right angles to each other, and reaches a height of 378m - 1240ft to cross the ridge separating the basins of the Seine and the Rhône by means of a tunnel 3333m - 3640yds long.

The Burgundy Canal is fairly busy with river shipping on the stretches between Laroche and Tonnerre, and Dijon and St-Jean-de-Losne. There are 189 locks along its course. Pleasure cruising has increased all along the canal *(p 8)*.

FROM BLIGNY TO DIJON 57km - 35 miles — about 1 1/2 hours

The road follows the green valley of the Ouche through a countryside of vales between wooded slopes strewn with rocks.

Bligny-sur-Ouche. — Pop 776. Gothic church with a Romanesque belfry.

Take the D 33 north.

South of Pont-d'Ouche the road passes under the flyover which carries the A 6 motorway across the Ouche Valley. North of the village the road runs parallel with the Burgundy Canal which is carried over the Ouche by an aqueduct. The valley widens and the bottom becomes wooded and rocky. Soon large rock outcrops appear on the left among the hillsides covered with the forest of Bouhey.

La Bussière-sur-Ouche. — Pop 180. *7km - 4 1/2 miles north of Pont d'Ouche.* The Romanesque **church** is topped by a fine slate belfry. Inside, the broken-barrel vaulting of the nave has transverse arches. The aisles have more primitive domical vaulting. There are tombs, tombstones, low-reliefs and numerous statues. In the choir 17C painted panels are surmounted by two interesting statues of St Barbara to the left and St Sebastian to the right.

The restored buildings of a 13C Cistercian abbey, in a pleasant setting, now serve as a retreat for those wishing to get away from it all.

Continue north on the D 33.

North of Auvillard the imposing ruins of Marigny Château are visible on a rocky spur *(left)*. In Ste-Marie-sur-Ouche the river is spanned by a pretty hump-back bridge *(right)*.

In Pont-de-Pany cross the river; make a detour southeast by the D 35.

Montculot Château. — This château is an elegant 18C building with a park and lakes. One of them, the source of the river Foyard, was praised by the Romantic poet Alphonse de Lamartine, who inherited this family property on the death of his uncle, Abbot de Lamartine. He wrote many of his poems at Montculot between 1801 and 1831.

From Pont-de-Pany take the D 905 east.

On the opposite side of the Burgundy Canal, the engineering works required to carry the main Paris-Dijon railway line along the limestone cliffs are visible.

In La Cude turn right into the D 10^F^.

Notre-Dame d'Étang. — *1/2 hour Rtn on foot starting from the psychotherapeutic centre.*

From the *corniche* road in front of the centre there is a good panorama of the whole valley of the Ouche.

A monument (24m - 79ft high), bearing an immense statue of the Virgin Mary, was built on the top of the hill of Étang in 1896. The miraculous statue, found in 1435, is in the church at Velars-sur-Ouche.

Take the D 10^F^ north across the canal and east to join the D 10.

Shortly before Dijon the Ouche widens to form an artificial lake.

★★★ **Dijon.** — *Time: 4 hours. Description p 91.*

★ PANNESIÈRE-CHAUMARD DAM

Michelin map 🖥 south of fold 16 or 🖥🖥🖥 folds 23 and 24 — Local maps pp 73 and 124

The Pannesière-Chaumard dam (340m - 1115ft long and 50m - 164ft high) is supported on a multiplicity of narrow arches flanked by massive concrete embankments; twelve supporting buttresses rise from the bottom of the gorge. It controls the flow of water in the Seine basin. Downstream a hydro-electric power station produces nearly 18 million kWh annually.

The reservoir (7.5km - 5 miles long), which has a capacity of 18145 million gallons, forms a glorious expanse of water in an attractive **site★** amid wooded hills. A road runs right round it and along the top of the dam, providing a **view** of the numerous inlets of the lake while the summits of the Upper Morvan (Haut Morvan) stand out against the sky.

Downstream from the principal dam (near the D 944) is a control dam (220m - 722ft long) composed of 33 slender arches. Although the turbines consume water in accordance with the demand for electricity, the control dam enables the discharged water to be returned to the Yonne at a constant rate and supplies water to the Nivernais Canal.

★★ PARAY-LE-MONIAL   Pop 11 312

Michelin map 🖥 fold 17 or 🖥🖥🖥 fold 37 — Local map p 63

Paray-le-Monial, cradle of the worship of the Sacred Heart of Jesus, is situated on the boundary between the Charollais and Brionnais regions, on the banks of the river Bourbince beside which flows the Central Canal.

The town's Romanesque basilica is a magnificent example of the architecture of Cluny.

The building materials industry, which is concentrated in the valley of the Bourbince, is represented at Paray by factories producing tiles and sandstone pavings as well as fireproof products.

Margaret-Mary Alacoque. — Although her desire to become a nun was obvious at a very early age, Margaret-Mary Alacoque, the daughter of a royal notary in Verosvres-en-Charollais, could not carry out her intention until she was 24.

On 20 June 1671 she entered the convent of the Visitation at Paray-le-Monial as a novice and two months later took the veil.

From 1673 onwards, Sister Margaret-Mary received a succession of visitations that continued up to her death. Helped by her confessor, Father Claude de la Colombière, she revealed the messages she had received – writing out the revelations that were made to her: "Here is this heart, which so loved mankind" – and advocated the worship of the Sacred Heart. She died on 17 October 1690.

Devotion to the Sacred Heart. – It was not until the beginning of the 19C, when the turmoil of the French Revolution had died down, that devotion to the Sacred Heart began to develop. In 1817 hearings began before the Vatican Tribunals which ended in 1864 with the beatification of Sister Margaret-Mary. In 1873, when the first great pilgrimage in Paray-le-Monial took place in the presence of 30 000 people, the decision was made to dedicate France to the Sacred Heart of Jesus. This event was linked to the vow made in 1870 to build a church dedicated to the Sacred Heart with money raised by national subscription; this was the basilica which now stands on the hill of Montmartre. Pilgrimages have been repeated each year since 1873. Sister Margaret-Mary was canonised in 1920.

Many religious orders have communities at Paray-le-Monial which has become one of the great centres of Christianity.

★★ BASILICA OF THE SACRED HEART
(BASILIQUE DU SACRÉ-CŒUR) *time: 1/2 hour*

On the right bank of the Bourbince, approached by a promenade flanked by flowers and weeping willows, stands the church; it was originally dedicated to the Virgin Mary but in 1875 it was raised to the level of a basilica and consecrated to the Sacred Heart.

The church was built without interruption between 1090 and 1109 under the direction of St Hugues, Abbot of Cluny, and restored in the 19C and 20C; it constitutes a contemporary model on a smaller scale of the famous Benedictine Abbey at Cluny. Only the architectural style is similar; the builders eschewed decorative splendour and large-scale design to the glory of God, in favour of abstract beauty, composed of the rhythmic combination of light and shadow, space and simplicity, which is conducive to contemplation. The rare sculptures make generous use of the geometric motifs found in Islamic art; its enchanting perfection was probably discovered by St Hugues during two visits to Spain.

From the bridge spanning the Bourbince there is a fine view of the basilica; its golden stone is used in many of the churches in the neighbouring Brionnais *(p 62)*.

Exterior. – The façace is of a great simplicity: two square towers surmount the narthex. Supported at the corners by powerful buttresses, the towers have four storeys of windows, of which the first tier lights the narthex.

The right-hand tower, built in the early 11C, has sober decoration; the tower on the left, which is of a later date, is more richly decorated: the upper storeys are separated by a moulded cornice and the third storey is pierced by two twinned openings, divided by columns ornamented with capi-

Paray-le-Monial. – Basilica of the Sacred Heart.

tals; on the top storey, the arch of the opening is formed by two recessed orders instead of three, while the capitals of the small columns are joined by a cordon of ovoli (quarter-section mouldings) and lozenges. The octagonal tower which stands over the transept crossing was restored in 1860.

A good vantage point from which to admire the decorative harmony of the chevet is the top of the steps of the old Pageboys' House (Maison des Pages) which now houses the Relics Chamber *(see p 134)*.

Enter the basilica by the north arm of the transept; the beautiful Romanesque doorway is decorated with floral and geometric designs.

Interior. – One is struck by the height of the building (22m – 72ft in the main nave) and the simplicity of its decoration. Here, one finds all the characteristics of the art of Cluny *(p 27)*. Huysmans (French novelist 1848-1907) saw the symbol of the Trinity in the three naves, composed of three bays supporting above the great arches three arcades surmonted by three windows.

The choir and its ambulatory with three small apses – the gallery of the Angels – is a graceful ensemble. The historiated capitals of the delicate columns are a typical example of 12C Burgundian art. The semi-domed apse is decorated with a 14C fresco, representing a benedictory Christ in Majesty, which was brought to light only in 1935. The transept crossing, covered by a dome on squinches, is of a graceful height.

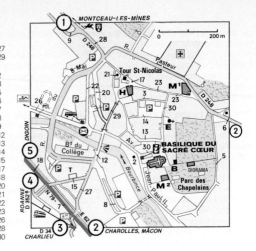

THE PILGRIMAGE

Relics Chamber (Chambre des Reliques) (B). — In the former house of the pages of Cardinal de Bouillon, many souvenirs of St Margaret-Mary have been assembled. The saint's cell has been faithfully reconstructed.

Parc des Chapelains. — It is in this large park, containing a Way of the Cross, that the great pilgrimage services take place. A **diorama** in the park depicts the life of St Margaret-Mary.

Chapel of the Visitation (E). — It was in this little chapel, also called "Sanctuary of the Apparitions", that St Margaret-Mary received her principal Revelations. The silver-gilt reliquary in the chapel on the right contains the relics of the saint.

ADDITIONAL SIGHTS

★ **Town Hall (Hôtel de ville) (H).** — The façade of this fine Renaissance mansion, built in 1525 by a rich draper, is decorated with shells and medallion portraits of French kings.

Hiéron Museum(M¹). — The theme of this museum of sacred art is the Eucharist reflected in the life of Christ, the Virgin Mary and the saints. The collection of 13C to 18C Italian art includes primitive paintings; works from the schools of Florence (Donatello, Bramante), Venice, Rome and Bologna; sculptures including a 13C Tuscan Christ and a 13C and 16C ivory eucharistic tabernacle; gold and silver ware. There are also a few works from Flanders and Germany (engravings by Lucas of Leyden and Dürer) as well as from France: a very beautiful 12C **tympanum★** from the Brionnais priory at Anzy-le-Duc *(p 38)*. In the revolutionary turmoil of 1791 the doorway was transported to the park of Château d'Arcy and then given to the Hiéron Museum. The tympanum shows Christ in Majesty enthroned in a mandorla supported by two angels. On the lintel the Virgin bares her breast to the Infant Jesus in her lap; to the left are four virgins bearing a crown and to the right four apostles and disciples. The technical achievement of the sculpture is as remarkable as its iconographic richness.
Liturgical items: gold and silver ware, ivory, enamels.

Charollais Faience Museum (M²). — The museum is devoted to the history of a product which has altered many times in shape and decoration between 1836 and now. In 1879 Élisabeth Parmentier, a decorative artist who had worked with Majorelle, settled in Charolles and established a style which became the hallmark of Charollais earthenware: delicate bouquets flanked by insects or butterflies and bordered with a blue frieze. At the same time part of the production followed the stylistic development of the decorative arts.
The first room presents moulds, tools, raw material and firing errors *(diorama of the production process)*. The following rooms contain many pieces in chronological and thematic order; the last section is devoted to the factory archives.

St Nicholas Tower (Tour St-Nicolas). — This square 16C tower was originally the belfry of the church of St Nicholas, now deconsecrated. The façade which overlooks Place Lamartine is adorned with a beautiful wrought ironwork staircase and a corbelled turret at the apex of the gable.

EXCURSIONS

Digoine Château. — *15km - 9 miles northeast of Paray-le-Monial by the D 248 and the D 974. Cross the Central Canal when level with Varennes and continue for 1km - 1/2 mile.*
This beautiful 18C mansion, built on the site of an ancient fortress, has two entirely different façades. The main façade is preceded by a courtyard that is closed off by finely worked railings; it has an elegant sculptured fronton and is flanked by two projecting pavilions. The façade facing the park, built in the first years of the 18C, has a two-storey portico as its centrepiece; two cylindrical towers with domes stand at either end.

★**The Romanesque churches of the Brionnais.** – *Round tour of 69km - 43 miles south of Paray-le-Monial – allow half a day. Michelin maps* 🔟 *fold 17 and* 🔟 *folds 7 and 8 – Local map p 62. Leave Paray-le-Monial by* ④ *on the town plan, the D 352bis; turn left shortly after St-Yan into the road which follows the Arconce Valley.*

Montceaux-l'Étoile. – *Description p 63.*

    Continue south by the D 174.

★ Anzy-le-Duc. – *Description p 38.*

    Take the D 10 and the D 982 towards Marcigny then the D 989 to reach Semur.

★ Semur-en-Brionnais. – *Description p 153.*

    The D 9 then the D 8 lead to St-Julien.

St-Julien-de-Jonzy. – *Description p 143.*

    Follow the D 8 then turn left into the D 20 to reach the D 34.

Varenne-l'Arconce. – *Description p 63.*

    Return to Paray-le-Monial by the D 34.

PERRECY-LES-FORGES
Pop 2 205

Michelin map 🔟 fold 17 or 🔟 fold 25 – 12km - 8 miles east of Gueugnon

The Romanesque **church** of this small industrial town was originally part of a Benedictine priory.

It is entered through a very large **narthex-porch★** which is beautifully designed. The tympanum of the main doorway shows Christ in Majesty framed in a mandorla supported by two angels. In contrast with the austerity of this apocalyptic representation the carvings on the lintel (the Passion) and on the capitals are livelier and less rigid. The transept crossing is lit by twin bays and surmounted by a dome on squinches.

The ground south of the church has been laid out with grass banks and bushes to indicate the position of the cloisters.

⊘An **exhibition** about the town and priory is on show in the gallery on the first floor of the porch.

The main through-routes are clearly indicated on all town plans.

★ PIERRE-DE-BRESSE CHÂTEAU
Pop 2 097

Michelin map 🔟 fold 3 or 🔟 fold 29

Pierre Château is set in a park (30ha - 74 acres); it is a handsome 17C building constructed of limestone bricks with a slate roof. The moat and U-shaped plan, guarded by four round corner towers capped by domes, reveal that it stands on the foundations of a fortified building. The central block is ornamented by an arcade of round-headed arches opening into a gallery. The pediment above the delicate central section is detached from the high mansard roof.

In the 18C the axis of the courtyard was extended by the addition of an outer court bordered by extensive outbuildings encircled by a second moat.

⊘The left wing of the château houses the **Burgundian Bresse Museum**. Only the stairs in the entrance lobby with their beautiful wrought-iron bannister and two rooms (18C and 19C) restored in period show how the interior of the château used to be. The exhibitions on three floors cover the natural environment, history, the traditional way of life and the present economic situation in Burgundian Bresse *(several audio-visual presentations including one 18 min long at the end of the tour).*

The museum, which illustrates the activities and traditions of Bresse, has established several branches throughout its territory at Louhans, Rancy *(p 109)*, St-Germain-du-Bois, Perrigny *(p 136)*, Verdun-sur-le-Doubs *(p 148)*, and Cuiseaux (Vines and Viticulture, see Green Guide Jura Franche-Comté).

Pierre-de-Bresse. – Château.

Terrans Château. — *3km - 2 miles west by the D 73 and a left turn into a small road.* The sober style of the château dates from 1765. The elegant façade with two lions flanking the steps to the front door is visible through the beautiful wrought-iron screen which encloses the courtyard.

⏱**St-Germain-du-Bois Museum of Agricultural Machines.** — *17km - 10 1/2 miles south by the D 13.* This branch of the Burgundian Bresse Museum *(see above)* is devoted to the rural life of Bresse; it traces the development of agricultural machinery in the 19C and 20C and presents the traditional products of the region — predominantly maize and poultry. The section on horses includes a reconstruction of a saddler's and harness-maker's workshop.

⏱**Perrigny Forest and Woodland Museum.** — *27km - 17 miles southwest by the D 13, D 313, D 970 and D 35.* This branch of the Burgundian Bresse Museum *(p 135)* situated in the centre of the woodland of Bresse is devoted to the timber trade and its attendant crafts and to different aspects of the Bresse forest (sculptures by Alan Mantle).

★ **PIERRE-PERTHUIS**   Pop 72

Michelin map 🔢 fold 16 or 🔢 fold 23 — 6km - 4 miles south of Vézelay — Local map p 124

The little village of Pierre-Perthuis with its church looking straight down into the valley of the Cure is in a very picturesque **site★** at the edge of the Morvan country. The river Cure flows boisterously at the bottom of a narrow gorge, spanned 33m - 108ft above by a modern single-arched bridge. From the bridge one can see Vézelay in the distance and, on the east bank, the pierced rock (Roche Percée) forming a natural arch, to which the village of Pierre-Perthuis owes its name.
Upstream from the modern bridge the Cure is spanned by an 18C humpback bridge. In Pierre-Perthuis itself stand the ruins of a feudal castle dating from the 12C.

PIERRE-QUI-VIRE ABBEY

Michelin map 🔢 folds 16 and 17 or 🔢 fold 24 — 10km - 6 miles east of Quarré-les-Tombes

This monastery, founded in the middle of the last century, is built in a wild and lonely part of the Morvan, on a hilly bank of the Trinquelin, the local name for the river Cousin, a small stream of clear water flowing at the foot of granite rocks in the middle of thick woods.
Foundation of the Abbey. — The name of **Father Muard** is closely associated with the foundation of the abbey. He was born in 1809 in the diocese of Sens and showed a desire to enter holy orders at an early age.
In 1850 Father Muard laid the foundations of his monastery on land donated by the Chastellux family. It took its name of "Pierre-Qui-Vire" (the Rocking Stone) from a druidic monument, an enormous block of granite, placed on another rock, which could be made to rock with a push of the hand.
Father Muard's death in 1854, when he was Superior of the abbey, did not stop the development of the community which joined the Benedictine Order in 1859. The present buildings — the church and monastery buildings — were built from 1850 to 1953.
⏱Although the rules of monastic enclosure forbid tours of the monastery, the **exhibition room** is always open to visitors interested in the life of the monks and their work, mainly editing the Zodiaque books on religious art *(audio-visual presentation on the life of the monastery)*. The church is open for **services** and one can visit the **druidic stone** which is outside the monastery walls.

★ **PONTIGNY**   Pop 825

Michelin map 🔢 fold 5 or 🔢 fold 11 — 18km - 11 miles northeast of Auxerre

This little village on the edge of the river Serein is celebrated for its former abbey, the second daughter-house of Cîteaux, founded in 1114. Whereas Cîteaux is now in ruins, the abbey of Pontigny (a retraining centre since 1968) has preserved its church intact.

The foundation. — At the beginning of the year 1114 twelve monks with the Abbot Hugues de Mâcon at their head were sent from Cîteaux by St Stephen to found a monastery on the banks of the Serein, in a large clearing at a place known as Pontigny. The abbey was situated on the boundaries of three bishoprics (Auxerre, Sens and Langres) and three provinces (counties of Auxerre, Tonnerre and Champagne) and thus from its beginning benefited from the protection and the generosity of six different masters. An old saying recalls that three bishops, three counts and an abbot could dine on the bridge of Pontigny, each one remaining on his own territory. Thibault the Great, Count of Champagne, was the abbey's most generous benefactor: in 1150 he gave the abbot the means to build a larger church than that existing at the time (the chapel of St Thomas), which had become too small for the monks. He enclosed the abbey buildings with a wall (4m - 13ft high) of which sections still remain.

A refuge for archbishops. – During the Middle Ages Pontigny served as a refuge for ecclesiastics fleeing from persecution in England; three Archbishops of Canterbury found asylum there. Thomas Becket, Primate of England, came to Pontigny in 1164 having incurred the anger of his sovereign, Henry II. He returned to his country in 1170 but was murdered in his cathedral two years later.

Stephen Langton took refuge at Pontigny from 1208 to 1213 because of a disagreement with King John.

Edmund Rich, St Edmund of Abingdon, lived in Pontigny in saintly exile for several years until his death in 1240, when he was buried in the abbey church. He was canonised in 1247 and is venerated throughout the region.

The decades of Pontigny. – Abandoned during the French Revolution, the abbey served as a quarry for the nearby villages up to 1840. The ruins were then bought back by the Archbishop of Sens and put at the disposition of the Congregation of Missionary Fathers founded by Father Muard *(see p 136: Abbey of Pierre-Qui-Vire)*, who restored the church and other buildings.

At the start of the 20C, the fathers were expelled and the property was bought by the philosopher, Paul Desjardins (1859-1940), who organised the famous "Décades" which brought together the most eminent personalities of the period including Thomas Mann, André Gide, T S Eliot and François Mauriac, who had lengthy literary conversations in the celebrated avenue of arbours.

★THE ABBEY *time: 1/2 hour*

Opposite the War Memorial in the village an 18C entrance, flanked by small pavilions, opens into a shady avenue which leads past the conventual buildings to the abbey church.

★ Church.

– Built in the second half of the 12C in the transitional Gothic style by Thibault, Count of Champagne, it is austere, in conformity with the Cistercian rule *(p 20)*. Of impressive size (108m - 354ft long inside, 117m - 384ft with the porch, and 52m - 171ft wide at the transept), it is almost as large as Notre-Dame in Paris.

Exterior. – A lean-to porch, festooned with arcades standing on consoles and small columns, takes up the whole width of the façade. Closed at the sides, it is pierced by twin, double-semicircular bays and a central doorway with a low arch.

The façade, decorated with a tall lancet window and two blind arcades, ends in a pointed gable with a small oculus. The sides of the church are typically bare; no belfry breaks the long line of the roof. The transept and the aisles are of a great simplicity; flat-sided buttresses and flying buttresses support the chevet and the north side.

Interior. – The long, two-storey nave has seven bays; it is the earliest Cistercian nave with pointed vaulting to have survived to the present day. The perspective of the nave is interrupted by the wooden screen of the monks' choir.

The squat side aisles of groined vaulting contrast with the more unrestricted nave. The transept, lit at either end by a rose window, is very characteristic with its six rectangular chapels opening on to each arm of the transept.

The choir, rebuilt at the beginning of the 13C, is very graceful with its ambulatory and its eleven apsidal chapels. The crocketed capitals of the monolithic columns are more elaborate than those of the nave where water-lily leaves, of somewhat rudimentary design, constitute the main decorative element.

At the end of the choir under a heavy baldaquin is the 18C shrine of St Edmund; the earlier wooden shrine, made during the Renaissance, is kept in one of the apsidal chapels.

The beautiful **stalls★**, the transept grille and the organ case date from the end of the 17C. The organ loft, which is heavily ornamented, the choir parclose and the altar date from the end of the 18C.

Monastery buildings. – All that is left of the 12C Cistercian buildings is the wing of the lay brothers' building; the rubblestone and delicate Tonnerre stone harmonise well in the façade, which is supported by buttresses.

Of the other buildings, only the southern gallery of the cloisters, rebuilt in the 17C, remains today *(access via the church)*.

EXCURSION

Ligny-le-Châtel. – Pop 1 020. *4.5km - 3 miles southeast*. The **church** dates from the 12C. The chancel was added in the 15C; the chevet is modelled on Pontigny Abbey although the apse is polygonal whereas at Pontigny it is circular.

In the second chapel on the north side there is a 16C painting on wood (restored) of St Jerome. There are also two early-16C painted wooden statues and a 16C St John and the Virgin at the foot of the cross.

POUGUES-LES-EAUX
Pop 2 269

Michelin map 🔢 fold 3 or 🔢🔢🔢 fold 33 – 11km - 7 miles northwest of Nevers

Set near the Loire, this health resort is in an agreeable spot in a shady valley overlooked by Mount Givre.

Its parks with age-old trees and the terrace of the Bellevue park on Mount Givre, from which there is a wide **view** over the valley of the Loire and the Berry countryside, are charming for a walk or a rest for the holidaymaker, for whom there is also a whole variety of distractions and sports.

POUILLY-EN-AUXOIS

Pop 1516

Michelin map 65 fold 18 or 243 fold 14

This little town has developed at the foot of the Pouilly Mount (altitude 559m - 1 834ft) at the end of the tunnel (3 333m - 10 925ft long) through which the Burgundy Canal passes from the Rhône basin to that of the Seine. The barges are drawn through the tunnel by means of a towing chain anchored to the bottom of the canal. In 1867 the first steam warping tug went into service on the canal.

Notre-Dame-Trouvée. – This little church of the 14C and 15C, a centre of pilgrimage and a sanctuary, was built to shelter an ancient statue of the Virgin, called "Our Lady Discovered" because of its miraculous discovery. The building stands halfway up St Peter's Hill in the middle of a graveyard. It possesses a beautiful 16C Entombment, with nine figures, which shows the influences of Burgundian art (the fall of the draperies), Champagne art (the holy women grouped in the centre of the composition) and Italian art (numerous figures completing the scene: sleeping soldiers and angels carrying the instruments of the Passion).
Near one of the entrances to the graveyard stand a stone pulpit, an altar and a calvary, forming an original 15C ensemble.

EXCURSIONS

Éguilly Château. – *5km - 3 miles north.* There has been a castle on the site since the 12C. The surviving medieval features are the four-square design flanked by towers and the **13C gateway,** which contains the vertical shafts for the arms of the drawbridge. The courtyard with its domed Renaissance well is separated into two distinct parts down the entrance axis. On the south side the outbuildings back on to the walls of the original precinct; traces of the sentry walk are visible in the stables which project at a right angle. The range is completed by a small Gothic chapel which on the north side abuts the living quarters, altered in the 17C. In summer there are temporary exhibitions.

Croix St-Thomas. – *About 18km - 11 miles northwest.* Vast **panorama★** over the Auxois and the Morvan.

Mont St-Jean. – Pop 271. *18km - 11 miles northwest.* The remarkable **site★** of the feudal town includes the 12C castle surrounded by pleasant tree-shaded avenues.

Chailly-sur-Armançon. – Pop 231. *6.5km - 4 miles west.* The handsome Renaissance **château** has an attractively decorated façade.

Ste-Sabine. – Pop 193. *9km - 5 1/2 miles southeast.* The Gothic **church** has a surprisingly tall porch.

PRÉCY-SOUS-THIL

Pop 592

Michelin map 65 fold 17 or 243 fold 13 – 16km - 10 miles north of Saulieu

Précy is situated in a pleasant beauty spot in the valley of the Serein, at the foot of the Thil mountain. It is in the centre of a region that used to be important for the processing of iron ore, with more than eighty ironworks.

★Thil. – *2.5km - 1 1/2 miles east by the D 10ʲ turning left on leaving Maison Dieu.* The avenue bordered with lime trees leads to the former collegiate church (right) and the outer walls of the castle (left).

Former Collegiate Church (Ancienne Collégiale). – Founded in 1340 by John II of Thil, Constable of Burgundy, the collegiate church was consecrated four years later by the Bishop of Autun.
Of a simple plan the church has a flat east end with three windows. The vaulting with the stones placed edgewise is quite remarkable.
Some of the capitals rest on corbels. A small room under the tower, to the left on entering, contains three tombstones.
To admire the exterior, walk round the building anti-clockwise: fine roof-level frieze and square tower. There is a good **panorama** of the Auxois.

Castle. – The castle was built on the site of a Roman camp and follows its oval shape. The outer walls pierced by loopholes date from the 9C and 12C; the keep is 14C. The great square tower provides a good view for 50km - 31 miles round; it was nicknamed the "spy of the Auxois". To the south are more 12C fortifications. From the foot of the watch-tower there is a good view of the surrounding area and the foothills of the Morvan.

PRÉMERY

Pop 2603

Michelin map 65 south of fold 14 or 238 fold 22

In a pretty setting of hills on the banks of the river Nièvre, Prémery owes the greater part of its development to a large factory specialising in the distilling of wood alcohol and the production of chemicals.

St-Marcel. – This building of the 13C and 14C, a former collegiate church, is surmounted by a massive belfry.
The interior has flattened Gothic vaulting and wide side aisles. The apse has two storeys of windows.

Former château. – This used to belong to the bishops of Nevers. Built in the 14C, 16C and 17C, the château has a fine 14C fortified gateway.

PUISAYE

Michelin map 🔢 folds 3, 4, 13 and 14 or 🔢🔢🔢 fold 9

The Puisaye is a region of forests, water and scrubland, which has a reputation for being monotonous and even austere. The uniformity is however only superficial and the visitor will find a variety of scenery; St-Fargeau is the chief town of the region.

The countryside. – The word "Puisaye" appears to be the combination of two Celtic words: *poel*, meaning lake, marsh or pool, and *say*, meaning forest. The forest that once covered most of the area has now disappeared but the damp climate and the marl and sand soil still favour the existence of numerous pools. From Toucy to Bléneau and from Arquian to St-Sauveur, water is the dominant element and oozes everywhere: a multitude of rivers and pools are hidden in the greenery. From St-Sauveur through St-Fargeau and Bléneau to Rogny-les-Sept-Écluses runs a watery chain: Moutiers Pool, Bourdon Reservoir, La Tuilerie Pool, La Grande Rue Pool etc.

The meadows and fields, enclosed by quickset hedges, the wooded hills and the silhouettes of the many châteaux – Ratilly, St-Fargeau, St-Sauveur and St-Amand – all add to the interest of a drive in the Puisaye.

The country of Colette. – It was in **St-Sauveur** that Colette was born and spent her childhood. On the façade of a large house with a flight of steps, in Rue Colette, a red marble plaque carries the simple inscription: "Colette was born here".

She described this village, which she used to know so well, in *La Maison de Claudine* and in *Sido* with an exactitude and a reality that never sought to hide or embellish. Those days however have passed and St-Sauveur no longer has the appearance that the author knew.

Pottery in the Puisaye. – The soil of the Puisaye contains uncrushed flint coated with white or red clays which were used in the Middle Ages by the potters of St-Amand, Treigny, St-Vérain and Myennes.

It was in the 17C that the pottery trade really began to develop; the fine pieces of pottery, known as the "Bleu de St-Verain" (Blue of St Verain), were followed in the next century by utility products. In the late 19C craftsmen-potters built up a new reputation.

Pottery making is now concentrated in **St-Amand-en-Puisaye,** where there is a training centre, and on the outskirts of the town where several potters' shops produce first-rate stoneware. Moutiers, near St-Sauveur, is known for the earthenware and stoneware produced at La Batisse. At Ratilly Castle *(p 140)* those interested in ceramic art can observe the different stages of the potter's craft: casting, moulding and throwing on the wheel.

Le PUITS XV

Michelin map 🔢 fold 19 or 🔢🔢🔢 fold 15 – 7km - 4 miles northeast of Sombernon

The Blaisy-Bas Tunnel (4.1km - 2 3/4 miles long) is used by the main Paris-Dijon railway to cross the ridge separating the basins of the Rhône and the Seine. The course of the tunnel is marked by twenty-two shafts, used for the extraction of rock and earth during the digging of the tunnel. Eleven of these now provide sufficient ventilation. The fifteenth shaft, **Puits XV**, is the deepest (197m - 646ft).

From the plateau *(access by the D 16)* near Puits XV, the view spreads over the **Baulme-la-Roche Cliff** (popular among climbers since its rock walls are the highest in the Dijon region), the Mâlain signal station and, beyond it, to Mount Afrique.

QUARRÉ-LES-TOMBES   Pop 772

Michelin map 🔢 fold 16 or 🔢🔢🔢 fold 24 – Local map p 124

Quarré-les-Tombes is situated on the narrow plateau separating the valleys of the Cure and the Cousin, in a picturesque region of the Morvan. It is an excellent place to stay and a good centre for excursions.

The township owes its name to the numerous limestone sarcophagi (112 stone coffins or covers) which were found in the vicinity of the church. These are the remains of over 1 000 tombs which date from the 7C-10C. No one seems to know their exact origin although it is supposed that the local population specialised in making such sarcophagi or that the original sanctuary, dedicated to St George, patron of horsemen, was surrounded by a necropolis to which the dead were brought from great distances to be buried under the protection of their saint. It seems that in the past the sarcophagi may have contained bones.

EXCURSIONS

St-Léger-Vauban. – *5.5km - 3 1/2 miles northeast by the D 55. Description p 143.*

Les Isles Ménéfrier. – *5km - 3 miles south via Bousson.* In this beauty spot, near the old village, the Cure tumbles in a torrent from rock to rock.

La Roche des Fées. – *3.5km - 2 miles south, plus 1/4 hour on foot Rtn.* This pleasant walk passes through Le Duc Forest (Forêt du Duc) to the granite area known as the Fairies' Rock.

★ RATILLY CASTLE

Michelin map 🔢 northeast of fold 13 or 🔢🔢🔢 fold 21

⊘The first sight of this large 13C castle, placed well away from the main roads in a setting of magnificent trees in the heart of the Puisaye region, will charm visitors. Massive towers and high walls of an austere appearance overlook the dry moat surrounding the castle, which is built in fine ochre-coloured stone that time has mellowed.

In 1653 La Grande Mademoiselle (Mademoiselle de Montpensier), who had been exiled to St-Fargeau *(p 141)*, stayed for a week at Ratilly. A little later Ratilly served as a refuge for the Jansenists, who published a clandestine paper there, safe from the pursuit of the royal police.

The left wing now houses a stoneware workshop (courses available). Both the workshop and the showroom, with its small exhibition on the original Puisaye stoneware, are open to the public. Other premises have been refurbished to house temporary art exhibitions.

EXCURSION

Treigny. – Pop 917. *2km - 1 mile east*. This town has a beautiful **church** built in the 15C and 16C in the Flamboyant Gothic style. Owing to its enormous size – astonishing for a country church – it has been nicknamed the "Cathedral of the Puisaye region".

Some hotels have their own gardens, tennis courts,
swimming pool beach facilities;
consult the current **Michelin Red Guide France.**

★ La ROCHEPOT   Pop 272

Michelin map 🔢🔢 fold 9 or 🔢🔢🔢 fold 27 – 5km - 3 miles east of Nolay

The village, now by-passed by the main road, is set at the foot of a rocky promontory on which stands the feudal castle which has been restored. It was the birthplace of Philippe Pot (1428-94), famous statesman and ambassador in London of the Dukes of Burgundy. His tomb is a masterpiece of the Burgundian school and is now to be seen in the Louvre Museum.

⊘**Castle.** – The castle is in an impressive **setting★**. The original 12C building was altered in the 15C but the keep was razed during the French Revolution. The complete rebuilding of the castle was undertaken by M. Sadi Carnot, son of Président Carnot.

The outer defences are dominated by huge but graceful towers. The inner courtyard, beyond the drawbridge, contains a well with a wrought-iron wellhead; the turrets of the Renaissance wing are roofed with glazed coloured tiles. The tour includes the Guard Room with its vast chimney and handsome ceiling beams, the chamber of the Captain of the Guards, the kitchens, the dining room, which is richly furnished and contains numerous *objets d'art*, the former chapel, the northern tower with its apartments and the watchpath.

From a small terrace at the far end of the courtyard on the right, there is a view over the village and its encircling hills.

Church (Église). – This 12C priory church was built by the Benedictine monks from Flavigny. The historiated capitals are similar in style to those at Autun and represent Balaam's ass, the Annunciation, a knight and an eagle in combat. It contains a number of interesting works of art including a 16C triptych by the Dijon painter, Quentin, with a Descent from the Cross on the central section.

La Rochepot. – Château.

ST-FARGEAU

Michelin map 🔲 fold 3 or 🔲🔲🔲 fold 9

The clearing of the forests made possible the establishment of smelting works at St-Fargeau, chief town of the Puisaye *(p 139)* to treat the minerals extracted from the ferruginous soil.

St-Fargeau has a fine château filled with memories of Anne-Marie-Louise d'Orléans, cousin of Louis XIV, better known under the name of Mademoiselle de Montpensier or "La Grande Mademoiselle". She was an incorrigible supporter of the Fronde (a rising of the aristocracy and parliament, 1648-53).

★ **Château.** – The present château is built on the site of a fortress erected at the end of the 10C; the system of fortifications was completed two centuries later. The present building was begun in the Renaissance period and was built in several stages. The largest tower was built by Jacques Cœur, treasurer to the royal household of Charles VII (reign 1422-61), who owned St-Fargeau for some time.

Antoine de Chabannes, who acquired the château when Jacques Cœur fell into disgrace, carried out many improvements but it is **"La Grande Mademoiselle"** who can claim the honour of completely changing the appearance of the buildings.

Mademoiselle de Montpensier was exiled to St-Fargeau for several years on the orders of Louis XIV as punishment for her attitude during the rising of the Fronde. When she arrived in 1652 she had "to wade through knee-high grass in the courtyard" and found a dilapidated building. To make her place of exile more comfortable, she called in Le Vau, the king's architect, who laid out the inner courtyard and completely refurbished the interior of the château.

In 1681, Mademoiselle de Montpensier made a gift of St-Fargeau to the Duc de Lauzun, a man of questionable background, whom she later married in a secret ceremony.

In 1715 the property was bought by Le Pelletier des Forts. His great-grandson, **Louis-Michel Le Pelletier de St-Fargeau**, became deputy to the National Convention in 1793 and voted for the death of Louis XVI. He was assassinated on the eve of the king's execution by the Paris bodyguard and considered by the revolutionaries as the first martyr of their cause; his corpse is buried in the chapel.

🕑**Tour.** – *40 min.* The warm rose-coloured brick does much to dispel the grim aspect that the massive towers of the main gateway and the corner towers give to this impressive building, surrounded by a moat. With the exception of the largest tower, known as that of Jacques Cœur, these squat towers are surmounted by slender, pierced lanterns.

Within the feudal enclosure is a huge courtyard of rare elegance bordered by five ranges of buildings (the most recent on the right of the entrance dates from 1735).

A semicircular stair in the corner between the two main wings leads to the entrance rotunda. The chapel is housed in one of the towers: on the left is the portrait gallery which led into the apartments of the Grande Mademoiselle until they were burned in 1752; on the right is the 17C guardroom. A grand stair leads to the rooms on the first floor.

In addition there are the timber-roofed attics. In the park (118ha - 292 acres) with its handsome groves there is a large lake, fed by the small Bourdon river.

Clock Tower (Tour de l'Horloge). – This tower of brick and stone is a former fortified gateway dating from the end of the 15C.

Church (Église). – The church was built and altered or added to during the 11C, 13C and 15C. The Gothic west front has a radiant rose window set in a square.

In the nave, note on the right a 16C polychrome *Pietà* in stone and the choir stalls of the same period. At the far end of the choir the wooden statue of Christ dates from the 14C. The chapel in the south aisle contains three sculptures in wood, a 15C triptych representing the Passion, a 16C painted statue of the Virgin Mary and a remarkable 16C carving of St Martin sharing his cloak.

EXCURSIONS

Bourdon Reservoir (Lac de Bourdon). – *3km - 2 miles southeast. Lakeside walks, sailing, canoeing, fishing and swimming.* The beautiful Bourdon reservoir (220ha - 494 acres) supplies the Briare Canal.

🕑 **St Hubert Wildlife Park** (Parc St-Hubert). – *9km - 6 miles southeast by the D 185.* This wildlife park (400ha - 988 acres) in the grounds of the **Boutissaint Château** allows visitors to see at close quarters, either free-ranging or in enclosures, deer, fallow deer, wild boar, European bison and moufflon.

Moutiers. – *10km - 6 miles southeast.* The village **church,** which formerly belonged to a priory dependent on the Abbey of St Germain in Auxerre, has retained a few works of art from its various periods of prosperity between the 10C and 16C: the sculpted ornaments decorating the window embrasures in the narthex (13C refurbished in the 16C) and the medieval frescoes in the nave; the two superimposed painted cycles, Romanesque and Gothic, were discovered in 1982 under a coat of 17C whitewash.

The Romanesque frescoes (2nd half of the 12C) are painted on the north wall (the Annunciation, the Nativity, the Visitation of the Shepherds, Christ surrounded by angels), on the west wall (enigmatic figures) and on the first bay of the south wall (scenes of adoration). The south wall is completed by three rows of Gothic frescoes (*c*1300): a procession *(above),* scenes from Genesis *(centre),* the history of John the Baptist and Noah's Ark *(below).*

ST-FLORENTIN

Michelin map 🗺 south of fold 15 or 🗺 fold 46
Town plan in the current Michelin Red Guide France

St-Florentin stands terraced on a hill overlooking the confluence of the Armance and the Armaçon and is served by the Burgundy Canal. It was once the main town of a large bailiwick and, during the French Revolution, was called Mont-Armance. This small industrial centre, where the well-known cheeses Soumaintrain and St-Florentin are made, is a popular place for anglers. The proximity of the forests of Othe *(see the Michelin Green Guide Champagne Ardennes, in French only)* and Pontigny and the open-air theatre are added attractions.

⊘ **Church (Église).** — At the top of the hill stands the church surrounded by picturesque streets. Its construction, disrupted by the Hundred Years War and the Wars of Religion, lasted from 1376 to 1614. The nave, still incomplete, consists of two bays while the chancel, extended by a semicircular ambulatory, consists of three. The late-Gothic style of the main structure is embellished by decorative features in the Renaissance style: the transept doorways, the triple-arched rood screen, the high altar retable and the choir screen.

The 16C **stained glass windows** are uncommonly uniform. The work of the flourishing Troyes school is characterised by its taste for intense colours, its frequent evocation of the lives of the saints and the re-use of cartoons to make the studio's stock profitable (similar compositions are found in several churches including Ste-Madeleine in Troyes — *see the Michelin Green Guide Champagne Ardennes, in French only)*. The most remarkable are Genesis and the Tree of Jesse *(right of the chancel)* and the Apocalypse, inspired by engravings by Dürer *(left of the rood screen)*.

Fountain. — This is a 20C (1979) copy of the original Gothic-Renaissance fountain which was destroyed in the 19C. The three bronze griffins (1512) spouting water are original.

Promenade du Prieuré. — From this terrace there is a fine **view** over the Armançon valley and the old town with one of its 12C rampart towers, Bell Tower, clearly visible.

EXCURSION

Neuvy-Sautour. — Pop 1 023. *7km - 4 miles northeast of St-Florentin by the N 77.* The village is dominated by the 15C-16C **church** with its two fine side doorways. The choir and transept are both Renaissance. The architectural styles of Burgundy and Champagne are both clearly visible in this church.

Note on the south side of the choir a large 16C cross ornamented with several figures.

★ # ST-HONORÉ-LES-BAINS

Michelin map 🗺 fold 6 or 🗺 fold 35 — Local map p 124

The **health resort** of St-Honoré, which was used by the Romans, has grown increasingly popular since the last century. Its sulphurous, arsenical and radioactive waters are used against all forms of asthma, bronchitis and emphysema. Those taking the cure can enjoy the shady spa park set in a small valley or make use of the many sports facilities at their disposal.

Its situation on the edge of the Morvan region makes St-Honoré an excellent excursion centre *(p 126).*

EXCURSIONS

Vieille Montagne. — *8km - 5 miles southeast. Description p 126.*

Vandenesse. — Pop 396. *Round tour of 16km - 10 miles. Leave St-Honoré by the D 106.*
The road runs through forest nearly all the way.
On arriving in Vandenesse, one can see the huge castle from the road. It was built in 1475 and is flanked by numerous towers.
Return to St-Honoré by the D 3 and the D 403 which afford good views of the Lac de Chèvre.

*The current **Michelin Red Guide France** offers*
a selection of pleasant hotels in convenient locations.
Each entry specifies the facilities available (gardens,
tennis courts, swimming pool, beach facilities)
and the annual opening and closing dates.

There is also a selection of establishments recommended for their
cuisine – well-prepared meals at moderate prices; stars for good cooking.

ST-JULIEN-DE-JONZY

Michelin map 73 fold 8 or 243 fold 37 – 12km - 8 miles north of Charlieu – Local map p 63

The village dominates the horizon of the Brionnais with the Beaujolais mountains in the distance.

CHURCH
time: 1/4 hour

The village church, a 12C Romanesque building, has a fine carved doorway. Some of the detail is similar to the sculptures in the porch at Charlieu.

St-Julien-de-Jonzy. – Tympanum of the church doorway

★**The doorway.** – The sculptures on the tympanum and the lintel are carved from a single block of sandstone. The craftsmanship is outstanding.
The lintel represents the Last Supper: the heads of all save two of the figures were mutilated with hammers during the French Revolution in 1793. The folds of the tablecloth have been executed with consummate skill and at either end there is a scene of the Washing of the Feet.

Interior. – The former transept crossing, covered by a dome on squinches, now serves as the narthex. The four engaged columns have beautiful capitals, that on the right before the nave has a decoration of water-lily leaves, reminiscent of Cistercian art.

ST-JULIEN-DU-SAULT

Michelin map 61 south of fold 14 or 237 fold 45

This little township stands on the west bank of the river Yonne.

Church (Église). – Dating from the 13C and 14C, this building was partly altered in the 16C. Note the side porches on the exterior.
The choir, altered during the Renaissance, is of bold proportions. The stained glass windows date from the 13C (those with medallions) and from the Renaissance (those with figures).

Wooden House (Maison de bois). – *From Place du Général-Leclerc in front of the church take Rue Notre-Dame (D 107) towards Courtenay; turn left into Rue du Puits-de-la-Caille going towards Place Fontenotte.* The 16C timber-framed house has flint infill on the ground floor and brick on the first floor.

Vauguillain Chapel. – A road climbs steeply to the chapel and to the remains of a château built on the hillock. From the ramparts there is a good view of St-Julien and the valley of the Yonne.

ST-LÉGER-VAUBAN

Michelin map 65 fold 16 or 238 fold 24 – 5.5km - 3 miles northeast of Quarré-les-Tombes

Sébastien le Prestre, who under the name of the **Marquess of Vauban** became one of the outstanding figures of a great century, was born in 1633 in this little village which was then called St-Léger-de-Foucheret.

Vauban, "the most honest man of his century". – Sébastien le Prestre was left a penniless orphan early in life, and at the age of seventeen joined the army of the Prince of Condé, then in revolt against the court, and was taken prisoner by the royal forces.
From that time onwards, he entered the service of Louis XIV. As a military engineer, he worked on 300 ancient fortified places and built 33 new ones; he successfully directed 53 sieges, thus justifying the saying: "a town defended by Vauban is an impregnable town: a town besieged by Vauban is a captured town". Created Brigadier General of the royal armies and then Commissioner General of fortifications, he was made a Field Marshal in 1704. He protected France's frontiers with a belt of fortresses which were entirely new in conception, utilising such tactics as cross-fire, ricochet fire, hollow bullets, parallels, trenches and many other innovations of a character revolutionary for the period.
Saint-Simon (writer: 1675-1755), who was not renowned for his kind remarks, wrote of Vauban: "A man of medium height, rather squat, who had a very warlike air, but at the same time an appearance that was loutish and coarse, not to say brutal and ferocious. Nothing could be further from the truth; never was there a gentler man, more compassionate, more obliging, more respectful, more courteous, and most sparing in the use of men's lives, a man of great worth capable of giving himself in the service of others..."

The last years of this man's life, who never denied his humble origin, were unhappy. Deeply affected by the great misery of the common people, he sent his *Projet d'une Dîme Royale* (Plan for a Royal Tithe) to the king, in which he proposed ways and means of bettering the living conditions of the lower classes. The work was banned and Vauban, relegated virtually to disgrace by Louis XIV, died of grief on 30 March 1707.

In 1808 Vauban's heart was placed in the Invalides in Paris by Napoleon I; the rest of his body lies in the church in **Bazoches**, a village in the Morvan *(20km - 12 miles southwest of Avallon)*, near the château which was in large part reconstructed by his efforts and from which the view extends to Vézelay.

SIGHTS

St Leger's Church. — The church, in which Vauban was baptised, was originally built to a cruciform plan in the Renaissance period; it was transformed in the 19C and boasts some interesting modern additions by the sculptor Marc Hénard: carved wooden panels in the south door; the sculptures and stained glass window in the chapel (1625), left of the chancel; the beautiful blue and pink ceramic **tiles★** (1973) which surround the high altar and depict the planets, animals, tools etc revolving round the triangle of the Holy Trinity.

⊘**Vauban's House.** — *Community centre.* In a small room information panels and an audiovisual presentation *(20 min)* retrace the life and work of this great Frenchman.

EXCURSIONS

Pierre-qui-Vire Abbey. — *4km - 2 1/2 miles south by two local roads, the V 5 and the V 16. Description p 136.*

St-Agnan Reservoir (Lac de St-Agnan). — *10km - 6 miles south by Trinquelin and the local road, the V 7 and the access road.*
From the retaining dam there is an attractive view over the reservoir encircled by its forested banks (firs and deciduous trees). There is access to the water's edge on the north bank and via St-Agnan to the south bank.

*The **Michelin Green Guide France**
aims to make touring more enjoyable
by suggesting several touring programmes
which are easily adapted to personal taste.*

★ ST-PÈRE   Pop 356

Michelin map 🔢 fold 15 or 🔢 fold 23 — 2km - 1 mile southeast of Vézelay — Local map p 124

The little village of St-Père, standing at the foot of the hill of Vézelay, on the banks of the river Cure, possesses a beautiful Gothic church.

★ CHURCH OF THE VIRGIN (ÉGLISE NOTRE-DAME) *time: 1/4 hour*

The church, which was begun in about 1200 and completed in 1455, shows all the stages in the development of the Gothic style between the 13C and 15C. In the 16C it became the parish church in place of St Peter's Church (from which the name St-Père is derived) which burned down in 1567 during the Wars of Religion and was never rebuilt.

Exterior. — The gable, surmounting a rose window of beautiful design, is hollowed out by arches forming niches. Those in the centre contain statues of Christ being crowned by two angels, and St Stephen, framed on one side by the Virgin and Sts Peter, Andrew and James, and on the other by St Mary Magdalene with St John and two Evangelists.
The delicately worked 13C belfry is graceful. At the corners angels sound trumpets. The porch added at the end of the 13C and restored by Viollet-le-Duc (1814-79) has three doorways. The centre one, which has a trefoiled archway, depicts the Last Judgment: on the right of Christ, the blessed are being welcomed by Abraham, while on His left the damned are being devoured by Satan.
Under the porch housing the tomb of the donors (dating from 1258) note the size of the arches and the design of the tracery of the side windows.

Interior. — The overall effect is one of great purity of style. Rebuilt in the 15C the choir is encircled by an ambulatory with five radiating chapels. On entering note the two 14C cast-iron fonts shaped like upturned bells.
The vaulting of the nave has painted bosses and corbels carved in the form of expressive faces.
A narrow gallery leads round the building at the height of the clerestory windows. In the north aisle there is a defaced recumbent figure dating from the 13C and in a chapel on the south side of the choir a 10C stone altar which probably belonged to the original church. On leaving the church note the curious painted baptismal font dating from the Carolingian period.

ADDITIONAL SIGHTS

⊘**Regional Archaeological Museum (Musée archéologique régional).** — The museum is installed in the former presbytery, built in the 17C, and contains objects excavated at Fontaines-Salées, in particular sections of a water conduit made from tree trunks hollowed out by fire to carry mineral water from a spring; it dates from the Hallstatt period (First Iron Age). Also on display are a 4C Gallo-Roman weighing device, enamelled bronze fibulae in the form of seahorses or wild ducks, Merovingian weapons and jewellery found in the tombs at Vaudonjon near Vézelay, and Gratteloup near Pierre-Perthuis. The medieval room contains sculpture from the 12C to 16C from the Vézelay region including a statue of St James the Great and a 13C statue of Christ conferring His Blessing.

⊘**Excavations at Fontaines-Salées.** — *2km - 1 mile.* The excavations, which are near the D 958, have unearthed Gallo-Roman baths, built on to what was once a Gallic sanctuary (a 2C BC circular temple with a lustral basin) enclosed within a vast precinct dedicated to the gods of the springs.
These saline springs, which were used in the Iron Age, by the Romans and again in the Middle Ages, were filled in by the salt tax authorities in the 17C. Nineteen wooden casings dating from the first millennium BC have been preserved by the high mineral content of the water. A stone duct from the Roman period gives access to the waters of a spring which is once again being used for treating arthritic complaints.

ST-PIERRE-LE-MOUTIER   Pop 2261

Michelin map 🔢 southeast of fold 3 or 🔢🔢🔢 fold 33

Set astride the N 7 this former royal barony is now an important market town; it has several quiet little squares and sections of the 15C ramparts.

Joan of Arc's last victory. — After the coronation in Rheims, the king's council, jealous of Joan's success and growing fame, forced a period of inaction on the Maid who was impatient to retake Paris. In October 1429 it was decided to send her to rid the Nevers district of Perrinet-Gressard's *(p 70)* marauding bands. A small band of Royalists buoyed up by the Maid's enthusiasm set out from Berry in early November and took St-Pierre-le-Moutier. After having to wait in Moulins for reinforcements of men and arms, the small army set out again in December but failed to recapture La Charité-sur-Loire *(p 70).* The following year the Maid was taken prisoner at Compiègne *(see the Michelin Green Guide Flandres, Artois, Picardie, in French only).*

Church (Église). — The church was part of a Benedictine priory which was founded during the time of Queen Brunhilda (7C). Set square and solid it stands uncluttered by other buildings on the market place. The mutilated north doorway represents Christ and the four Evangelists with their symbols, surrounded by angels on the recessed arches. Some of the capitals in the nave are carved with picturesque scenes; 14C recumbent effigy.
The presbytery doorway, overlooking the church parvis, has a Gothic doorway with delicate Flamboyant decoration.

EXCURSION

Mars-sur-Allier. — *Pop 264. 9.5km - 6 miles northwest by the D 108.* The small Romanesque church of Mars was part of a Cluniac priory in the 12C. Standing alone on a small square it has a simple rectangular plan. The tympanum of the doorway portrays Christ in Glory surrounded by the symbols of the Evangelists and the Apostles. Walk around the church to admire the carved brackets and the chevet.

ST-RÉVÉRIEN   Pop 315

Michelin map 🔢🔢 fold 15 or 🔢🔢🔢 fold 22 — 17km - 11 miles southwest of Corbigny

This little Nivernais village has a Romanesque church of considerably greater interest than the other country churches of the region. For the best view of the church approach the town from the northeast, the road from Guipy (D 977*bis*).

Church. — The original mid-12C church was largely destroyed by fire in 1723; all that remains is the chancel with its ambulatory and radiating chapels which show that it once belonged to a Cluniac priory. The nave was rebuilt in the 19C and the central belfry was replaced by a porch-belfry.
The doorway is surmounted by two angels with double wings in the Byzantine style, originally part of an earlier doorway. The **interior★** shows great purity of style. Note the arches of the nave with alternating thick and thin columns. Among churches where the nave has no clerestory, this is one of the few with an ambulatory, a well-lit prolongation of the aisles. The springing of the arches is supported by fine foliated capitals. The three small chapels have beautiful historiated capitals. The apsidal chapel and St Joseph's Chapel (right) contain 16C frescoes. Tombstones taken from other parts of the church and the graveyard have been placed in the aisles.

EXCURSION

Étang de Vaux. — *10km - 6 miles southeast by the D 977bis, the D 277 to the right via Vitry and Laché and the D 135.*
The **Vaux Pool** and the adjacent **Baye Pool,** south of the dyke, both flow into the Nivernais Canal. The Vaux pool, which is larger and surrounded by woodland, is popular for fishing; the Baye Pool is used for sailing.

★★ ST-ROMAIN (MOUNT)

Michelin map 🗺 fold 19 or 🗺 fold 39 — 7km - 4 miles northwest of Lugny — Local map p 113

> *From the D 187 a steep side road climbs to Mount St-Romain; turn right to the car park beside the tower adjoining the farm buildings.*

From the top of the tower *(viewing table)* there is a magnificent **panorama★★**: east across the Saône plain to the Bresse, the Jura and the Alps; south over the Mâconnais and the Beaujolais; west over the Charollais.

ST-SAULGE   Pop 1019

Michelin map 🗺 northwest of fold 5 or 🗺 fold 34

This little township once belonged to the Counts of Nevers.
The Gothic-style **church** has fine pointed vaulting above the nave and aisles. There are beautiful 16C stained glass windows in the aisles.

EXCURSION

Jailly. — Pop 92. *4km - 2 1/2 miles.*
The Romanesque **church** of Jailly, which was once part of a Cluniac priory, stands on an attractive site on the slope of a hill.
A magnificent tree grows beside the door of the church which is surmounted by an octagonal belfry. In front of the church stands an old Romanesque doorway surmounted by a small frieze of roses.

ST-SEINE-L'ABBAYE   Pop 339

Michelin map 🗺 fold 19 or 🗺 fold 15

This little place, situated about six miles from the source of the Seine, has perpetuated the name of the holy man who founded a Benedictine abbey on his land in the 6C. The abbey church has survived.

⊙**Abbey Church.** — This early-13C abbey church marks the transition from the Burgundian-Romanesque style to the Gothic style which came from the Île-de-France. The church was restored in the 14C after a fire; the façade dates from the 15C. The porch is set between two towers, supported by buttresses; the right-hand tower is incomplete.
The nave is lit by a clerestory; the flat chevet is pierced by a beautiful rose window, rebuilt in the 19C. The chapels in the flat-ended transept communicate with the side aisles of the choir by means of stone screens pierced by window apertures. There are numerous tombstones in the transept. At the end of the choir stands the former rood screen.
The 18C carved stalls are set against a Renaissance screen, on the reverse side of which are paintings representing the story of St Seine (Sequana).
On leaving the church, note the fountain of the Samaritan Woman; the basin is surmounted by an 18C bronze.

ST-THIBAULT   Pop 145

Michelin map 🗺 fold 18 or 🗺 fold 14 — 19km - 12 miles southeast of Semur-en-Auxois

This Auxois village is named after St Theobald whose relics were presented to the local priory in the 13C. The priory church has a choir of great elegance and a main doorway which is considered among the most beautiful examples of 13C Burgundian architecture.

★ CHURCH *time: 1/2 hour*

⊙The church is approached from the north side. The original church was built to house the relics of St Theobald at the expense of Robert II, Duke of Burgundy, and his wife, Agnes of France, daughter of St Louis; all that remains are the choir, an apsidal chapel and the carved doorway from the old transept which collapsed together with the nave in the 17C.
The **doorway★**, once protected by a porch, is a picture-book in itself. The sculptures of the tympanum, executed during the second half of the 13C, are devoted to the Virgin. Those in the recessed arches, dating from the same period, represent, on the inner arch, the Wise Virgins to the left and the Foolish Virgins to the right.
About the year 1310, five great statues were added: St Theobald stands with his back to the pier; the other four have been identified as true likenesses of Duke Robert II and his son, Hugh V, benefactors of the church, the Duchess Agnes, and the Bishop of Autun, Hugues d'Arcy. The expressions on the faces and the modelling of the features show great skill; the door itself has beautifully carved 15C panels.

Interior. — The nave, which was rebuilt in the 18C, is decorated with period woodwork from Semur-en-Auxois. The chief interest lies in the choir and apse, masterpieces of bold and skilful design, which date from the end of the 13C and the beginning of the 14C.

The five-sided **choir**★ is the most graceful Burgundian construction of that period. From the ground to the vault each slender column rises in an unbroken upward movement linking the blind arcades at the lowest level, the lower windows with their delicate tracery, the triforium and the clerestory *(illustration p 30)*. In the choir (left) stands a late-14C painted wooden statue of St Theobald when young, in a slightly affected pose, one finger on the page of a book.

To the right, in a recess, is the 13C tomb of the founder of the church, Hugues de Thil. The low-reliefs on the back wall of the recess were restored in 1839. Nearby is the piscina for the high altar, with two 16C basins.

The **furnishings**★ are interesting: the altar is decorated with two carved wooden retables representing episodes from the life of St Theobald.

At the far end of the choir is a large 14C Crucifixion and above the high altar a beautiful crosier, decorated with a 16C eucharistic dove.

On the right of the nave, standing against the wall of the choir, is an attractive 14C statue of the Virgin watching Jesus playing with a bird.

In the chapel of St Giles, which is the oldest part of the church, stands the 14C wooden shrine of St Theobald and statues of personages from the Old and New Testaments.

EXCURSIONS

Vitteaux. – Pop 1 138. *7km - 4 miles northeast by the D 26 and the D 70.* The **church of St-Germain** has a well-proportioned 13C doorway and 15C carved doors. The fine carvings of the 15C organ loft portray the Passion according to St Matthew.

Posanges Castle. – *10km - 6 miles northeast by the D 26 and the D 70; in Vitteaux turn left into the D 905.*

This imposing 15C castle was built by Guillaume Dubois, Chamberlain and Chancellor to Philip the Good *(p 18)*. The fortified entrance is overlooked by a postern and retains the slots for the arms of the former drawbridge. Four great round corner towers are linked by curtain walls.

STE-MAGNANCE   Pop 336

Michelin map 🖾 fold 17 or 🖾🖾 fold 24 – On the N 6, 25km - 16 miles northwest of Saulieu

The Gothic **church** of this small village was built *c*1514. Both the chancel and the apse have Flamboyant Gothic vaulting.

The church contains the beautiful 12C **tomb**★ of St Magnance. The low-reliefs recount the tale of the miracles of the saint, who together with St Camilla and three Roman ladies accompanied the body of St Germanus of Auxerre *(p 45)* from Ravenna, where he died, to Auxerre in the mid-5C. The low-reliefs have been restored since they were destroyed during the Revolution.

SAÔNE PLAIN

Michelin maps 🖾🖾 folds 13 and 14 🖾🖾 folds 1 to 3 and 🖾🖾 fold 3 or 🖾🖾🖾 folds 17 and 28

The Saône rises at Vioménil (395m - 1 296ft) at the junction of the Lorraine Plateau and the Vosges. The river enters Burgundy near Pontallier and then after 480km - 298 miles joins the Rhône at La Mulatière on the outskirts of Lyons.

The Saône is a placid river and navigable for over three quarters of its length owing to its gentle gradient and regular flow.

The landscapes. – The Saône flows slowly in the broad depression between the Massif Central and the Jura. Each year the winter floods leave a layer of silt which is exploited for market gardening (Auxonne) and pasturing. The Ouche and Tilles Valleys were a vast marsh until the 18C but now they are exploited for cash crops such as tobacco and sugar beet.

Beyond Seurre the Saône approaches the Côte but is separated from it by a partially wooded zone (Forests of Cîteaux and Gergy) which was partially cleared by the Cistercian monks during the Middle Ages.

A natural route. – Already in the Bronze Age (2nd millennium BC) Burgundy was on the principal trade routes from north to south: the Amber Road from the Baltic shores, the Tin Road from Cornwall via the Seine Valley and the Salt Road from Italy. Under the Roman Empire trade developed and the Via Agrippa from Lyons to Trier passed through Mâcon, Tournus, Chalon-sur-Saône and Langres. The Saône itself was also much used as a waterway and Chalon-sur-Saône became a busy river port and 'warehouse' for the powerful Saône rivermen's guild.

Wine was one of the numerous imports from Italy; the number of bases of amphorae found in the river bed at Chalon-sur-Saône has been estimated at 24 000. In the 13C and 14C Chalon-sur-Saône was already famous for its fairs, then centres of international trade where the cloth merchants of Dijon, Châtillon and Beaune traded with drapers from Flanders and Italy. The Saône was linked by canal to the Loire in 1793, the Seine in 1832, the Rhine in 1833 and the Marne in 1907. The Saône valley is the only natural north-south route in western Europe and is in consequence followed by numerous roads (the A 6, N 5 and N 6) and the railway (the Paris-Lyons-Marseilles line). Convoys of up to 4 000 tonnes can at present ply upstream from Fos-sur-Mer to Mâcon, but there is a project to extend the navigable reach as far as Auxonne. In the future, once the capacity of the Saône-Rhine link has been increased convoys of up to 4 000 tonnes will be able to travel by water from Fos to Rotterdam.

FROM PONTAILLER TO VERDUN-SUR-LE-DOUBS

69km - 43 miles – about 2 3/4 hours.

Pontailler-sur-Saône. – Pop 1 370. From the nearby summit of Mount Ardoux there is a good view over the Saône plain to the Jura on the eastern horizon.

Take the D 961 and D 976 south and the N 5 east (16km - 10 miles).

Auxonne. – *Description p 47.*

Take the D 20 south down the west bank of the Saône.

St-Jean-de-Losne. – Pop 1 476. This town is a veritable crossroads of the inland waterway network. The Burgundy Canal starts here while that of the Rhône-Rhine begins not far away.

In 1636 this fortified town withstood a siege by the Austro-Spanish armies during the Thirty Years' War, as the Saône then marked the boundary between France and Franche-Comté, which was part of the Habsburg Empire. Several hundred resisted victoriously against an army of 60 000 under the Austrian General Matthias Gallas, imperial commander in chief.

The 15C-16C church has a belfry with small turrets and steeply pitched roofs.

Take the D 976 southwest down the east bank of the Saône.

Seurre. – Pop 2 795. This busy little town stands near the confluence of two arms of the Saône. The far end of Rue Beauraing is a good vantage point. The 17C **hospital** with its one communal ward is a smaller version of the one at Beaune *(p 50)*. The 14C St Martin's Church, some half-timbered houses and no 13, the parental home of the well-known 17C preacher Bossuet, are worth seeing. No 13 is now the Tourist Information Centre and the Saône Museum (temporary exhibitions).

South of Seurre take the D 35^D southwest for 20km - 12 1/2 miles.

Verdun-sur-le-Doubs. – Pop 1 139. This little town is in a charming spot near the confluence of the smooth-flowing Saône and the turbulent Doubs, and surrounded by meadows.

This is the country of the *pauchouse*, a fish stew made with wine, onions and herbs, a well-known speciality of the region.

⊘Overlooking the confluence is the **Wheat and Bread Centre,** a branch of the Burgundian Bresse Museum *(p 135);* Verdun-sur-le-Doubs is on the edge of the wheat belt in the Valley of the Saône. The centre describes the origins and development of wheat cultivation as well as the history of milling and breadmaking; collection of loaves. Further south **Chalon-sur-Saône** *(p 66),* **Tournus★★** *(p 162)* and **Mâcon** *(p 110)* are other places of interest in the Saône plain.

★ SAULIEU   Pop 3 183

Michelin map ▦▦ fold 17 or ▧▧▧ fold 13 – Local map p 125

Saulieu is pleasantly situated on the boundaries of the Morvan and the Auxois, beside the N 6. The art lover will find interest in the Basilica of St Andoche and also in the works of François Pompon, the animal sculptor, who was born at Saulieu in 1855.

A gastronomic centre. – The gastronomic reputation of Saulieu is linked to the history of road travel and goes back to the 17C. In 1651 the Burgundian States decided to restore to the old Paris-Lyons road, which passed along the eastern edge of the Morvan, the importance that it had before the Middle Ages. Saulieu set about increasing its prosperity by developing local industry and fairs. The town became a post house on the route and felt it its duty to treat travellers well. Rabelais had already praised Saulieu and its excellent meals. **Madame de Sévigné** stopped in the town on her way to Vichy on 26 August 1677, and she avowed later that for the first time in her life she had become a little tipsy.

The timber of the Morvan. – Although Saulieu's economic activity has always been to a great extent based on forestry there has been a considerable transformation in this sector. There is an ever-growing trade in Christmas trees; each year more than a million of these trees (spruces in particular) are sent to Paris and other large towns in France, Europe and Africa. Despite this shift to conifers there are still large areas of oak and beech. Large tree nurseries now produce several hundreds of thousands of saplings for the French and foreign markets.

The state forest of Saulieu (768ha - 1 898 acres) now has many recreational facilities: picnic sites, adventure playgrounds, walks and trails, riding tracks and small lakes providing trout fishing.

★ BASILICA OF ST ANDOCHE
(BASILIQUE ST-ANDOCHE) *time: 1/2 hour*

The basilica stands in Place du Docteur-Roclore where there is a pretty 18C fountain. The church, which dates from the beginning of the 12C, is slightly later than the one in Vézelay; it was built to replace an abbey church founded in the 8C on the site of the martyrdom of St Andoche, St Thyrse and St Felix, and was influenced by St Lazarus in Autun of which it was a sister house.

St-Andoche Basilica. – Capital.

This fine Romanesque building has been sadly maltreated; the main doorway was mutilated during the French Revolution and rebuilt in the 19C. Inside, the bases of the pillars are buried nearly three feet deep. The choir was burnt by the English in 1359 and rebuilt in 1704 without any attempt at coherence of style.

Interior. – The main point of interest is the series of historiated or decorated **capitals★**, inspired by those in Autun. Here one can see: the Flight into Egypt, the Temptation of Christ in the Desert, the Hanging of Judas, Christ appearing to Mary Magdalene, the false prophet Balaam.

The choir stalls date from the 14C and the organ loft from the 15C. After its restoration, the tomb of St Andoche was placed in the last chapel in the right aisle. To the right of the choir, note a Renaissance Virgin in stone and a 14C statue of St Roch. In the north aisle, there is a handsome tombstone and painted *Pietà*, presented, so it is said, by Madame de Sévigné as a penance *(p 148)* for over-indulgence.

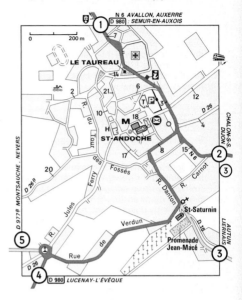

ADDITIONAL SIGHTS

Museum (M). – The museum, which is housed in a 17C mansion abutting the basilica, contains archaeological and ethnological collections about Saulieu and its neighbourhood.

Ground floor: in the entrance hall a collection of fragments offers a visual survey of the history of the site; the rooms following display Gallo-Roman tombstones from the old necropolis, fragments of the Romanesque doorway from St Andoche's Basilica, a collection of sacred statues (12C-18C) and obsolete tools (hemp working, clog making, forge).

First floor: one room is devoted to a Gallo-Roman water source (discovered near Saulieu) believed to have curative powers, as is evident from the considerable collection of small wooden votive offerings in the shape of human limbs and organs; the large oak casing of the well is on show together with a model of the site. Souvenirs of **François Pompon** (Saulieu 1855 - Paris 1933) as well as some of his original work are displayed in the following rooms; he was a pupil of Rodin *(Bust of St Catherine and Cosette)* and is best known for the smooth finish of his large animal sculptures (one of his masterpieces, the **Bull★**, was erected in 1948 in a square on the north side of the town). Old crafts, souvenirs of 19C Saulieu and a reconstruction of a traditional Morvan domestic interior complete the ethnological collections on the ground floor.

St Saturnin. – This charming 15C church, with its pointed belfry covered with shingles, stands in the middle of a terraced graveyard.

Beyond the east end of the church is the tomb of François Pompon, surmounted by one of his own works representing a condor.

Promenade Jean-Macé. – A pleasant walk, shaded by age-old lime trees.

SEIGNELAY   Pop 1 485

Michelin map 🔢 fold 5 or 🔢 folds 10 and 11

The town spreads over the slopes of a wooded hillside, which overlooks the Serein meandering below. In the Middle Ages Seignelay was the chief town of an important barony. Colbert purchased the said barony in 1657 and soon after had it raised to the status of a marquisate. Anxious that his greatness should be reflected in his surroundings, Colbert commissioned the royal architect to restore the château.

Château. – The castle was destroyed during the Revolution but the park has survived together with part of the fortified curtain wall, a tower restored in the 19C and one of the two entrance lodges built at the end of the 18C by the Montmorency family.

Place Colbert. – A lime-tree-shaded avenue opens into this square which has retained its 17C aspect and offers an attractive view of the Serein.

The present town hall occupies the former court house built by Colbert. The façade is adorned with a pediment and heavily moulded doorways. The building next door, now an income tax office, was originally the governor's residence and was built by the Duc de Montmorency. The whole forms an attractive ensemble of two wings with slated mansard roofs. The château gatehouse stands at right angles to the governor's residence. Facing the town hall is the 17C **covered market** with its unusual double-pitched roof; each section of roof differs in shape and angle of incline from the seven others. The fine timberwook roof rests on 32 columns.

⊘**St Martial.** — The present church was rebuilt in the 15C incorporating parts of the fabric of an earlier Romanesque church, notably the buttress. A fine belfry flanks the west front and is topped by a lantern turret. The plan of the church is unusual in that it has only one aisle. The choir, the Lady Chapel, apsidal and baptismal chapels all date from the 15C. The nave was altered in the 16C and the vaulting of the aisle was raised to the level of that of the nave. The Renaissance doorway is protected by an overhanging roof.

The churchwarden's pew is of the Louis XIII period. The six silver chandeliers in the sanctuary are in the Louis XVI style and came from the château, as did the three stools and two small reliquaries emblazoned with Colbert's arms. The painted statue of the Virgin is 17C. The windows in the south wall and in the choir contain fragments of 16C tracery designed by the Veissières brothers and their pupil, Mathieu, all natives of Seignelay.

SEINE (SOURCE)

Michelin map 🗓 fold 19 or 🗓🗓 folds 3 and 15 — 10km - 6 miles northwest of St-Seine-l'Abbaye

The source of the Seine, one mile west of the N 71 by the D 103, flows in a little valley planted with fir trees. The city of Paris owns the area. The main spring bubbles up from a cave containing the statue of a nymph, a copy of the statue personifying the Seine sculptured in 1865 by Jouffroy.

Immediately downstream, excavations have uncovered the ruins of a Gallo-Roman temple and bronzes including a faun and the goddess Sequana, proof that the source of the river was worshipped during Roman times.

Other finds include numerous wooden statues and votive offerings, including around 200 flat sticks carved to resemble human figures which are now in the Archaeological Museum in Dijon.

SPRING

On the Langres Plateau *(see the Michelin Green Guide Champagne Ardennes, in French only)* there are numerous resurgent springs, known locally as *dhuys* or *douix*. These springs owe their existence to the presence of marl or clay below beds of limestone.

La Coquille Source. — This springs forth in an attractive spot at Étalante *(27km - 17 miles north of the source of the Seine)*.

⊘A few miles from this spot the village of **Aignay-le-Duc** has a 13C Gothic **church** with a belfry roofed with shingles. In the choir is an early-16C stone retable portraying scenes from the Passion.

★ SEMUR-EN-AUXOIS   Pop 5 364

Michelin map 🗓 folds 17 and 18 or 🗓🗓 fold 13

The **setting★** and the town of Semur, main centre of the Auxois region, form a picturesque scene if approached from the west or the north. From the Paris road, there is a good view of the ramparts and the town during the downhill run to the Joly ⊘Bridge. The main buildings are **floodlit** in the evenings.

A tightly-packed mass of small light-coloured houses stand on the top of a rose-tinted granite cliff, overlooking a deep ravine at the bottom of which flows the river Armançon. Above the houses and cascade of gardens rise the great red-slated towers of the castle keep and the slender spire of the Church of the Virgin (Église Notre-Dame).

A stronghold. — Semur became the strong-point of the duchy in the 14C when the citadel was reinforced by ramparts and eighteen towers. The town was divided into three parts each with a perimeter wall. Occupying the whole width of the rock spur and towering above all else was the keep, a citadel in itself and reputedly impregnable. It had a sheer drop both to the north and the south to the Armançon valley and was flanked by four enormous round towers: the Golden Orle Tower, the Gehenna Tower, the Prison Tower and the Margot Tower. The château stood to the west, on the upper part of the peninsula, encircled by a bend in the river — the ramparts can still be seen. To the east was the town, still the most densely populated district although the town has spread on to the west bank.

★ CHURCH OF THE VIRGIN (ÉGLISE NOTRE-DAME) *time: 1/2 hour*

The church stands in Place Notre-Dame, flanked by old houses. The church was founded in the 11C, rebuilt in the 13C and 14C, altered in the 15C and 16C, extended by the addition of chapels to the north aisle and restored by Viollet-le-Duc (1814-79).

Exterior. — The 14C façade, dominated by two square towers, is preceded by a vast porch. In Rue Notre-Dame, the 13C door in the north transept (Porte des Bleds) has a beautiful tympanum depicting Doubting Thomas. Surmounting the doorway is a statue of an angel, arms open in a welcoming gesture. On one of the slender engaged piers which flank the doorway are two sculptured snails, symbolising Burgundian cooking.

The 15C porch shelters three doorways. Although the sculptures of the recessed arches and the niches disappeared at the Revolution, various low-relief figures line the base of the engaged piers.

From the garden behind the church there is a view of the chevet which, with the narrow and steeply roofed apse and conically roofed chapels, show great purity of line.

The octagonal transept crossing tower is surmounted by a beautiful stone spire.

⊘ Interior. – The narrowness of the central nave, dating from the 13C and 14C, emphasises the soaring height of the vaulting supported by slender columns.

There are several interesting chapels opening off the north aisle. In the second chapel (1) is a polychrome Entombment dating from the late 15C with monumental figures typical of Claus Sluter *(p 31)*. The third chapel (2) with its stellar vaulting has 16C stained glass illustrating the legend of St Barbara. The last two chapels contain panels of stained glass given in the 15C by local guilds: the butchers (3) and eight panels from the drapers (4).

Behind the pulpit is a 15C stone canopy (5), remarkably carved with a 5m - 16ft high pinnacle.

A blind triforium decorates the 13C choir and the transept; its elegant and slender columns are surmounted by capitals in the form of sculptured human heads. The hanging keystone of the choir is brightly painted and represents the crowning of the Virgin amidst foliage and angels' heads.

The choir is flanked by double aisles; the

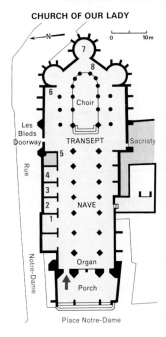

CHURCH OF OUR LADY

three chapels radiating from the ambulatory are separated by triple lancets. The Grantin-Riepp-Callinet organ dates from the 17C-19C.

In the last chapel of the outer north aisle is a painted retable (6) dating from 1554, representing the Tree of Jesse. The retable is surmounted by a Gothic canopy of carved wood. The Lady Chapel (7) is lit by very beautiful stained glass windows of the 13C restored by Viollet-le-Duc. In the ambulatory is a late-15C polychrome statue (8) of Christ bearing the Five Wounds; with a theatrical gesture He indicates the spear thrust in His side; two angels carry His mantle.

ADDITIONAL SIGHTS

⊘ Golden Orle Tower and Museum (M¹). – This tower, which is now cracked on the north side, was once part of the keep which was razed in 1602. The tower owes its name to its battlements (demolished), which used to be covered with coppered lead *(ourlée d'or* – trimmed with gold). Its dimensions are impressive (44m - 144ft high, walls 5m - 16ft thick at the base tapering to about 2.2m - 7ft at the top). Prior to the construction of the Joly Bridge (1787), this tower was one of the main entrances to the town. It now houses a local and natural history **museum.** The different floors provide good views of the keep and the town. The top floor has a fine chestnut timber ceiling.

Promenade des Remparts. – The former ramparts along the edge of the granite spur have been converted into a promenade shaded by lime trees which overlooks the valley of the Armançon. To reach the promenade, go past the hospital, a pleasant 18C building, which was once the mansion of the Marquis du Châtelet, Governor of Semur, whose priggish wife was Voltaire's sweetheart.

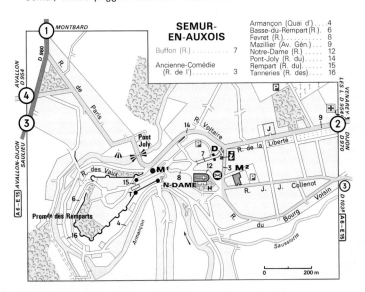

SEMUR-EN-AUXOIS

Buffon (R.) 7
Ancienne-Comédie (R. de l') 3

Armançon (Quai d') ... 4
Basse-du-Rempart (R.). 6
Fevret (R.) 8
Mazillier (Av. Gén.) ... 9
Notre-Dame (R.) 12
Pont-Joly (R. du) 14
Rempart (R. du) 15
Tanneries (R. des) 16

Semur-en-Auxois

Joly Bridge (Pont Joly). – From the Joly Bridge there is an overall **view★** of the little medieval city. It is particularly charming in the light of the setting sun. The bridge crosses the Armançon at the foot of the castle keep, which once guarded the narrow isthmus joining the rose-coloured cliff, where the city first started, to the granite plateau on which the town has now spread. In the foreground the view sweeps up the valley with gardens, rocks, parks and small cascades on either side.

Tour of the ramparts. – Rue Basse-du-Rempart skirts the foot of the ramparts. Their grandeur is emphasised by the enormous blocks of red granite, sparkling with mica and quartz, which serve as the foundations of the keep.

⊘Museum (M²). – An old Jacobin convent houses the museum and library. The ground floor displays a collection of 13C to 19C sculpture, including many original plaster figures, mostly by Augustin Dumont, who created monumental sculptures and commemorative statues (*Spirit of Liberty* in Place de la Bastille in Paris). The first floor houses a rich collection on natural science, particularly zoology and geology (fossils – rare fish fossils – and mineral samples). The second floor contains articles found during the archaeological excavation of prehistoric, Gallo-Roman (votive offerings from the source of the Seine) and Merovingian sites. The gallery contains 17C to 19C paintings (*Portrait of a Prophet* by Vignon and three works by Corot) and a few 19C sculptures; a small room is devoted to the Middle Ages and the Renaissance (*Angels* by Le Moiturier).

Sauvigny Gateway (D). – This 15C gateway, preceded by a postern, marked the main entrance to the district known as the Bourg Notre-Dame.

EXCURSIONS

Pont Lake (Lac de Pont). – *3km - 2 miles south by ③, the D 103ᴮ.*
This artificial reservoir (80ha - 198 acres), stretching over 6km - 4 miles from Pont-et-Massène to Montigny, was created in the 19C to supplement the waters of the Burgundy Canal. The shores of the lake (bathing beach and water sports) are pleasantly surrounded by rocks and shrubs and trees.

⊘Bourbilly Château. – *9km - 6 miles southwest by ④ on the plan and then the D 9 to the left.* The 14C château, set in the Serein valley, belonged to Jeanne-Françoise Frémyot de Chantal (1572-1641), who with St Francis de Sales co-founded the Order of the Visitation in 1610 and was canonised in 1767 as St Jeanne de Chantal. Her granddaughter, the future Marquise de Sévigné, spent some of her childhood holidays here. The château was despoiled at the Revolution and restored in the 19C and again in 1952 following a fire. Set in fine parkland the château comprises three ranges around a courtyard, quartered by round towers with conical roofs. The very tall slender chimneys are unusual.
The tour includes the guard room, formerly the chapel's crypt with a Louis XIII billiard table and a rare photograph of fighting during the First World War; the refurbished chapel with its fine timberwork roof and an attractive 18C wrought-iron grille decorated with roses and crosses; the library; the dining room with its painted French-style ceiling and 17C Flemish tapestry portraying *The Capture of Tyre by Alexander the Great;* the Venetian Room which is named after the 19C Venetian glass chandeliers and lamps with their fantastic forms; the furniture is 17C and 18C.

Venarey-les-Laumes. – *13km - 8 miles northeast by ② on the plan, the D 954.*
On the esplanade near the station stands a modern **church** (1968) designed by the architect Jacques Prioleau. The austere building is lit by a huge window in the chancel and two side windows overlooking two small gardens.

★ SEMUR-EN-BRIONNAIS

Michelin map **73** north of folds 7 and 8 or **243** fold 37 — Local map 63

The village stands on a promontory which is covered with vines and fruit trees. The château, the Romanesque church, the former priory and 18C court room (now the town hall) make an attractive ensemble in pinkish stone.

SIGHTS

★ St Hilary's Church (St-Hilaire). — The church, which was built in the Cluniac style, has a very fine chevet; its squat appearance is relieved by the height of the gable walls at the end of the chancel and the transept arms, and its austerity is offset by the carved cornice below the roof. The elegant octagonal belfry is decorated with a double band of twin Romanesque arcades; the upper band is framed by a series of recessed arches.

The west doorway is richly decorated although the sculptures show a certain lack of skill in the modelling. As at Charlieu, a haloed lamb is carved on the external key-stone. The lintel depicts a scene from the life of St Hilary of Poitiers: condemned by a council of Arian bishops, he sets off into exile, a begging bag on his shoulder; on the road he meets an angel who gives him hope and returns him to his place among the bishops; meanwhile the devil makes off with the soul of the Council President.

The nave is very attractive; at the west end the triforium, which consists of an arcade with twin arch stones, forms a bowed gallery which is supported by an impressive corbel springing from the keystone of the west door.

The gallery may be an imitation of St Michael's Chapel above the west door of Cluny abbey church.

The dome on squinches above the transept crossing is decorated with arcades similar to those of the triforium.

⊘ St Hugues' Castle. — The 9C rectangular keep was the birthplace of the famous abbot, St Hugh of Cluny *(p 80)*. The two round towers served as a prison in the 18C.

There is a view of the vineyard-covered slopes and in the distance the summits of Le Forez and La Madeleine.

★★ SÈNE (MOUNT)

Michelin map **69** fold 9 or **243** fold 27 — 10km - 6 miles west of Chagny

Sène Mount is also known as Three Cross Mount **(Montagne des Trois-Croix)** owing to the three crosses which stand on the summit. It is approached by a turning (east) off the road between Dezize-lès-Maranges and the N 6 (north); the road is narrow with sharp bends and steep gradients near the top.

★★ Panorama. — From the top one can see (north) the famous vineyards of the Côte beyond La Rochepot, (east) the Saône Valley, the Jura and the Alps, (south) the Cluny district dominated by Mount St Vincent and (west) the Morvan.

SENNECEY-LE-GRAND

Michelin map **69** northeast of fold 19 or **243** fold 27

The Town Hall occupies all that remains of a former feudal castle, standing on the edge of a large square surrounded by a moat. A church of monumental appearance, with tall interior columns, was built in the classical style in the 19C on the remainder of the site once occupied by the castle.

West of the town are two Romanesque churches *(see below)* of very simple design with Lombard arcading on the exterior and roofs of lava flagstones; in both cases the transept crossing is covered by a dome on squinches surmounted by a solid square belfry.

⊘ St-Julien. — *Between the town and the motorway.* Both the nave and belfry are 11C but the rest of the church is 15C.

⊘ St-Martin-de-Laives. — *2.5km - 1 1/2 miles west by the D 18; after passing under the motorway turn left into a track.*

The church stands on a spur with a view over the Bresse, the Jura, Chalon and its surroundings, the valley of the River Grosne and the Charollais region. Like St-Julien it dates from the 11C; the chapels were added in the 15C and 16C.

Admission times and charges for the sights described are listed at the end of the Guide.

Every sight for which there are times and charges is indicated by the symbol ⊘ in the margin in the middle section of the guide.

Michelin map ⬛⬛ fold 14 or ⬛⬛⬛ fold 45
Plan of built-up-area in the current Michelin Red Guide France

Today, a sub-prefecture in the Department of Yonne, Sens is the seat of an archbishopric, proof of its past grandeur. The old town is girdled by boulevards and promenades that have replaced the ancient ramparts. In the city centre stands St Stephen's Cathedral. The approach from the west (D 81) provides a fine view of the town as the road descends from the heights on the left bank of the Yonne.

HISTORICAL NOTES

The Country of the Senones. – The tribe of the Senones, who gave their name to the town, was for long one of the most powerful in Gaul. In 390 BC, under the command of Brennus, they invaded Italy and seized Rome. When the Romans were masters of all Gaul, they made Sens the capital of a province of the Lyonnaise, known as Lyonnaise IV or Senonia.

An Important Diocese. – Up to 1622, the year in which Paris was elevated to the rank of an archbishopric, Sens had pre-eminence over the bishoprics of Chartres, Auxerre, Meaux, Paris, Orléans, Nevers and Troyes, giving the initials forming the device of the metropolitan church: "Campont". During the residence in Sens of Pope Alexander III in 1163-64 the city became the temporary capital of Christianity. The church council that condemned Abelard was also held at Sens and the marriage of St Louis and Marguerite of Provence was celebrated in the cathedral in 1234. With the elevation of Paris, the diocese of Sens lost the bishoprics of Meaux, Chartres and Orléans.

★★ CATHEDRAL OF ST STEPHEN (CATHÉDRALE ST-ÉTIENNE)
time: 1/2 hour

Although the cathedral was started *c*1130 by Archbishop Henri Sanglier, most of the construction took place between 1140 and 1168; it was the first of the great Gothic cathedrals in France. Many other buildings have borrowed largely from the design (the plan, the alternating pillars, the triforium): William of Sens, architect, used it as his model when reconstructing the chancel of Canterbury Cathedral (1175-92).

Exterior. – The west front, despite the loss of a tower, has nevertheless preserved its imposing majesty and harmony of balance. The north tower (Lead Tower), built at the end of the 12C, used to be surmounted by a timbered belfry covered in lead, which was destroyed last century.
The south tower (Stone Tower), which collapsed at the end of the 13C, began to be rebuilt in the following century and was completed in the 16C. Topped by a graceful campanile, it is 78m - 256ft high. The tower houses two bells, weighing 13 3/4 tons and 15 3/4 tons.
The statues on the upper gallery, which were added in the 19C, represent the leading archbishops of Sens. An immense radiant window, a rose window of smaller size, and a Christ conferring His blessing, framed by two angels (modern statues), rise in tiers above the central doorway.

North doorway. – The tympanum of this 12C doorway recalls the history of St John the Baptist. Generosity and avarice are portrayed at the bottom of the low-reliefs.

Central doorway. – A beautiful statue of St Stephen, in the costume of a deacon and carrying the Gospel, fortunately spared during the Revolution, stands with its back to the pier of the main doorway. This work, dating from the end of the 12C, marks the transition period between the sculptures of Chartres and Bourges and those of Paris and Amiens, and is thus an interesting sign of the beginning of Gothic sculpture.

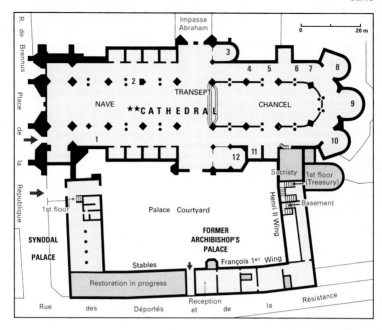

The low-reliefs of the engaged piers framing the doorway represent the Foolish Virgins on the right and the Wise Virgins on the left. The statues of the Apostles, which used to occupy the twelve niches in the splaying of the doorway, have disappeared. The original tympanum, which it is believed portrayed the Last Judgment, was remade in the 13C: it is devoted to scenes from the life of St Stephen. Statuettes of saints decorate the arches.

South doorway. – The tympanum of the right-hand doorway (early-14C) is devoted to the Virgin. The statuettes, representing the prophets, have been decapitated. A decoration of angels ornaments the arching.

Enter by the south doorway.

Interior. – The nave is impressive for its size and unity; it is divided from the aisles by magnificent arches surmounted by a triforium and roofed with sexpartite vaulting. The alternating stout and slender pillars are characteristic of the early-Gothic style. The original appearance of the church has been somewhat lost in successive alterations: the clerestories in the choir were extended upwards in the 13C and in the nave in the 14C; in the 15C Archbishop Tristan de Salazar added the transept marking the division between the nave and the choir.

The **stained glass windows★★**, dating from the 12C-17C, are magnificent.

In the third bay of the south aisle is a window (1) by Jean Cousin, dating from 1530. On the north side of the nave is a Renaissance retable and a monument (2) given by Archbishop de Salazar in memory of his parents.

The stained glass windows of the south transept (1500-02) were made in Troyes: those portraying the Tree of Jesse and legend of St Nicholas are outstanding; the rose window represents the Last Judgment. Those in the north transept were made in 1516-17 by Jean Hympe and his son, glaziers from Sens; the rose window represents Paradise.

The choir is enclosed by handsome bronze screens (1762) bearing the arms of Cardinal de Luynes. The large high altar is 18C by Servandoni and the stained glass of the clerestory dates from the 13C.

Leave the cathedral by the north transept.

North transept. – From the Impasse Abraham one can admire the magnificent Flamboyant-style façade built by Martin Chambiges and his son between 1500 and 1513. The sculptured decoration is very graceful. The statue of Abraham, surmounting the gable, is modern.

Re-enter the cathedral by the same door.

Both St John's Chapel, which contains a fine 13C calvary (3), and the blind arcade round the ambulatory are part of the original building. The oldest stained glass, dating from the late 12C, is in the four windows overlooking the ambulatory: the story of Thomas Becket (4), the story of St Eustace (5) and the parables of the Prodigal Son (6) and the Good Samaritan (7). The tomb (8) of the Dauphin, father of Louis XVI, by Guillaume Coustou is placed in the next chapel. The 13C apsidal chapel has stained glass windows (9) of the same period. In the chapel of the Sacred Heart (10) one of the windows is attributed to Jean Cousin. In the chapel beyond the sacristy is a Renaissance retable (11). The Lady Chapel contains a 14C seated statue of the Virgin (12) above the altar.

Leave by the south transept.

South transept. – This was built by Martin Chambiges, master mason who had worked at both Beauvais and Troyes. It is a fine example of the Flamboyant style (1490-1500). The decoration of the Moses Doorway is quite remarkable. The gable is surmounted by a modern statue of Moses.

★MUSEUM, TREASURY AND SYNODAL PALACE (M)

The Sens Museums are housed in the **former archbishop's palace** (16C-18C) and the Synodal Palace which stand on the south side of the cathedral.

François I and Henri II Wings. – These galleries are devoted to the history of Sens and the Sens district. The first rooms display prehistoric and protohistoric articles: Palaeolithic stone tools, Neolithic house and burials (7500 to 2500 BC), Bronze Age objects (2500 to 750 BC) including the Treasury from Villethierry (jeweller's stock), many Iron Age weapons and ornaments.

The basement contains pieces of Gallo-Roman stonework re-used in the construction of the town walls of Sens: architectural pieces, sculptures, tombstones. It is noticeable that the sculpture on the public monuments is in the official Roman style (façade of the baths) whereas funerary sculpture, a more popular art, provides a picture of ancient Sens society. Excavations under the courtyard have revealed the foundations of a 4C bathhouse including a collection of bone combs. 18C sculpture is displayed on the first floor: reliefs from the Porte Dauphine which was erected in memory of the Dauphin, Louis XV's son, and of the Dauphin's wife, and a rood screen removed from the cathedral in the 19C.

The second floor is hung with 17C to 19C paintings.

★★ **Cathedral Treasury.** – *Access via the museum.* This treasure house, along with that in Conques *(see the Michelin Green Guide Gorges du Tarn, in French only)* is one of the richest in France. It contains a magnificent collection of materials and liturgical vestments: the shroud of St Victor, a 13C white silk mitre embroidered with gold thread; handsome 15C high warp tapestries *(Adoration of the Magi* and the *Crowning of the Virgin)*; ivories (5C and 6C pyx, the 7C liturgical comb of St Lupus, an 11C Byzantine coffret and a 12C Islamic one) as well as goldwork.

Synodal Palace. – This beautiful 13C (*c*1230-40) palace was restored by Viollet-le-Duc. The great vaulted chamber on the ground floor was the seat of the ecclesiastical tribunal *(officialité).* In the 13C two bays were converted into a prison and there are still traces of graffiti on the walls.

The magnificent hall on the first floor was where the bishops deliberated. The archaeological collection on the ground floor and the collections of the adjoining treasury (Lemoine paintings, tapestries...) will be rearranged once the rooms of the new museum are ready.

ADDITIONAL SIGHTS

Covered market. – The metal framework filled with pink brick standing opposite the cathedral is typical of the architectural style in fashion during the latter half of the 19C. The conspicuous pitched roof is ornamented with pinnacle turrets.

Old houses (Maisons anciennes). – Among the many old buildings in the town, two are particularly noteworthy. At the corner of Rue de la République and Rue Jean-Cousin, stands a 16C house (**E**) known as the House of Abraham. The carved corner post is decorated with a Tree of Jesse. The next-door house, at 50 Rue Jean-Cousin, known as the House of the Pillar (Maison du Pilier) (16C), has a curious porch. In Rue Abélard there are several 16C and 18C mansions.

St-Pierre-le-Rond. – Beside the church stands the belltower (1728) and a building which in 1928 was faced with the 13C façade of the Sens charity hospital (Hôtel-Dieu). The high spear-shaped windows in the gables provide a point of harmony between the two façades. The wooden-roofed 13C nave of the church leads to a rectangular chancel. The aisle, built in the Gothic style, is lit by five windows which have largely retained their 16C stained glass. The wrought-iron screens date from the 17C.

St Maurice. – The church was built in the latter half of the 12C on an island in the Yonne. The square east end is half-timbered; the slate spire rising from the asymmetrical roof is seen to advantage from the right bank of the river. The choir, which was refurbished in the 16C, contains a large low-relief sculpture composed of several panels dating from 1567.

St Savinien. – *East of the town plan in Rue Alsace-Lorraine, 750m - 820yds from Boulevard du Mail on the left.* The church was built in the 11C on the site of an earlier church. It is basilical in plan with a steep-pitched roof over the nave and three apsidal chapels but no transept. A flight of steps in front of the central apsidal chapel leads to a small crypt. The plain exterior of the building contrasts with the graceful belfry which has two storeys; the lower one in the Romanesque style is pierced by twin bays with round-headed arches; the upper one has tall bays with pointed arches.

★ Les SETTONS RESERVOIR

Michelin map 🖽 southwest of fold 17 or 🖾🖾 fold 24 – Local maps pp 73 and 124

Les Settons Reservoir (34 359ha - 887 acres) was created in the Cure Valley (alt 573m - 1 880ft) in one of the most isolated parts of the Morvan. It is a peaceful place, surrounded by pine and larch woods, where wildfowl congregate in the autumn. Footpaths and a lakeside road provide easy access for walking, fishing and water sports.

The dam (277m – 909ft long) was built in 1861; the dyke (227m - 745ft) was added in 1901. The reservoir has a potential capacity of 4 619 million gallons of water. It was created originally to facilitate logging on the River Cure *(pp 77 and 89)* but is now used to regulate the flow of the River Yonne.

The small resort of **Les Settons** is a pleasant place to spend the summer holidays.

SOLUTRÉ

The **Rock of Solutré★**, a superb limestone escarpment with a distinctive profile, figures largely in prehistory. It was here that a particular type of flint tool was first identified and given the name Solutrean (18000 to 15000 BC). The tools were created by knapping, i.e. knocking off flat flakes to obtain bifaced stones with sharp edges, sometimes called "laurel leaves" (fine examples in the Denon Museum in Chalon-sur-Saône – *p 66*). The end of this period is marked by the appearance of stone needles with eyes.

Excavations. – The first excavations at the foot of the rock in 1866 brought to light a pile of horse bones which, together with a few bison, auroch, deer and mammoth bones, formed a layer between 0.5m - 2m (18in - 6 1/2ft) thick covering an area of 4000m² - 4784sq yds. This hunting ground was used for 25000 years by the different generations of the Upper Palaeolithic Age (Aurignacian, Gravettian, Solutrean and Magdalenian).

Rock of Solutré.

At the end of the last century it was supposed that the horses were rounded up on the top of the rock and forced by noise or fire to jump to their death; this theory is no longer maintained. Excavations carried out between 1968 and 1976 suggest that the wild horses were hunted during their spring migrations to the foot of the rock where they were slaughtered and dismembered.

Panorama. – *From Mâcon take the D 54 southwest through Solutré; beyond the cemetery take the second road on the right to a car park; 3/4 hour on foot Rtn.* A path leads through Crot du Charnier (where the museum is situated) to the top of the Rock of Solutré (495m - 1624ft). Although the range is limited the view embraces the Valley of the Saône, the Bresse, the Jura and on a clear day the Alps.

⊙**Museum.** – The museum, which is buried at the foot of the rock, is devoted to the prehistoric archaeology of the south Mâconnais, the horses and hunting at Solutré in the Upper Palaeolithic Age and Solutrean man in the European context. In between the three sections are two viewpoints overlooking the surrounding countryside: the Valley of the Saône and the Rock of Solutré.

Many camping sites have:
shops, bars, laundry, games rooms,
playground, mini-golf, paddling pool, swimming pool.
Consult the Michelin Guide, Camping Caravaning France.

★★ SUIN HILL

The hill, **Butte de Suin** (593m - 1946ft) stands halfway between Charolles and Cluny, north of the D 17. It is one of several tors or rocky hilltops which rise from the sandstone and granite ridge to the east of the Charollais region. These hilltops (Les Carges, Suin, Chaumont) are often crowned by great blocks of stone.
From the car park by the War Memorial take the path to the right of the church; when level with the statue of the Virgin take the steps (right) which lead to the viewing table (1/4 hour Rtn on foot).
From this vantage point there is a magnificent **panorama★★**: to the north, Mount St-Vincent (603m - 1978ft); to the northeast, the depression formed by the valley of the Grosne, and beyond, the valley of the Saône; to the east, the line of the Mâconnais highlands; to the southeast lies the Mère Boitier (758m - 2487ft); to the south, Mount St-Rigaux and the mountain of St-Cyr; to the west, in the foreground, Mount Botey (561m - 1841ft), and beyond it, the Brionnais, the Charollais and the valley of the Loire.
The rock is now a popular venue for hang-gliding.

★ SULLY CHÂTEAU

Michelin map 🔢 fold 8 or 🔢 fold 26 – 4km - 3 miles northwest of Épinac

⊙Sully Château is a Renaissance mansion flanked by its outbuildings and set in a vast park; in its lay-out and decoration it is similar to the château of Ancy-le-Franc *(p 37)*. The building was begun early in the 16C by Jean de Saulx, who had already acquired the land at Sully, and continued by his son, the Maréchal de Tavannes.

The surrounding moat is fed by the River Drée. Four wings, flanked by four square corner towers set at an angle, enclose an inner courtyard.

The west façade, containing the entrance, consists of wide bays separated by pilasters at first-floor level. Two turrets flank the chapel in the south façade. From the north façade, which was rebuilt in the 18C, a monumental stair gives access to a terrace, bordered by a handsome balustrade, overlooking a stretch of water.

The château was the birthplace of Marshal **Mac-Mahon,** Duke of Magenta and President of the French Republic from 1873 to 1879.

TAIZÉ

Pop 140

Michelin map 🔢 fold 19 or 🔢 fold 39 – 10km - 6 miles north of Cluny

In 1940 Pastor Schutz (now called Brother Roger) settled at Taizé and established an ecumenical community which now numbers over 80 brothers, who take lifelong vows and are drawn from various Christian churches (Catholic and Protestant) and from about twenty different countries.

Their mission is to be involved worldwide with young people in the search for unity and reconciliation; the brothers organise youth meetings throughout the world. Pope John-Paul II visited Taizé in 1986.

The community is a highly active one with a tented village and group of bungalows to accommodate the visitors, and many craft workshops and stands.

SIGHTS

⊙**Church** (Église). – The low-lying, flat-roofed Church of the Reconciliation was consecrated in 1962 and serves as a place of worship. The five-bell peal is out in the open air. This concrete building has a large main doorway but small and narrow windows.

The nave is flanked to the right by a passageway leading to the crypt. The stained glass in the windows opening into this passage represent the main feast days: the Easter Lamb, a yellow and flame-coloured composition; the last window, of the Transfiguration, has ochre-coloured figures against a pale blue-green background with touches of red.

The first crypt, revolving round a central pillar supporting the choir, is a place of prayer and silence; the second crypt is an orthodox chapel.

Parish Church (Église paroissiale). – This Romanesque church is starkly simple and is lit by narrow windows. The church is also used by the community.

EXCURSIONS

Ameugny. – Pop 148. *2km - 1 1/4 miles north.* The massive 12C **church** is built of the attractive local red sandstone. Pointed vaulting covers the three bays of the nave. Above the transept crossing a dome on squinches supports the heavy square belltower with its open belfry.

Besanceuil. – *13km - 8 miles northwest.* At the foot of a wooded ridge overlooking the Guye Valley are grouped the pale stone houses of the village, the 14C château (inhabited) with its square towers, and the 11C Romanesque chapel with its timberwork porch.

St-Hippolyte. – *10km - 6 1/4 miles northwest.* Visible from afar dominating the hill and the hamlet is the singular and powerful belltower of the half-ruined priory church of St Hippolyte which was built in the Romanesque style in the 11C with a triple apse; the adjoining convent buildings are now used by a farm.

The tower is pierced by two storeys of arcades over round-headed arches (twinned on the second storey); it was enlarged and fortified at the sides (arrow slits) during the Wars of Religion.

The body of the church was built of small pale stones; the walls of the nave and the choir surmounted by a dome on squinches are all that remain.

Traces of frescoes are visible on the central apse. From the east end there is an extensive view of the Guye Valley.

Malay. – Pop 219. *8km - 5 miles north.* The 12C Romanesque **church,** standing in its graveyard, boasts a solid square belltower with twin bays; the transept arms end in high gables. The nave is roofed with barrel vaulting, the choir with a dome and the apses with oven vaulting.

An old bridge leads to the main courtyard.

Gourmands or gourmets

*Each year the **Michelin Red Guide France** gives an up-to-date selection of establishments renowned for their cuisine.*

French gastronomic specialities and fine wines are described on page 33.

★ TALMAY CHÂTEAU

Michelin map 📖 fold 13 or 📗 fold 17 – 6km - 4 miles north of Pontailler-sur-Saône

The great 13C square keep (46m - 151ft high), topped by a Louis XIV roof and surmounted by a lantern tower, is all that remains of the feudal castle destroyed in 1760 and replaced by the present charming residence in the classical style.

There is a curious decoration on the fronton of the 18C main building: the Phrygean goddess, Cybele, mother of the gods, stands in the centre with the sun and the moon on either side. The gardens are laid out in the French style.

The different floors of the keep are furnished with taste; first there are fine Renaissance rooms with sculptured ceilings and 17C woodwork; on the upper floors are a library, a room decorated with Louis XIV wainscoting, and the guard room, which has a handsome fireplace.

From the top of the tower there is a wide panorama: La Côte to the west prolonged to the north by the Langres Plateau with the Jura mountains rising to the southeast.

★ TANLAY CHÂTEAU

Michelin map 📖 fold 7 or 📗 fold 12 – 9km - 6 miles east of Tonnerre

The château of Tanlay, built about 1550, is a magnificent architectural composition. The château was built shortly after Ancy-le-Franc *(p 37)*, the first example of the classical Renaissance style, and is a fine monument to French Renaissance architecture at a time when it had broken away from the Italian influence.

Approaching Tanlay from the east by the D 965, there is a good general view of this handsome residence and its park; it is particularly attractive in the evening light.

TOUR *time: about 3/4 hour*

Exterior. – The small château, an elegant building of Louis XIII style, gives on to the "Cour Verte" (Green Courtyard), which is surrounded by arches except on the left where a bridge crosses the moat and leads to the great doorway opening on to the main courtyard.

Tanlay. – Château.

Built by François de Coligny d'Andelot (1531-69) on the site of an ancient feudal fortress, the château was completed and decorated by Michel Particelli d'Hémery (d1650), Superintendent of Finances. Though a genius in money matters, he was dismissed by Mazarin (1602-61) because the tax rates he imposed caused such discontent. Since the late 17C the château has belonged to the Thévenin de Tanlay family.

The main living quarters are joined by two staircase towers to two wings. These are lower and built at right angles to the main building. Each wing ends in a round tower covered with a dome and lantern.

The Archive Tower is on the left, the Chapel on the right.

Interior. – The tour includes: on the ground floor, the hallway known as the Hall of the Caesars, which is closed off by a handsome 16C wrought-iron grille, the beautiful drawing room with 17C woodwork, and the dining room with period furnishings and portraits.

The spiral staircase has a slender handrail. The rooms on the first floor are well decorated and furnished. Most of them, like the rooms on the ground floor, are ornamented with sculptured fireplaces. A great gallery, painted in *trompe l'œil*, is covered with monochrome frescoes.

On the top floor, a corner room in the turret was the meeting place for Huguenot conspirators at the time of the Wars of Religion. The dome ceiling is covered by a painting attributed to the School of Fontainebleau; the figures include outstanding 16C Catholics and Protestants.

★ TERNANT

The art lover visiting the Nivernais or the Morvan should not miss going to Ternant to see the two magnificent 15C Flemish triptychs in the little village **church.**

★★THE TRIPTYCHS IN THE CHURCH *time: 1/2 hour*

⊘The triptychs were given to the church between 1432 and 1435 by Baron Philippe de Ternant, Chamberlain to Philip the Good, Duke of Burgundy, and his son Charles de Ternant. They are made of wood — carved, painted and gilded.

Large triptych. — This is devoted to the Passion of Christ. The centre panel portrays Christ's death. Below, a fainting Virgin Mary is supported by St John and the holy women; the donor Charles de Ternant and his wife Jeanne are shown kneeling in the foreground. The left-hand panel is a *Pietà* including the figures of St John, Mary Magdalene and the holy women. To the right is the Entombment. The folding panels show scenes from the Passion: the Agony in the Garden, Christ carrying the Cross, the Resurrection, the Descent into Hell.

Small triptych. — This triptych, which is older, is devoted to the Virgin Mary. In the centre of the carved panel is a scene from the Assumption: a little angel, his head covered by a hood, draws out from her head the Virgin's soul, depicted as a little girl at prayer. Above this is shown the later scene of the Assumption of the Virgin, when she is carried to heaven on a crescent moon held by an angel: this particular detail is unique.

The last meeting of the Virgin with the Apostles is shown on the left of the central motif; on the right is her funeral procession.

The panel paintings are remarkable. Besides the scenes from the life of the Virgin — the Annunciation, the crowning of the Virgin, Christ holding the world, the Virgin's funeral — one can see the donor, Philippe de Ternant, dressed in chequered material — the arms of his house — the Order of the Golden Fleece *(p 18)* about his throat, and his wife Isabella, in full state dress, accompanied by the crowned Virgin, her patron saint.

Smokers and campers please take care
Fire can spread rapidly and cause extensive damage.

TIL-CHÂTEL

Here the river Ignon joins the Tille, a tributary of the Saône.

St-Florent. — This 12C Romanesque chapel has a beautiful doorway. On the tympanum, Christ in Majesty is surrounded by the symbols of the Evangelists. The side door, based on the same theme, is not so ornate.

Inside, note the capitals in the nave, the dome on squinches over the transept crossing and the semi-domed apse with its apsidal chapels. The 12C altar is placed over the enormous stone block which was used for the beheading of St Florent. Other points of interest include two wooden statues (a 12C Christ Reviled and a 17C Italian calvary), the tomb of St Honorius and his 16C reliquary as well as five engraved tombstones.

EXCURSION

⊘**Grancey Château.** — *26km - 16 miles by the D 959 west through Is-sur-Tille and north via Marey-sur-Tille.*
The present château of Grancey was built in the 17C and 18C on a terrace overlooking a fine park, beside the ruins of a castle dating from the 12C and 15C — moats, drawbridge and chapel.

TONNERRE

Tonnerre is a pleasant little town, terraced on one of the hills that form the west bank of the Armançon and surrounded by vineyards and green scenery. Both the old town and the newer quarters are dominated by St Peter's Church and the Notre-Dame Tower. From the terrace behind St Peter's there is a good view of the town and its surroundings.

Few monuments have survived the fire that ravaged the town in the 16C but the old hospital and the beautiful sepulchre it contains are among the treasures of Burgundy.

The Knight of Éon. — It was at Tonnerre that Charles-Geneviève-Louise-Auguste-Andrée-Timothée Éon de Beaumont, known as the knight or the lady-knight of Éon, was born in 1728. After a brilliant military and diplomatic career, during which he sometimes had to wear women's clothes, he met with reversals of fortune and was forced to flee to London. He was refused permission to return to France except dressed as a woman. Returning to England, he died there in 1810. To the end of his life, there was widespread speculation as to his sex. The announcement of his death gave rise to a wave of great curiosity ended only by an autopsy. Charles d'Éon was unquestionably a man.

FORMER HOSPITAL (ANCIEN HÔPITAL) *time: 1/2 hour*

⏱This beautiful building, erected between 1293 and 1295 by Margaret of Burgundy, widow of Charles d'Anjou, king of Naples and Silicy and brother of St Louis, has survived intact, apart from minor modifications.

From the outside, the walls of the hall, despite their buttresses, seem to be crushed by the tall roof which covers an area of 5 400 sq yds. The west face was changed in the 18C.

Interior. – Although shortened by 20m - 66ft in the 18C, the great hall is of impressive size (80m - 262ft long and 18.2m - 60ft wide). The broken-barrel vaulting and the **oak timbering★** are remarkable. The

Tonnerre. – The Entombment.

forty beds for the sick were set in wooden alcoves built in lines along the walls as at Beaune, which was built 150 years later. The walls themselves were pierced by high semicircular bays, divided by pointed arches. From 1650, the hall was put to many different uses and often served as the parish church. Many citizens of Tonnerre were buried there, which explains the presence of the numerous tombstones.

Note the gnomon (sundial) on the paving, designed in the 18C by a Benedictine monk and the astronomer Lalande (1732-1807).

The chapel opens off the end of the hall. The tomb of Margaret of Burgundy, rebuilt in 1826, is in the centre of the choir. Above the altar is a 14C stone statue of the Virgin. To the right of the high altar, a little door leads to the sacristy which contains a carved **Entombment★**, presented to the church in the 15C by a rich merchant of the town *(illustration above)*. The figures of this Holy Sepulchre make up a scene of dramatic intensity. In the north side chapel is the monumental tomb of the French statesman Louvois, who acquired the county of Tonnerre in 1684 and served as Minister of War under Louis XIV. The bronze statues represent Vigilance by Desjardins and Wisdom by Girardon (1628-1715). The wooden statues in the niches at the end of the hall, above the gallery, representing Margaret of Burgundy and Margaret of Beaumont, Countess of Tripoli, who withdrew here with the foundress, are late 13C.

Among the objects on view in the Council Chamber of the hospital are the original documents of the Foundation Charter (1293), the queen's will (1305) and a great golden cross in which is mounted a reputed piece of the True Cross.

ADDITIONAL SIGHTS

⏱**St Peter's Church (St-Pierre).** – This stands on a rocky terrace affording a good view of the town and its surroundings. With the exception of the 14C chancel and the

15C square tower, the church was rebuilt in 1556 following the fire that ravaged the town. There is a handsome doorway on the south side with a statue of St Peter on the pier.

Inside, note the interesting 16C paintings on wood, representing scenes from the Passion, and the 17C pulpit, churchwarden's pew and organ loft.

Fosse Dionne. – This circular basin, filled with blue-green water, is used as a wash-house. It is fed by an underground river that flows through a steeply-inclined rock gallery (45m - 148yds long) to emerge in the centre of the pool; its flow varies considerably according to season and rainfall. The pool overflows into the Armançon by way of a small stream.

Hôtel d'Uzès (A). – A savings bank occupies this Renaissance dwelling, birthplace of the Knight of Eon; note the design on the doors.

Promenade du Pâtis. – Pleasant shady walk.

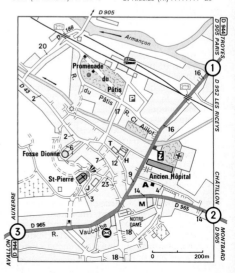

This township, built on the east bank of the river Ouanne, has a church which looks like a fortress: the chevet, flanked by two 12C towers, and the north wall of the building are part of the former fortifications of the castle of the Barons of Toucy. Toucy is the birthplace of the great lexicographer, **Pierre Larousse** (1817-75). This indefatigable man made his presence felt when he was still young by his intense desire for knowledge. At first he took up teaching but his wish "to teach everyone about everything" led him to compile a Dictionary of the French Language *(Dictionnaire de la Langue Française),* which was soon followed by other works on style and grammar. He was a glutton for work and dreamed of a universal dictionary that would "provide an answer to every query". Pierre Larousse died before the appearance of that gigantic work the Great Dictionary of the 19C *(Grand Dictionnaire du XIXe Siècle)* but he had made sure of its completion. It was an intellectual achievement of huge range that for many years had no equal abroad.

EXCURSIONS

Villiers-St-Benoît. — Pop 380. *8km - 5 miles northwest of Toucy by the D 950.* ⊘ A **regional art museum** contains (attic floor) a large collection of stoneware from the Puisaye region (17C-18C) and earthenware from the Yonne (18C-19C). On the ground floor Burgundian interiors are the setting for local furniture and examples of Burgundian sculpture, from the Romanesque period to the 16C including works from the 15C Dijon school, as well as 16C Flemish ivories (sacred objects).

Pourrain. — Pop 1 196. *10km - 6 miles east by the D 965 to Auxerre.* ⊘ The village has an interesting and well presented **Second World War Museum.** The collections include a variety of American, British and German items: vehicles, bayonets, regimental badges and medals. Other exhibits include a telephone exchange, a Mosquito cockpit and one of the Ruppert decoy parachutes as well as Wehrmacht and Luftwaffe uniforms.

The town stands on the right bank of the Saône between Chalon and Mâcon, near the agricultural land of the Mâconnais hills; the region, which is blessed with a gentle climate, is rich in old buildings and famous wines.

The original Gaulish city of the Aedui tribe became a *castrum* under Roman rule. The few surviving traces of the old fortifications are dominated by the tall towers of the abbey church. Tournus is one of the oldest and most important of the monastic centres in France owing to the architectural beauty and the harmonious proportions of the church and the conventual buildings, which date from the 10C.

Monastic centre. — When St Valerian, a Christian from Asia Minor, escaped from persecution in Lyons in 177, he travelled to Tournus to convert the people but was martyred on a hillside above the Saône; a sanctuary was built beside his tomb. In the Merovingian period it was converted into an abbey and dedicated to St Valerian. In 875 the monastery embarked on a period of development following the arrival of monks from Noirmoutier. They had led a wandering life fleeing from the Norsemen since the beginning of the 9C until they were invited by Charles the Bald to settle at St Valerian's abbey. They brought with them the relics of St Philibert, founder of Jumièges Abbey in Normandy, who died at Noirmoutier in 685; the dedication of the abbey was eventually changed from St Valerian to St Philibert.

A Hungarian invasion in 937 checked the prosperity of the abbey which was destroyed by fire and rebuilt. In about 945 the monastery was abandoned by the monks who retreated to St Pourçain in the Auvergne. In 949 following a decision in council, Abbot Stephen, formerly prior of St Philibert, was ordered to return to Tournus with a group of monks.

The reconstruction which he set in motion was completed in the 12C; it produced one of the most beautiful parts of the church.

Over the centuries the building underwent damage, repair and modification; in 1562 it was sacked by the Huguenots.

The abbey became a collegiate church in 1627 and in 1790 a parish church, so that it avoided irrevocable damage during the Revolution.

★ABBEY (ANCIENNE ABBAYE)
time: 1 hour

★★ **St Philibert.** — *Access from the main* ⊘ *road by Rue Albert-Thibaudet.* The street passes between two round towers, all that is left of Field Gate (Porte des Champs), the main entrance to the old abbey precinct.

Tournus. – Interior of St Philibert's Church.

Exterior. – The façade, dating from the 10C and 11C and built of beautifully cut stone, has almost the appearance of a castle keep with the dark loophole slits emphasising the warm colour of the stone. The bareness of the strong walls is broken by slightly projecting Lombard bands. The crenellated parapet with machicolations linking the two towers accentuates the military appearance of the building. Both this gallery and the porch are the work of Questel in the 19C.

The right tower is topped by a saddle-back roof; the other was heightened at the end of the 11C by the addition of a two-storey belfry surmounted by a tall spire.

The two column-statues, which decorate the corners of the upper storey, are among the oldest of their kind.

Enter the church by the doorway to the right of the main façade.

Narthex. – This is the place of transition from the outer world to the house of God, where reflection and preparation for prayer are encouraged by the half-light. Its rugged and simple architecture achieves a singular grandeur. Four enormous circular abacus pillars divide it into a nave and two aisles, each of three bays. The nave has groined vaulting while the two aisles are covered with transversal barrel vaulting.

One bay of the vault is painted in a black and white chequered pattern, the arms of Digoine, an old and powerful Mâcon family. On the wall above the entrance to the nave is a 14C fresco of Christ in Majesty (1); the end wall of the north aisle carries another 14C fresco portraying the Crucifixion (2).

The round tombstones are peculiar to this region.

The nave. – The luminous and rose-coloured nave, which dates from the beginning of the 11C, is now devoid of decoration.

Magnificently tall cylindrical pillars made from the rose-coloured stone of Préty (a small place near Tournus) are surmounted by ordinary flat capitals, like those in the narthex; they divide the five bays of the nave from the aisles.

A most unusual feature is the central vault which consists of five transverse barrel vaults resting on transverse arches with alternating white and pink archstones; great columns surmounted by slim columns support the arches, which obscure the clerestory, through which light enters the nave.

Pronounced transverse ribs sub-divide the vaulting in the aisles.

The side chapels in the north aisle date from the 14C and 15C.

A 15C niche in the south aisle contains a 12C statue-reliquary of the Virgin (3), Notre-Dame-de-la-Brune, which shows the artistic influence of the Auvergne. The statue, which is made of painted cedar wood (regilded in the 19C) retains an aura of calm and majestic beauty.

Transept and choir. – Built at the start of the 12C, the transept and choir contrast strongly with the rest of the building in the whiteness of the stonework; they show the rapid evolution of Romanesque art.

In the transept the contrast can be seen between the spaciousness of the nave and the narrowness of the choir which the architect restricted to the dimensions of the existing crypt.

The semi-domed apse is supported by six columns with capitals, surmounted by semicircular windows framed by delicately sculptured decoration. The ambulatory built at the beginning of the 11C has barrel vaulting and five radiating chapels with flat end walls; the axial chapel contains the shrine of St Philibert (4).

★ **Crypt** (a). – *Access by steps in the north transept.* The crypt with its thick walls was built by Abbot Stephen at the end of the 10C and restored by Questel in the 19C. The height of the crypt (3.5m - 12ft) is quite exceptional. The central part, flanked by two rows of slender columns (some have a typical archaic bulge) with delightful foliated capitals, is surrounded by an ambulatory with radiating chapels. The 12C fresco, decorating the chapel on the right and representing a Virgin and Child and a Christ in Majesty, is the best preserved in the whole church.

St Michael's Chapel (b). – The chapel occupies the upper room in the narthex which was built before the nave. In plan it is identical with the ground floor but the astonishing height of the central section and the amount of light give it an entirely different feel. The ancient sculpture on the capitals and the blocks which they support have survived from the Carolingian period: the Gerlannus inscription half-way up the archivolt may refer to the year 1000 and confirm that the room was built earlier than the nave. The great arched bay opening into the organ loft was once the entrance to a small oven-vaulted apsidal chapel which was built out on corbels at first-floor level; the chapel was suppressed when the organ loft was built in 1629.

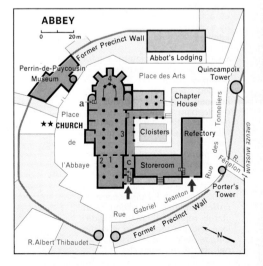

Conventual Buildings. – To reach the cloisters one passes through the old Alms Room (c) or warming room (13C) adjoining the south wall of the narthex. It contains a lapidary collection including the column-statues and capitals from the north tower as well as a few sculptures from the cloisters.

Chapter House. – This was rebuilt by Abbot Bérard following a fire in 1239 and now houses temporary exhibitions. The pointed vaulting is visible through the Romanesque apertures overlooking the cloisters.

The buildings on the south side, which hide the refectory, now house both the public and abbey libraries. They are dominated by the square Prior's Tower.

Leave the cloisters by Place des Arts.

Admire the east end with the chevet and five radiating chapels, all dominated by the 12C belfry over the transept crossing. This fine tower was inspired by Cluny.

Abbot's Lodging. – This is a charming late-15C building.

In Rue des Tonneliers stands the Quincampoix Tower which was built after the Hungarian invasion in 937; it was part of the wall of enclosure of the old abbey as was the neighbouring tower, called the Porter's Tower.

Refectory. – This magnificent 12C chamber (33m - 108ft long and 12m - 39ft high) has no transverse arches but is vaulted with slightly broken barrel vaulting. When the abbey was secularised in 1627 the hall was used for real tennis and was called the Ballon or ball. The hall is used for temporary exhibitions.

Storeroom. – The storeroom, also 12C, has broken barrel vaulting resting on transverse arches. It is lit by two small windows set high up. The vast cellars below are now occupied by various craftsmen.

ADDITIONAL SIGHTS

⊙**Perrin-de-Puycousin Museum** (M¹). – This folklore collection, donated to the town by Perrin de Puycousin in 1929, is displayed in a 17C family mansion, formerly the Treasurer's House, bequeathed to the town by Albert Thibaudet (1874-1936), the celebrated literary critic, who was born in Tournus. Wax models in Burgundian costume recreate scenes from daily life in past centuries (about forty figures in eight rooms).

The scenes include the interior of a Bresse farm, a local Tournus interior with nine variations of the regional costume, the large room of the Burgundian spinners, collections of headdresses, costumes, and, in the basement, the reconstruction of a Burgundian cellar.

⊙**Greuze Museum** (M²). – The museum is mostly devoted to the painter **Jean-Baptiste Greuze** (1725-1805), born in Tournus in the street which now bears his name.

His work, sentimental and edifying, is represented here by a fine collection of drawings, a few canvases (including seven original portraits) and many engravings illustrating the genre scenes with which he made his reputation. It also contains a regional archaeological section (prehistoric, Gallo-Roman and Merovingian relics) and rooms displaying 19C Tournusian sculpture.

Old houses. – Many old houses and mansions are to be found in Rue du Dr-Privey, Rue de la République and Rue du Midi.

View from the bridge and the quays. – From the bridge over the Saône at the end of Rue Jean-Jaurès there is a good view of the church of St-Philibert and the town.

La Madeleine. – This church stands at the heart of the Roman town and, despite the deterioration of the exterior, remains quite attractive. The east end, adjoined by a cluster of houses, should be admired from the banks of the Saône.

The 12C doorway is interesting for the decorative details. The columns supporting the round-headed recessed arches are adorned with beaded braids and overlapping vertical or slanting garlands; the capitals portray foliage or pairs of birds face to face.

The interior, uniformly white since the restoration, has 15C pointed vaulting. Opening off the north aisle is a Renaissance chapel; its vault is adorned with decorative coffers and ribs. The gilded wood statue represents Mary Magdalene and the tabernacle is in the Empire style. The baptismal chapel also dates from the 15C.

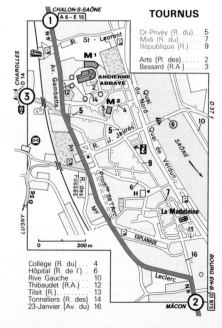

TOURNUS

Dr-Privey (R. du) . . 5
Midi (R. du) 7
République (R.) . . . 9

Arts (Pl. des) 2
Bessard (R.A.) 3

Collège (R. du) . . . 4
Hôpital (R. de l') . . 6
Rive Gauche 10
Thibaudet (R.A.) . . 12
Tilsit (R.) 13
Tonneliers (R. des) 14
23-Janvier (Av. du) 16

EXCURSIONS

The Region of St-Trivier-de-Courtes. – *Approximately 20km - 12 miles southeast.* This region, which is typical of the Bresse plain, is known for its **Saracen chimneys,** which were built on the estate of the lords of Bagé from the 13C onwards and which are particularly numerous beside the Ain.

The 30-odd which have survived date from the 17C and 18C. Within the house there is an enormous hearth, set away from the wall and covered by a hood, under which a man can stand upright; the flue is lined with wood panels. The chimney pots resemble small belfries or – more rarely – reliquaries built in the Romanesque, Gothic and sometimes Byzantine style; their shapes are round or square (modelled on the belfry of St Philibert in Tournus) or octagonal (the belfry of St Andrew in Bagé); they have one or two bands of vents and are capped by a cone, a pyramid or a Baroque belfry.

They are unusually high (3m to 5m - 10ft to 16ft) and surmounted by a wrought-iron cross. In the past some may have housed a bell, a useful feature in the daily life of these traditionally isolated farms. The adjective "Saracen" does not describe the chimneys' geographical provenance but is a survival of the medieval use of the word Saracen to mean "belonging to a foreign, old or unknown culture": the term was therefore quite naturally applied to these unusual chimneys.

Saracen chimneys are to be found at:

St-Trivier. – *1.5km - 1 mile west by the D 2.* **Grandval** Farm.

Vescours. – *5km - 3 miles west of St-Trivier; on the left at the entrance to the village.*

Vernoux. – *3km - 2 miles northeast of St-Trivier.* **Colombier** Farm.

⊘ **La Forêt Farm.** – *3km - 2 miles east of St-Trivier.* This attractive 16C-17C *(illustration p 14)* farm has been restored and converted into a Bresse farm museum. The small building with the wooden balcony contains a traditional interior; the chimney over the open hearth (4m² - 43sqft) is supported by a beam weighing 4 tonnes. The second building displays a collection of old agricultural implements.

St-Nizier-le-Bouchoux. – *6km - 4 miles east of St-Trivier.* **Bourbon** Farm *(beware of the dogs).*

The Mâconnais Heights. – *Round tour of 65km - 40 miles south of Tournus – about 2 1/4 hours. Follow the itinerary described on pp 113 and 114 as far as Lugny. Take the D 56 north; in Chardonnay turn right.*

⊘ **Uchizy.** – Pop 645. The **church** was probably built by the monks of Tournus at the end of the 11C. The building has a nave and two aisles and the transept crossing is surmounted by a tall belfry of five storeys of diminishing size; the top storey is not original.

Take the D 210 north.

Farges. – Pop 192. The village has an early-11C Romanesque **church** which though small has an interesting interior. The nave, with its beautiful pillars, resembles that of St Philibert in Tournus.

Continue on the D 210 which passes over the motorway (A 6-E 15) and under the N 6.

Le Villars. – Pop 269. The cemetery of this village, set on the banks of the Saône, is the final resting place of the pianist Alfred Cortot (1877-1962) and the aeronautical engineer Gabriel Voisin (1880-1973). Le Villars is the scene of the conclusion of Anatole France's short story, *Rôtisserie de la reine Pédauque.*

⊘ The curious village **church** (11C-12C) has two naves, one of which was reserved for the nuns from a neighbouring priory. The porch has two recessed arches. Inside there are some interesting sculptures: carved pulpit, Virgin in marble; polychrome Good Shepherd in wood.

Take the N 6 north to Tournus.

★ UCHON   Pop 67

Michelin map 🗗🗗 fold 7 or 🗗🗗🗗 fold 25 – 8.5km - 5 miles south of Mesvres

The **setting★** of the little village of Uchon is remarkable. Against a wild background of scattered granite boulders stand the ruins of a tower, an old church and an oratory containing a statue of the Virgin on a column, where pilgrims came in the 16C to pray for deliverance from the plague.

★ **Uchon Signal Station (Signal d'Uchon).** – *1.4km - 1 mile south by the D 275.* About 100m - 109yds beyond the Hotel Bernard turn right into a tarred lane to the car park. Walk to the viewing table on the rock (alt 650m - 2133ft).

The semicircular **view** extends over the wide green Arroux depression to the Madeleine and Dômes Mountains. Nearer are the Morvan summits: Mount Beuvray, Mount Preneley and the Haut-Folin.

*When driving in French towns use the plans in the **Michelin Red Guide France** which are revised each year; they show*

– through-routes and by-passes
– new roads and one-way systems
– car parks.

VALLERY

Michelin map 61 fold 13 or 237 fold 44 — 6km - 4 miles northeast of Chéroy

This small Gâtinais village has three main points of interest: the remnants of two châteaux and the Condé family vault which contains the funerary monument of the father of the Great Condé.

⊙**The châteaux.** – The austere **Renaissance château** with its imposing roof is more evocative of the Louis XIII style than of a Renaissance palace.
In the **Vallery Wood** stands an oak tree known as the **Grand Condé** which is over 350 years old.
The **ruins** of an earlier castle are represented by a tower, once part of the 13C ramparts.

⊙**Church (Église).** – The chapel off the south transept is dedicated to Henri II de Bourbon (1588-1646) the third prince of Condé. The parclose is in the form of a cenotaph, with the prince reclining on one arm. Against the parclose are the marble statues of four of the Cardinal Virtues: (left to right) Prudence, Temperance, Fortitude and Justice.

VARZY

Michelin map 65 fold 14 or 238 fold 22

Handsome shaded boulevards have now replaced the old ramparts that used to encircle this little town, the favourite residence of the bishops of Auxerre.

SIGHTS

⊙**St Peter's (St-Pierre).** – This church dates from the 13C and 14C. The nave, with its tall arches, has an elegant triforium. In the choir there is a coloured statue and 16C triptych of St Eugenia. In the south transept a second triptych dating from the 17C portrays scenes from the life of St Peter.
The treasury *(in a strongroom to the right of the choir)* contains several reliquaries from the former collegiate church of Ste-Eugénie. There are two 13C arm reliquaries: of Sts Eugenia and Regnobert, an early-13C octagonal coffer containing the skull of St Regnobert and an early-16C Christ Crucified in wood.

⊙**Museum (Musée).** – Six rooms display the various collections: furniture, paintings, sculpture, weapons, ceramics and earthenware (Nevers, Clamecy, Rouen, Delft...), sacred objects, 12C-16C wood sculpture, Egyptian sarcophagi and 17C-19C musical instruments.
The most interesting items are: an equestrian St Hubert in 18C Nevers earthenware; a canvas *(The Death of Comala)* by Girodet; a 14C Virgin and a 16C Aubusson tapestry *(Queen Zenobia).*

Washing Place. – The two wash-houses face one another across a small pool; their size is an indication of the past importance of the town.

*The **Michelin Detailed Map** Series (1:200 000)*
covers the whole of France. These maps show
   golf courses, stadiums, racecourses, beaches, swimming pools,
   viewpoints, scenic routes, state forests, interesting sights,
   long distance footpaths, high altitude mountain airfields.
*The perfect complement to the **Michelin Green Guides.***

VAULT-DE-LUGNY

Michelin map 65 fold 16 or 238 fold 23 — 5km - 3 miles west of Avallon

Vault-de-Lugny is in the picturesque valley of the river Cousin and has a 15C **church** with a flat east end.
Inside, a **mural painting** dating from the middle of the 16C goes right round the nave and the choir between the great arches and the bases of the pointed arches. This huge fresco (about 70m - 230ft long) presents thirteen pictures of the Passion of Christ. The scenes have been executed with great delicacy but the brilliance of the colours has been dimmed by time.
A **castle** with a moat and a 15C keep stands near the village.

VAUSSE PRIORY

Michelin map 65 fold 7 or 243 fold 1 — 20km - 12 miles west of Montbard

This Cistercian priory, which was dedicated to St Mary and St Denis, was founded in the 12C by the lord of Montréal and was of some importance until the 15C. Decline set in at the Renaissance. During the Revolution the monastery was deemed state property and sold to a potter who converted it into a factory. It was restored in 1869.
⊙The Romanesque **cloisters** and the small 14C **chapel** are both well preserved. The church was transformed into a library by the Burgundian historian, Ernest Petit.

The beautiful setting of Vézelay, the Basilica of St Mary Magdalene, the town with its old houses and ramparts, constitute one of the treasures of Burgundy and France *(illustration p 35)*.

HISTORICAL NOTES

Girart de Roussillon, the founder. — It was this Count of Burgundy, a legendary hero whose exploits were sung in the ballad-chronicles of the Middle Ages, who was the founder of the abbey of Vézelay.

In the middle of the 9C he established a group of monks where St-Père stands today. After the destruction of the monastery during the Viking invasions, Girart de Roussillon decided to establish a new monastery on a nearby hill, a natural position more easily defended, and this time he installed Benedictine monks.

Pope John VIII consecrated the foundation of the abbey of Vézelay in 878.

The call of St Bernard. — The abbey was at the height of its glory when St Bernard preached the Second Crusade at Vézelay on 31 March 1146. For a century the church had sheltered the relics of Mary Magdalene, "the beloved and pardoned sinner". Vézelay was then one of the great places of pilgrimage and the start of one of four routes that led pilgrims and merchants across France into Spain and Santiago de Compostella.

It was from the side of this "hill of inspiration" that St Bernard launched his vibrant call for the Crusade, in the presence of King Louis VII of France and his family and a crowd of powerful barons. Such was the authority of the Abbot of Clairvaux that he was considered as the real leader of Christianity. His call was received with great enthusiasm by all present who undertook to leave for the Holy Land without delay. Although the Third Crusade, undertaken in 1190, was not preached at Vézelay, it was there that King Philippe-Auguste of France and King Richard the Lionheart of England met before their departure.

It was also the place chosen by St Francis of Assisi for the first of his monasteries of Minorities in France. In about 1217 two of his friars, whom he had entrusted with the task, chose to settle near to the small church of St Cross, which had been built on the spot where St Bernard had addressed the crowd massed in the Asquins Valley; the church was later given into the care of the Franciscans. From 1248, the year of the Seventh Crusade, St Louis, who was a Franciscan tertiary, made several pilgrimages to Vézelay. Vézelay was the birthplace of **Theodore Beza** (de Bèze or Besze in French) (1519-1605) who preached the Reformation with Calvin. **Romain Rolland** (1866-1944), who loved "the breath of heroes" and wished to awaken the conscience of Europe, spent the last years of his life at no 20 Grande-Rue.

Restored after centuries of neglect, the church of St Mary Magdalene is once more the scene of great pilgrimages *(p 180)*. The Franciscans have charge of both the church and St Cross Chapel, which retains some of the original Romanesque arches.

★★★ BASILICA OF ST MARY MAGDALENE
(BASILIQUE STE-MADELEINE) *time: 1 hour*

> *By car from Place du Champ-de-Foire (lower end of the town) via Porte du Barle and a steep one-way street to a parking space near the church. On foot from Place du Champ-de-Foire via Promenade des Fossés (p 170) returning by Grande-Rue.*

The abbey church became a parish church in 1721 but was elevated to a basilica in 1920.

The different stages of the building. — The monastery founded in the 9C by Girart de Roussillon came under the control of Cluny in the 11C. The miracles that happened at the tomb of Mary Magdalene soon drew so great a number of penitents and pilgrims that it became necessary to enlarge the Carolingian church (1096-1104); in 1120 a fierce fire broke out on the eve of 22 July, day of the great pilgrimage, destroying the whole nave and engulfing more than 1 000 pilgrims. The work of rebuilding was immediately begun, the nave was soon finished and, about 1150, the "pre-nave" or narthex was added. In 1215 the Romanesque-Gothic choir and transept were completed.

The discovery at the end of the 13C of other relics of Mary Magdalene at St-Maximin in Provence created misgivings. Pilgrimages became fewer and the fairs and market lost much of their importance. The religious struggles caused the decline of the abbey, which was transformed into a collegiate church in 1538, was pillaged from cellar to roof by Huguenots in 1569 and finally partially razed during the French Revolution. In the 19C **Prosper Mérimée** (novelist: 1803-70), in his capacity as Inspector of Historical Monuments, drew the attention of the public works' authorities to the building, which was on the point of collapsing. In 1840 **Viollet-le-Duc**, who was then less than thirty years old, undertook the work, which he finished only in 1859.

Exterior

The façade. — This was reconstructed by Viollet-le-Duc according to plans contained in the ancient documents. Rebuilt about 1150 in pure Romanesque style it was given a vast Gothic gable in the 13C, consisting of a five-light window decorated with statues, also rebuilt in the 19C. The upper part forms a tympanum decorated with arcades framing the statues of Christ Crowned, accompanied by the Virgin Mary, Mary Magdalene and two angels.

The tower on the right — St Michael's Tower — was surmounted by a storey of tall twin bays in the 13C; the octagonal wooden spire (15m - 49ft high) was destroyed by lightning in 1819. The other tower remained unfinished.

Three Romanesque doorways open into the narthex; the tympanum of the centre doorway on the outside was remade in 1856 by Viollet-le-Duc, who took the mutilated original tympanum as his inspiration: the archivolt, decorated with plant designs, is authentic, but the rest of the arches and the capitals are modern.

Tour of the exterior. – Walk round the building anti-clockwise to appreciate its length and the flying buttresses which support it. This side of the church is dominated by St Anthony's Tower (13C) (30m - 98ft high) which rises above the junction of the nave and the transept; the two storeys of round-headed bays were originally intended to be surmounted by a stone spire.

The chapter house, built at the end of the 12C, abuts the south transept. The gallery of the cloisters (p 170) was entirely rebuilt by Viollet-le-Duc. Beautiful gardens (private property) now cover the site of the former abbey buildings. Remains of the 12C refectory still stand.

Château Terrace. – Access by Rue du Château. From this terrace, shaded by handsome trees, situated behind the church on the site of the old Abbot's Palace, there is a fine **panorama★** (viewing table) of the valley of the river Cure and the northern part of the Morvan.

Continue round the basilica past the attractive houses built by the canons of the chapter in the 18C.

⊙ Interior

Enter the basilica by the door on the south side of the narthex.

Vézelay. – Narthex tympanum: Christ in glory

Narthex. – This "pre-nave", consecrated in 1150 by the bishop of Rouen, is later than the nave and the interior façade. Unlike the rib-vaulted church (p 28), the Romanesque narthex is roofed with pointed arches and ogival vaulting. The narthex is so large it seems like a church in its own right. The nave is divided into three bays flanked by aisles surmounted by galleries. The four cruciform pillars of engaged columns decorated with historiated capitals are extremely graceful. The capitals portray scenes from both the Old Testament (Joseph with Potiphar's wife, Jacob, Isaac and Esau, the death of Cain and Samson slaying the lion) and the New Testament (the life of St John the Baptist and St Benedict resurrecting a dead man). Three doorways in the narthex open into the nave and the aisles of the church. When the central door is open, there is a marvellous perspective, radiant with light, along the full length of the nave and choir.

A detailed examination should be made of the sculptures of these doorways, executed in the second quarter of the 12C, and particularly of the tympanum of the central doorway. This is indisputably a masterpiece of Burgundian-Romanesque art, ranking with that of Autun (p 39).

★★★ **Tympanum of the central doorway.** – As the church is a place of pilgrimage, the decoration of the great doorway is devoted to the worldwide evangelical mission which Christ entrusted to his Apostles before His ascension into heaven. All pilgrims arriving at Vézelay, sometimes after a long journey, would learn that God had first approached them. At the centre of the composition a mandorla surrounds an immense figure of Christ Enthroned (1) extending his hands to his Apostles (2) assembled round him; the Holy Ghost is shown radiating from the stigmata to touch the head of each of the Twelve. All around, on the arch stones and the lintel, are crowded the converts to be received at the feet of Christ by St Peter and St Paul (3), symbols of the universal Church. People of every sort are called: on the lintel are (left) archers (4), fishermen (5), farmers (6), and (right) distant and legendary people: giants (7), pygmies (climbing a ladder to mount a horse – 8), men with huge ears (one with a feather-covered body – 9). The arch stones show Armenians (wearing clogs – 10), Byzantines perhaps (11), Phrygians (12) and Ethiopians (13); immediately next to Christ are men with dogs' heads (the cynocephalics converted by St Thomas in India – 14). The next two panels show the miracles that accompanied the divine word preached by the Apostles: two lepers show their regenerated limbs (15) and two paralytics their healthy arms (16). Lastly two Evangelists record all that they have seen (17).

The large-scale composition seeks to demonstrate that the word of God touches the whole world. The signs of the zodiac which alternate with the labours of the months on the outer arch stone (18) introduce the notion of time: the Apostles' mission must also be transmitted from generation to generation.

On the central pier John the Baptist (19) carrying the paschal lamb (unfortunately missing) is shown at the feet of Christ as if supporting Him and introducing Him to His rightful place in the centre. Below Him and on the flanking piers are more Apostles (20).

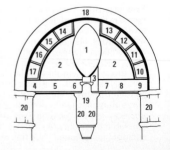

The power of the Holy Ghost which fills the Twelve Apostles is symbolised by a strong wind creating turbulence which ruffles the garments and drapes, and sways the bodies. The linear skill, which is the dominant feature of this masterly work, suggests that in the principal scene the sculptor was following the work of a calligrapher, whereas in the medallions, showing the signs of the zodiac and the months of the year, he felt free to carve humorous interpretations of his contemporaries at work.

Tympana of the side doors. — Two recessed arches with ornamental foliage and rosettes frame the historiated tympana on the side doors.

The one on the right represents the Childhood of Christ: on the lintel are the Annunciation, the Visitation and the Nativity; on the tympanum is the Adoration of the Magi. The one on the left represents the apparitions of Christ after His Resurrection; on the tympanum is the apparition to the Apostles; on the lintel is the apparition to the disciples at Emmaüs.

Nave. — Rebuilt between 1120 and 1135 after a terrible fire *(p. 167)*, this Romanesque nave is noteworthy for its huge size (62m - 203ft long), the use of different coloured limestone, the lighting, and above all, the fine series of capitals.

The nave is much higher than the side aisles and is divided into ten bays of groined vaulting separated by transverse arches with alternating light and dark stones. These do much to mitigate the severity of the lines.

The great semicircular arches, surmounted by windows, rest on cruciform pillars ornamented with four engaged columns decorated with capitals. A graceful decoration of convex quarter-section mouldings, rosettes and pleated ribbons goes round the arches, the main arches and the string-course that runs between the windows and the arches.

★★★ **The capitals.** — As they are more beautiful than those in the narthex they deserve to be examined in detail *(details and plan below)*.

The sculptors — five different hands have been detected in the work — must have had an astonishing knowledge of composition and movement; their genius is expressed with spirit and malice although their realism does not exclude lyricism, a sense of the dramatic and even of psychology.

Transept and chancel. — Built in 1096, when the original Carolingian church was enlarged, the Romanesque transept and chancel were demolished at the end of the 12C and were replaced by this beautiful Gothic ensemble completed in 1215. The arcades of the triforium continue into the transept.

The relics of Mary Magdalene ( ), preserved in the base of a column surmounted by a modern statue, are to be found in the south transept.

A vast ambulatory, with radiating chapels, surrounds the choir.

Right side

1) A duel.
2) Lust and Despair.
3) Legend of St Hubert.
4) Sign of the Zodiac: the scales.
5) The mystical mill (Moses and St Paul).
6) The death of Dives and Lazarus.
7) Lamach kills Cain, concealed in a bush.
8) The four winds of the year.
9) David astride a lion.
10) St Martin avoids a tree about to fall on him.
11) Daniel subdues the lions.
12) The angel wrestling with Jacob.
13) Isaac blessing Jacob.

Left side

14) St Peter delivered from prison.
15) Adam and Ève.
16) Two capitals of this pillar are devoted to the legend of St Anthony, a third represents the animals.
17) The execution of Agag.
18) Legend of St Eugenia: thanks to a disguise, she becomes abbot of a monastery of men; accused later of having outraged a woman, she shows her innocence by opening her robe.
19) Death of St Paul the hermit, for whom two lions dig a grave; above St Anthony prays for him.
20) Moses and the Golden Calf.
21) Death of Absalom : first caught by the hair in the branches of a tree and then decapitated.
22) Two scenes from the fight between David and Goliath.
23) Killing of the Egyptian by Moses.
24) Judith and Holophernes.
25) Calumny and Greed.

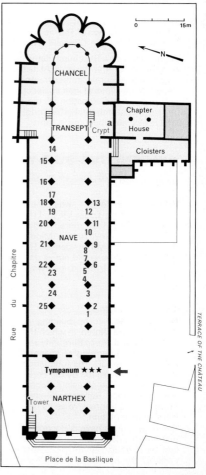

Place de la Basilique

Crypt. — The Carolingian crypt was completely altered during the second half of the 12C. It used to contain the tomb of Mary Magdalene at the time of the great medieval pilgrimages and still houses part of her relics *(see the Michelin Green Guide Provence, English edition)*. The painting on the vaulting is 13C.

Chapter house and cloisters. — Built at the end of the 12C, shortly before the choir of the basilica, the chapter house has pointed vaulting. It was completely restored by Viollet-le-Duc.

The cloisters, which were razed during the French Revolution, used to have a huge cistern in the centre of the close, the only water reserve for the town. Viollet-le-Duc rebuilt one gallery in Romanesque style.

⏱**Ascent of the tower.** — A staircase (200 steps) near the left-hand door, leads to the top of the tower, passing under the rafters above the narthex.

There is a more extensive **view★** from the platform than from the terrace: the old town, the valley of the Cure, the northern part of the Morvan (southeast) and the Auxerrois (north).

ADDITIONAL SIGHTS

Moat Promenade (Promenade des Fossés). — *From Place du Champ-de-Foire at the lower end of the town follow Promenade des Fossés.*

The road is laid out on the line of the ramparts which encircled the town in the Middle Ages and which were punctuated by seven towers.

The 14C-16C **New Gate** (Porte Neuve), which bears the coat of arms of the town of Vézelay, is flanked by two rusticated towers with machicolations and opens on to a charming promenade shaded by walnut trees.

From **St Cross Gate** (Porte Ste-Croix or Porte des Cordeliers), which provides a good view of the Cure Valley, a path leads down to La Cordelle where St Bernard preached the Second Crusade in 1146 *(p 167)*; a cross commemorates the great event. The promenade ends at the château terrace behind the basilica *(p 168)*.

Old houses. — *Walk up from Place du Champ-de-Foire to the Basilica of St Mary Magdalene.* The narrow winding streets still contain many old houses in the picturesque setting of the old town: sculptured doorways, mullioned windows, corbelled staircase turrets and old wells surmounted by wrought-iron wellheads.

VILLENEUVE-L'ARCHEVÊQUE   Pop 1 234

Michelin map 61 fold 15 or 237 fold 46 — 24km - 15 miles east of Sens

It was in this little town in the valley of the river Vanne, founded in the 12C by an archbishop of Sens, that St Louis and Blanche of Castille solemnly received from the Venetians the Crown of Thorns, for which the king was to build a magnificent shrine in Paris: the Sainte-Chapelle (Holy Chapel).

⏱**Notre-Dame.** — The church dates from the 12C, 13C and 16C. The façade is flanked by a tower roofed with slates. At its base is a beautiful 13C doorway, dedicated to the Virgin Mary: six great statues frame that of the Virgin and Child which has its back to the pier. Three lines of statues decorate the arches; the upper part of the tympanum represents the Coronation of the Virgin Mary.

Inside, the Entombment (1528) originally came from the nearby abbey of Vauluisant which has now become a farm.

VILLENEUVE-SUR-YONNE   Pop 4 980

Michelin map 61 fold 14 or 237 fold 45

Villeneuve-sur-Yonne was built entirely by King Louis VII in 1163 and was, at that time, called Villefranche-le-Roy. In the Middle Ages it was a royal residence. The ramparts have been laid out as gardens but two fortified gateways still exist.

SIGHTS

⏱**Notre-Dame.** — The building of this handsome church, in which the architectural styles of Burgundy and Champagne intermingle, spanned the 13C to the 16C. The foundation stone was laid in 1163 by the Pope, Alexander III. The pleasing proportions of the Renaissance-style façade are as impressive as its delicate ornamentation.

The huge Gothic nave is decorated with foliated capitals. The 13C choir and the ambulatory are the oldest parts of the church.

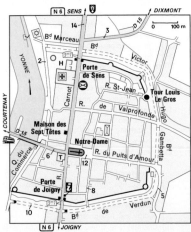

VILLENEUVE-S-YONNE

Bretoche (Quai) 2
Dixmont (R. de) 3

Espérance (Fg de l') .. 5
Joubert (R.) 6
Lemoce-Fraix (R.) 8
Peynot (Bd E.) 10
République (Pl. de la). 12
St-Nicolas (Fg) 14

The Chapel of the Holy Sepulchre in the south aisle contains an Entombment: a 14C wooden Crucifix and a group of Renaissance stone figures.
In the first chapel of the north aisle the stained glass portrays the life of the Virgin. The 14C statue shows the Virgin Mary with the Infant Jesus who is holding a dove.

Sens Gate (Porte de Sens ou Champagne). – The 13C gate is a good example of medieval military architecture.

Joigny Gate (Porte de Joigny ou Bourgogne). – The 13C gate, which was altered in the 16C, fits in well with the adjoining houses.

Louis le Gros Tower. – Despite its name, the enormous round keep, a relic of the old royal castle, was built by Philippe-Auguste early in the 13C both as a defensive work and as a lodging for the king.

Seven Heads House (Maison des Sept-Têtes). – 18C post-house which takes its name from the figures which adorn the street front.

EXCURSION

Dixmont. – Pop 584. *10km - 6 miles northeast by the D 15.*
Little remains of the early-Romanesque **church;** it was later altered and extended and contains elements from the 13C-16C. The doorway has two interesting statues portraying the Virgin Mary and the Archangel Gabriel.

*The **Michelin Motoring Atlas France**
provides the motorist in France
with the best possible information
for route-planning and choosing where to go.*

YONNE VALLEY

Michelin map 📕 fold 14 or 📕 folds 5, 15 and 16 and 📕 fold 6 or 📕 fold 45 and 📕 folds 10, 11, 22, 23 and 36

Of all the rivers of the Morvan, the Yonne is the biggest. Its picturesque valley from Auxerre to Château-Chinon is a pleasant way to approach the high summits of the Morvan.

A capricious stream. – From its source (alt 730m - 2 395ft) on the slopes of Mount Préneley southeast of Château-Chinon, the Yonne flows into the Seine at Montereau after a course of 273km - 170 miles. At its confluence with the Seine, the Yonne has the greater flow of the two rivers.
The frequent rains that fall on the Morvan and the impermeability of almost all the land over which the river flows are the cause of violent floods. The Yonne, a wayward stream, is the unpredictable factor of the hydrographic system of the Seine basin. The tributaries of the Yonne, of which the Cure is the largest, have almost torrential flows, which only emphasise the irregular character of the main river.
The construction of a certain number of dams and reservoirs, the largest of which is the Pannesière-Chaumard reservoir *(p 132)*, has made it possible to regulate the flow of the Yonne by holding back part of the flood waters and releasing them in the summer. Compensating dams have been built to facilitate the process.

Logging and navigation. – The use of the Yonne and the Cure as waterways with the invention of logging *(details pp 77 and 89)* in the 16C contributed to a period of great activity for the river towns. Since 1923, however, logging has ceased although barge traffic has increased.
The Yonne is classified as a navigable river below Auxerre. The Nivernais Canal links it with the basin of the Loire; the Burgundy Canal connects with the Saône basin.

FROM SENS TO AUXERRE *62km - 39 miles – about 1 hour*

★★**Sens.** – *Time: 1/2 hour. Description p 154.*
 Take the N 360 and then the N 6 south following the river.
Villeneuve-sur-Yonne. – *Description p 170.*
Between Villeneuve-sur-Yonne and Joigny the valley is particularly attractive and acts as a divide between the scattered woodlands of the Gâtinais and the forest of Othe.
 In Villevallier cross the Yonne.
St-Julien-du-Sault. – *Description p 143.*
 Continue south on the west bank.
Joigny. – *Description p 106.*
 Take the N 6 south.
Appoigny. – Pop 2625. The district was once under the control of the Bishops of Auxerre who built the **Collegiate Church of St Peter** in the 13C. The high square tower was added in the 16C. The interior, much restored, contains a handsome carved rood screen which dates from 1610.
 Continue south on the N 6.
★★**Auxerre.** – *Time: 3/4 hour. Description p 44.*

FROM AUXERRE TO CLAMECY 59km - 37 miles – about 3 hours.

Take the D 163 and then the N 6 south along the west bank of the Yonne.
From Auxerre to Cravant, the Yonne has the appearance of a river of the plains; its waters, swelled by those of the Cure, flow gently through a fairly wide valley. The nearby hillsides are covered with vineyards. Those overlooking the road on the right are planted with cherry trees.
South of Vincelles bear right into the D 100.
At the top of a slope, there is a view of the village of **Cravant** *(p 89)*, which stands at the confluence of the Yonne and the Cure.
After Bazarnes the road goes along the river edge, which is bordered by trees. The valley is often narrow and the river flows more swiftly.
Mailly-le-Château. – *Description p 115.*
After Mailly-le-Château the road crosses the Yonne by a pretty, double-humpback **bridge** with a chapel. From the bridge there is a good view of the cliff-like rocks of Mailly.

After crossing the Nivernais Canal the road follows the east bank, passing Merry charmingly situated on the west bank and skirting the foot of a steep rock face.

Le Saussois Rock Face. – The limestone forms a wall of rock used by climbers as a practice ground.

Châtel-Censoir. – Pop 677. This village is situated with its back to a hill which dominates the confluence of the rivers Chamoux and Yonne.

⊘**St-Potentien Collegiate Church** is built on top of a hill and surrounded by a tall wall. Enter by the postern. The Romanesque choir dates from the 11C while the nave and aisles are 16C. The two main doorways are Renaissance; the one representing the Last Supper is 16C; the other, which represents the Crucifixion and is badly damaged, is 15C. The sacristy in the south aisle provides access to the charming 13C chapter house. The choir, which is raised up over the crypt, has some ancient capitals, some of which were never completed.

Le Saussois. – Rock face.

From the terrace near the church there is a good view of the town.
Beyond Châtel-Censoir, the Faulin Château comes into view (left).
In Lucy-sur-Yonne turn left into the D 214.
Faulin Château. – This handsome late-15C building with mullioned windows is encircled by a wall with towers.
From Lucy continue east on the D 21. Turn left into the N 151 to cross the Yonne.
Surgy. – Pop 421. The 16C church has an attractive stone spire.
After this village, the road passes the foot of the rocks of Basseville – a succession of limestone cliffs and escarpments *(climbing school)* – and enters Clamecy through an industrial suburb.
Clamecy. – *Description p 77.*

FROM CLAMECY TO CORBIGNY
38km - 24 miles – about 2 1/2 hours

Clamecy. – *Description p 77.*
Take the D 951 east.
From Clamecy to Corbigny, the road follows a picturesque route along the east bank of the Yonne at the foot of small wooded hills.
Armes. – Pop 293. This small village is set in a charming beauty spot beside the Yonne and the Nivernais Canal.
Continue south; in Dornecy turn right into the D 985.
The road briefly follows the Armance Valley before rejoining the Yonne Valley and the Nivernais Canal in Brèves.
In Brèves take the D 280 east to Metz-le-Comte.
Church of Metz-le-Comte. – *Description p 78.*
Take the D 165 southwest to Tannay.
Tannay. – *Description p 78.*
Take the D 119 east and the D 985 south to reach Corbigny.
Corbigny. – Pop 2190. Situated on the borders of the Morvan and the Nivernais regions, Corbigny is a busy centre for local fairs. The little town was the home of the poet, Franc-Nohain (1873-1934). The church is of the 15C Flamboyant Gothic style.

FROM CORBIGNY TO CHÂTEAU-CHINON

45km - 28 miles — about 2 hours

Corbigny. – *Description p 172.*

From Corbigny take the D 985 south.

From Corbigny to Château-Chinon, the usual turbulent nature of the Yonne is harnessed by engineering works aimed at regulating its flow; the Yonne channel (Rigole d'Yonne) is also used to supplement the Nivernais Canal, the compensating dam and the Pannesière-Chaumard reservoir and dam.

Marcilly. – 15C château.

Turn left into the D 147 then right into the D 126, a winding road.

The Montreuillon aqueduct comes into view spanning the valley.

Montreuillon Aqueduct (Aqueduc Montreuillon). – The aqueduct (152m - 499ft long and 33m - 108ft high) carries the Rigole d'Yonne across the Yonne Valley.

East of the aqueduct the gorge ends and the valley widens into pastureland. The road is flanked by the River Yonne *(right)* and the Rigole d'Yonne *(left);* it then passes between a pool and the reservoir formed by the compensating dam built downstream of the Pannesière-Chaumard dam.

Turn right into the D 944; south of l'Huis-Picard turn left into the D 303; take the road across the dam.

★ **Pannesière-Chaumard Dam.** – *Description p 132.*

Upstream, the Yonne is nothing but a small undisciplined river.

Take the road along the east shore of the reservoir.

★ **Château-Chinon.** – *Description p 72.*

NOTES

Practical
Information

TRAVELLING TO FRANCE

Passport. – A valid national **passport** (or a British Visitor's Passport) is required.

Customs. – The UK Customs issue a leaflet on customs regulations and "duty free" allowances. The US Treasury Department ☎ 202 566 8195 offers a publication "Know before you go" for US citizens.
There are no customs formalities for bringing **caravans** into France for less than 6 months nor is a customs document necessary for **pleasure boats** and **outboard motors** for less than 6 months – only the registration certificate.

By air. – National and independent airlines operate services to Paris (Charles de Gaulle and Orly) and to the major provincial airports (Lyon for Burgundy). There are also package tour flights with a rail or coach link-up as well as Fly-Drive schemes – details available from the airlines and travel agents.

By sea. – There are numerous **cross-Channel services** (passenger and car ferries, hovercraft) from the United Kingdom and Eire – details from travel agencies.

By rail. – French Railways, 179 Piccadilly, London W1V OBA; ☎ 071 409 3518 and travel agencies arrange reservations and provide information on special air/rail packages and Rail passes (France Vacances Pass which offers unlimited travel). Eurorail Pass, Flexipass and Saver Pass which are available in the US for travel in Europe must be purchased in the US – ☎ 212 308 3103 (information) and 1 800 223 6 36 (reservations). Tickets bought in France must be validated *(composter)* in the orange automatic date-stamping machines at the platform entrance.

By coach. – Regular coach services are operated from London to Paris and large provincial towns in France:
Hoverspeed, Maybrook House, Queens Gardens, Dover CT17 9UQ. ☎ 0304 240241. Euroways/Eurolines, 52 Grosvenor Gardens, Victoria, London SW1W OAU. ☎ 071 730 8235.
It is advisable to book well in advance for the holiday season *(see below)*.

MOTORING IN FRANCE

Documents. – Nationals of EC countries require a **national** driving licence; nationals of non-EC countries require an **international** driving licence (obtainable in the US from the American Automobile Club).
Car **registration papers** (log-book) and a **nationality plate** of the approved size are required for the car.

Insurance. – Insurance cover is compulsory although an International Insurance Certificate (Green Card) is no longer a legal requirement in France. Certain UK motoring organisations (AA, RAC) run accident insurance and breakdown service schemes for members. Europ-Assistance (252 High St, Croydon CR0 1NF ☎ 081 680 1234) has special policies for motorists. Members of the American Automobile Club should obtain the brochure "Offices to serve you abroad".

Highway Code. – Traffic drives on the **right.** The minimum driving age is 18 years. It is compulsory for front seat passengers to wear **seat belts;** back seat passengers must wear seat belts where they are fitted. Children under ten must travel on the back seat. In case of a **breakdown** a red warning triangle or hazard warning lights are obligatory.
In built-up areas **priority** must be ceded to vehicles joining the road from the right but traffic on roundabouts and on main roads outside built-up areas has priority. At traffic lights vehicles may filter to the right only where indicated by an amber arrow.
The regulations on **drink-driving** and **speeding** are strictly enforced – usually by an on-the-spot fine and/or confiscation of the vehicle.
Although liable to modification **speed limits** are as follows:
– toll motorways 130kph – 80mph (110kph – 68mph when raining);
– dual carriage roads and motorways without tolls 110kph – 68mph – (100kph – 62mph when raining);
– other roads 90kph – 56mph (80kph – 50mph when raining) and in towns 50kph – 31mph;
– outside lane on motorways during daylight, on level ground and with good visibility: minimum speed limit of 80kph – 50mph.

Route Planning. – There is a full range of **Michelin Road Maps** covering France and Minitel 3615 Michelin provides detailed route planning. For 24-hour road traffic information: dial 48 94 33 33 or consult Minitel 3615 Code Route.
Many of the motorways are toll-roads *(autoroutes à péage)*. The A26 motorway from Calais to Reims by-passes Paris to the east.
To avoid congestion during the holiday period (particularly weekends in July and August) take the recommended secondary routes (Bison Futé – itinéraires bis).

ACCOMMODATION

Places to stay. – The **Michelin Red Guide France** provides a selection of hotels and restaurants.
Loisirs Accueil is an officially-backed booking and tourist information service. Loisirs Accueil, 2 Rue Linois, 75015 Paris, ☎ 40 59 44 12. Loisirs Accueil **Loiret**, 3 Rue de la Bretonnerie, 45000 Orléans, ☎ 36 62 04 88. Loisirs Accueil **Yonne**, 1-2 Quai de la République, 89000 Auxerre, ☎ 86 51 12 05.
The brochure 'Logis et Auberges de France' is available from the French Government Tourist Office.

Rural accommodation. – Apply to Maison des Gîtes de France, 35 Rue Godot-de-Mauroy, 75009 Paris, ☎ 47 42 20 20 or 47 42 25 43 (answering service) or to 178 Piccadilly, London W1V OAL. ☎ 071 493 3480 for a list of addresses and **bed and breakfast** accommodation.

Camping. – The **Michelin Guide Camping Caravaning France** lists a selection of the 11 000 officially graded camping sites.

Electricity. – The electric current is 220 volts. Circular two pin plugs are the rule.

GENERAL INFORMATION

Medical treatment. – Pharmacies (green cross sign) offer advice and first aid (night service rota). It is advisable to take out comprehensive insurance cover as the recipient of medical treatment has to pay the bill. American Express offers "Global Assist" for any medical, legal or personal emergency – call collect from anywhere 202 554 2639. British citizens should obtain **Form E 111,** available from the Department of Health and Social Security, which entitles the holder to urgent treatment for accident or unexpected illness in EC countries.

Currency. – Banks are open from 9am to 12 noon and 2 to 4pm and are closed on Monday or Saturday (except if market day). Banks close early on the day before a holiday. They usually charge the lowest rates of commission for changing currency; a passport is necessary as identification.

Credit Cards. – American Express, Carte Bleue (Visa/Barclaycard), Diners Cub and Eurocard (Mastercard/Access) are widely accepted (including bank cash dispensers).

Post. – Post Offices open Monday to Friday 8am to 7pm, Saturday 8am to 12 noon. Postage via air mail to: UK letter 2.30F; postcard 2.10F; US aerogramme 4.20F; letter (20g) or postcard 3.80F. Stamps are also available from newsagents and tobacconists.
Poste Restante mail should be addressed as follows: Name, Poste Restante, Poste Centrale, *department's* postal code followed by town name, France. The Michelin Red Guide France gives local postal codes.

Telephone. – Pre-paid phone cards *(télécarte)* (50 or 120 units), which are available from post offices, tobacconists and newsagents, can be used for inland and international calls. Calls can be received at phone boxes showing the blue bell sign.

Internal calls. – For calls within either of the two main zones (French provinces and Paris and its region) dial only the 8 digit customer's number. From Paris to the provinces dial 16 + 8 digit number. From the provinces to Paris dial 16 + 1 + 8 digit number.

International calls. – To telephone abroad from France dial 19; when the continuous tone recurs, dial the country code, dialling code and the number of the correspondent. For international enquiries dial 19 33 12 + country code.

Shopping. – The big stores and larger shops are open Monday to Saturday from 9am to 6.30-7.30pm. Small shops may close during the lunch hour. Food shops keep longer hours and some open on Sunday mornings.

Public holidays. – The following are days when museums and other monuments may close or vary their hours of admission:

New Year's Day	France's National Day (14 July)
Easter Sunday and Monday	Assumption (15 August)
May Day (1 May)	All Saints' Day (1 November)
V E Day (8 May)	Armistice Day (11 November)
Ascension Day	Christmas Day
Whit Sunday and Monday	

National museums and art galleries are closed on Tuesdays; municipal museums are closed on Mondays. School holidays occur at Christmas, in the spring and summer and also (10 days to a fortnight) in February and early November.

Consulates: British – 24 Rue Childebert, Lyon 69002, ☎ 78 37 59 67.
US – 22 Cours du Maréchal-Foch, Bordeaux 33080 ☎ 56 52 65 95.

Embassies: British – 35 Rue du Faubourg-St-Honoré, 75008 Paris, ☎ 42 66 91 42.
US – 2 Avenue Gabriel, 75008 Paris, ☎ 42 96 12 02.

TOURIST INFORMATION

French Government Tourist Offices. – These offices in Sydney, Toronto, Montreal, Dublin, London, Chicago, New York, Los Angeles and Dallas, provide information, brochures, maps and other assistance, including the brochures published by the Regional Tourist Offices.
FGTO, 178 Piccadilly, London W1V OAL. ☎ 071 499 6911 (24 hour answering service), ☎ 071 491 7622 (urgent enquiries only).
FGTO, 6120 Fifth Avenue, New York 10020-2452, ☎ (212) 757 1125; 1-900-420-2003 for information on hotels, restaurants, transportation.

Regional Tourist Offices (Comités Régionaux de Tourisme) :
Côte-d'Or : Hôtel du Département, BP 1601, 21035 Dijon Cedex, ☎ 80 73 81 81.
Loiret : 3 Rue de la Bretonnerie, 45000 Orléans, ☎ 38 66 24 10.
Nièvre : Conseil Général, Hôtel du Département, 58019 Nevers, ☎ 86 36 39 80.
Saône-et-Loire : 389 Avenue du Maréchal-de-Lattre-de-Tassigny, 71000 Mâcon, ☎ 85 39 47 47.
Yonne : 1 Quai de la République, 89000 Auxerre, ☎ 86 52 26 27.

Tourist Information Centres 🏛. – See the admission Times and Charges *(p 182)* for the addresses and telephone numbers of the Local Tourist Information Offices (Syndicats d'Initiative); they provide information on craft courses and itineraries with special themes – wine tours, history tours, artistic tours.

Tourism for the Disabled. – Sights which are accessible to disabled people are listed in the publication 'Touristes quand même! Promenades en France pour les Voyageurs Handicapés' which covers nearly 90 towns in France and is published by the Comité National Français de Liaison pour la Réadaptation des Handicapés (30-32 Quai de la Loire, 75019 Paris).
The **Michelin Red Guide France** and **Michelin Camping Caravaning France** indicate hotels and camping sites suitable for disabled people.

SPORTS AND LEISURE ACTIVITIES

Information and brochures on sporting and leisure facilities may be obtained from the French Government Tourist Office or from the organisations listed below.

Rambling. – Topo-Guides, published by the Fédération Française de la Randonnée Pédestre, which give detailed maps of the short, medium and long distance footpaths and other valuable information, are on sale at the Centre d'Information de la Randonnée Pédestre : 64 Rue de Gergovie, 75014 Paris. ☎ 45 45 31 02.

Riding and Pony Trekking. – Information from the Fédération des Randonneurs Équestres, 16 Rue des Apennins, 75017 Paris, ☎ 42 26 23 23. An annual handbook is published by the Association Nationale de Tourisme Équestre (ANTE), 170 Quai de Stalingrad, Ile-St-Germain, 92130 Issy-les-Moulineaux, ☎ 45 54 29 54.

Golf. – The **Michelin Golf Map** of France gives comprehensive details about golf courses. An annual guide is published by Éditions Person, 34 Rue de Penthièvre, 75008 Paris. The Fédération Française de Golf, 69 Avenue Victor-Hugo, 75016 Paris, ☎ 45 02 13 55, also publishes a map.

Cycling. – Information and itineraries available from the Fédération Française de Cyclotourisme: 8 Rue Jean-Marie-Jégo, 75013 Paris, ☎ 45 80 30 21. Information on cycle hire available from Tourist Information Centres. Cycles, which can be hired at one main railway station and returned at another, available at Auxerre-St-Gervais, Avallon, Beaune, Bourg-en-Bresse, Chalon-sur-Saône, Châtel-Censoir, Clamecy, Cosne, Dijon, Joigny, Louhans, Mâcon, Montargis, Montbard, Nevers, Paray-le-Monial, Tonnerre.

Cruising. – *See page 8.*

Water-skiing. – Enquire at the local Tourist Information Centre.

Sailing. – Information on clubs, training and boat hire available from the Fédération Française de Voile: 55 Avenue Kléber, 75016 Paris. ☎ 45 53 68 00.

Wind surfing. – Information from sailing clubs. Wind-surfing is permitted on lakes and in sports and leisure centres subject to regulations.

Canoeing. – Information available from the Fédération Française de Canoë-Kayak, 87 Quai de la Marne, 94340 Joinville-le-Pont. ☎ 48 89 39 89, and from Comité de l'Yonne de Canoë-Kayak, Avenue Yver prolongée, 89000 Auxerre, ☎ 86 52 13 86.

Fishing. – Folding map "Fishing in France" (Pêche en France) is available from the publisher, Conseil Supérieur de la Pêche, 134 Avenue de Malakoff, 75016 Paris, ☎ 45 01 20 20. Information on regulations is available from Tourist Information Offices and from departmental fishing organisations : Fédération de Pêche, 25 Rue Charles-Gille, 37000 Tours, ☎ 47 05 33 77.

BOOKS TO READ

Titles which are out of print can be obtained through public libraries.

Burgundy by A Turner and C Brown *(Batsford – 1977)*
Burgundy Landscape with Figures by P Gunn *(Victor Gallancz Ltd – 1978)*
Phoenix Frustrated: The Lost Kingdom of Burgundy by C Cope *(Constable)*
Burgundy (Faber book on wine) by A Hanson *(Faber & Faber)*
The Century Companion to the Wines of Burgundy by G Chidgey *(Century – 1984)*
The Wines of Chablis and the Yonne by R George *(Sotheby's Publication – 1988)*
The Food Lover's Guide to France by P Wells *(Eyre & Spottiswoode – 1988)*
The Wine Lover's Guide to France by M Busselle *(Pavilion, Michael Joseph – 1986)*
Burgundy (Architecture) by Ian Dunlop *(Hamish Hamilton – 1990)*

PRINCIPAL FESTIVALS

Saturday after 22 January

La Côte . . . .
St-Vincent "Rotating" Festival. Procession in honour (venue changes annually) of the patron of vine-growers. *Further information from the Brotherhood of the Knights of the Tastevin, BP 12, 21701 Nuits-St-Georges*

Late January

Chablis . . . .
St-Vincent "Rotating" Festival ☎ 86 42 40 08

During February

Montargis . . . .
Flower Market

27 February

Chalon-sur-Saône . . . .
International common pelt fair *(p 66)*

For one week in March

Chalon-sur-Saône . . . .
Carnival: musical parade and day of the Goniots; procession and children's fancy-dress ball. *Information:* ☎ 85 43 08 39

April to October

Beaune . . . .
Son et lumière spectacle at the Hôtel-Dieu every evening. *Information from the Tourist Office* ☎ 80 22 24 51

3rd or 4th week in May

Mâcon . . . .
French national wine festival

31 May

Semur-en-Auxois . . . .
Ring Festival: a horse race (dating from 1639)

Friday and Saturday after Corpus Christi Sunday

Paray-le-Monial . . . .
Sacred Heart Pilgrimage

June, July, August

Autun . . . .
Son et lumière spectacle at the Roman theatre: *Once upon a time Augustodunum.* About ten shows during the season. *Information:* ☎ 85 52 20 34

3rd Sunday in June or 1st Sunday in July

St-Jean-de-Losne . . . .
Boatmen's Festival

Sunday nearest to 24 June

Mont-St-Vincent . . . .
Celtic Fire Festival on the Feast of St John

Late June

Escolives-Ste-Camille . . . .
Cherry Fair

Late June to 3rd Sunday in July

Beaune . . . .
International Baroque and Classical Music Festival

Two evenings in July and two in August

La Clayette . . . .
Son et lumière spectacle at the castle

July, August

St-Fargeau . . . .
Fridays and Saturdays at 10pm: son et lumière spectacle (600 actors, 50 horsemen; *information* ☎ 86 74 05 67); Sundays at 8.30pm: chamber music concerts

July

Mâcon . . . .
French Rowing Championship on the Saône

14 July

Clamecy . . . .
Jousting on the Yonne in memory of log floating *(p 77)*

2nd fortnight in July

Autun . . . .
Music in the Morvan

3rd Sunday in July

Mont-St-Vincent . . . .
Wine and Pancake *(crapiaux)* Fair

22 July

Vézelay . . . .
Feast of St Madeleine: pilgrimage

Late July

Joigny . . . .
Festival of the free commune of St-André

Rogny-les-7-Ecluses . . . .
Fireworks at the locks. ☎ 86 74 52 34

Early August

Accolay . . . .
Great water jousts

Etigny . . . .
Harvest Festival

1st Sunday in August

Semur-en-Auxois . . . .
Lake Pont Festival

1st Saturday and Sunday in August in odd years

Charolles . . . . International Folklore Festival

1st Sunday in August

Clamecy . . . . Traditional chitterling sausage and white wine festival in Vauvert Park

1st Monday in August

Château-Chinon . . . . International Cycling Championship

August

Cluny . . . . Recitals and concerts. *Information from the Tourist Office* ☎ 85 59 05 34 and from Grandes Heures de Cluny ☎ 85 59 00 58

St-Sauveur-en-Puisaye . . . . Potters' Fair

9 and 15 August

Dijon . . . . Bell Ringing Festival

15 August

Coulanges-sur-Yonne . . . . Water jousts
Pouilly-sur-Loire . . . . Wine Festival
Seurre . . . . Horse Show

Mid August

Treffort map **70** fold 13 *(1)* . . La Côte Car Race
St-Honoré-les-Bains . . . . Flower Festival

Saturday and Sunday after 15 August

Saulieu . . . . Charollais Show

Last two Fridays, Saturdays and Sundays in August

Ferrières . . . . Historical Pageant in period costume at 9.30pm

Late August to early September

Dijon . . . . Wine Festival. International Popular Music and Dance Festival

Saturday and Sunday nearest to 7 September

Alise-Ste-Reine . . . . St Reina's Pilgrimage: Gaulish and Gallo-Roman costume procession. Mystery play at Les Roches Theatre

1st weekend in October

Auxerre . . . . Ballooning

Sunday nearest to 16 October

Paray-le-Monial . . . . Feast of St Margaret-Mary

One week in the 2nd fortnight in October

Chalon-sur-Saône . . . . October Festival

Last weekend in October

St-Léger-sous-Beuvray
map **69** fold 7 *(1)* . . . . Chestnut Festival

First two weeks in November

Dijon . . . . International Gastronomic Fair

10 November

Auxerre . . . . Martinmas Fair

Weekend before 11 November

St-Bris-le-Vineux . . . . Auxerrois Wine Festival

3rd Saturday, Sunday and Monday in November

Nuits-St-Georges . . . . 1st of the "Three Glorious Days" at Le Clos de Vougeot Château
Beaune . . . . 2nd of the "Three Glorious Days": auction sale of the wines of the Hospices in the covered market
Meursault . . . . 3rd of the "Three Glorious Days": "Paulée" de Meursault *(p 87)*

4th Sunday in November

Chablis . . . . Chablis Wine Festival

3rd Saturday in December

Bourg-en-Bresse . . . . Plucked and Drawn Poultry Show *(p 57)*

---

(1) The Michelin Map and fold number are given for places not described in this guide.

ADMISSION TIMES AND CHARGES

As admission times and charges are liable to alteration, the information below is given for guidance only.

The information applies to individual adults. Special conditions for groups are common but arrangements should be made in advance. In some cases there is no charge for admission on certain days, eg Wednesdays, Sundays or public holidays.

Churches are usually closed from noon to 2pm; they should not be visited during services. Admission times are indicated if the interior is of special interest. Visitors to chapels are usually accompanied by the key-holder; a donation is welcome.

Most tours are conducted by French-speaking guides but in some case the term "guided tours" may cover group visiting with recorded commentaries. Some of the larger and more frequented sights may offer guided tours in other languages; enquire at the ticket office or book stall. Other aids for foreign visitors are notes, pamphlets or audio guides.

Enquire at the tourist information centre for local religious holidays, market days, etc.

Every sight for which there are times and charges is indicated by the symbol ⊘ in the margin in the alphabetical section of the guide. The entries appear in the same order as in the alphabetical section of the guide.

A

ALISE-STE-REINE

Excavations. – Open 1 July to 10 September, daily, 9am to 7pm; end March to 30 June, 11 September to 11 November, daily, 10am to 6pm. F20, ticket also valid for the Alésia Museum. ☎ 80 96 10 95 or 80 30 54 60.

Alésia Museum. – Same times as for the excavations, combined ticket.

ANCY-LE-FRANC

Château. – Tour (3/4 hour) 1 April to 15 September, daily, 10am to 12 noon and 2pm to 6pm (7pm 1st May to 14 September). F32. ☎ 86 75 14 63.

Motor and Carriage Museum. – Tour (1/2 hour) daily, 1 April to 30 September, 10am to 12 noon and 2pm to 6pm; 1 October to 11 November, 10am to 12 noon and 2pm to 5pm. F16. ☎ 86 75 14 63.

ANZY-LE-DUC

Church. – All year. Guided tour for three weeks in July and the first two weeks in August.

ARCHÉODROME

Tour. – Open daily, June to August, 9am to 8pm (7pm June), September to May, 10am to 6pm (7pm May and September, 5pm January and December). F22. ☎ 80 21 48 25.

ARCY-SUR-CURE   🄴 Mairie – 89650. ☎ 86 40 91 69

Chastenay Château. – Guided tour (3/4 hour) at Easter and from 15 June to 1 September, 10am to 12 noon and 2.30pm to 6pm. F25. ☎ 86 81 93 41.

Great Cave. – Guided tour (3/4 hour) March to October, daily, 9am to 12 noon and 2pm to 6pm. F30. ☎ 86 81 90 63 (out of season: 86 81 92 24). Fax 86 81 91 07.

ARNAY-LE-DUC   🄴 Mairie – 21230. ☎ 80 90 11 59

Regional Tableware Exhibition. – Tour (3/4 hour) 14 April to 14 October, daily, 10am to 6.30pm. F12. ☎ 80 90 11 59.

AUTUN   🄴 3 Avenue Charles-de-Gaulle – 71400. ☎ 85 86 30 00

Guided tour of the town organised by the local authority. ☎ 85 52 20 34 or 85 86 30 00.

Cathedral Belfry. – Open Easter to 1 November, 8am to 6.30pm except during services. F3.

Rolin Museum. – Open 1 April to 30 September, daily except Tuesdays, 9.30am to 12 noon and 1.30pm to 6pm; October, daily, 10am to 12 noon and 2pm (Sundays, 2.30pm) to 5pm; 1 November to 31 March, daily except Tuesdays, 10am to 12 noon and 2pm to 4pm (Sundays, 2.30pm to 5pm). Closed 1 January, 1 May, 14 July, 1, 11 November, 25 December. F10. ☎ 85 52 09 76.

Town Hall Library. – Exhibitions, Mondays, Tuesdays, Thursdays at 2.30pm, 6.30pm, Wednesdays, 10am to 6.30pm, Fridays, 10am to 12 noon and 2.30pm to 6.30pm, Saturdays, 10am to 12 noon and 2pm to 5pm. F35.

Lapidary Museum. – Open 1 January to 15 April and 1 October to 31 December, 10am to 12 noon and 2pm to 4pm (4.30pm Sundays). Closed February, Tuesdays, public holidays. No charge. ☎ 85 52 35 71.

Natural History Museum. – Open all year, daily except Mondays and Tuesdays, 10am to 12 noon and 2pm to 6pm (5pm, 1 October to 30 June). Closed public holidays. F10. ☎ 85 52 09 15.

AUXERRE
🛈 1-2 Quai de la République – 89000. ☎ 86 52 06 19

Guided tour of the town organised by the Tourist Office.

No charge for museums on Wednesdays. Combined ticket for St Germanus Abbey, the crypt, the Art and History Museum, the Leblanc-Duvernoy Museum and the temporary exhibitions at the Coche d'Eau Museum.

Cathedral. – **Crypt and treasury:** open 1 June to 1 November, daily, 9am to 7pm, otherwise, 9am to 12 noon and 2pm to 6pm; also Easter to 1 November, Sundays, 2pm to 6pm. **Crypt:** F5; **Treasury:** F5. **Tower:** access temporarily suspended for restoration work. ☎ 86 52 31 68, ext 14.

St Germanus Abbey. – **Church:** closed Tuesdays and public holidays (☎ 86 51 09 74). **Crypt:** guided tour (1/2 hour) Holy Saturday to 30 September, 9am to 12.30pm and 1.30pm to 6.30pm. 1 October to Good Friday, 9am to 12 noon and 2pm to 6pm. Closed Tuesdays, 1 January, Easter and Whit Mondays, 1 and 8 May, Ascension Day, 14 July, 15 August, 1, 11 November, 25 December. F16. ☎ 86 51 09 74. **Archæological Museum:** same as for the crypt.

Leblanc-Duvernoy Museum. – Tour (3/4 hour) Holy Saturday to 31 August, 9am to 12 noon and 1.30 to 6.30pm; 16 September to Good Friday, 2pm to 5pm. Closed same days as the abbey crypt. F10. ☎ 86 51 09 74.

Natural History Museum. – Open all year, daily, 8am to 12 noon and 2pm to 6pm (afternoons only at weekends). Closed 1 January, 1 May, 25 December. No charge. ☎ 86 51 51 64.

Coche d'Eau Museum. – Guided tour all year, daily except Tuesdays and public holidays, 2pm to 6pm. No charge. ☎ 86 51 09 74.

Excursion

St-Bris-le-Vineux. – **Church:** Apply to Mme Lhéritier, 3 Rue de Grisy.

AUXONNE

Bonaparte Museum. – Open 2 May to 15 October, daily, 2.30pm to 4.30pm. Closed Thursdays except from mid-July to the end of August. F8. ☎ 80 31 10 65.

AVALLON
🛈 4 Rue Bocquillot – 89200. ☎ 86 34 14 19

Guided tour of the town organised by the Tourist Office.

St Lazarus Church. – Open Palm Sunday to early December.

Avallonnais Museum. – Open 1 June to 30 September, daily except Tuesdays, 10am to 12 noon and 2pm to 7pm; during the winter and spring school holidays, 2pm to 6pm. F10. ☎ 86 34 03 19.

B

BEAUMONT-SUR-VINGEANNE

Château. – Guided tour (1/4 hour) 15 July to 31 July and September. F10. Otherwise external visit free of charge.

BEAUNE
🛈 Rue de l'Hôtel-Dieu – 21200. ☎ 80 22 24 51

Guided tour of the town organised by the Tourist Office.

Hospital (Hôtel-Dieu). – Open 29 March to 17 November, daily, 9am to 6.30pm; 1 January to 28 March and 18 November to 31 december, daily, 9am to 11.30am and 2pm to 5.30pm. F25. ☎ 80 24 45 00. Fax 80 24 45 99.

Burgundy Wine Museum. – Open all year, daily, 9.30am to 5.30pm. Closed Tuesdays, December to end February, 1 January. F10. ☎ 80 22 08 19.

Town Hall Museums. – Open 1 June to 30 September, 9.30am to 1pm and 2pm to 6pm; 1 April to 31 May and 1 October to 21 November, 2pm to 6pm. Guided tour only of the Marey Museum only. F10. ☎ 80 24 56 92.

Excursions

Combertault. – **Church:** restoration in progress. Apply to Mme Pelletier near the church.

BERZÉ-LA-VILLE

Monks' Chapel. – Open 9.30am to 12 noon and 2pm to 6pm. F10. ☎ 85 36 66 52.

BÈZE

Caves. – Guided tour (1/2 hour) 1 May to 30 September, 10am to 7pm. Admission charge unavailable. ☎ 80 75 31 33.

BLANOT

Caves. – Tour (1 hour) 15 March to 30 September, daily, October, Sundays, 9.30am to 12 noon and 1.30pm to 7pm. F16. ☎ 85 50 03 58.

BOURBON-LANCY
🛈 Place d'Aligre – 71140. ☎ 85 89 18 27

St Nazaire Church and Museum. – Open July and August, Tuesdays, Thursdays to Sundays, 3pm to 7pm. Closed Mondays and Wednesdays. No charge. ☎ 85 89 23 23.

Military Museum. – Open July and August, 10am to 12 noon and 3pm to 6.30pm; Easter to 30 June, 1 September to 15 October, 3pm to 6.30pm. Closed Mondays. F12. ☎ 85 89 12 21.

Bourbon-Expo. – Open July and August, 3.30pm to 6.30pm (also 9am to 12 noon Tuesdays and Saturdays); September to June, Tuesdays, 9am to 12 noon, Saturdays 9am to 12 noon and 2pm to 6pm. Closed Sundays and Mondays. No charge. ☎ 85 89 23 23.

Excursion

St-Aubin-sur-Loire Château. – Guided tour (1/2 hour) July to September, daily except Tuesdays, 2pm to 5pm. Closed 15 August. F15. ☎ 85 53 91 96. No entry for cars to the courtyard.

BOURG-EN-BRESSE
🛈 6 Avenue Alsace-Lorraine – 01005. ☎ 74 22 49 40

Guided tour of the town organised by the Tourist Office.

Brou Church. – Open April to September, 8.30am to 12 noon and 2pm to 6.30pm; otherwise 10am to 12 noon and 2pm to 4.30pm. October to March, weekends, 12.30pm to 5pm. Closed 1 January, 1 May, 1, 11 November, 25 december. F24. ☎ 74 22 26 55.

Brou Museum. – Open April to September, 9am to 12.30pm and 2pm to 7pm; otherwise 9am to 12 noon and 2pm to 5pm. Closed same days as for church. F11. ☎ 74 35 49 00.

Excursion

Buellas Church. – Keys available from the grocery / petrol station (épicerie-station-service) opposite or at the clergy house.

Vandeins Church. – Apply locally to M. and Mme Bertillot. ☎ 74 30 25 72.

Montfalcon Church. – When closed apply to M. or Mme Perret.

BRANCION

No entry for cars. Car park outside the walls.

Castle. – Open 15 March to 15 November, 9am to 7pm. F12. ☎ 85 51 03 83.

St Peter's Church. – Open Holy Week to 11 November; otherwise apply in advance to the castle. ☎ 85 51 03 83.

BRIARE
🛈 Place de l'Église – 45250. ☎ 38 31 24 51

Car Museum. – Open 1 March to 31 July, daily, 12 noon to 6pm; 11 November to 28 February, weekends, 2pm to 6pm. F30. ☎ 38 31 24 51 (Tourist Office) or 38 31 20 34.

Ecomuseum. – Same as for the Car Museum; combined ticket.

Excursion

Pont-Chevron Château. – Guided tour (1 hour) 15 June to 15 September, daily except Tuesdays, 2pm to 6pm. F20. ☎ 38 31 92 02.

La BUSSIÈRE

Les Pêcheurs Château. – Guided tour (3/4 hour) late March to 11 November, daily except Tuesdays, 10am to 12 noon and 2pm to 6pm. F23. ☎ 38 35 93 35.

BUSSY-RABUTIN

Château. – Guided tour (3/4 hour) 1 April to 30 September, daily, at 10am, 11am, 2pm, 3pm, 4pm, 5pm, 6pm; October to 31 March, daily except Tuesdays and Wednesdays at 10am, 11am, 2pm 3pm. Closed 1 January, 1 May, 1, 11 November, 25 December. F18. ☎ 80 96 00 03.

Information in this guide is based on data
provided at the time of going to press. Improved facilities and changes in the cost of
living make alterations inevitable; we hope our readers will bear with us.

C

CHABLIS ∄ Chapelle de l'Ancien Hôtel-Dieu – 89300. ☎ 86 42 11 73

St Martin's Church. – Apply to the Tourist Information Office.

CHALON-SUR-SAÔNE ∄ Boulevard de la République – 71100. ☎ 85 48 37 97

Guided tour of the town organised by the Tourist Office.

Denon Museum. – Open daily except Tuesdays and public holidays, 9.30am to 12 noon and 2pm to 5.30pm. F10; no charge Wednesdays. ☎ 85 48 01 70 ext 4239.

Nicéphore-Niepce Museum. – Open daily except Tuesdays, 9.30am to 11.30am and 2.30pm to 5.30pm. Closed 1 January, 1 May, Ascension Day, 14 July, 15 August, 1, 11 November, 25 December. F10; no charge Wednesdays. ☎ 85 48 41 98.

St Vincent's Cathedral. – Restoration work in progress.

Hospital. – Tour (1 hour) last Wednesday of the month at 2.30pm or on application to the Association Abigaïl Mathieu, C.H. Quai de l'Hôpital, 71100 Chalon-sur-Saône. F10. ☎ 85 44 66 88.

Deanery Tower. – Open 2 May to 1 September, 2pm to 4.30pm. ☎ 85 43 07 75.

Excursion

Germolles Château. – Guided tour (1 hour) July and August, daily except Tuesdays, 10am to 12 noon and 2pm to 6.30pm. F20. ☎ 85 45 10 55.

CHAPAIZE (Excursion)

Lancharre Old Church. – Apply to M. Marcel Malagola next door. ☎ 85 50 13 92.

LA CHARITÉ-SUR-LOIRE

Guided tours of the town organised by the local authority. ☎ 86 70 16 12, in summer 86 70 15 06.

Priory Church of the Virgin. – Open all year, daily. Guided tours, July and August, 10am to 12 noon and 3pm to 6pm. Details from the Tourist Information Office. ☎ 86 70 16 12.

Museum. – Guided tour (1/2 hour), 25 June to 15 September, 10am to 12 noon and 3pm to 7pm; otherwise during school holidays weekends only, 3pm to 7pm. Closed Tuesdays. F10. ☎ 86 70 16 12 or 86 70 34 83.

Excursion

Champvoux Church. – Closed temporary for maintenance work.

CHÂTEAU-CHINON ∄ Porte Gudin – 58120. ☎ 86 85 06 58

Septennate Museum. – Open Ascension Day to the last weekend in September, daily, 10am to 6pm (7pm July and August); otherwise, weekends, public holidays and school holidays. Closed in January. F16. ☎ 86 85 19 23 or 86 57 80 90.

Costume Museum. – Closed temporarily for maintenance work. ☎ 86 85 15 05 (town hall).

CHÂTEAUNEUF

Castle. – Guided tour April to end September, daily, at 9.30am, 10.30am, 11.30am, 2pm, 3pm, 4pm, 5pm; October to 31 March, except Tuesdays and Wednesdays, at 10am, 11am, 2pm, 3pm. Closed 1 January, 1 May, 1, 11 November, 25 December. F18. ☎ 80 49 21 89.

CHÂTILLON-COLIGNY ∄ 2 Place Coligny – 45230. ☎ 38 96 02 33

Guided tour of the town organised by the Tourist Office.

Museum. – Open Easter to 31 October, Tuesdays to Saturdays, 2pm to 5.30pm, Sundays and public holidays, 10am to 12 noon and 2pm to 5.30pm; 1 November to Easter, Sundays and public holidays, 2pm to 5.30pm. F8. ☎ 38 92 64 06.

Excursion

Les Barres Arboretum. – Open 10 January to 20 December, daily, 10am to 12 noon and 2pm to 6pm. F15. ☎ 38 97 60 20.

CHÂTILLON-SUR-SEINE ∄ Place Marmont – 21400. ☎ 80 91 13 19

Museum. – Open 16 June to 15 September, daily, 9am to 12 noon and 1.30pm to 6pm; 16 September to 15 june, daily except Mondays, 9am (10am 16 November to 31 March) to 12 noon and 2pm to 6pm (5pm 16 November to 31 March). Closed 1 January, 1 May, 25 December. F12.50. ☎ 80 91 24 67.

St-Vorles Church. – Open 16 June to 15 September, daily, 10.30am to 12 noon and 2.30pm to 5.30pm; 31 March to 15 June, Wednesdays, weekends and public holidays only; 16 September to 11 November, Saturdays, Sundays and public holidays, 2.30pm to 4.30pm. Closed 1 May and 12 November to 30 March. ☎ 80 91 24 67.

Montigny-sur-Aube Château. – **Exterior and Chapel:** guided tour (1/4 hour) all year, daily, 8am to 12 noon and 2pm to 6pm. F7.

CÎTEAUX

Abbaye. – Only the abbey church is open to visitors; audio-visual presentation (20 min) in French, English and German.

CLAMECY
🖪 Rue du Grand-Marché – 58500. ☎ 86 27 02 51

Guided tour of the town organised by the Tourist Office.

Romain-Rolland Museum of Art and History. – Open all year, daily except Tuesdays, 10am to 12 noon and 2pm to 6pm. Closed 14 July and Sundays from 1 November to Easter. F3. ☎ 86 27 17 99.

Metz-le-Comte Church. – Key available from the Mayor of Metz or M. Garnaud, Presbytère de la Maison-Dieu, 58190 Tannay.

CLOS DE VOUGEOT

Château. – Guided tour (1/2 hour) April to September, 9am to 7pm; otherwise, 9am to 11.30am and 2pm to 5.30pm (5pm Saturdays). Closed 1 January, 24, 25, 31 December. F12. ☎ 80 62 86 09. Following the tour, audio-visual presentation (1/4 hour) about the Confrérie des Chevaliers du Tastevin.

CLUNY
🖪 6 Rue Mercière – 71250. ☎ 85 59 05 34

Guided tour of the town organised by the Tourist Office.

Old Abbey. – Guided tour (1 1/4 hours) July to September, 9am to 7pm; April to June, 9.30am to 12 noon and 2pm to 6pm; October, 9.30am to 12 noon and 2pm to 5pm; November to March, 10.30am to 11.30am and 2pm to 4pm. Closed 1 January, 1 May, 1, 11 November, 25 December. F24. ☎ 85 59 12 79.

Ochier Museum. – Tour (3/4 hour) April to September, 9.30am to 12 noon and 2pm to 6.30pm; otherwise, 10am to 12 noon and 2pm to 6pm. Closed 1 May and 21 December to 14 January. No charge.

Cheese Tower. – Tour (1/4 hour) March to October, daily, 9.30am to 12 noon and 2.30pm to 6.30pm; otherwise, 2pm to 6pm only. F5. ☎ 85 59 05 34.

National Stud. – Open all year, 9am to 7pm. No charge. ☎ 85 59 07 85. Display of tack and stallions, last Sunday in August. Audio-visual presentation on request.

St Marcel's Church. – Open in summer; otherwise apply to the Priest of Notre-Dame Church.

COMMARIN

Château. – Guided tour (3/4 hour) April to October, daily except Tuesdays, 10am to 12 noon and 2pm to 6pm. F30. ☎ 80 49 23 67 or 80 49 24 20.

CORMATIN

Château. – Guided tour (3/4 hour) 15 June to 1 November, daily, May and June, weekends and public holidays only, also at Easter, 10am to 12 noon and 2pm to 6.30pm (5pm in October). F25. ☎ 85 50 16 55.

COSNES-SUR-LOIRE

St Agnan Church. – Apply to the clergy house: Le Presbytère, Place Agnan, Cosnes-sur-Loire. ☎ 86 28 27 95.

Museum. – Tour (1/2 hour) 1 July to 31 October, daily except Tuesdays, 10am to 12 noon and 3pm to 7pm. F16. ☎ 86 26 71 02.

Cadoux Estate. – **Museum:** tour (3/4 hour) 1 May to 30 September, daily, 2pm to 7pm; otherwise by appointment. F20. ☎ 86 39 22 84.

LA CÔTE

Chenôve. – **Duke of Burgundy's Cellar:** tour (1/4 hour) 15 June to 30 September, daily, 2pm to 7pm; otherwise by appointment. No charge. ☎ 80 52 82 83 (out of season 80 52 51 30).

Reulle-Vergy. – **Museum:** open July to mid September, daily, 2pm to 7pm; otherwise, Sundays and public holidays or by appointment during the week. F10. ☎ 80 61 40 95 or 80 61 42 93.

St Romain. – **Town Hall Museum:** guided tour (1 hour) 1 July to 15 September, daily except Wednesdays, 4pm (2pm Sundays and public holidays) to 8pm; otherwise by appointment. ☎ 80 21 28 50. No charge.

Santenay. – **St John's Church:** restoration work in progress.

Le CREUSOT

La Verrerie Château. – Guided tour (1 hour comprising the courtyard, the pocket theatre and the technical centre) 1 April to 30 September, 9am to 12 noon and 2pm to 7pm; 1 October to 31 March, 10am to 12 noon and 2pm to 6pm. Closed Tuesdays, Saturday mornings, Sundays and public holidays. F15. ☎ 85 55 02 46.

Museum. – Tour (1 1/2 hours) Mondays to Fridays, 9am to 12 noon and 2pm to 6pm; weekends and public holidays, 2pm to 6pm. F15. ☎ 85 55 02 46.

Excursion

Brandon Château. – Tour (1/2 hour) July and August, daily except Tuesdays, 2pm to 6pm; otherwise by appointment in writing to M. de Masin, Château de Brandon, 71670 St-Pierre-de-Varennes. F10. ☎ 85 55 45 16.

Couches Château. – Guided tour (1 hour) July to September, daily, 10am to 12 noon and 2pm to 6pm; April to June, Sundays and public holidays, 2pm to 6pm; October to March, by appointement. F25. ☎ 85 49 68 02.

Écuisses. – **Canal Museum:** open 1 April to 31 October, daily except Mondays, 3pm to 6pm; otherwise by appointment. F10. ☎ 85 78 92 56.

CURE VALLEY

Cravant Church. – When closed apply to "Les Hortensias" Hotel, Place de l'Église, Cravant.

D

DECIZE

Guided tour of the town organised by the local authority ☎ 86 25 03 23.

St Aré Church. – Apply to the clergy house (Presbytère) for the key to the crypt.

DIGOIN

Pottery Documentation Centre. – Guided tour (1 1/2 hours) 1 June to 31 October, 10am to 12 noon and 2.30pm to 6.30pm; 1 April to 31 May, 10am to 12 noon and 2pm to 4pm. F15. ☎ 85 53 00 81.

DIJON

Guided tour of the town organised by the Tourist Office. ☎ 80 43 42 12. Combined ticket for all the museums except the Grévin Museum: F13.

Fine Arts Museum. – Tour (1 1/2 hours) Mondays, Wednesdays to Saturdays 10am to 6pm (except the modern art section which closes 12.15pm to 2.15pm); Sundays and public holidays, 10am to 12.30pm and 2pm to 6pm. Closed 1 January, 1 May, 14 July, 1 November, 25 December. F10. ☎ 80 74 52 70.

Philip the Good's Tower. – Restoration in progress until 1993. Thereafter open Easter to 1 November, daily except Tuesdays, 9.30am to 11.30am and 2.30pm to 5.30pm; otherwise, Wednesdays, 2.30pm to 5.30pm, Sundays and public holidays 9.30am to 11.30am and 2.30pm to 5.30pm. Closed 1 January, 1, 8 May, 14 July, 1 November, 25 December. F6; no charge Sundays and public holidays. ☎ 80 74 52 70.

Hôtel de Vogüé. – Access to the inner courtyard only.

Municipal Library. – **Courtyard and chapel** (lecture room): open Tuesdays to Saturdays, 9.30am to 12.30pm and 1.30pm to 6.30pm (all day Wednesdays and Saturdays). Closed Saturdays, July and August. **First floor rooms** provisionally closed. ☎ 80 30 36 39.

Magnin Museum. – Tour (1 hour) 1 June to 30 September, daily except Mondays, 10am to 6pm. Closed 1 January, 25 December. F12. ☎ 80 67 11 10.

Charterhouse of Champmol. – Open all year, 9am to 6pm. No charge. ☎ 80 42 48 48.

St Benignus' Cathedral Crypt. – Tour (1/4 hour) daily, 9am to 7pm. F3. ☎ 80 30 39 33.

Archæological Museum. – Tour (1 hour) all year, daily except Tuesdays, 9.30am to 6pm (closed 12 noon to 2pm, September to May). Closed 1 January, 1, 8 May, 14 July, 1, 11 November and 25 December. F 9. ☎ 80 30 88 54.

Natural History Museum. – Tour (1 1/2 hours) all year, daily except Tuesdays, 2pm to 5.15pm. Closed 1 January, 1, 8 May, 14 July, 1, 11 November, 25 December. F 3.50; no charge Sundays and public holidays. ☎ 80 41 61 08.

Grévin Museum. – Open all year, daily, 9.30am to 12 noon and 2pm to 7pm. Closed 1 January, 25 December. F 38. ☎ 80 42 03 03.

Rude Museum. – Tour (1/2 hour) June to September, daily except Tuesdays, 9.30am to 12 noon and 2pm to 5.45pm. Closed 14 July. Otherwise apply to the Fine Arts Museum. No charge. ☎ 80 66 87 95 or 80 74 52 70.

Burgundian Folklore Museum. – Tour (1 1/2 hours) daily except Tuesdays, 9am to 12 noon and 2pm to 6pm. Closed 1 January, 1, 8 May, 14 July, 1, 11 November, 25 December. F 9. ☎ 80 30 65 91.

Museum of Sacred Art. – Tour (1 hour) daily except Tuesdays, 9am to 12 noon and 2pm to 6pm. Closed 1 January, 1 May, 25 December. F 8. ☎ 80 30 06 44.

DONZY (Excursion)

Les Granges Château at Suilly-la-Tour. – **Exterior** and **chapel** only, open 1 to 20 July and 1 to 20 September, Mondays to Fridays, 9am to 12 noon and 2pm to 5pm. No charge. ☎ 86 26 30 71.

Menou Château. – Guided tour (1/2 hour) July to September, daily, 2pm to 6pm. F 28. ☎ 86 39 84 33.

DRUYES-LES-BELLES-FONTAINES

Castle. – Guided tour (1 1/4 hours) July and August, weekends and public holidays, at 3pm, 4pm, 5pm, 6pm; 1 to 15 September, Sundays only, at 3pm, 4pm, 5pm. F 15. ☎ 86 41 57 86.

E – F

ÉPOISSES

Château. – **Interior:** guided tour (1/2 hour) July and August, daily except Tuesdays, 10am to 12 noon and 3pm to 6pm. F 25. **Exterior:** all year, F 5. ☎ 80 96 40 56 and 80 96 42 65.

LA FERTÉ-LOUPIÈRE

Church. – For a guided tour, apply to M. and Mme A. Breton, Rue Basse, La Ferté-Loupière, 89110 Aillant-sur-Tholon or ☎ 86 63 41 86.

FIXIN

Noisot Park. – Open 16 March to 28 June, daily, 2pm to 7pm; 1 July to 14 November, Wednesdays to Sundays afternoons only. Closed mid-November to mid-March. F 5. ☎ 80 52 45 52 or 80 52 45 62. Guided tour available (1/2 hour).

FLAVIGNY-SUR-OZERAIN

St-Genest Church. – Apply to Mlle Gerbenne.

Crypt of the Former Abbey. – Guided tour (1/4 hour) Mondays to Saturdays, 8.15am to 11.15am and 1.30pm to 5.15pm; Sundays and public holidays, 10am to 12 noon and 2pm to 6pm. F 7. ☎ 80 96 20 88.

Excursion

Frolois Château. – Guided tour (1/2 hour) July and August, daily, 2pm to 6pm (last admission 5.30pm). F 14.

FLEURIGNY

Château. – Guided tour Easter to 17 September, daily except Wednesdays, 2.30pm to 5.30pm. F 20. ☎ 86 97 60 09.

FONTAINE-FRANÇAISE (Excursion)

Rosières Castle. – Open all year, daily. F 5. ☎ 80 75 82 53.

FONTENAY

Abbey. – Guided tour (3/4 hour) all year, 9am to 12 noon and 2pm to 6pm, every hour; also July, August, 2pm to 6pm, every half hour. ⚐34. ☎ 80 92 15 00.

G – J

GEVREY-CHAMBERTIN

Château. – Guided tour (1/2 ·hour) 10am to 12 noon and 2pm to 6pm (4.30pm 15 November to 31 March). Closed Sundays till 2.30pm, Easter, 15 August and 1 November, 25 December. F 20. ☎ 80 34 36 13.

JOIGNY (Excursions)   🚌 Gare routière, Quai Ragobert – 89300. ☎ 86 62 11 05

Guided tour of the town organised by the Tourist Office.

Laduz Folk Museum. – Tour (1 1/2 hours) June to September, daily, 2pm to 7pm; Easter to 31 May and 1 October to 2 November, weekends and public holidays only. F 25. ☎ 86 73 70 08.

Fabulous Museum at Dicy. – Guided tour (1 1/2 hours) July and August, daily, 2pm to 6pm; Easter to June and September to November, weekends, 2pm to 6pm. F 25. ☎ 86 63 64 21.

L

LOUHANS

Hospital. – Guided tour 1 March to 30 September, Mondays, Wednesdays to Saturdays, at 10.30am, 2.30pm and 4pm, Sundays and public holidays, at 2.30pm, 4pm; 1 October to 28 February, Wednesdays to Saturdays, at 10.30am. F 17. ☏ 85 75 54 32.

Print-Room of the Old "Indépendant". – Tour (1 hour) 15 May to 30 September, daily except Tuesdays, 3pm to 7pm. F 10. ☏ 87 76 27 16.

Excursion

Rancy Museum of Makers and Menders of Chairs. – Open 15 May to 30 September, 3pm to 7pm. F 10. ☏ 85 76 27 16.

LUZY

Tapestries in the Town Hall. – Tour (1/4 hour) Mondays to Fridays, 9am to 12 noon and 1.30pm to 5.30pm (4.30pm, Fridays). Closed weekend and public holidays. No charge. Apply to the town hall. ☏ 86 30 02 34.

Excursion

Tibetan Monastery of Kagyu-Ling. – Open all year, daily, 10am to 12 noon and 2pm to 6pm (afternoons only in winter). F 10. ☏ 85 79 43 41.

M

La MACHINE

Mining Museum. – Open 15 June to 14 September, daily, 10am to 12 noon and 3pm to 7pm; 1 March to 14 June and 15 September to 31 October, Sundays, 2pm to 6pm; otherwise by appointment. F 12. ☏ 86 50 91 08.

Simulated mine. – Guided tour. Same times as the museum. F 12.

MÂCON   🛈 187 Rue Carnot – 71000. ☏ 85 39 71 37

Ursuline Municipal Museum. – Open daily except Tuesdays and Sunday mornings, 10am to 12 noon and 2pm to 6pm. Closed 1 January, 1 May, 14 July, 1 November, 25 December. F 10. ☏ 85 38 18 84.

Lamartine Museum. – Open 1 March to 31 October, daily, 10am to 12 noon and 2pm to 6pm. Closed January, February and the same days as the Ursuline Museum. F 10.

Hospital. – Tour (1/4 hour) all year, daily except Tuesdays, Sundays and public holidays, 10am to 12 noon, on prior application to Ursuline Municipal Museum, 5, Rue des Ursulines, 71000 Mâcon (☏ 85 38 18 84). Otherwise apply to the Centre Hospitalier des Chanaux (medical centre), Boulevard de l'Hôpital, 71000 Mâcon. (☏ 85 20 30 40.) No charge.

Excursion

St Andrew. – When closed apply to the farm next to the church. Details of guided tours from the town hall. ☏ 85 30 41 94.

Le MÂCONNAIS

Tour 1: the Mountain

Lugny. – **Church:** apply to the Centre Pastoral, Rue du Pont. ☏ 85 33 24 34.

Azé. – **Caves and Museum:** Guided tour (1 1/2 hours) Palm Sunday to 30 September, daily, October, Sundays only, 10am to 12 noon and 2pm to 7pm. F 22. ☏ 85 33 32 23.

Clessé. – **Church:** Keys available from Épicerie Sivignon (grocery) or the café in the square.

Tour 3: Lamartine

Monceau Château. – **Exterior** (courtyards and terrace) and **chapel,** 15 June to 30 September, 9am to 12 noon and 2pm to 6pm; otherwise exterior only (chapel by appointment), 9am to 12 noon and 2pm to 5pm. No charge. ☏ 85 37 81 52.

Berzé-le-Châtel Castle. – Open 14 July to 31 August, daily, 2.30pm to 6.30pm. No charge.

St Point Château. – Guided tour (1/2 hour) 1 March to 15 November, daily except Wednesdays, Sunday mornings, 10am to 12 noon and 2pm to 6pm. Closed public holidays. F 20. ☏ 85 50 50 30.

Pierreclos Château. – Guided tour (1 hour) daily, 9.30am to 12 noon and 2pm to 6pm. F 15. ☏ 85 35 73 73.

MARCIGNY

Mill Tower Museum. – Open March to October, daily, 2pm to 6pm (also July and August, 10am to 12 noon). F 10. ☎ 85 25 21 87.

Excursion

St-Martin-du-Lac Carriage Museum. – Tour (1/2 hour) 15 June to 15 September, daily, 2pm to 6.30pm; Easter to 14 June and 16 September to 1 November, Sundays only; otherwise by appointment. F 15. ☎ 85 25 03 72.

MONTARGIS
🖪 Place du 18-Juin – 45200. ☎ 38 98 00 87

Girodet Museum. – Tour (1 hour) Wednesdays to Sundays, 9am to 12 noon and 1.30pm to 5.30pm. Closed public holidays. F 10. ☎ 38 98 07 81.

Gâtinais Museum. – Open Wednesdays to Sundays, 9am to 12 noon and 1.30pm to 5.30pm. Closed public holidays. F 10. ☎ 38 93 45 63.

MONTBARD
🖪 Rue Carnot – 21500. ☎ 80 92 01 34

Buffon Park. – Guided tour 1 April to 30 September, daily except Tuesdays, at 10.15am, 11.15am, 2.15pm, 3.15pm, 4pm, 5pm; 1 October to 31 March, Tuesdays to Saturdays, 10.15am, 11.15am, 2.15pm, 4pm. F 10. ☎ 80 92 03 75.

Fine Arts Museum. – Open April to October, daily except Tuesdays, 3pm to 6pm. F 10. ☎ 80 92 01 34.

Old Stable Museum. – Open April to October, daily except Tuesdays, 10am to 12 noon and 3pm to 6.30pm. F 10. ☎ 80 92 01 34.

Excursion

Buffon Forge. – Open June to September, daily except Tuesdays, 2.30pm to 6pm; also July and August, Wednesdays to Fridays, 10am to 12 noon. F 20. ☎ 80 89 40 30.

Château de Nuits. – Tour (3/4 hour) April to October, daily, 10am to 11.30am and 2pm to 5.30pm. F 20. ☎ 86 55 71 80.

MONTCEAU-LES-MINES

Fossil Museum. – Tour (3/4 hour) Wednesdays, Saturdays and 1st Sunday of the month, 3pm to 6pm. Closed 14 July to 15 September, 1 January, 25 December. F 10. ☎ 85 57 29 73 or 85 57 38 51.

Blanzy. – **"Men and mining":** Guided tour (1 1/4 hours) 1 July to 15 September, daily, 2pm to 6pm (3pm to 7pm, Sundays and public holidays); 15 March to 30 June and 16 September to 15 November, weekends and public holidays, 3pm to 7pm. Otherwise apply to Montceau-les-Mines Tourist Information Office (☎ 85 57 38 51). F 15. ☎ 85 58 40 02.

Excursion

Gourdon Church. – Key available from the town hall. ☎ 85 79 80 83.

MONT-ST-VINCENT

J. Régnier Museum. – Tour (1/2 hour) 15 April to late September, Sundays and public holidays, 3pm to 7pm. No charge. ☎ 85 57 38 51.

MOULINS-ENGILBERT (Excursion)

Commagny. – **Priory:** open Whitsun to 1 October, daily, 10am to 6pm. No charge. Otherwise apply to the town hall. ☎ 86 84 21 48.

N

NEVERS
🖪 31 Rue du Rempart – 58000. ☎ 86 59 07 03

Guided tour of the town organised by the Tourist Information Office.

Pottery Workshops. – **Montagnon Workshop** (10, Rue de la Porte-du-Croux): open 1st Wednesday of each month, at 2.30pm. ☎ 86 59 27 16.

Nivernais Archæological Museum. – Tour (3/4 hour) 1 April to 1 December, daily except Tuesdays, 2pm to 6pm. F 10. ☎ 86 59 17 85.

Municipal Museum. – Tour (1 hour) February to December, daily except Tuesdays, 10am to 12.30pm and 2pm to 6.30pm. F 10. ☎ 86 68 46 46.

Cathedral. – The 6C Baptistry is not open.

St Gildard Convent and Museum. – Open April to October, 6.30am to 7.30pm, November to March, 7am to 12 noon and 1.30pm to 7pm. No charge. ☎ 86 57 79 99.

Ste Bernadette du Banlay. – When closed see notice attached to gates.

Excursions

Magny-Cours Racing Circuit. – For information ☏ 86 21 20 74 or 86 54 17 33.

Chevenon Castle. – **Exterior:** Open 1 April to 31 October, daily. No charge. **Interior:** for a guided tour write to M. Bardin, Château de Chevenon, 58100 Imphy.

NOYERS

Guided tour of the town organised by the local authority ☏ 86 82 83 72.

Museum. – Open June to September, daily, 2.30pm to 6pm; 1 October to 31 May, weekends and public holidays, 2.30pm to 6pm. F 10. ☏ 86 82 89 09.

NUITS-ST-GEORGES
🛈 Rue Sonoys – 21700. ☏ 80 61 22 47

Archæological Museum. – Open 2 May to 31 October, daily except Tuesdays, 10am to 12 noon and 2pm to 6pm. F 8. ☏ 80 61 12 54.

Military Museum. – Same details as for the archæological museum.

Excursion

Cussigny Château. – Guided tour (1/2 hour) 14 July to 1 September, Mondays to Saturdays, 10am to 12 noon and 2pm to 6pm; Sundays and public holidays, 12 noon to 1pm and 2.30pm to 6.30pm. F 15.

O - P

OUCHE VALLEY

La Bussière-sur-Ouche. – **Church:** open only for retreats and other religious activities.

PARAY-LE-MONIAL
🛈 Avenue Jean-Paul-II – 71600. ☏ 85 81 10 92

Guided tour of the town organised by the Tourist Information Centre.

Relics Chamber. – Open April to October, daily, 9am to 6pm. No charge.

Parc des Chapelains Diorama. – Tour (1/2 hour) 1 June to 15 September, daily, 9.30am to 3pm and and 1.30pm to 7pm; Palm Sunday to 31 May, daily, 1.30pm to 7pm; 16 September to 31 October, 1.30pm to 5.30pm. F 8. ☏ 85 88 85 80.

Chapel of the Visitation. – Silence must be observed. Closed during services. Guided tour available by appointment ☏ 85 81 09 95.

Hiéron Museum. – Closed until 31 December 1993.

Charollais Earthenware Museum. – Tour (1/2 hour) 20 March to 20 October, daily except Tuesdays, 10am to 12 noon and 3pm to 7pm. F 13. ☏ 85 81 10 92.

PERRECY-LES-FORGES

Exhibition. – Open July to October, daily except Mondays, 3pm to 6pm; November to June by appointment. F 7. ☏ 85 55 01 11.

PIERRE-DE-BRESSE

Château. – **Museum:** open daily, 2pm to 6pm. Closed 1 January, 25 December. F 30. ☏ 85 76 27 16.

Excursion

St Germain du Bois Museum of Agricultural Machines. – Open 15 May to 30 September, Sundays, 3pm to 7pm. F 10. ☏ 85 76 27 16.

Perrigny Forest and Woodland Museum. – Open 15 May to 30 September, Sundays, 3pm to 7pm. F 10. ☏ 85 76 27 16.

PIERRE-QUI-VIRE ABBEY

Exhibition Room. – Open February to December, Mondays to Saturdays, 10.30am to 12 noon and 2.30pm to 5pm, Sundays 11.30am to 12.30pm and 3pm to 5pm. Audio-visual presentation. ☏ 86 32 21 23.

Mass in the abbey church. – Mondays to Saturdays, 9.20am; Sundays and feast days, at 10am.

PONTIGNY

Church. – Guided tour, July and August, 10am to 12 noon and 3pm to 7pm, except during Sunday mass at 11am. ☏ 86 47 41 76.

POUILLY-EN-AUXOIS

Notre-Dame-Trouvée. – On prior application to the town hall or the clergy house (Presbytère).

Excursion

Éguilly Château. – Guided tour (3/4 hour) March to October, 10am to 12 noon and 2pm to 6pm. No charge.

R

RATILLY

Castle. – Tour (3/4 hour) 15 June to 30 September, daily, 10am to 6pm; otherwise, Mondays to Saturdays, 3pm to 6pm, Sundays (November to April closed) 4pm to 6pm. F 15. ☎ 86 74 79 54.

La ROCHEPOT

Castle. – Guided tour (3/4 hour) Palm Sunday to 31 May, daily except Tuesdays, 10am to 11.30am and 2pm to 6.30pm; 1 June to 1 November, daily except Tuesdays, 9.30am to 11.30am and 2.30pm to 6.30pm. F 15. ☎ 80 21 71 37.

S

ST-FARGEAU

Castle. – Open (partial guided tour: 1 hour) early April to mid November, 10am to 12 noon and 2pm to 7pm. F 25. ☎ 86 74 05 07.

Excursion

St Hubert Wildlife Park. – Open April to September, 8am to 8pm; October to March, sunrise to sunset. Closed Sundays, 15 November to 31 December. F 35. ☎ 86 74 71 28.

ST-FLORENTIN

Church. – Apply to the Tourist Information Office, Rue de la Terrasse.

ST-JULIEN-DU-SAULT

Church. – When closed apply to the clergy house: le Presbytère, 13 Faubourg de la Croix (☎ 86 63 23 29) or to Mlle Cagne, 17 place de la Mairie. ☎ 86 63 25 89.

Vauguillain Chapel. – Not open.

ST-LÉGER-VAUBAN

Vauban's House. – Tour (3/4 hour) 1 June to 15 September, daily, 10am to 12 noon and 2pm to 7pm; otherwise by appointment F 13. ☎ 86 32 26 94.

ST-PÈRE

Regional Archæological Museum. – Tour (1/2 hour) 15 March to 15 December, daily except Wednesdays, 10.30am to 12.30pm and 2.30pm to 6.30pm. F 18 (ticket also valid for Fontaines-Salées). ☎ 86 33 23 14.

Excavations at Fontaines-Salées. – Open 15 March to 30 November; otherwise as above. Ticket also valid for the Archæological Museum.

ST-SEINE-L'ABBAYE

Abbey Church. – When closed apply to the Épicerie Najean-Siroey (grocery) near the abbey.

ST-THIBAULT

Church. – Open 15 March to 15 November.

SAÔNE PLAIN

Verdun-sur-le-Doubs. – Wheat and Bread Centre. – Open 15 May to 30 September, daily, 11am to 12 noon and 3pm to 7pm. F 10. ☎ 85 76 27 16.

SAULIEU   🛈 Rue d'Argentine – 21210. ☎ 80 64 09 22

Museum. – Tour (1 hour) Mondays, Wednesdays to Saturdays, 9am to 12 noon and 2pm to 6pm, Sundays, 9.30am to 12 noon. F 15. ☎ 80 64 09 22.

St Saturnin. – On prior application to the town hall. ☎ 80 64 09 22.

SEIGNELAY

St-Martial. – On prior application to the clergy house (Presbytère). ☎ 86 47 75 66.

SEINE (Source)

Aignay-le-Duc Church. – When closed apply to the clergy house (Presbytère).

SEMUR-EN-AUXOIS   🛈 Place Gaveau – 21140. ☎ 80 97 05 96

Guided tour of the town organised by the Tourist Information Centre.

Floodlighting of the main buildings: July and August weekends and public holidays.

Church of Our Lady. – Closed Wednesday afternoons during school termtime.

Golden Orle Tower and Museum. – Guided tour (1/2 hour) July and August, 10am to 12 noon and 3pm to 6pm. F 10.

Museum. – Tour (1 hour) 15 May to 15 September, Wednesdays to Sundays, 2pm to 5.45pm; 1 October to 14 May, Wednesdays and Fridays, 2pm to 5.45pm. Closed public holidays. F 10. ☎ 80 97 24 25.

Excursion

Bourbilly Château. – Guided tour (1/2 hour) 1 July to 15 September, daily except Sunday mornings, 10am to 12 noon and 3pm to 6pm. F 20.

SEMUR-EN-BRIONNAIS

St Hugues Castle. – Open 1 March to 11 November, daily, 10am to 12 noon and 3pm to 7pm. F 8. ☎ 85 25 13 57. Guided tour on request.

SENNECEY-LE-GRAND

St Julien. – Apply to the Tourist Information Office for a guided tour. ☎ 85 44 82 54.

St Martin de Laives. – Sundays only. Guided tour May to November, 3pm to 7pm; otherwise apply to the Tourist Information Office ☎ 85 44 82 54 or 85 44 81 07.

SENS
🛈 Place Jean-Jaurès – 89100. ☎ 86 65 19 49

Guided tour of the town organised by the Tourist Information Centre.

Museum, Treasury and Synodal Palace. – Open 1 June to 30 September, daily except Tuesdays, 10am to 12 noon and 2pm to 6pm; 1 October to 31 May, Wednesdays, weekends, 10am to 12 noon and 2pm to 6pm, Mondays, Thursdays, Fridays, 2pm to 6pm. Closed 1 January, 25 December. F 12. ☎ 86 64 15 27.

St-Pierre-le-Rond. – Closed for restoration work.

St Maurice. – When closed apply to 12 Rue de l'Ile-d'Yonne. ☎ 86 64 25 72.

St Savinien. – The church may be closed for restoration work. To check that it is open, ☎ 86 65 19 27 (71, Rue d'Alsace-Lorraine); key available from 137 bis Rue d'Alsace-Lorraine.

SOLUTRÉ

Museum. – Tour (1/2 hour) 2 May to 30 September, daily except Tuesdays, 10am to 1pm and 2pm to 7pm; otherwise 10am to 12 noon and 2pm to 5pm. Closed 1 May, 31 December to 29 February. F 17. ☎ 85 38 85 24 and 85 35 83 23.

SULLY

Château. – **Exterior** only, open from the Saturday before Palm Sunday to 1 November, daily, 8am to 8pm. F 10. ☎ 85 82 01 08.

T

TAIZÉ

Church. – Open day and night. Prayers Mondays to Saturdays, at 8am, 12.30pm, 8.30pm. Sundays, at 10am, 5pm, 8.30pm. ☎ 85 50 14 14.

TALMAY

Château. – Guided tour (3/4 hour) July and August, daily except Mondays, 3pm to 5pm. F 18. Otherwise apply to M. Louis Bordeaux Montrieux, Château de Talmay, 21270 Pontailler-sur-Saône.

TANLAY

Château. – Guided tour (3/4 hour) April to 1 November, daily except Tuesdays, at 9.30am, 10.30am, 11.30am, 2.15pm, 3pm, 3.45pm, 4.30pm and 5.15pm. F 32. ☎ 86 75 70 61.

TERNANT

Church. – When closed key available from Mme Masse at the clergy house, near the War Memorial.

TIL-CHÂTEL (Excursion)

Grancey Château. – Guided tour on prior application to M. de Bazelaire, 54 Rue des Forges, 21000 Dijon. ☎ 80 75 60 30.

TONNERRE
🛈 42 Rue de l'Hôpital – 89700. ☎ 86 55 14 48

Guided tour of the town organised by the Tourist Information Office.

Former Hospital. – Guided tour (1/2 hour) Easter to 1 November at 10am, 11.30am, 2pm and 5.30pm. Closed Tuesdays (except in July and August), 1 May. F 10. ☎ 86 55 14 48.

St Peter's Church. – Maintenance work in progress.

TOUCY (Excursion)

Villiers-St-Benoît. – **Regional Art Museum:** Tour (1 hour) 1 February to 15 December, daily except Tuesdays, 10am to 12 noon and 2pm to 6pm. Closed 1 May, 15 August, 1, 11 November. F 15. ☎ 86 45 73 05.

Pourrain. – **Second World War Museum:** Guided tour (1 hour) daily, 9am to 12 noon and 2pm to 6pm. F 15. ☎ 86 41 13 27.

TOURNUS   🛈 Place Carnot – 71700. ☎ 85 51 13 10

Guided tour of the town organised by the Tourist Office.

St Philibert. – Guided tour July and August, Mondays to Fridays, 10.30am to 3pm. Lighting of the crypt by time switch (F 1).

Perrin-de-Puycousin Museum. – Scheduled to re-open in April 1992 on completion of maintenance work. Open same times as the Greuze Museum. Charge not available. ☎ 86 57 80 90.

Greuze Museum. – Tour (1/2 hour) April to October, daily except Tuesdays and Sunday mornings, 9.30am to 12 noon and 2pm to 6.30pm. Closed 1 May. F 5.50. ☎ 85 51 30 74.

St-Trivier-de-Courtes. – **La Forêt Farm:** open 15 June to 25 September, daily, 2pm to 7pm; Easter to 14 June and 26 September to 1 November, Sundays and public holidays, 2pm to 7pm. No charge. ☎ 74 30 71 89.

Uchizy Church. – When closed apply to Mme Grozeillier in the fabric shop (boutique de tissage) opposite.

Le Villars Church. – When closed apply to Épicerie Mathey (grocery) in Grand'rue, or to Mme Nicot, cour du Prieuré (☎ 85 51 14 06). Information from the town hall ☎ 85 51 00 57.

V – Y

VALLERY

Châteaux. – Guided tour (3/4 hour) 1 April to 31 October, Sunday afternoons and public holidays, 3pm to 6pm. F 16.

Church. – Tour on prior application to M. Sottiaux. ☎ 86 97 53 09.

VARZY

St Peter's. – Open Sundays in the summer. Otherwise on prior application to the town hall. ☎ 86 29 43 73.

Museum. – Partial opening scheduled for July 1992 following maintenance work.

VAUSSE PRIORY

Cloisters and Chapel. – Guided tour (1/2 hour) 15 March to 15 November, daily except Tuesdays, 2pm to 7pm. F 10. ☎ 86 55 86 84 or 86 82 86 84.

VÉZELAY   🛈 Mairie – 89450. ☎ 86 33 23 69

Basilica of St Mary Magdalene. – Guided tour on request to the clergy house (Presbytère) (☎ 86 33 24 36). Closed during services; Sunday mornings; 15 August. Ascent of the tower, July and August, 10am to 12 noon and 2pm to 5.30pm. F 5.

VILLENEUVE-L'ARCHEVÊQUE

Notre-Dame. – When closed apply to Pâtisserie Betsch (cake shop), 10 Rue de la République, or to the clergy house: le Presbytère, 20 Rue Voltaire. For information ☎ 86 86 71 86, 86 86 77 85 or 86 86 75 22.

VILLENEUVE-SUR-YONNE   🛈 4 bis Rue Carnot – 89500. ☎ 86 87 36 28

Notre-Dame. – For groups apply in writing to M. le Curé (89500 Villeneuve-sur-Yonne).

Excursion

Dixmont Church. – Key available from M. Evezard, Rue de la Mairie. ☎ 86 96 01 10.

YONNE VALLEY

Appoigny. – **Collegiate Church of St Peter:** apply to the clergy house (Presbytère). ☎ 86 53 00 12.

Châtel-Censoir. – **St-Potentien Collegiate Church:** apply to the town hall or to Mme Schuh, 6 Rue du Presbytère. ☎ 86 81 01 98.

INDEX

ACKNOWLEDGEMENTS – ILLUSTRATIONS

p. 9   J Sierpinski/SCOPE, Paris.
p. 14   A Gaël, Paris.
p. 16   Tourist Office, Le Creusot.
p. 18   Musée des Beaux-Arts, Dijon.
p. 26   LAUROS GIRAUDON, Paris.
p. 27   After photo by Trincano, Arthaud/PIX, Paris.
p. 28   After photo by CNMHS, Paris © SPADEM.
p. 29   A Wolf/EXPLORER, Paris (above).
p. 29   J-L Barde, SCOPE, Paris (below).
p. 30   After photo by H Veiller/EXPLORER, Paris (above).
p. 30   J Sierpinski/SCOPE, Paris (below).
p. 31   After photo Trincano, Arthaud/PIX, Paris.
p. 35   J Guillard/SCOPE, Paris.
p. 42   S Chirol, Paris.
p. 44   After photo by A Gaël, Paris.
p. 51   J D Sudres/SCOPE, Paris.
p. 57   After photo by CNMHS, Paris © SPADEM.
p. 59   After photo by CNMHS, Paris © SPADEM.
p. 64   After photo by J Feuillie/CNMHS, Paris © SPADEM.

p. 68   After photo by S Chirol, Paris.
p. 69   After drawing by Deroy, photo by Delayance.
p. 76   Ph Beuzen/SCOPE, Paris.
p. 80   After photo Jouvry.
p. 83   R Guillemot/CDA EDIMEDIA, Paris.
p. 94   LAUROS GIRAUDON, Paris.
p. 102 S Chirol, Paris.
p. 104 After photo by Pélissier/VLOO, Paris.
p. 115 LAUROS GIRAUDON, Paris.
p. 117 P Viard/PIX, Paris.
p. 120 Pélissier/VLOO, Paris.
p. 127 J Guillot/CDA EDIMEDIA, Paris.
p. 133 After photo by J Bottin, Paris.
p. 135 J Cartier, Pierre-de-Bresse.
p. 140 A Gaël, Paris.
p. 143 J-L Barde/SCOPE, Paris.
p. 148 After photo by Combier, Mâcon.
p. 152 Ch Olivier, Nice.
p. 157 A Gaël, Paris.
p. 159 J Guillard/SCOPE, Paris.
p. 161 After photo by La Cigogne/PIX, Paris.
p. 172 A Gaël, Paris.
p. 175 Musée des Beaux-Arts, Dijon/Bourquin, Dijon.

MANUFACTURE FRANÇAISE DES PNEUMATIQUES MICHELIN

Société en commandite par actions au capital de 2 000 000 000 de francs

Place des Carmes-Déchaux - 63 Clermont-Ferrand (France)

R.C.S. Clermont-Fd B 855 200 507

© Michelin et Cie, Propriétaires-Éditeurs 1992

Dépôt légal 1er trim. 1992 - ISBN 2-06-013082-4 - ISSN 0763-1383

Printed in France 03-92-30/1
Photocomposition : APS, Tours – Impression : MAME Imprimeurs, Tours
Brochage : S.I.R.C., Marigny-le-Châtel